Heidegger's Nietzsche

Heidegger's Nietzsche

*European Modernity and the Philosophy
of the Future*

José Daniel Parra

LEXINGTON BOOKS
Lanham • Boulder • New York • London

Published by Lexington Books
An imprint of The Rowman & Littlefield Publishing Group, Inc.
4501 Forbes Boulevard, Suite 200, Lanham, Maryland 20706
www.rowman.com

6 Tinworth Street, London SE11 5AL

British Library Cataloguing in Publication Information Available

Library of Congress Cataloging-in-Publication Data Available

ISBN 978-1-4985-7672-7 (cloth)
ISBN 978-1-4985-7673-4 (electronic)
ISBN 978-1-4985-7674-1 (pbk.)

To my family, for being such a profound constellation
of unconditional love.

Contents

Acknowledgments

The original version of this text was written at the University of Toronto during my doctoral studies. I would like to thank especially Ronald Beiner, Peggy Kohn, Ed Andrew, and Fred Dallmayr for their generous support for the project. The revised version benefitted from the time I spent as a postdoctoral research scholar at Universitat Pompeu Fabra, Barcelona, in 2016–2018. Those two years based in Spain allowed me to experience cultural life in Europe and in the Mediterranean, for which I am truly grateful. I would like to thank Victoria Cirlot and Fernando Pérez-Borbujo for their kind invitation to do research in Barcelona, and also Montserrat Herrero and Alejandro Martinez for their warm hospitality at Universidad de Navarra. My thanks as well to the staff of the Biblioteca Eugenio Trías, in Madrid, where I was able to read leisurely and enjoy many wonderful walks along El Retiro.

I should also acknowledge the institutional support of the Centro de Investigaciones y Proyectos Especiales, FIGRI, Universidad Externado de Colombia, where the project was completed in the first semester of the year 2019.

Over the years, I've had the opportunity to learn from and share with remarkable mentors, teachers, and friends. I would like to express my gratitude to: Tom Darby, Horst Hutter, Paul Mier, James Moore, Maben Poirier, Waller Newell, Fernando Estrada, Ryan Knighton, Juan Camilo Rodriguez, Ravi Ravindra, Lou Pauly, Peter Emberley, Clifford Orwin, Gary Mangel, Travis Smith, Craig Hathaway, Juan Esteban Ugarriza, Domingo Araya, Graham Forst, and Kenneth Green.

Joseph Parry, Bryndee Ryan, and Ashleigh Cooke at Lexington Books were very diligent with my editorial queries, and I am grateful for their terrific work on the manuscript.

Introduction

READING HEIDEGGER'S *NIETZSCHE*

This study has the character of an *untimely meditation* on two key figures in the history of political philosophy. The thoughts of Martin Heidegger and of Friedrich Nietzsche pose, independently of one another and in theoretical proximity, some of the most pressing challenges to modern western thought. Granted the provocative, indeed liminal mode of reason and style of these two radical thinkers, it is in the spirit of intellectual open-mindedness—to dialogically persist in the pursuit of the examined life—that I propose this study at the interstice between hermeneutics and political philosophy. Heidegger and Nietzsche bring to our attention a "spiritual crisis" of epic proportions that in their account originates in European culture and that has become increasingly global in the contemporary world. It is my intent to shed light on the ontological sources of this potentially transformative event, to understand and test the soundness of its claims, while pursuing a dialogue and apprenticeship with the towering figures at the forefront of the ongoing history of political philosophy.

This is a meditation that employs Heidegger as "interpretative lens" by means of which to read Nietzsche. The largest portion of the text, Parts I–III, offers an interpretative reading of Heidegger's study of book 1 of Nietzsche's *The Will to Power* titled "European Nihilism." Generally speaking, the aim of Parts I–III is to focus on Heidegger's reading of Nietzsche in an attempt to shed light on this particular portion of Nietzsche's writings. The original source of the text comes from Heidegger's lecture-course delivered in the first trimester of the year 1940 at the University of Freiburg. Heidegger divided the published lectures into twenty-nine subsections: the book offers a detailed reading of each of these sections, focusing on the problem of nihi-

1

lism or "lost spirit" that Heidegger pursues in great detail through his engagement with the thought of Nietzsche. Part IV runs a commentary on Heidegger's treatise, "The Determination of Nihilism in Accordance with the History of Being" (*Die Seinsgeschichtliche Bestimmung des Nihilismus*), written between 1944 and 1946, and first published in 1961.[1] This fourth chapter, titled "Hermeneutics and Political Philosophy," seeks to add a more rounded set of themes, some of which may resonate with Heidegger's "later thought." It is a philosophical meditation that may be a beginning of our journey out of the nihilistic labyrinth[2] toward "the philosophy of the future."

This is therefore a study anchored in an exegesis of texts. My suggestion at the outset is that it is hermeneutically crucial that Heidegger is not writing a self-standing treatise like *Being and Time*, but that he is pursuing a dialogue with Nietzsche—a dialogue, which, granted, takes place in Heidegger's own terms. Although the book dwells on an interpretation of a work by Martin Heidegger, the aim has been to see how Heidegger's ontological perspective may contrast and expand upon Nietzsche's thinking. I have studied Heidegger's text in an attempt to elicit thoughts latent in Nietzsche.

Now, one difficulty of an interpretative endeavor of this sort is to figure out the primary object of study. Is this an interpretation of Heidegger, of Nietzsche, or of Heidegger's Nietzsche? Although the three alternatives seem distinctly possible, the book aims to develop the last option. To focus on *Heidegger's reading of Nietzsche* has the advantage that it appears to do the most justice to the fabric of the text. On the downside, at times it will seem difficult to distinguish whether a given line of reasoning should be taken to be Heidegger's or Nietzsche's. I would like to propose, however, that this ambiguity is part of the reason Heidegger chose to lecture and publish two volumes on the thought of Friedrich Nietzsche. Heidegger seems to be trying to think his way into and out of the world-shaping thinking drawn by Nietzsche's artful philosophy. Heidegger is after the true "face" of Nietzsche—a Nietzsche that, perhaps unexpectedly, might be both pluralist and ontological *Versucher*.

The more attentive we are to his mode of reasoning and the rhythm of his interpretation, we find that Heidegger's reading of Nietzsche orchestrates a paradox: it partakes in Apollonian delineation ("clarity," "distinctness") and Dionysian fusion ("roundedness," "fulfillment"). Heidegger is proposing to interpret Nietzsche's thinking to its limit, encompassing classical depth in tandem with a hermeneutic of singularity that sees texts as open letters for philosophical fulfillment.[3] This might sound complex, so let me explain what I mean. In this particular text, Heidegger partakes in a mode of interpretation where his intent is not only to understand the author's mind in its own right but also to participate in an ongoing encounter, propitiated by a seminal text, but ultimately driven by the reader's concerns. If I understand him correctly, the aim of Heidegger is therefore not to be a close reader, but to make the transition from the act of reading toward what he calls "thinking."[4] Nietzsche's text, in other words, is not an end-in-itself but a gateway to the experience of thought. More to the point, Heidegger explains his mode of reading Nietzsche thus:

> In the following text exposition and interpretation are interwoven in such a way that it is not always immediately clear what has been taken from Nietzsche's words and what has been added to them. Of course, every interpretation must not only take things from the text but must also, without forcing the matter, be able quietly to give something of its own, something of its *own* concerns.[5]

It is Heidegger's intent to take the reader toward a manner of interpretation that weaves itself into the fabric of the text, signaling a distinct set of concerns. We also note that to some or even a large extent Heidegger becomes Nietzsche's "sparring partner," entering into a spirited encounter with Nietzsche's writings, immersing himself in them while apparently leading Nietzsche's manner of thinking toward its "fulfillment."[6] At times, however, the experience of reading Heidegger's lectures gives the impression that we are partaking in an "attempt" or "experiment" (*Versuch*) in a Nietzschean sense. We are confronted with a sustained and extensive reading of one philosopher by another philosopher not in terms of some oblique remarks, such as, say, Aristotle's critique of Plato in the *Politics,* or Rousseau's references to Hobbes in the *Social Contract,* but at full length, in a manner and mode of study that resembles the practice of medieval commentaries of classical texts.[7] I invite the reader to remain with this image of the "medieval commentator," as a kind of approach that might well be analogous to Heidegger's intent. Note that this is only a qualified suggestion: my point here is that in his interpretation Heidegger is neither a close reader tout court, nor is he a deconstructionist for whom it would be misguided to search for true meaning or authorial intent. Perhaps it would not be altogether inaccurate to call Heidegger a *transfiguring interpreter*, unfolding lines of reasoning that could be taken to be latent in the text. Heidegger is trying to uncover the essential in Nietzsche's philosophy.

This might also be consistent with Nietzsche's view in *Beyond Good and Evil* aphorism 211 that for the philosopher, in contrast to the mere philosophical laborer, "knowing is creating." A critic, however, may point out that in the self-understanding of the medieval exegete interpretation is humanly speaking not a creative act. The function of the medieval commentator is to explain and incorporate a philosophical text into a given (theological) tradition. There seems to be a delicate "tight-rope walk," a balancing act, instead of necessarily a "quarrel," between genuine exegetical or thoughtful discovery (philosophy) and the power of authentic creative unfolding (poetry). In broad strokes, Heidegger's study of Nietzsche resembles this consideration.

INTERPRETATIVE APPROACH

Not surprisingly, the secondary literature is ambivalent about how to come to terms with Martin Heidegger's interpretation of the thought of Friedrich Nietzsche. Broadly speaking, commentators tend to take three approaches: (1) Non-synthetic confrontation: a continuum that goes from an *Auseinandersetzung* to a possible "dialogue" of some kind. (2) Veiled self-expression: Heidegger employing his interpretation of Nietzsche as "mask" for his own thinking. (3) Hermeneutic expansion or development: Heidegger's engagement with the text drawing out trains of reasoning potentially underlying or latent in Nietzsche's thinking. In this section of the introduction I offer a selection of authors that represent these interpretative positions and provide a scholarly and literary space that situates the book in the context of more recent studies.

Hans-Georg Gadamer makes the claim that Heidegger's *Nietzsche* is "the true counter-part to *Being and Time*." Gadamer is of the view that the lectures are mostly about Heidegger's thought and not about Nietzsche.[8] More generally, Gadamer reads Heidegger and Nietzsche on the basis of Kant's *Critique of Judgment*: for him both are responding to the "radical subjectivization" put forth by the Kantian compartmentalization of the human mind.[9] Gadamer is also of the view that Heidegger reads Nietzsche with the aim to orient the spirit from such mode of subjectivity towards a hermeneutical question that is latent in Nietzsche's mature thinking: the symbol of the eternal return.[10]

Gianni Vattimo, who studied with Gadamer and Karl Löwith at the University of Heidelberg, and later became an influential scholar of hermeneutics and Nietzsche-Heidegger studies in Italy,[11] writes in the early 2000s that "the problem of the Heidegger-Nietzsche relationship" might be *the* central theme, of current philosophical debate, in the continental European tradition." Although this may sound overstated, Vattimo reminds us that from the 1960s onward, broadly speaking, the continental tradition has tried to come to terms with two key and not unrelated themes: Nietzsche's rhetorical critique of foundationalism, and the later Heidegger's "poetic thought," which led to probing debates on rethinking the distinction between philosophy and literature.[12] Vattimo argues that, hermeneutically speaking, the influence of Heidegger and Nietzsche has worked both ways: "in addition to the explicit positions taken by Heidegger in his interpretation of Nietzsche, Nietzsche himself opens the door to an understanding of the meaning of Heidegger's philosophy." While Heidegger takes Nietzsche to be the last metaphysician, Vattimo also notes that Nietzsche was taken over as the precursor of "post-metaphysical philosophy."[13]

In contrast to the hermeneutic and post-modern appropriation of Nietzsche, Lawrence Hatab offers a triangular dialogue between Heidegger and

Nietzsche in relation to the figure of Aristotle.[14] In Hatab's view, the main moral tension between Heidegger and Nietzsche stands on the difficulty of bringing to common terms "creativity and normalcy." Hatab makes the more moderate case that "inspired by Nietzsche, Heidegger wanted to contest the common patterns of everydayness and *das Man* on behalf of the innovative work of artists and thinkers."[15] Hatab focuses on the ethical possibilities that the liaison between Heidegger and Nietzsche might make possible in so far as it is interpreted in the key of Aristotelian *phronesis*. Hatab's aim is to let the question of ontology recede in the background (perhaps in some form of tacit knowing) to bring to the forefront particular questions of ethical life that respond to "limit-conditions" in terms of our singular and shared sense of human finitude.

Michael Allen Gillespie[16] contends that Heidegger's reading is not a mere interpretation but an *Auseinandersetzung* or "setting-apart-from-one-an-other"—a vigorous encounter between "hermits of the spirit" "across the gulf that separates the two peaks."[17] The notion of *Auseinandersetzung* can be a rather forceful word for Heidegger: at times conveying a "setting of ac-counts," "confrontation," "clash"; it is Heidegger's term for the Greek word *polemos*.[18] At times, however, Gillespie seems to take a somewhat Gadamer-ian interpretation of the expression, perhaps based on Heidegger's explicit and more attenuated use of the word in his study of Nietzsche. According to Gillespie, Heidegger's interest in Nietzsche is "not scholarly but philosoph-ic." What he seems to mean by this distinction is that Heidegger's aim is "not to interpret Nietzsche but 'to let our thinking enter into the matter' that bears the name Nietzsche."[19] Heidegger's encounter with Nietzsche from Gilles-pie's perspective also takes the reader from the question of nihilism to con-sider new forms of culture founded upon the thought of eternal return.

Although Stanley Rosen[20] grants that "without a doubt, the most influen-tial interpretation of Nietzsche in [the twentieth] century is that of Heideg-ger," he finds himself at the antipodes of Heidegger's view that Nietzsche was "the last of the Platonists who constitute the history of western meta-physics." The problem of interpreting Nietzsche's texts seems to lie on the trope of "masks" which, at some level, make every reading of Nietzsche "an attempt and a temptation."[21] Although Rosen correctly resists the simple equation between Plato and Nietzsche, he grants that for both Plato and Nietzsche "contrary to Heraclitus, the way up is not the same as the way down," and therefore there is an affinity in both philosophers in that they try to grapple, in the context of their own times, with the problem of re-compos-ing and re-shaping the *polis* and the *psyche*. For Rosen, however, Heideg-ger's interpretation of Nietzsche is "too 'rationalist.'"[22] There is a marked rhetorical difference between Nietzsche and Plato in that "Plato says nothing in his own name," whereas Nietzsche (with the exception of *Zarathustra*) "states everything in his own name." But Rosen's Plato is not a "Nietzschean": in his account the fundamental difference between Plato and Nietzsche is that for Plato, unlike Nietzsche, there are eidetic "originals." Platonic "pre-discursive vision that somehow allows us to regulate our discourse" is contrasted by Rosen from Nietzsche's "interpretations," which he takes to be "derivative notions." [23] For Rosen, however, neither Plato nor Nietzsche are "Platonists," and that is at the center of his objection to Heidegger's historicizing of philosophy.

Also from the perspective of "perennial philosophy" Laurence Lampert[24] notes that in Heidegger's lectures Nietzsche emerges as "metaphysician, Platonist, and nihilist," even though he claims to be none of the three.[25] Lampert seems to take issue with Heidegger's interpretative strategy: the notion that it may be possible to understand a first rate author better than he understood himself (perhaps something hubristic in its own right) seems to uphold the principle of difference and novelty above the understanding of authorial intent. In Lampert's critical view, Heidegger's interpretative emphasis seems to lie on an "other" rather than a "better" reading.[26] Lampert contends that Nietzsche becomes a caricature in Heidegger's hands, not with a polemical but with a historical intent: for Heidegger, Nietzsche is "one of a small number of men who can disclose the real meaning of western history."[27]

In a compelling intellectual biography, Rudiger Safranski[28] claims that Heidegger read Nietzsche in a developmental manner. Heidegger "presents his own thinking as an overcoming of Nietzsche, in Nietzsche's footsteps."[29] Safranski's Nietzsche, however, seems to have lost sight of the question of Being that is central to Heidegger by affirming the sphere of values—values which are a product of the will to power. From the viewpoint of "valuative thought," the world for Nietzsche seems to be "reduced to the quintessence of 'preservation and enhancement of conditions.'"[30] Heidegger, on the other hand, would seem to overcome Nietzsche's thinking by rejoining the question of Being to the mystery of human freedom.

From a perspective "between hermeneutics and deconstruction" Alan Schrift[31] argues that although in his view it may be unfeasible to clearly and distinctly separate the thought of both thinkers in these lectures, in his reading he has chosen to view "Heidegger's works on Nietzsche to be works about Nietzsche and not about Heidegger." Schrift provides a series of exegeses that try to steer clear of either dogmatic or relativistic positions, examining the tension between Nietzsche's pluralist temper and the mode of concentrated ontological analysis initiated by Heidegger.

There are a variety of modes to craft and bring to the fore the Heidegger/Nietzsche relation. Let me state concisely my own view. The book proposes to develop an ontological exploration: we are looking at a study undertaken by Heidegger to offer a reading that could serve the quest for truth latent in Nietzsche's philosophy. This study therefore makes the case that situating these two philosophical titans "in tandem" can offer insights that would otherwise be lost if taken at further interpretative distance. [32]

The study has the character of a serene reading of a text, a text that, in turn, deals with key ontological themes and problems in the history of modern thought. More to the point, however, the primary aim and interpretative limits of most of the exegesis are bound by Heidegger's reading of Nietzsche's aphoristic writings on "European Nihilism." Although the book offers various references to seminal texts in the history of political philosophy, theology, and comparative literature, its core purpose is to offer an immersion in the slow "rumination" of what Heidegger has to say about relatively few pages in Nietzsche's oeuvre. This is therefore not primarily a study on Heidegger's philosophy, nor is it a study of Heidegger's entire interpretation of Nietzsche. Rather, the text engages in a bounded exercise to auscultate Nietzsche's diagnosis of *der europäische Nihilismus* from Heidegger's perspective, for the most part by focusing on a specific collection of aphoristic texts devoted to the problem.

Now, a major difficulty of this kind of interpretative exercise lies in the estimation of the primary sources. To what extent and in what ways is the study of Nietzsche's posthumous texts a scholarly sensible endeavor? Several challenges are possible on this front.

R.J. Holingdale takes Nietzsche's unpublished writings to be for the most part outside the purview of his role as commentator: the rationale for this is that he finds unpublished and unauthorized work hard to distinguish.[33] To some extent, this seems a compelling interpretative position, especially with regards to Nietzsche's *Nachlass*. On the other hand, it also seems reasonable to grant that some interpretative latitude is called for, especially in the case of seminal writers. Think, for instance, of Franz Kafka's works, a number of which (altogether 6 volumes, including manuscripts of *The Trial, The Castle, Amerika,* etc.) were published posthumously by his friend and literary executor Max Brod without authorial consent. Hegel's posthumously published lecture courses, perhaps not unlike Aristotle's *Politics* which might be a series of students' notes, are also cases in point. Circumstances of this kind may give us second thoughts about Hollingdale's position. Also, restricting our focus only to an author's published works would possibly compromise the legitimacy of scholarly research of unpublished or posthumously published correspondence, which often can be illuminating and (depending on the date, circumstance of composition, and addressee) perhaps decisive.

Heidegger claims that Nietzsche's thinking was moving in the direction of a "major work." It is on this basis that Heidegger contends that he is following in the "thought-paths" of Nietzsche. As such, his interpretation would be an attempt to pursue lines of thought initiated by Nietzsche's texts, especially from the post-Zarathustra period (1884–1888). Heidegger makes the case that the "innermost core" of Nietzsche's "metaphysics" is to be found to a large extent in the posthumous writings.[34] Despite their accidental and very problematic editorship, Heidegger's attempt is to try to "make public" and discuss at length what was to be found in inchoate and arbitrarily assorted form in Nietzsche's notebooks.

Allow me to signal also at the outset that the material of *The Will to Power*, seminal and useful for scholarly purposes as it is, should nevertheless be taken with caution: Nietzsche's sister, the infamous anti-Semite Elisabeth Förster-Nietzsche, was in charge of the initial editorial work of the text.[35] Again, right from the outset, the study of Heidegger's interpretation seems to be mired with not inconsiderable interpretative risks and difficulties.[36] The reader should always keep in mind that the "ground" of Heidegger's interpretation of Nietzsche remains open to question. My argument, of course, is not that I am offering a definitive and final interpretation of Heidegger's Nietzsche, let alone that I am bringing to closure the intention of Nietzsche's philosophy. But what I am indeed arguing is that despite the interpretative difficulties, the approach I am pursuing—a liaison between hermeneutics and political philosophy—can be a fruitful way to stay true to the liveliness and depth of the thought of Heidegger and of Nietzsche. It can also bring us to a closer view of the ontological sources, conditions, limitations, and aspirations brought forth in this seminal moment in the tradition of European intellectual culture and history.

Now, a caveat seems required here: in their writings, Nietzsche and Heidegger convey a relentless critique of liberal democracy. There are plenty of allusions in which they are resolute critics of modernity,[37] critics of Socrates, of Descartes, and severe opponents of the legacy of the French Revolution.[38] What are we to make of this potentially uncompromising critique? Both Heidegger and Nietzsche thought that left to its own devices the immanent movement of modernity would foreclose the higher regions of "self-over-coming" and "authenticity" leading to the social hegemony of the "last man."[39] At some level, what nihilism seems to mean therefore is that, increasingly, in our late-modern social consensus the calculus for predictable security, comfortable self-preservation, and economic interest maximization seems to become everybody's necessary and sufficient condition for self-actualization. Broadly and provocatively put, the hegemony of secure self-preservation as axiomatic postulate of the modern social condition, in their view, falls into an ever-increasing latitude toward consensually regulated homogeneity (a pluralism of sameness), technologically induced conformism (what Heidegger calls "enframing"), and an irreverent attitude of boundless pragmatic relativity (whatever "works"). These are of course sweeping remarks on the meaning of nihilism, and the text itself will develop a hermeneutic definition of what nihilism might mean philosophically. The point I want to bring up for now is that Heidegger and Nietzsche seem to be onto something when they don't let us assume a complacent and self-congratulatory attitude in our late-modern way of life: Heidegger and Nietzsche muster all their philosophical energies to revive the question of the soul, and of Being, and what it means to meaningfully "be-there."[40]

In terms of the history of political thought, the text attempts to highlight that the careful study of controversial authors such as Heidegger and Nietzsche can partake in a descriptive and prescriptive exploration of a high order. It is also a strong dose of a mode of thinking that tests and perhaps unsettles the "overlapping consensus" of contemporary liberal theory, bringing back to our attention key questions such as "what is the good life, and what political regime can make it possible?" As long as we approach these "high-octave" authors with a sense of Platonic *sophrosyne* and Aristotelian *phronesis*, we might well be realizing the highest purpose of liberal democracies: to protect, foster, and whenever possible encourage men and women to "follow the logos," living the examined life in authentic and genuine manners open toward "harmonious development."[41]

The book gathers Heidegger's reading of Nietzsche as a thought experiment in this overarching cultural context. Moreover, the text also intends to be a propaedeutic in the "craft of thinking."[42] Studying Heidegger's Nietzsche can be a philosophical apprenticeship: an immersion into how a first-rate thinker interprets another, distinct, towering mind.[43] Despite their differences in tone and content, both Heidegger and Nietzsche are joined in their deep care for the presence of the spirit in the modern world. It is that common focus that grounds this work of interpretation.[44]

SYNOPSIS: FROM THE RHETORIC OF NIHILISM TO THE *SEINSFRAGE*

Let me summarize the two main reasons for writing a book on Heidegger's *Nietzsche*. First, the possibility to gain a comprehensive and contrasting view with respect to Nietzsche's thought: getting a sense of clarity on how to come to terms with insights that in Nietzsche tend to be phrased too provocatively and elliptically. In a way, reading Nietzsche through Heidegger provides a series of hermeneutic resources to pursue a consistent line of interpretation that may rein in Nietzsche's paradoxical reversals, shocking turns of phrase, and constant passionate *non sequiturs*. This is not to imply that Heidegger doesn't engage in his own kind of intense philosophical rhetoric. No doubt he does. Nevertheless, Heidegger's reading is useful because his language, with all its apparent idiosyncrasies and obscurities, provides a sense of contrast, even critical distance, and, oft-times, further precision and development with regards to the philosophical problems Nietzsche highlights and urges upon the reader.

The essential problem—the "spiritual crisis" that Nietzsche diagnosed in the late nineteenth century, and which he claimed would persist for the next two hundred years[45]—is the overarching concern of the book. To use a medical image: the book takes its bearings from Nietzsche's diagnosis and seeks in Heidegger a second view. The attempt, however, is not only to understand the diagnosis but to begin to foresee a prognosis and what might be called a "philosophical therapy." Having said that however, the reader should also bear in mind that neither Heidegger nor Nietzsche are neutral spectators in this world-historical drama: their own rhetoric in many ways also exacerbates the problem they so powerfully disclose. Hence the need for some serene consideration. Is the cultural diagnosis they are presenting true? If so, to what extent and in what measure?

This takes me to the second reason to study Heidegger's Nietzsche. The text investigates the problem of cultural foundations in terms of speculative "ontology." For Nietzsche and for Heidegger "European nihilism" is not an abstract problem of "pure reason" but an *essentially* historical predicament—a question, in Heidegger's language, of Being-and-time. Unlike Kant, for whom time, like space, is a product of the autonomous human mind,[46] for Heidegger time seems to have the character of a mystery. Although it may sound paradoxical, for Heidegger it is the failure to get out of our autonomous subjectivities to "think the nothing" that is at the origin of "nihilism."[47] For Heidegger *Sein* and *Zeit* need not be unrelated: we are timed by time, time becomes our there-being, in so far as we stay in front of the question of Being.[48] It is by remembering the question that we may find our measure.[49]

The meaning behind Heidegger's "question of Being" is a difficult, perhaps intractable aspect of his thought. What does "Being" mean for Heidegger?[50] In his draft notes on Heidegger's *Nietzsche*, George Grant discusses the distinction between non-capitalized being (*das Seiende*) taken to be particular beings or entities, and capitalized Being (*das Sein*) as the German infinitive for "the to be" (*Esse, l' etre*), and for the substantive noun derived from it.[51] In her study of *Being and Time*, Magda King proposes to translate *das Seiende* for the Greek *to on*: not only as "beings," but also sometimes as "things" or "the things that are."[52] Throughout the book references to "Being" (*das Sein*) will refer to the realm of "ontology" or the underlying and overarching "ground" that for Heidegger has the character of an existential question for man[53] (qua *Dasein*, being-there, being-in-the-world), and "being" (*das Seiende*) will make reference to "what presences" (*das Anwesende*), that is, to all the "ontic" concrete entities of sense experience.

In *Sein und Zeit* Heidegger analyzes the Being of *Dasein* as existentially structured on the basis of three aspects: finite "projection," "thrownness," and being in relation with beings ("being-with"). In the relational finitude of *Dasein's* "transcending projection," *Dasein* finds itself thrown into a world of concrete possibilities and can seek to be liberated from the determination of every-day things by recollecting itself ("staying in front of the lack"). This implies an existential constitution of *Dasein* occurring in temporality: the ontological may be disclosed in the ontic if *Dasein* is gripped by authentic "anticipatory resoluteness" of caring to have a conscience of its "ownmost possibility of Being." Such possibility has the character of an existential question for Heidegger. But the key event might be that the Being of *Dasein* is intimated in the call of care: "an ontic attestation for *Dasein's* ontological possibility of Being-a-whole."[54]

In the context of Heidegger's reading of Nietzsche, the problem of ontology seems to produce the following difficulty: while in Heidegger's thought ontology is a question of the mystery of "the ground," for Nietzsche (in Heidegger's account) it seems to be a manifestation of the "will to power." The book is in many ways an extended meditation on this distinction. Heidegger contends that the *Seinsfrage* is a fundamental predicament that has been occluded since the foundation of metaphysics in the thought of Plato and by means of the history of Platonism has found its culmination in Nietzsche's "valuative thought." The view that all thought is subservient to the faculty of willing seems to have led to the mistaken juxtaposition of "ideas" and "values." Although this theme will be developed at length in the text, allow me to say a few preliminary remarks to clarify the issue.

IDEAS AND VALUES

The misunderstanding that puts the Platonic ideas and Nietzschean values on the same footing[55] seems to be an offshoot of taking the Hegelian concept as a paradigm of universal thought. The key implication of reasoning in terms of concepts is that the concept "grasps" phenomena, thereby shaping experience in the act of cognition. Reason thereby becomes a species of "knowing as making," apparently molding the given in our cognitive self-image. In the beginning of modernity this mode of reasoning seems to have been put forth by Giambattista Vico to challenge the Cartesian division between (historical) body and (cognitive) mind. Vico's method of historically infused reasoning seems to have influenced the thought of Hegel, who in a sense tried to effect a synthesis between Vico ("new science" of historical tradition) and Descartes (methodical subjectivity).[56]

Ideas, in contrast to concepts, don't directly attempt to modify phenomena: ideas "illuminate" the mind, enabling it to exercise "collection and division" according to what Plato calls "natural kinds."[57] While the intellection of ideas is contemplative or mindfully receptive, the grasp of concepts is active, forthcoming to shape the given. Intellection in terms of ideas or "genuine thought" is reflective of a classical disposition, and reasoning in terms of concepts is decisively modern.

There seems to be, however, a further complication: it has been argued that "no one has ever succeeded in giving a satisfactory account of the ideas."[58] Although this is a formulation I find unsatisfactory—I am much closer to the view that the Platonic ideas have a *notissimum* character[59]—we could still ask ourselves why it might make sense to have a more modest or somewhat unruffled interpretation of the ideas. In my reading, one of the reasons for having a skeptical *zetetic* attitude might be that if we take the ideas as "permanent problems," that is, as self-standing, yet open-to-question sources of aspiration and longing, then we could be in a position to reflect, ponder, deliberate about what they might mean. The view that the ideas are straightforwardly self-evident and in no possible contradiction would seem to preclude the opportunity to debate about and think through the "permanent problems." A 'supple' yet steadfast interpretation of the ideas seems to mirror the figure of Socrates,[60] and may also be a salutary corrective for the ever-recurrent downturn of neo-scholastism and thick-headed dogmatism (of all sorts). In the *zetetic* interpretation of Plato, the "idea of justice" is a "permanent problem" that highlights the possibility of genuine thought disclosing the "noetic heterogeneity" of the whole. In other words, not everything is governed by the idea of justice: some events are not political. Our sense of justice might be fairer and more soundminded if we see the limits of what is just, and what therefore is pertinent or not to our judgment. My point here is not to demerit the universality of the idea of justice. I am trying to highlight the Aristotelian understanding that it might well be our disagreements about the meaning of justice which elevate our thought from mere moralism toward the pursuit of intellectual virtue, as well as a humane sense of compassion.[61] As non-relative, trans-subjective, supra-historical, unconstructed, yet real sources of longing independent of our volition, the ideas are illuminated by *eros*.

Concepts, on the other hand, seem to drive us to configure our future: they appear to be a by-product of willing. Taken in a secular mode, concepts provide a frame of reference for our active pursuit to shape the world in a way that would have seemed unfitting for ancient thinkers; our conceptual mind does not assume that the world is a cosmos, an orderly whole, but seems to start from the Cartesian premise that the *ego cogito* can be disengaged from "matter," and as such can methodly impose its rational will onto it for the betterment of man.[62] This makes a certain amount of sense from a modern angle: if the world is not orderly, if we seem to be somehow on our own, then why not use our cognitive powers to secure our welfare in the "here and now"? The modern project as Heidegger conceives it has taken this line of reasoning as its starting point to make the "conditions of possibility" (*die Bedingungen der Möglichkeit*) for human living a matter of rational planning. Our problem—a problem particularly acute in the modern research university—is that increasingly *theoria* seems to lose ground vis-à-vis practical specialization.[63] This mode of technical reasoning conceived for the means of mastering human and non-human nature to a large extent drives contemporary global "enframing." The reason for the relative length of this discussion on the distinction between "ideas" and "values" is to signal, right from the outset, that to take both "values" and the "ideas" as manifestations of "will" or "the will to power" seems to be at the core of Heidegger's thought-provoking and questionable juxtaposition of Plato and Nietzsche.

HEIDEGGER AND POLITICS

Although the book unfolds at an "architectonic" level of enquiry, given that this is an interpretation at the interstice between hermeneutics and political philosophy, it is fitting to offer a number of clarifying remarks on Heidegger's thought in relation to the deep problem of practical judgment and political history. Although the book focuses on the ontological realm in Heidegger's interpretation of Nietzsche, in Heidegger's thought "Being" and "time" are not necessarily unrelated, therefore it seems fitting to express in this introductory chapter some remarks regarding this delicate and unsettling concern.

An insightful account to begin making sense of Heidegger and "the political" is Fred Dallmayr's *The Other Heidegger*.[64] Dallmayr offers an even-handed treatment of a series of political and ethical implications originating from Heidegger's thinking. Such themes include: the problem of "post-metaphysical" politics, Heidegger's relationship to democracy, his "poetic turn," and the dialogue between "East and West." More to the point for the purposes of this part of the introduction, Dallmayr offers a persuasive and sensible political interpretation, arguing for a reading of Heidegger at the paradigmatic level of "ontology," rather than on the ontic plane of concrete decision-making.[65]

Dallmayr begins his reflections on "Heidegger and politics" offering a sense of historical geo-political context: an obsolescent *Pax Britannica* of the nineteenth century and the various modes of expansive utilitarianism encompassed under this broad political power. The twentieth century, by contrast, was marked by "deep stirrings and epochal ruptures," and socio-political "paradigm shifts." In the first half of the twentieth century, the times fostered experimentation, risk-taking: at a general sociological level, they were not conducive for a settled orientation to cultivate prudent habits and routine practices. Ontologically speaking, twentieth-century thought exposed the "fragility of traditional conceptions of subjectivity." Out of this open and contested cultural context, the need seems to have arisen to explore philosophical thinking "resolutely" (following the *logos* to the outmost) by seminal twentieth century thinkers, such as Ludwig Wittgenstein, Martin Heidegger, and others. In particular, Heidegger's thought originated in the apparent possibility of "overcoming metaphysics," which he took to be a mode of cogitation in terms of structural generality conditioning and stipulating the typology of all "things."

Dallmayr offers a distinction that might be useful to try to come to terms with the problem of Heidegger's relation to political thought. The distinction between: (a) Ontological "polity" (*le politique*, the political, *das Politische*: "Politics as regime, or paradigmatic framework"), and (b) Ontic "policy" (*la politique*, politics, *die Politik*: "Politics as concrete decision-making and action").

Dallmayr follows up on this distinction arguing that there are four general areas that permeate "the political" perspective in the thought of Heidegger: (1) the individual "subject" in relation to political agency; (2) the "character" or shape of the political community; (3) the tension and relation between the cultural and political community and "modernization"; and (4) the developing shape of global politics taken as the problem of an "emerging *cosmopolis*, or world-order beyond the confines of Western culture."[66] Indeed, these themes will be part of the horizon of questions that the book explores in liaison with the history of political philosophy.[67]

Dallmayr's distinction between "ontological" or systemic (we might perhaps even say qualifiedly Aristotelian) and ontic, concrete, policy-driven levels of analysis is not necessarily superimposable with traditional political distinctions between left and right. Dallmayr also notes that in his reading the ontological/ontic distinction is related *only obliquely* to Heidegger's "ontic-ontological difference."[68] The bottom line, in Dallmayr's view, is that the ontic "can never be a derivation or simple application of the ontological dimension." Differently put: perhaps "Being" and "time" need not be unrelated, but their mediation—their bridge in *Dasein*—would require a manner of carefully being-there free from political *ressentiment* which clearly evaded Martin Heidegger. I find myself in agreement with Dallmayr's contention that if we don't qualify the distinction between the ontological and the ontic, Heidegger's account can become "dismal, to the point of nearly eclipsing the rest of his work."

In the process of writing the book, a series of posthumous *Schwarze Hefte*, "Black Notebooks," appeared in print in the year 2014. The Black Notebooks contain Heidegger's previously unpublished notes from the years 1931–1941, and have brought renewed attention to the problem of Heidegger's political biography.[69]

Allow me to clarify that it is outside the scope of this study to discuss in detail the appalling political opinions of Martin Heidegger. Perhaps I should add that I am not a historian of ideas, and therefore I acknowledge that I am philosophically unequipped to describe in detail the particular sources, conditions, and timely circumstances that would account for Heidegger's political biography, mainly, for our purposes in this discussion, from 1933 on-wards. Nevertheless, I would refer the reader to Gregory Fried's pointed and thorough discussion in the *Los Angeles Review of Books* (September 13, 2014), which traces Heidegger's views in a critically probing and persuasive manner. Fried brings our attention to Heidegger's unrepentant antipathy against what he refers to as Jewish cosmopolitan "rootlessness," "Platonic universalism,"[70] and "world-historical" motivations, which would allegedly at some level explain Heidegger's opinions regarding this delicate historical matter. In a review essay for the *Frankfurter Allgemeine Zeitung* (July 25, 1953), the then twenty-four-year old graduate student Jürgen Habermas, upon reading the *Introduction to Metaphysics* where Heidegger callously refers to the "inner truth and greatness" of the National Socialist movement, reacted with strong critical conviction to Heidegger's "silence" on his parti-san Nazi engagement. Although Heidegger added in the original publication that what he meant to assert in that line was the movement's "encounter between global technology and modern humanity," Habermas is correct in pointing out that this apparent explanation is far from satisfactory.

Decades later, Habermas described his reaction in the following way: "what is irritating is the unwillingness and the inability of this philosopher, after the end of the Nazi regime, to admit his error with so much as one sentence—an error fraught with political consequences."[71] The dismal his-torical record of political actions, opinions, and omissions of Martin Heideg-ger gives us more than sufficient reasons to be open-eyed in the attempt to articulate our understanding of his thinking.[72] In Heidegger's biography, we seem to find a conjunction of a towering intellect together with a staggering lack of humane political sensibility. Let me close this section by saying that the ground and purpose of this book is to propose that we can learn from the thought of Heidegger and Nietzsche while being mindful of the central im-portance of the study of Platonic-Aristotelian political philosophy.

GENERAL OVERVIEW

The book is divided into four main parts. Part I, "European Fragmentation and the Problem of Valuative Thought," offers a series of accounts on the sources of the problem of European nihilism at several levels, ranging from physics and the meaning of nature, to psychology and metaphysics. In this context, Nietzsche offers the following definition: "What does nihilism mean? That the highest values devalue themselves. The aim is lacking; 'why?' finds no answer" (*Will to Power* I.2). The overall discussion of the problem is framed in the unfolding of an epochal change and period of transition that in Heidegger's interpretation of Nietzsche's philosophy is in the process of "fulfillment" (*die Vollendung*). The reader will note that Heidegger's thinking partakes in a kind of movement: Heidegger begins by making a thought-experiment from the origin to the potential outcome of "valuative thought" (*der Wertgedanke*). Such exploration leads him to see that "values" are a product of "will," and that in order to grasp the link between "willing" and the modern subject he has to revisit the philosophy of Descartes.

Part II, "Cartesian Re-Founding," explores Heidegger's claim that the Cartesian *ego cogito* as a mode of disembodied reason lies at the source of modern subjectivity. It gives an account of the metaphysics of Cartesian subjectivity in relation to and contrast with the philosophical anthropology of the ancient Greeks. The key predicament of our time, in Heidegger's view, is the identification of the Cartesian subject with the ontological *hypokeimenon* or "ground." The second part of the book is therefore an attempt to explain from a variety of angles Heidegger's analysis of the distinction between "truth" in the modern mode of reflective representation, and a more classically attuned "truth" as "unconcealment," on the basis of his reading of Nietzsche.

Part III, "Metaphysics to the *Seinsfrage*," offers an expanded meditation on the problem of inter-subjectivity also from classical and modern perspectives. Heidegger explores the conceptual origins of the Kantian *a priori* and considers a liaison with what we might call an ontological "post-critical trust" to account for a way of thinking and sounding out of experience that clears the duality between universals and particulars at the center of the history of western metaphysics. The third part expands, therefore, on Heidegger's critique and re-composition of metaphysics. Heidegger returns in full circle to the language of "Being," not only signaling the problem as in previous sections, but now impressing upon the reader the essential importance, in *logos*, of the word "is." Part III therefore addresses the need to (sensibly) recollect the question of Being anew in the midst of the contemporary world.

It is Heidegger's way of philosophizing to stay with "the question," which means to remain thinking within a "hermeneutic circle" until the gist of the inquiry hits home. Part IV, "Hermeneutics and Political Philosophy," initially reiterates and elaborates upon some of the arguments previously presented and discussed, particularly the critique of "valuative thought." But it also goes beyond the scope of Heidegger's primary exegesis on "European nihilism" to begin considering a mode of thinking less reliant on voluntarism and more open to meditative receptivity. Part IV highlights the role of poetic thinking and the distinction between the "what" of traditional metaphysics and the "who" of existential singularity. It also underlines the thoughtful experience of care and conscience (*Gewissen*) in Heidegger and in Nietzsche. The book concludes with an overall summary and a rejoinder of the themes of enlightenment, hermeneutics, and political philosophy in our period of transition toward new forms of time.

NOTES

1. Martin Heidegger *Nietzsche* 2 Vols. (Pfullingen: Verlag Günther Neske, 1961). References by page number in the text, with some amends, are from Martin Heidegger *Nietzsche* Vol. IV Trans. Frank Capuzzi. Edited with Notes and Analysis by David Farrell Krell (New York: Harper, 1991). I have also relied on the Spanish translation by Juan Luis Vermal: Martin Heidegger *Nietzsche* (Barcelona: Ariel, 2013). For the titles of the 29 sections in Parts I-III, I relied on Capuzzi's translation, with some adjustments. Although I have endeavored to offer a bounded interpretation of Heidegger's "der Europaïsche Nihilismus" and "Die Seinsgeschichtliche Bestimmung des Nihilismus," occasionally, in order to clarify certain passages, I also make reference to the rest of the text: Martin Heidegger *Nietzsche* Volumes I and II. Trans. with Notes and Analysis by David Farrell Krell. (New York: Harper 1979). *Nietzsche* Volumes III and IV. Trans. Frank Capuzzi. Edited with Notes and Analysis by David Farrell Krell. (New York: Harper, 1991). With the exception of the *Untimely Meditations* which refer to specific page numbers, references in the text to the works of Nietzsche are by book title and section or aphorism number.

2. The secondary literature on "nihilism" is extensive. This is only a small representative sample of recent works. For an analysis of the different accounts of nihilism as a spiritual crisis in the nineteenth and twentieth centuries see Franco Volpi *Il Nichilismo* (Roma: Laterza, 2004); an interpretation from both poetic and philosophical angles aiming at the prospect of "healing" the nihilist malaise is offered by Ofelia Schutte *Beyond Nihilism: Nietzsche without Masks* (Chicago: University of Chicago Press, 1984); an Oriental-Heideggerian account is put forth by Nishitani Keiji *The Self-Overcoming of Nihilism.* Trans. Graham Parkes with Setsuko Aihara. (Albany: SUNY Press, 1990); other pertinent interpretations are: Karl Löwith "The Historical Roots of European Nihilism" in *Nature, History, and Existentialism* (Evanston: Northwestern University Press, 1966); Alan White *Within Nietzsche's Labyrinth* (New York: Routledge, 1990); Tom Darby et al. eds. *Nietzsche and the Rhetoric of Nihilism* (Ottawa: Carleton University Press, 1989); Stanley Rosen *Nihilism* (New Haven: Yale University Press, 1969); Michael Gillespie *Nihilism Before Nietzsche* (Chicago: University of Chicago Press, 1994). Two pertinent recent compilations of essays around this theme are: Jeffrey Metzger ed. *Nietzsche, Nihilism and the Philosophy of the Future* (London: Continuum, 2009), and Laurence Paul Hemming et al. eds. *The Movement of Nihilism: Heidegger's Thinking after Nietzsche* (London: Continuum, 2011).

3. References to Heidegger's *Being and Time* are from the John Macquarrie and Edward Robinson translation (New York: Harper, 1962). Heidegger discusses "hermeneutics" in Sections 31 and 32: "Being-there as understanding," and "Understanding and interpretation." The hermeneutic approach attempts to participate in the pursuit of understanding in a manner that is not based on Cartesian disengaged subjectivity. Rather, the human interpreter configures a "hermeneutic circle," gathering the "parts" and the "whole" of his experience in a dynamic but stable interdependence that seeks to further understanding. Henri Bortoft *The Wholeness of Nature: Goethe's Way toward a Science of Conscious Participation in Nature* (New York: Lindisfarne Press, 1996), p. 9-11; 331, makes a persuasive account in the following terms. Bortoft distinguishes between (a) the "meaning" of the hermeneutic circle of constitutive parts-in-the-whole "unfolding" (*explicatio*) and "enfolding" (*complicatio*), in contrast to (b) the analytical logic of linear *either/or*. Bortoft describes the hermeneutic experience as "the unfolding of enfolding, so that the parts are the place of the whole where it bodies forth into presence. The whole imparts itself; it is accomplished through the parts it fulfills." Hans-Georg Gadamer defines the hermeneutic experience in Heidegger as the ontological "disclosure of the forestructure of understanding" in *Truth and Method* Sheed and Ward Trans. (New York: Continuum, 1975), p. 235-45.

4. Martin Heidegger *What is Called Thinking?* Trans. J. Glenn Gray. (New York: Harper, 2004), p. 244.

5. Heidegger *Nietzsche* Vol. III. "Nietzsche's Metaphysics," Intro. p. 191. Critics, on the other hand, have noted that Heidegger's reading is more forceful than this passage concedes. See for instance Bernard Williams "Nietzsche's Centaur" *London Review of Books*, l. 3 No. 10, 4 June 1981. For an interpretation that focuses more on the shared themes and continuities in

Nietzsche and Heidegger cf. Robert Pippin "Heidegger on Nietzsche on Nihilism" in *Interanimations: Receiving Modern German Philosophy* (Chicago: University of Chicago Press, 2015), Ch. 8.

6. The sense of "agon" *tout court* between Heidegger and Nietzsche might lack sufficient nuance to characterize Heidegger's reading. The image of "chess opponents" also depicts, in many ways, the spirit of their confrontation. On the other hand, a critic who might want to stress their differences may perhaps think of Thomas Mann's masterful depiction of Naphta and Settembrini in the novel the *Magic Mountain.* Granted that there is some power to this allusion of distinct uncompromising views, but Heidegger's reading offers more sources of possible agreement with Nietzsche's philosophy than we might have otherwise expected. Differently put: Heidegger's aim is to take up Nietzsche to the level of "ontology." In many ways, this seems to go against the grain of Nietzsche's rhetoric, to the extent that the suggestion seems implausible. But then again, what are we to make of a thinker who asserts: "go away from me and protect yourselves from Zarathustra! [. . .] perhaps he has deceived you [. . .] I bid you to lose me and find yourselves; and only when you have all denied me, I will return to you" *Ecce Homo*, Preface, 4. Cf. *Gay Science,* 100. Although Nietzsche would have possibly been appalled by Heidegger's intricate language, the case can be made that many of Nietzsche's poetic allusions and "songs," upon meditation, resonate with Heidegger's philosophy. At some level, perhaps the expression "polyphonic confrontation" might also come close to the heart of the Heidegger/Nietzsche encounter.

7. See for instance Armand Maurer *Medieval Philosophy: An Introduction.* With Preface by Etienne Gilson. (Toronto PIMS, 1982). Ralph Lerner and Muhsin Mahdi eds. *Medieval Political Philosophy* (Ithaca: Cornell University Press, 1963). Umberto Eco *The Aesthetics of Thomas Aquinas* (Cambridge: Harvard University Press, 1994). Richard Rubenstein. *Aristotle's Children: How Christians, Muslims and Jews Rediscovered Ancient Wisdom and Illuminated the Middle Ages* (New York: Harcourt, 2003).

8. Hans-Georg Gadamer "Martin Heidegger—85 years" in *Heidegger's Ways.* Trans. John Stanley. With intro. by Dennis Schmidt. (Albany, New York: SUNY Press, 1994), p. 118. For a recent set of essays interpreting Heidegger from a hermeneutical perspective cf. Michael Bowler and Ingo Farin, eds. *Hermeneutical Heidegger* (Evanston, IL: Northwestern University Press, 2016).

9. Immanuel Kant *Critique of Judgment* (Part I, Division I.1-5). Nietzsche, however, examines critically the Kantian notion of disinterested moral and aesthetic action in *Beyond Good and Evil,* 33 and 220. The puzzle here seems to be not unrelated to the status of "asceticism" in Nietzsche's thinking: the closer the approximation of aesthetics to disinterestedness, the closer judgment seems to lead toward a "practical" approximation to the "ascetic ideal" (presumably beyond earthly interests). Nietzsche, however, agrees with Stendhal that beauty is *"une promesse de bonheur"* (*Genealogy of Morals* III.6), hence for him it is not unrelated to desire and interest: the question would be how to manifest the relation between beauty and interest in an uplifting manner. Nietzsche discusses at length the "ascetic ideal" in part III of the *Genealogy of Morals.* For a pluralistic and non-puritan interpretation of philosophy in terms of "ascetic practices" or "spiritual exercises," see the discussion of Pierre Hadot *Philosophy as a Way of Life.* Ed. with Intro. by Arnold I. Davidson. (Oxford: Blackwell, 1995).

10. Hans-Georg Gadamer "The Drama of Zarathustra," in Michael Allen Gillespie, and Tracey Strong eds. *Nietzsche's New Seas: Explorations in Philosophy, Aesthetics, and Politics.* (Chicago: University of Chicago Press, 1991), p. 220-231. *Truth and Method*, p. 60; 87-89; 214. The link between eternal return, the "Dionysian," and "ontological practice" across Nietzsche's works is explored in Eugen Fink *Nietzsche's Philosophy* (London: Continuum, 2003). In Fink's Heideggerian reading of Nietzsche the key question is whether Nietzsche is "merely an inverted metaphysician or whether a new ontological understanding announces itself through him" (p. 6).

11. Gianni Vattimo *Dialogue with Nietzsche.* Trans. William McCuaig. (New York: Columbia University Press, 2006), p. 181-189.

12. This is the starting point of Jürgen Habermas' critique of the French appropriation of Nietzsche and Heidegger in *The Philosophical Discourse of Modernity.* Trans. Frederick Lawrence. (Cambridge: MIT Press, 1990). David Wittenberg *Philosophy, Revision, Critique: Re-*

reading Practices in Heidegger, Nietzsche, and Emerson (Stanford: Stanford University Press, 2002), Chs. 1-3, proposes a study of Heidegger's Nietzsche from the perspective of literary criticism, describing Heidegger's reading as a textual effort of historicist revision and Ciceronian "paralipsis."

13. Michel Foucault's position also seems to partake in the line of interpretation that brings together Heidegger and Nietzsche: "For me Heidegger has always been the essential philosopher [. . .] my entire philosophical development was determined by my reading of Heidegger. I nevertheless recognize that Nietzsche outweighed him [. . .] My knowledge of Nietzsche is certainly better than my knowledge of Heidegger. Nevertheless, these are the two fundamental experiences I have had. It is possible that if I had not read Heidegger, I would not have read Nietzsche [. . .] Nietzsche alone did not appeal to me—whereas Nietzsche and Heidegger: that was a philosophical shock!" Michel Foucault *Politics, Philosophy, Culture: Interviews and Other Writings 1977-1984*. Ed. with Intro. by Laurence Kritzman. (New York: Routledge, 1990), p. 250.

14. Lawrence Hatab *Ethics and Finitude: Heideggerian Contributions to Moral Philosophy* (Oxford: Rowman and Littlefield, 2000).

15. Ibid. p. 123.

16. Michael Gillespie "Heidegger's Nietzsche" *Political Theory*, Vol. 15 No. 3 August 1987, p. 424-435. In *Nietzsche's Final Teaching* (Chicago: University of Chicago Press, 2017), Gillespie explores the political, philosophical, and theological thoughts and musings of the "late Nietzsche" centered around the notion of eternal recurrence, Nietzsche's "musical politics," and his kinship with Plato. See Gillespie's exchange with Ronald Beiner in *Interpretation: A Journal of Political Philosophy* (Spring 2018, Vol. 44, Issue 3), p. 425 ff.

17. Gillespie "Heidegger's Nietzsche," p. 424.

18. Martin Heidegger *Introduction to Metaphysics*. Trans. Gregory Fried and Richard Polt. (New Haven: Yale University Press, 2000), p. 153. David Farrel Krell offers an insightful analysis of why Heidegger, in his Foreword to the *Nietzsche* lectures, might have chosen the term *Aus-einander-setzung* to characterize his encounter with Nietzsche. Particularly relevant is Heidegger's interpretation of *Auseinandersetzung* as *polemos* in Heraclitus, fragments B53 and B80. Krell takes this to mean a "confrontation" that also partakes in a *koinonia* or community between the two thinkers: a "setting apart from one another that serves essentially to bring together, a contest that unites." *Nietzsche* Vol. I "The Will to Power as Art," p. 230-31.

19. Gillespie "Heidegger's Nietzsche," p. 427.

20. Stanley Rosen "Remarks on Nietzsche's 'Platonism'" in Tom Darby, Bela Egyed, Ben Jones eds. *Nietzsche and the Rhetoric of Nihilism*. (Ottawa: Carleton University Press, 1989), p. 147.

21. Ibid. p. 161. Eric Blondel *Nietzsche: The Body and Culture*. Trans. Sean Hand. (Stanford: Stanford University Press, 1991), also grants that although Heidegger is Nietzsche's "greatest commentator," he seems to overlook the genealogical resonances and nature of Nietzsche's philosophy. Blondel contends that Heidegger is apparently "blind to the interpretative, non-instrumental and anti-technical aspects of the body and genealogy in Nietzsche [. . .] the price paid is the effacement of the *Versuch* [. . .] Reduced in this way to a few concepts, Nietzsche's work becomes valuable only as an example of metaphysics and as such has to be superseded by the thought of Heidegger" (5).

22. Rosen "Remarks on Nietzsche's 'Platonism,'" p. 155.

23. Rosen references Plato's *Phaedo* 100a-b, where Socrates refers to the ideas as the "strongest hypotheses" and the "safest response." Rosen claims that "there is no ontology in Plato, no univocal sense of Being as presence. There are of course, fragmentary, inconclusive and playful discussions of what we could call *fragments* pointing toward ontology" (160). Rosen's view is that the Platonic ideas are "silent paradigms of what eludes discourse even when regulating it . . . human beings are not Ideas but lovers of the Ideas. We desire what we lack, yet what we lack 'structures' or directs our desire" (162-63).

24. Laurence Lampert "Heidegger's Nietzsche Interpretation." *Man and World*, 11/1974, Vol. 7, Issue 4, p. 353-378.

25. Ibid, p. 353. Contrast, however, with Louis P. Blond *Heidegger and Nietzsche: Overcoming Metaphysics* (London: Bloomsbury, 2011).

20   *Introduction*

26. Ibid. p. 354.
27. Ibid. p. 355.
28. Rüdiger Safranski *Martin Heidegger: Between Good and Evil.* Trans. Ewald Osers. (Cambridge: Harvard University Press, 2002).
29. Ibid. p. 302.
30. Ibid., p. 304.
31. Alan Schrift *Nietzsche and the Question of Interpretation: Between Hermeneutics and Deconstruction* (New York: Routledge, 1990), p. 14. To a large extent, Schrift appears to be taking his bearings from Jacques Derrida especially in *Of Grammatology.* Trans. Gayatri Chakravorty Spivak. (Baltimore: Johns Hopkins, 1974). But there are also Gadamerian aspects to Schrift's interpretation, in so far as he seems to find in hermeneutics an alternative to the Scylla and Charybdis of dogmatism and relativism.
32. According to Vattimo this is consistent with Karl Löwith's perspective: "Löwith too thinks of Nietzsche and Heidegger as substantially in tandem, as driven by the same purposes." *Dialogue with Nietzsche,* p. 183. Malcolm Bull *Anti-Nietzsche* (London: Verso, 2014), p. 90, notes that "in taking his distance from Nietzsche, Heidegger may be continuing his trajectory." Alejandro Vallega also signals the question of "how much of a metaphysical reading Nietzsche's thought accepts, and how much of a Nietzschean reading Heidegger's thought withstands." "'Beyng-Historical Thinking' in Heidegger's *Contributions to Philosophy,*" in Charles E. Scott et al. eds. *Companion to Heidegger's Contributions to Philosophy* (Indianapolis: Indiana University Press, 2001), p. 62.
33. R.J. Hollingdale. *Nietzsche* (London: Routledge, 1939), p. xii.
34. Heidegger *Nietzsche* Vol. III, "The Will to Power as Knowledge," Section 2. Cf. Nietzsche's letter to Carl Fuchs (December 14, 1887). Heidegger's conception of Nietzsche's *Nachlass* also seems consistent with the judgment of the leading editor of Nietzsche's *Kritische Gesamtausgabe: Werke,* Giorgio Colli, whom, despite many reservations, comparatively speaking finds in the notebooks a mode of argument and tone "unusually sober, almost contemplative." Colli refers to the published texts as "productions of Nietzsche the *artist* and the notebook materials as meditations of Nietzsche the *philosopher.*" (Cited in Krell's Analysis to Heidegger *Nietzsche* Vol. III, p. 271, footnote 9). Walter Kaufmann, on the other hand, comments that in the *Nachlass* "we look into a vast studio, full of sketches, drafts, abandoned attempts, and unfinished dreams. And in the end we should be less tempted than ever to mistake a random quotation for an ultimate position." Friedrich Nietzsche *The Will to Power.* Kaufmann ed. (New York: Vintage, 1968), p. 557.
35. For further evidence of Heidegger's disclaimer cf. *Nietzsche* Vol. IV, Section 1, p. 11-12. Nietzsche's stormy relation to his sister is vividly described in H.F. Peters *Zarathustra's Sister: The Case of Elisabeth and Friedrich Nietzsche.* (New York: Crown, 1977). For a historical overview of the reception and appropriation of Nietzsche's philosophy in Germany see Steven Ascheim *The Nietzsche Legacy in Germany 1890-1990* (Berkeley: University of California Press, 1994).
36. From the perspective of intellectual biography, Julian Young discusses the *The Will to Power* under the rubric "history of a failed literary project" in *Friedrich Nietzsche: A Philosophical Biography.* (Cambridge: Cambridge University Press, 2010), p. 540-549. Young cites Nietzsche's letter to his friend and close collaborator Heinrich Köselitz (a.k.a. Peter Gast), dated February 13th 1888, where Nietzsche relates that "the final version of my 'attempt at a revaluation' is ready: it was, all in all, a torture, I haven't had the audacity for it. In ten years-time I'll make it better." But Nietzsche just a few days later also tells Köselitz that he has apparently "abandoned all thought of publishing the work" (541). Later in the year, however, in the month of September 1888, Nietzsche seems to have found renewed courage, writing to Paul Deussen that the work he was preparing, was his "life-defining task," which would "split the history of humanity in two halves" (541). Tracy Strong comments that "any sense of the arrangement of these selections, any resonances they seem to acquire by being beside each other on paper are to be radically distrusted . . . interpretation is therefore difficult." *Friedrich Nietzsche and the Politics of Transfiguration* (Berkeley: University of California Press, 1988), p. 220-21.

37. Heidegger goes as far as to equate modernity with the "history of the non-essence of Being," which for him centers on the notion of man as "subiectum" that begins with "Platonism," and seems to find its culmination in Nietzsche's "valuative thought." This sweeping claim makes Heidegger not only a critic of modernity, but a critic of what he takes to be the entire history of western metaphysics. If modernity is identical with the "history of the non-essence of Being," then for Heidegger "modernity" would begin not with Machiavelli or the Lutheran Reformation but with the ancient Greeks, presumably with the "Greek enlightenment" in Periclean Athens. Cf. Heidegger *Nietzsche* Vol. III, Part 3, "Nietzsche's Metaphysics," Section 5. Contrast with Nietzsche *Gay Science*, 358.

38. See, for instance, Nietzsche *Dawn* 534; Heidegger *Basic Concepts* Trans. Gary Aylesworth (Indiana: Indiana University Press, 1998), p. 76. Contrast with Edmund Burke *Reflections on the Revolution of France* (Oxford: Oxford University Press, 2009), p. 10: "it looks to me as if I were in a great crisis, not of the affairs of France alone, but of all of Europe, perhaps of more than Europe. All circumstances taken together, the French revolution is the most astonishing that has hitherto happened in the world." Now, philosophically speaking, Heidegger and Nietzsche are concerned with the *best of possible worlds*, including what might be higher, or at any rate "other," than man. His furious rhetoric notwithstanding, the case can also be made that Nietzsche might not be an anti-modern *tout court* (cf. *Twilight of the Idols*, "Expeditions of an Untimely Man", 43-44; *Beyond Good and Evil*, 242). Granted that he is a strong critic of the modern condition, how to characterize Nietzsche's views on modernity? I am sympathetic toward Karl Löwith's view that Nietzsche, in the spirit of his colleague at Basel, Jacob Burkhardt, has in mind something like "repeating antiquity at the peak of modernity." Strauss-Löwith Correspondence *Independent Journal of Philosophy* Vol 5/6 (1988), p. 183. Heidegger grasps the tension of "sensibilities" in Nietzsche in the following way: "Nietzsche in an immediate way comes closer to the essence of the Greeks than any metaphysical thinker before him . . . at the same time he thinks in a modern way." Vol. III "The Will to Power as Knowledge and as Metaphysics," Section 17, p. 113. In *Time as History* (Toronto: Hunter Rose Company, 1969), p. 44, George Grant offers the following statement: "in thinking the modern project [Nietzsche] did not turn away from it. His critical wit about modern society might lead one to believe that he condemned its assumptions. Rather, he expressed the contradictions and difficulties in the thought and life of western civilization, not for the sake of turning men away from that enterprise, but so that they could overcome its difficulties and fulfil its potential heights." Nietzsche's thought in Grant's view makes explicit the meaning of modernity, that is, the experience of "time as history." Grant, however, is wary of this distinct conception of "time as history" as it is expressed in Nietzsche, and also has strong reservations about the voluntarism at the origin of modernity ("endless time"), and about much that he finds in Nietzsche's thinking (45). More specifically, Grant expresses moral concern and incomprehension about Nietzsche's view of "redemption," and its apparent lack of perfection, or fulfilment, or goodness, in willing *amor fati* (46-47). Perhaps a way to begin addressing Grant's concerns would involve a comparative study of Nietzsche and Leibniz.

39. Nietzsche *Thus Spoke Zarathustra*, Prologue, 5. Heidegger *Being and Time*, Section, 27.

40. Cf. Magda King *A Guide to Being and Time*. John Llewelyn ed. (New York: SUNY Press, 2001), p. xiv; 122-25. Consider also Nietzsche's notion of "the great health" in *Gay Science* 381-82.

41. Nietzsche uses the expression "harmonious development" in *Schopenhauer as Educator*, Section 2 (p.131). cf. Heidegger *Nietzsche* Vol. III "Nietzsche's Metaphysics," Section 4. Contrast with Plato *Timaeus* 44d ff.

42. As Heidegger put it in a letter to a young student (June 18th, 1950): "Everything here is the path of a responding that examines as it listens. Any path always risks going astray, leading astray. To follow such paths takes practice in going. Practice needs craft. Stay on the path, in genuine need, and learn the craft of thinking, unswerving, yet erring." *Poetry, Language, Thought,* Trans. Albert Hofstadter. (New York: Harper, 2001), p. 184.

43. The closest analogies I can think of to illustrate these kinds of towering encounters are Thomas Aquinas' reading of Aristotle, or Al-Farabi's interpretation of Plato, or perhaps even Plato's characterization of Socrates (cf. Plato *Second Letter* 314 a-c).

44. Cf. Martin Heidegger "Letter on Humanism," Capuzzi Trans., in William Mcneil ed. *Pathmarks* (Cambridge: Cambridge University Press, 1998), p. 241. All references to the "Letter on Humanism" refer to this translation, with occasional amendments from the original *Brief über den Humanismus* (Frankfurt am Main: Vittorio Klostermann, 1974).

45. Nietzsche *Ecce Homo*, "Why I am Destiny," 1. Cf. Leo Strauss "German Nihilism," Lecture delivered at the New School for Social Research (February 26, 1941), published in *Interpretation* Spring 1999, Vol. 26, No. 3, p. 363-64. In that lecture, Strauss tells his students to "not lose hope; what appears to you the end of the world, is merely the end of an epoch, of the epoch which began in 1517 or so." In this passage, Strauss equates the "spiritual crisis" with what he takes to be the origin of modernity. Notice that neither Heidegger nor Nietzsche focus on the events of "1517 or so" with the emphasis that Strauss' writings convey.

46. Kant *Critique of Pure Reason* Part I, Sections 1 and 2. Nietzsche *Birth of Tragedy*, Section 18.

47. Heidegger *Nietzsche* Vol. IV "Nihilism and the History of Being," p. 226. Magda King *A Guide to Being and Time*, p. 9-10.

48. Heidegger *Being and Time* II.3.65; Nietzsche *Thus Spoke Zarathustra* III "The Other Dance Song." Also, Gadamer *Truth and Method*, p. 228. Nietzsche discusses the "Lust des Fragen" in *Gay Science*, 344. Contrast with *GS,* 351.

49. Heidegger *Nietzsche* Vol. I "Will to Power as Art," Section 23. *Poetry, Language, Thought*, p. 68-69.

50. Cf. Heidegger *Being and Time* II.4.68d, p. 401; II.4.69b, p. 408. In *Contributions to Philosophy: An Introduction* (Bloomington: Indiana University Press, 2003), Daniela Vallega-Neu offers a helpfully synthetic sketch of *Being and Time* in conversation with the *Beiträge* that sheds light on the "ontological difference" from the perspective of both texts. For commentaries on Heidegger's terminology, see Thomas Sheehan *Making Sense of Heidegger* (New York: Rowman and Littlefield, 2014). Michel Haar *Heidegger and the Essence of Man.* Trans. William McNeill. (New York: SUNY Press, 1993). William Richardson S.J. *Heidegger: Through Phenomenology to Thought.* With Preface by Martin Heidegger. (New York: Fordham, 2003). Richard Capobianco *Heidegger's Way of Being* (Toronto: University of Toronto Press, 2014). Gianni Vattimo *Introducción a Heidegger.* (Barcelona: Gedisa, 2002). Julian Young *Heidegger's Later Philosophy* (Cambridge: Cambridge University Press, 2002), especially Ch.1. A reviewer of the book has helpfully suggested that the text seems to fall into what Thomas Sheehan calls the "first generation paradigm" of Heidegger interpretation, which is mainly based on the ontological structure of *Being and Time.* That could be a plausible characterization if it is also considered within a larger Heidegger/Nietzsche hermeneutic context.

51. *George Grant: A Reader.* Ed. William Christian and Sheila Grant. (Toronto: University of Toronto Press, 1998), p. 307.

52. Magda King *A Guide to Being and Time*, p. 11-12.

53. See Martin Heidegger *Basic Problems of Phenomenology.* Trans. Albert Hofstaedter. (Bloomington: Indiana University Press, 1988), p. 227 ff. The German noun *Mensch* can be rendered in both male and female form. Although the Krell/Capuzzi version of the *Nietzsche* lectures consistently translates it as man, whenever grammatically and stylistically possible I have endeavored to render *Mensch* also as human being. Note, however, that for Heidegger being human (man or woman) itself is not identical to *Dasein*: our humanity opens the possibility for the ontological meditation concerning the Being of *Dasein* but is not reducible to it.

54. Heidegger *Being and Time*, Section 41. Cf. Vallega-Neu, *Contributions to Philosophy: An Introduction*, p. 14 ff. Gregory Fried "What's in a Word? Heidegger's Grammar and Etymology of 'Being' in *A Companion to Heidegger's Introduction to Metaphysics.* Richard Polt and Gregory Fried eds. (New Haven: Yale University Press, 2001), p. 125-142. In footnote 4, Fried references resonances of the *Seinsfrage* with the Sanskrit word "sat."

55. To offer a preliminary snapshot of the argument: Heidegger seems to be making the Hegelian inference that since Nietzsche's thinking is "inverted Platonism," it remains tied to the mode of thinking which he is "negating." For Heidegger that is the reason why Nietzsche's values, as "metaphysical" antitheses of the ideas, would be on the same plane as the Platonic forms. But this association would only be persuasive from a perspective that gives primacy to willing over classical *theoria*. Plato would have disagreed with this characterization (see for

instance *Symposium* 210a-212b). For further references in relation to "ideas" and "values" in Nietzsche cf. *Beyond Good and Evil*, Preface; *Gay Science*, 372. *Will to Power*, 12; 14; 37; 46; 53; 54; *WP* aphorism 715 contains a concise definition: "the stand point of 'value' is the standpoint of conditions of preservation and enhancement for complex forms of relative life-duration within the flux of becoming."

56. Karl Löwith discusses the thought of Vico in contrast to Descartes in *Meaning in History* (Chicago: University of Chicago Press, 1949), Ch. 6. Cf. Mark Lilla *G.B. Vico: The Making of an Anti-Modern.* (Cambridge: Harvard University Press, 1993), p. 35; 131; 177. Charles Taylor analyzes the cognitive implications of thinking under the rubric of concepts in *Hegel* (Cambridge: Cambridge University Press, 205), p. 297-349. As Taylor puts it: "that the world is for a subject means that the world-as-object-of-knowledge is structured by concepts." The conceptual mind appears to rule the history of modern philosophy from Baconian science and the Cartesian method all the way to Foucault's power/knowledge. Heidegger wants to question the distinction between ancients and moderns by claiming that this mode of thinking originates already with "Platonism." Contrast with Gadamer *Truth and Method*, p. 387, where Gadamer describes "the process of concept formation": on the one hand, it is associated with "accidents," but on the other with the apparent advantage that it involves multiplying "freedom to form an infinite number of concepts and to penetrate what is meant ever more and more." In this passage Gadamer is indeed closer to Husserl than to Heidegger.

57. Plato *Phaedrus* (246a3-257a2).

58. Leo Strauss *The City and Man* (Chicago: University of Chicago Press, 1978), p. 119. In that passage Strauss references Plato's Socrates in *Republic* 509d1-510a7 (the analogy of the line) and *Phaedrus* 247c3 (the plain of *aletheia*). Kant refers to ideas as "presentations of the imagination" in the *Critique of Judgment* (Part I, Division I, 49). For Plato unlike Kant, there is an epistemic distinction between imagination (*eikasia*) and the *noetic* contemplation of the ideas (*Republic* 509d11- 511e-5).

59. Cf. Heidegger *Nietzsche* Vol. IV, Section 19, "Nietzsche's Position vis-à-vis Descartes," p. 126. On this speculative note, I have found intriguingly persuasive the accounts by Marsilio Ficino *Platonic Theology* Trans. Michael J.B. Allen. (Cambridge: Harvard University Press, 2004), Vol. IV. Bk. XII. iii.9, and *Commentaries on Plato: Phaedrus and Ion.* Ed. and Trans. Michael J.B. Allen (Cambridge: Harvard University Press, 2008), Chs. 27-33. Also, Stephen Menn *Plato on God as Nous* (South Bend, Indiana: St. Augustine Press, 1995), Ch. 3.

60. Cf. Aristotle *Metaphysics* 1078b20-30. Also, Plato *Symposium* 206a-212c4.

61. Aristotle *Nicomachean Ethics.* Bk. I, i.2-3; I, iv.2-3; X, viii.13. Nietzsche *Thus Spoke Zarathustra* I. 22 "On the Gift Giving Virtue"; *Gay Science*, 328-29.

62. Charles Taylor *The Sources of the Self: The Making of Modern Identity* (Cambridge: Harvard University Press, 1989), p. 181-182, discusses the universality of Cartesian "disengaged reason" from ordinary experience, in contrast to the search for singularity in the "intensely individual" mode of reflection and expression, the "deeper engagement in particularity," in Montaigne. According to Taylor, there may be two distinct kinds of "modern individualism": on the one hand the Cartesian "quest . . . for an order of science, of clear and distinct knowledge in universal terms," and on the other Montaigne's "aspiration to ... loosen the hold of such general categories . . . so that the shape of our originality can come to view."

63. Martin Heidegger "The Age of the World Picture" in *The Question Concerning Technology and Other Essays.* Trans. William Lowitt (New York: Harper, 1977), p. 118-124; George Grant *Technology and Empire* (Toronto: House of Anansi, 1969), p. 113-133.

64. Fred Dallmayr *The Other Heidegger* (Ithaca: Cornell University Press, 1993), especially Chs. 1-3. I would like to thank Professor Dallmayr for his generous reading of an earlier version of the book.

65. Dallmayr *The Other Heidegger*, p. 50-51.

66. Ibid. p. 52.

67. Edward Andrew "Heidegger's Führerprinzip: Leadership out of and into Nihilism," in Joseph Masciulli, Mikhail Molchanov and W. Andy Knight eds. *The Ashgate Research Companion to Political Leadership.* (Farnham: Ashgate, 2009), p. 123-34, interprets Heidegger as heir of a tradition of charismatic leadership stretching from Machiavelli to Hegel. According to Andrew, Heidegger's *Rectoral Address* of 1933 should be understood in the historical context

of a counter-movement against "the effects of the French Revolution in Germany." Philippe Lacoue-Labarthe also focuses on Heidegger's "commitment" in 1933, but he goes further back in time to the ancient world to contend that Heidegger's radicalism was "founded on the idea of a hegemony of the spiritual and the philosophical over political hegemony itself, which leads us back to the Platonic *basileia*, if not to Empedocles." *Heidegger, Art and Politics* (Oxford: Blackwell, 1990), p. 13.

68. Heidegger *Being and Time* I.5. Section 29 explores the ontological-ontic distinction. Politically speaking, the distinction may be expressed in terms of "existential" understanding attuned to structures that are (presumably) not of human making (e.g., "divine law," or perhaps some higher harmony), and "ontic" or "existentiell" grasp of entities that appear in the world (e.g. human codes in their various positive renditions). At I.6. Section 43, Heidegger analyzes the distinction in terms of "ontological understanding" and "ontic experience." Dallmayr, on the other hand, seems to take the "ontological" perspective as it is nomothetically constituted in Aristotle's *Politics* (Bks. II and III) or in Plato's *Laws*.

69. In the secondary literature, critical reactions to Heidegger's politics include Victor Farías *Heidegger and Nazism* (Philadelphia: Temple University Press, 1989); Emmanuel Faye *Heidegger: L'introduction du Nazisme dans la Philosophie* (Paris: Albin Michel, 2005); also, Philippe Lacoue-Labarthe *La Fiction du Politique* (Paris: Bourgeois, 1987). Charles Bambach *Heidegger's Roots: Nietzsche, National Socialism, and the Greeks* (Ithaca: Cornell University Press, 2003) reads Heidegger's ontological study on Nietzsche as a situated cultural response to the misappropriation of Nietzsche's philosophy in terms of "biologism." p. 283-84. In a recent text, *Dangerous Minds: Heidegger, Nietzsche and the Return of the Far Right* (Pennsylvania: Penn State University Press, 2018), Ronald Beiner makes a critical examination of Heidegger and Nietzsche (to a large extent based on current world affairs), which attempts to forestall their political misappropriation while validating their philosophical import. Alexander Duff *Heidegger and Politics: The Ontology of Radical Discontent* (Cambridge: Cambridge University Press, 2015), critically remarks that there may be two kinds of political import derived from Heidegger's thought: purgative/foundational and expectant of a new dispensation. Theoretically speaking, both signal a kind of political radicalism that might be evocative Machiavelli.

70. Heidegger's aversion to "rootless cosmopolitanism" apparently extended beyond Judaism, and included Catholics, communists, and in general liberal cosmopolitans whom, from Heidegger's perspective, conceive metaphysics in ways that for structural reasons would uproot people from their homeland of origin. Cf. Otto Pöggeler *The Paths of Heidegger's Life and Thought.* Trans. John Bailiff. (New Jersey: Humanities Press, 1992), p. 174; Charles Bambach *Heidegger's Roots*, p. 53 ff. In an unpublished paper, Richard Polt has made a compilation of references to Jews and Judaism in Heidegger's *Black Notebooks* [*Gesamtausgabe* vols. 94-96 (2014) and 97 (2015)]. Cf. also *Ingo Farin and Jeff Malpas eds. Reading Heidegger's Black Notebooks 1931-1941* (Cambridge: MIT Press, 2016). On this note, Nietzsche and Heidegger would have differed strongly: see, for instance, Nietzsche's thoughts on the key role of Judaism in the Greek formation of Europe in *Human All Too Human, 475; Beyond Good and Evil, 250*. Unlike Heidegger, Nietzsche cherished the resilience to be found in the Jewish way of life. On the other hand, Nietzsche's disparaging views on Christianity might, at some level at least, become less stringent if read in dialogue with the writings of Søren Kierkegaard. On this note I have learned much from William Hubben *Dostoievsky, Kierkegaard, Nietzsche and Kafka* (New York: Collier, 1972), p. 11 ff.

71. Habermas *The Philosophical Discourse of Modernity*, p. 155.

72. In reference to the history of political philosophy, Mark Blitz remarks that "whether the Platonic understanding that Heidegger tries to overcome can, if suitably attentive to Heidegger's questions, separate what is compelling in his thought from what must be rejected in his politics is, of course, a central issue." "Heidegger During the War" *The Political Science Reviewer*, Vol. 2, Number 1, June 2018, p. 85.

I

European Fragmentation and the Problem of Valuative Thought

THE FIVE MAJOR RUBRICS OF NIETZSCHE'S THOUGHT

Heidegger begins his lecture-course, "European Nihilism," with a puzzle. What did Nietzsche understand by "nihilism," and why is this significant? Heidegger takes Nietzsche's thought to be a constellation of the following five categories: "nihilism," "revaluation of values," "will to power," "eternal recurrence of the same," and the "overman." Presumably, in order to grasp Nietzsche's "unthought thought" or "teaching," it would be necessary to see the links between these five categories.

Heidegger notes the word "nihilism" appears to have been coined by the late eighteenth- and early nineteenth-century thinker Friedrich Jacobi. Later, the expression "nihilism" became associated with gathering natural knowledge only by means of sense perception: Turgenev popularized this view in his novel *Fathers and Sons.*[1] Dostoevsky, in the foreword to his Pushkin lectures, links nihilism with "rootless society which seems to hover high above the common people" (3). In this opening sketch nihilism seems to be associated with two related movements: (1) Active skepticism about received tradition. Heidegger associates this critical disposition and active negation of traditional grounds of authority with "positivism," and, (2) Romanticism that passionately reacts against the dryness of positivism and attempts to imagine "reality" as completely "other" from the apparently given. Romanticism appears to be a direct consequence of positivism, but the more relevant observation here seems to be that both are products of "nihilism."

Heidegger, however, adds that for Nietzsche nihilism means something "substantially 'more'" (4). Nihilism is not an abstract notion. Nietzsche situates the malaise at a supra-national level, speaking in terms of "European nihilism." Heidegger notes that "European" does not only stand for nineteenth-century positivism: it is not a "scientific" but a "historical" category akin to the notion "western" as in "western history." In this account, nihilism is the name of a historical movement that Nietzsche recognized, and depicted with the dramatic expression: "God is dead."[2] What this means, according to Heidegger, is that apparently "the Christian God has lost its power over beings and over the determination of man." With the critique of the Christian God all transcendental referents—"ideals," "principles," "rules," "norms," "ends," "values" set "above"—also seem to lose their uncontestable ground.[3]

Perhaps for rhetorical effect in this opening section Heidegger links together theology and metaphysics. What appears to be lost is the order and purpose, the "meaning," of Being. Nihilism is a historical process by means of which the "'transcendent' in the form of the Christian God seems to become "null and void," losing its uncontested "worth" and meaning as the settled inter-generational, inter-social, inter-racial, supra-national pillar of European civilization. This has not been a sudden process: Heidegger uses the image of a "fading star," which, although it may already have been "extinguished for millennia," might still give some gleaming appearance.[4]

Heidegger also speaks of the "determination" (*Bestimmmung*[5]) of the nihilist movement. The implication from this language of "determination" is that, apparently, there would be a traced course that "the truth of being as a whole" has to traverse in its historical manifestation. Heidegger adds, however, that this "truth of being as a whole" has traditionally been referred to as "metaphysics": every epoch is contained by some metaphysics. A given transcendental frame of reference runs its course at the end of every epoch, disclosing the "collapse of its reign," as well as of the "ideal" that springs from it. History doesn't end with the end of metaphysics: Heidegger notes that Nietzsche understood his own philosophy as an "introduction to the beginning of a new age" (5).

This transformation, at a historical or political level, in Nietzsche's account will produce tremendous upheavals, which Nietzsche, in the second part of the nineteenth century, foresaw as our destiny for the next two centuries to come.[6] Heidegger notes, however, that this period of transition, the structural shift in cultural aims, is "no longer experienced as sheer annihilation and deplored as wasteful and wrong, but is rather greeted as liberation, touted as an irrevocable gain, and perceived as *fulfillment*"[7] (*die Vollendung*, Heidegger's emphasis). Paradoxically, nihilism makes it possible to explore in an honest way the "free and genuine task" of experimenting with new kinds of guiding structures. This stage of the "historical process," which lays the groundwork open for architectonic novelty, Heidegger defines as "classical nihilism." Here nihilism not only is a product of the "negating concept," but also becomes a "negation of the negation," whereby new unprecedented kinds of affirmation presumably become possible.[8]

The "revaluation of values" is not a mere mechanical replacement of old for new. While the postulated "transcendental" embeddedness of previous values seems to fade away, there appears to occur a simultaneous opening of the mind. In Heidegger's terms there is, at first, a tentative motion towards thinking "Being for the first time as value" (6). Metaphysics devolves from "ontology" into "value thinking." Heidegger associates this with a structural metamorphosis, in the historical plane presumably akin to the fall of Rome and the epochal shift away from the pagan gods of antiquity.[9] Such kinds of revaluation apparently are in need of a "new principle" that would "authoritatively" anchor and establish a new basis, a new "standard of measure," for defining "beings as a whole." This would presumably produce in due course a new "table of values" that would make possible to rank sensibly different objects of striving. Heidegger seems to allude to historical echoes of the ancient Mosaic story under the form of a future metaphysics grounding anew "the truth of being as a whole."[10]

Now, according to Heidegger, Nietzsche posits the basic character of being(s) as a whole (*das Seiende im Ganzen*) as "will to power." Nietzsche's interpretation of the *essence of power* (Heidegger's emphasis) is a striving of "will." Power is not a static fact. The essence of power is to increase or to grow in power: "every power is only power as long as it is more power . . . as soon as power stalls at a certain power-level, it immediately becomes powerless" (7). Heidegger claims the essence of power itself is power's "own overpowering." This definition, Heidegger tells us, stems from Nietzsche's thought in an experience of self-knowledge: will to power as the basic character of being is a fundamental experience of Nietzsche's thought. A "thinker" in this context is someone who might have "no choice" but to try to give words for "what a being *is* in the history of its Being" (7). Such thought therefore appears to be some kind of compulsion: the thinking that names being, names it "will to power." Will to power would be the realm "from which all valuation proceeds and to which it returns."

The new valuation is a product of the "overpowering" of power. Paradoxically, for Heidegger this is not a blind process: "power and only power posits values, validates them," and produces "decisions about the possible justifications of a valuation." Somehow, however, this needful, all-encompassing process is also endowed with a conscious capacity to "choose," and therefore to offer some sort of validation and justification for its choices. Choice and "necessity" find themselves juxtaposed at the core of the essence of power—its process of "incessant self-overpowering," turns therefore into constant "becoming," without end, producing thereby a "cycle" of "power-conforming becoming" that apparently must "always recur." If the nature of reality is will to power, and the essence of such power is to overpower itself, it seems to follow that one can establish a pattern of recurrence of power as the essence of the nature of reality. This, Heidegger seems to be saying, would be an appropriate characterization of Nietzsche's thought if the basic character of beings were will to power.

If Nietzsche's thought of will to power as the basic character of beings holds, then it would seem to follow that the basic character of beings may also be defined as the "eternal recurrence of the same." For Heidegger this seems to imply that if will to power is an essential feature of reality, and the essence of such power is to overpower itself constantly, then what this would mean is that will to power recurs always, that is to say, eternally. It would follow that the essence of will to power—the essence of the "Being of beings as a whole"—is eternal recurrence. The "necessity" of the will to power would therefore be mirrored by the essence of eternal recurrence of the same. Will to power that "necessarily" recurs is the essence of the eternal recurrence of the same. At this juncture, Heidegger seems to be saying that "eternal recurrence of the same" defines the "ontology," the "what," of beings in their "essence" or "constitution," while "will to power" defines their "how," or the manner in which such beings as a whole become. What is apparently decisive according to Heidegger in this self-referential definition of will to power as eternal recurrence is that Nietzsche had to think eternal recurrence, which Heidegger takes to be Nietzsche's "most essential thought," first. The "what" or essence precedes the "how" or way(s) in Nietzsche's thinking.

Heidegger also notes that Nietzsche contends that Being as "life" is in essence "becoming." He does not identify becoming with inchoate accident or chaos, nor as some asymptotic progression to some unknown goal. "Becoming" as "life" is the essence of power: the overcoming of power which continually "returns to itself in its own way" (8). At the same time, under the rubric of "classical nihilism," Heidegger notes that this "ontological" identification of eternal recurrence and will to power seems to be coeval with a contemporary sociological fact: the apparent impotence of transcendental referents—the beyond, heaven, hell, etc.—to shape men's frame of mind and conduct. Now "only the earth remains." We seem to have lost the "old world," and the kind of man that went with it; our predicament poses the problem of a new kind of man with apparently no genuine point of cosmological reference.[11] Nihilism understood as the revaluation of all prior values on the basis of understanding beings as will to power, and "in light of the eternal recurrence of the same," makes also needful, according to Heidegger, to "posit a new essence of man" (9). For Heidegger the essence of man is not permanent. The essence of man seems to be a by-product of the "uppermost categories."

According to Heidegger this does not only imply an anthropological speculation. It also carries political implications—global implications in our time of boundless technology. In "classical nihilism" eternal recurrence of the same is the ultimate and sole end of will to power. But this perspective shifts, once we adopt an anthropocentric angle: the "overman" seems to become the goal. The overman, in Heidegger's interpretation, becomes the "meaning of the earth." The overman would be "the most unequivocally singular form of human existence": absolute will to power embodied in every person to "some degree." As such, the overman becomes the measure for membership and overcoming in being as a whole—that is, in will to power, and thereby in (eternal) "life." The overman "overtakes" the anthropology of traditional values, launching a new source of justification of will to power as eternal "life."[12]

In Heidegger's interpretation, each of the five rubrics of Nietzsche's metaphysics—"nihilism," "revaluation of values," "will to power," "eternal recurrence of the same," and "overman"—conveys an angle of that teaching.[13] Each perspective could be singular and perhaps definitive. However, grasping what Nietzsche thought under these five rubrics seems to require that we think them all in tandem as it were through an "intimated conjunction."[14] For Heidegger this is an essentially historical event and not an exercise of *philosophia perennis*: to partake in such a knowledge is to "stand within the moment that the history of Being has opened up for our age" (10).

In order to explain this assertion, Heidegger claims that there is a distinction between the use of propositions and experiential "grasp" of thought. An account or *logos* may or may not follow from the conscious experience before which the thinker "stands" in "thoughtful knowing." This form of thoughtful "dispositional knowledge" is in itself a "comportment" that is "sustained by Being." It thinks "nihilism" from the perspective that grants this era the basic categories of "time and space, its ground and background, its means and ends, its order and justification, its certainty and its insecurity—in a word, its 'truth'" (10). Heidegger here seems to be saying that the genuine thinker becomes the *nunc stans* not only of thought thinking itself (the *noesis noeseos* of Aristotelian metaphysics), but also of thought thinking its determining nothingness as it has shaped the horizon of western history, recognizing now the cross-roads where it lies, in full-openness, in the midst of our world-historical drama. Heidegger is saying that by means of Nietzsche's thought he is thinking the history of western metaphysics "as the ground of our own history" (11).

On the other hand, "classical nihilism" also seems to be a defensive strategy. It seems to assume that no account or *logos* of its own essence (of the essence of the *Nichts*) needs to be given. It thereby has a certain degree of *naiveté*, of juvenile self-affirmation without apparent justification: rebellion without cause.[15] Heidegger claims that an explanation of what constitutes the essence of *nihil* is warranted—"as the veil that conceals the truth of the Being of beings." Through a study of Nietzsche's "reflections, meditations, definitions, maxims, exhortations, predictions, sketches for longer trains of thought, and brief reminders," Heidegger attempts to bring together and share in the "contemplat[ion of] Nietzsche's thoughts about nihilism, as the knowledge of a thinker who thinks in the direction of world history" (12). Heidegger acknowledges Nietzsche's thought as being more than an "expression of his times": rather, it expresses "reverberations of the still unrecognized history of Being in the world which that historical man [Nietzsche] utters in his 'language'" (12).

NIHILISM AS THE "DEVALUATION OF THE UPPERMOST VALUES"

Heidegger's interest in nihilism is a corollary of his focus on the question of Being. Heidegger is attempting to think through the "innermost essence that is called *nihilism* to theoretically approach the Being of what is" (13). To elaborate on this point, Heidegger refers us to Nietzsche's *Will to Power* aphorism 12 "Decline of Cosmological Values," where the essence or definition of nihilism seems to be that "the uppermost values devalue themselves"[16] (14). Heidegger gathers that since nihilism is a "process" or an "ism,"[17] it would appear to be a species of becoming, thereby lacking stability in the ultimate analysis. In other words, nihilism taken as a self-referential process of becoming—a thoroughgoing flux of becoming, "in becoming and of becoming," as it were—in itself would seem to offer no stable lens to reflect upon the problem of the evanescence of the "uppermost values."

The main difficulty in this process, what distinguishes it from "evolution" or "development," is that "an aim is lacking" (15). Heidegger questions why there should be an aim at all: what is the inner link between value and aim? By "aim" Heidegger presumably understands a *telos* in the Aristotelian sense. An aim refers to "why" something takes place in some specific way, or perhaps what would be the "ground(s)" for a thing to occur the way it does. Heidegger poses the foundational question: what are the grounds of such grounds? In other words, what is the relation between "ground (*der Grund*) and value (*der Wert*)"? Value is a "concept" that plays a major role in Nietzsche's thought. *Prima facie* values seem to be akin to "goods": "values" would be particularized, nominal, specific "goods." This would mean that "a good is a good on grounds of value." It is apparently on associations of this sort—the still unexplained relation between "goods" or "the good" and "value"—that Heidegger's Nietzsche would presumably be in line with Plato.

Now, what would be an example of "value"? Heidegger surprisingly asserts that "we know" that the "freedom of a people is a 'value'" (15). A value is something "worthwhile," something we esteem—"something that 'matters' for our behavior" (16). In this specific passage, values refer to particular *conceptual* entities that appear to "matter" to us because they seem to provide a viable and optimal set of aims we can usefully share and reciprocate. But for Nietzsche to think in terms of values takes place in the sphere of the *all-too-human*. Or, as Heidegger puts it in the *Letter on Humanism:* "by the assessment of something as a value what is valued is admitted only as an object for human estimation."[18]

Heidegger reads into Nietzsche a dynamic circular view of the uppermost categories: "value is what validates." The valid is what becomes a "standard of measure" on the basis of shared need. Are there permanent standards of measure that make values valuable, or are values what make standards of measure valid? In other words: what makes a value *valid*? Heidegger now raises the speculative stakes and suggests values to be "modes of *Being.*" What this seems to mean is that values are perhaps not merely intersubjective inventions or postulates of "practical reason," but might be grounded on the "question of Being." The question of value as well as the essence of such question are grounded on the question of Being. Values are a product of our estimation, of our reckoning, and on a larger scale they are a product of history: "such esteeming and valuing occurs only when something 'matters' for our behavior" (16). Apparently, values have to matter. Ideas, on the other hand, "can be without mattering" because presumably their reality is not subject to our apprehension, nor to our need. Perhaps at some level, like geometric figures or Euclidean theorems, ideas are there whether we grasp them or not—but values have the particularity that they "matter," because they derive from our esteem, particularly and collectively. To illustrate, Heidegger offers the example of the "freedom of a people" as a paradigmatic value.[19]

Such reckoning of valuation also seems to imply a direction, and therefore—in contrast to Cartesian asymptotic geometry—a specific aim. There seems to be a distinction of planes between "values" that matter to us and the "ground" that offers a "why" for what we esteem or value. Value and ground are "determined" by different planes: presumably the former is historical, while the latter is speculative or ontological. Heidegger is puzzled, however, as to why the language of values has dominated our "world view" since the end of the nineteenth century (and, indeed, remains dominant in the first two decades of the twenty-first century). Heidegger highlights that "in truth, the role of valuative thought is *by no means self-evident*" (16). Despite this fact the language of values has become a "truism." From this Heidegger draws a parallel with different "modes of thought." The moderns use modes of thought in terms of "culture" or "spirit" or "values" that, according to Heidegger, are essentially foreign to the Middle Ages or to the ancient Greek world (17).

NIHILISM, *NIHIL*, AND *NICHTS*

Heidegger now offers an ontological analysis of nihilism and its possible side effects. Nihilism seems to indicate that Being (*das Sein*) and by implication being (*das Seiende*) do not matter anymore for our understanding of entities in their singularity. In the philosophy of science this change in perspective receives the name of "positivism." Positivism assumes that only "factual" entities ("sense data") have "epistemologically" probable status, and enquiry into the meaning of Being lacks sense and therefore should partake in the realm of phantasy, or mere counterfactual imagination. But Heidegger claims that if we forgo the question of Being we also forfeit the meaning of beings.

Nihilism equates Being with *nihil*, nothing: Being seems to not be worth anything, because it does not seem to "matter." Whether something is or is not indexically "there" appears to be a necessary condition to decide whether something matters, and therefore whether it may or may not have value. "Nothing" for Heidegger implies a "thing's not being at hand," as when we search or explore something that is not found (18). Nihilism seems to be concerned with "beings in their non-being." But he wonders: the "nothing 'is'" that which "we at least never lose?" (19). Heidegger moves from nothing as absence of a given entity to "nothingness" as an infinitive noun that "is," yet seems to not be taken as a possible referent. In that case we could not attribute Being to such no-thing, because it is-not-at-hand.

This seems to lead Heidegger to the following question: "What, then, do 'Being' and the 'is' mean"?[20] Western metaphysics gives the impression of having a hold of knowing what "Being" and "is" are—this constitutes the ground of metaphysics—assuming as well that "nothingness" is the "opposite of all being" (20). But if there were no such thing as nothingness, there would be no opposite to Being: thus, perhaps either Being is not (Heraclitus) or all is Being (Parmenides). Heidegger, however, claims that, "on closer inspection" (i.e., perhaps relying on Aristotle *On Interpretation* 17a 1-4), there could be another option: "nothing" is also the negation of beings. The "nothing" would thereby be akin to the concept of negation, "nay-saying," the opposite of affirmation. Negation and affirmation are kinds of practical judgment. Contemplation does not affirm or negate: it "sees." In contemplation of "necessities" there would be no room for such judgment. Heidegger seems to take the "nothing" as a category of practice and not of contemplation. If we take the "nothing" to be a "product of negation," it could have a practical and/or strictly logical origin. Heidegger doesn't overlook the importance of "logic" to think correctly and methodically—to "give an account"—but, contrary to Anselm of Canterbury,[21] at this point he asserts that "what one thinks does not have to be." There seems to be a possible nominal distinction between thought and "something actual in reality" (21). The "nothing of negation," the "nay-saying," in the form of meditative abstraction, does not necessarily "matter," and therefore, Heidegger concludes, seems not to be worth our "attention or respect." Unlike the (Hegelian) negation of historical practice, the contemplative nothing (*Nichts*) appears to be a kind of illusion.

Thus, perhaps we would be able to move on "practically" from the nihilistic impasse. But Heidegger is not sure this is such a straightforward process. He refers to Nietzsche's *Will to Power* Preface, 1: "Nihilism stands at the door: whence comes to us this uncanniest of guests?" followed by aphorism 2: "what I shall relate is the history of the next two centuries." In Heidegger's interpretation the question at this juncture rests on the "Being of nothing"— whether there is nothingness. [22] Some preliminary questions come to mind: is such nothingness an immaterial substance of some sort? If so, would it be atomistic, monadic, individual, collective, holistic? Some combination thereof? How to establish its distinctiveness? At an interpretative moral level: is nothingness some kind of curse or an opening? Can such nothingness have attributes (e.g., substance, quantity, quality, relation, place, time, posture, condition, action, affect)? If the nothing has or is substance, then the problem of nihilism is to equate the no-thing with "nullity," making therefore "nihilism an apotheosis of the merely vacuous." If this were the case then, Heidegger argues, it would mean that "a negation can be set to rights at once by an energetic affirmation": practically speaking, a non-essential affirmation would respond "decisively" to a non-essential negation. Perhaps therefore the "essence of nihilism consists in *not* taking the question of the nothing seriously" (21). Heidegger wants to move past the *either/or* of whether nothingness is or is not. But it remains unclear what alternative he might foresee.

Now, "logic" would dictate that either "nothing" is Being, or it is not (therefore "nothing" would be null). But this *either/or* does not signal the "what" or the "thisness" of the no-thing Heidegger seems to be taking to heart. Could the nothing not be a being without nullifying it? "What if the *default* of a developed question about the essence of the nothing were *the grounds* for the fact that western metaphysics had to fall prey to nihilism?" (Heidegger's emphases) (22). The problem of nihilism seems to be that we misunderstand the essence of the *Nichts*. Nihilism could be defined then as "the essential non-thinking of the essence of the nothing." Nietzsche apparently grasped this process in its historical manifestation.

For Heidegger, Nietzsche's experience of nihilism is inextricably linked with the fact that "Nietzsche himself thought nihilistically." Nietzsche takes his bearings from "valuative thought," which occludes the question of the essence of nothing, bringing to conclusion what for Heidegger is the structure of western metaphysics from Plato onwards. What this seems to imply is that, from Heidegger's perspective, the Platonic ideas are not only metaphysical essences beyond human control or human will. Rather, Heidegger asserts that they are closer than expected to Nietzschean values, values which in turn have subsequently been translated into social science literature as the Weber-ian realm of "axiology." This would mean that there is no genuine "suprahis-torical" set of metaphysical ideas grounded on a transcendental genus or Archimedean point. Instead, there would be a variety of points of reference that we esteem or value because they matter to us, and which we embrace as long as they reflect our historical needs and aspirations. Logos therefore would not be disembodied logos, but logos of somebody somewhere and for something. The Socratic expression "virtue is knowledge" already seems to suggest this correlation: forms are virtues that may shape moral conduct and intellectual understanding. Although virtues and values remain distinct—forms of virtue are envisioned by the intellect and values are a product of will—presumably virtues make "the forms" matter in ways we may value because we trust that they are good. So far in this section, what Heidegger seems to be saying is that both Nietzschean values and Platonic forms are "metaphysical" configurations that aim at some good that apparently need not be trans-historically fixed.[23] Perhaps this juxtaposition might be at the origin of new kinds of modern virtue (e.g., compassion, generosity, sincerity, honesty, mindfulness, etc.).

Heidegger associates Nietzsche's "valuative thought" with metaphysics (23). This seems to create a puzzle: in his account, didn't values necessarily have to "matter"? If that is so, how could values be "meta-physical" or beyond "physics"? So far in this discussion, it is still unclear how Heidegger understands "physics" or "nature."[24] For Heidegger the question of the es-sence of nothingness offers a third possibility distinct from the *nomos/phusis* division of the ancient sophists. This third "metaphysical" possibility that seems to ground values is therefore distinct from either nature or convention as classically understood.

NIETZSCHE'S CONCEPTION OF COSMOLOGY AND PSYCHOLOGY

Heidegger begins this section with a rather strange assertion: nihilism is a "lawful" process. Nihilism is the lawful process of devaluation of the "upper-most values." By "lawful" Heidegger appears to mean that this process has a "logic." Nihilism is therefore a lawful or logical process through which the uppermost values become devalued. This is a process that follows from Nietzsche's "concept" of nihilism: that is, a conceptual or intersubjective "valuative interpretation" of "the being" (24). Heidegger takes this to mean that the "matter in question is the decline in '*cosmological*' values" (Heideg-ger's emphasis). In Nietzsche's words in aphorism 12 of *Will to Power*, the "faith" that gave man "a deep feeling of standing in the context of, and being dependent on, some whole that is infinitely superior to him" is no longer self-evident. By "cosmology" Heidegger refers to the "particular region of be-ings," or "nature," encompassing "the earth and stars, plants and animals" (26). Curiously, Heidegger excludes men (qua Dasein?) from the province of cosmology. The province of men pertains to the realm of "psychology, as the study of the soul and spirit, the study of man as a rational creature" (26). Cosmology, the logos about the cosmos, appears to be a necessary but insuf-ficient condition for the study of men. Theology, however, "parallels and surpasses psychology and cosmology," not understood as exegesis of the biblical canon, but as a "rational" or "natural" (Heidegger here seems to use both terms interchangeably) interpretation of God as first cause of nature, man, and history, according to biblical doctrine (26).[25] Heidegger's natural or rational theology is not "enlightened" or "free-thinking"—at this point of the analysis he seems to rely on biblical revelation to account for the "whence" (*woher*) of men, nature, and history. Biblical revelation, unlike "pagan wisdom," seems to take for granted a marked distinction between cosmology on the one hand, and theology, psychology, and history on the other.[26]

Heidegger explores what Nietzsche might mean when he refers to the "cosmos," as apparently distinct from "nature," "man," and "God." By "cos-mos" Nietzsche seems to mean a "world," whereby "God, man, and nature are constituent qualified parts." The "world" in this view is more than the "earth" as the natural substratum where man stands. The "world" would be a "whole": the "widest circle that encloses everything that is and becomes" (27). Nihilism is the decline of the uppermost referents that anchor the cos-mos, understood as an orderly "world." The decline seems to begin at the level of cosmological values: cosmological values lose their hold as points of reference opening the possibility (the "freedom") to conceive of new sources of valuation.

The dissolution of cosmological values is coeval with the possibility of a new valuation. However, the cosmological interregnum (the entire Coperni-can revolution?) also produces a psychological reflection or effect. Heideg-ger, however, notes Nietzsche is not writing here as a nineteenth-century behaviorist, making the *psyche* a species of the physical realm of Newtonian determination, "characteriology," or physiological experimental condition-ing. Heidegger claims the way to capture Nietzsche's psychology would be to focus on the realm of anthropology, specifically philosophical anthropolo-gy. By philosophical anthropology Heidegger seems to mean the "metaphys-ics" of man. Heidegger, however, is aware that Nietzsche, in contrast to a distinctly Christian philosophical anthropology, does not conceive "man" as a metaphysical entity exclusive from the rest of animate beings. Nietzsche's psychology therefore "in no way restricts itself to man, but neither does it extend simply to plants and animals" (28). There are distinctions in the natural realm, "natural kinds" of some sort, but the question seems to be how they are organized and qualitatively shown.

Furthermore, by "psychical" Heidegger seems to interpret that which is "living." All living beings are psychical entities, determined by the "basic character of all beings," which for Nietzsche is "will to power." This fundamental fact is "coterminous with metaphysics" in so far as it is "the truth of the whole of beings." For Heidegger's Nietzsche, psychology, will to power, and metaphysics are "coterminous," or have the same "end." The conceptual shift of metaphysics into a differentiated "transversal psychology," in which man is preeminent but perhaps not ultimately incommensurate, "lies grounded in the very essence of modern metaphysics"[27] (28). What does Heidegger mean by "modern metaphysics"? This appears to be a process of contraction, whereby the cosmological points of reference lose their hold, and man becomes qualifiedly naturalized, turning himself by default into "the measure and the center of beings."

According to Heidegger this anthropocentric revolution coeval with the modern project begins with Descartes. In Cartesian philosophy, the "ego" or "subject" by a process of radical doubt seems to become coeval with the ultimate ground, the ground of grounds, the *hypokeimenon* or *subiectum*.[28] According to Heidegger, however, this interpretation of the ultimate ground as ego is not sufficiently subjectivist for Nietzsche. At this juncture Heidegger interprets Nietzsche as a hyper-Cartesian thinker: turning somehow the *cogito* into the figure of the *Übermensch*. At bottom, in Heidegger's estimation, Nietzsche's "teaching" proclaims the overman as the *hypokeimenon,* the ultimate ground and expression of "will to power." This manifestation of the "most spiritual will to power" seems to encompass a *logos* of the psyche or account of the soul, therefore becoming a "psychological" manifestation of "the realm of the *fundamental questions of metaphysics.*"[29]

Following the identification of the overman's *psyche* with the *hypokeimenon,*[30] Nietzsche concludes that psychology becomes again the "queen of the sciences" and the "path to the fundamental problems" (29). Heidegger interprets this to mean that such path would imply a radicalized re-reading of the Cartesian *Meditations,* taking the "I" as somehow non-separate from "the whole" and as coeval with the ultimate "ground." Psychology would thereby be a species of metaphysics with the "overman" as mediating "measure." On the other hand, the contraction of the scope of man as mere historical locus of intersubjective reckoning, viewed as a configuration of the will to power, becomes the "psychological state" of nihilism. The historical movement of nihilism is not autonomous: it is derived from a cosmological interregnum whereby our grasp of "beings as a whole" seems open for re-interpretation.

THE ORIGIN OF NIHILISM AND ITS THREE FORMS

The apparent cosmological interregnum is the context from which Heidegger attempts to understand the "origin" (*die Herkunft*) of nihilism. Heidegger's question at this point, however, is not "whence," but "how" nihilism comes to be essentially. For Heidegger *die Herkunft* is not merely a matter of intra-historical genesis, but is a question of the "cause of nihilism" or the provenance of its essence.[31] The devaluation of uppermost values also seems to devalue the beings that are grounded on them. Heidegger notes that Nietzsche divides the unfolding of nihilism into three stages: as a psychological state, as the obsolescence of a world-system, and as the critique of dualism and subsequent occlusion of metaphysics.

The devaluation of the uppermost values is not only a conceptual, but also a physio-psychological process: nihilism first emerges as a "feeling" (*das Gefühl*) or as a "psychological state" (30). Nihilism appears as a feeling derived from the apparent lack of meaning of "all events" and possibly of "beings as a whole." Here Heidegger takes Nietzsche to closely associate "meaning" with "value." By "meaning" Nietzsche seems to understand "purpose," the "why and wherefore" of actions or events. Values understood as purposes therefore appear to be categories of action. Values give meaning to action. If values are categories of action, then they would be practical categories: categories of practical reason that bring about events. According to Heidegger, there are a number of possible grand purposes that can give meaning to action: an "ethical world order," "growth of love and harmony in social intercourse," "pacifism," "eternal peace," "'the gradual approximation to a state of universal happiness' as the greatest good for the greatest number," "or even the departure toward a state of universal nothingness." All these propositions, Heidegger claims, imply a goal or "meaning" (31).

Heidegger pauses to ask: is nothingness a goal? (*das Nichts ist ein Ziel?*) Instead of elaborating on what such (presumably substantive) no-thing could possibly refer to, Heidegger takes a step back and tries to explain this assertion in terms of efficient causation: *das Nichts* can be an aim "because the will to will nothingness still allows the will its *volition*" (31). It is willing that requires meaning or purposes for itself to be. Heidegger quotes Nietzsche's closing lines of the *Genealogy of Morals*: the "human will needs an aim—and will soon will nothingness than not will at all." Will here is to be taken to mean "will to power" as well as *horror vacui*: the "fundamental fact" that for Aristotle is the main feature of nature itself. At this juncture of Heidegger's interpretation, for Nietzsche Aristotelian nature and willing appear to overlap: therefore "meaning," "aim," and "purpose" (all apparently synonymous with Aristotelian *telos*) "are what allow and enable the will to be will" (31).[32] Upon reflection, however, the "way" or "process" or "becoming" in their absolute meaning "achieve nothing and attain nothing." The rhetoric of purpose seems to lack substance. This seems to produce a "new consciousness": a change in the relation of man both to himself and to "being as a whole" that is *felt* as genuine lack of direction.

In the second stage nihilism morphs from a physio-psychological state, from the "'feeling' of the valuelessness" of beings as a whole, to the awareness of the failure of the all-encompassing structure or organization ("the world") to offer a believable set of purposes (32). This critique reaches the uppermost point of unitary reference of the "structural" model: the Archimedean point. We wonder: "why and to what extent man 'posits' such a 'ruling' and 'dominant' 'unity'"—how such unity (*Einheit*) is grounded, and whether it has legitimacy. Here Heidegger seems to introduce a potential distinction between theory and practice: between the source of "unity" and the "quest for meaning" or purpose. Are these two the same? Heidegger's Nietzsche appears to assimilate the concept of "unity" with the term "universality": the ground of the value of man within a system encompassing the totality of beings. This seems to reinforce man's belief in his own value, which, in turn, would be the basis for his self-assertion.

Values are a projection of willing. Unified or non-contradictory willing seems to be a prerequisite for self-assertion. The "concept" of unity reflects upon man enabling him to make himself "the uppermost value" for beings as a whole. The belief in the "value" of unity seems to make architectonically possible distinctly human kinds of self-assertion. But if the belief in such unity is undermined, if unity and therefore meaning or purpose are lacking, all "realizing" would seem to become self-referential and possibly "unreal" in the last analysis. We seem to steer clear of both dogmatism and relativism by postulating a *conditional* notion of unity (33).[33]

In the third stage nihilism assumes its "final form." This follows from the supposed discovery that the distinction between the real and apparent world was crafted to satisfy "psychological needs." The critique of dualism at this stage undermines the postulates of "unity and totality" conceived as partaking in some kind of transcendent beyond. The notions of unity and totality, understood now as mental concepts, seem to become postulates produced by human needs that are not inherent in the structure of the "real" world. As a result, the experience of nihilism shifts from the realm of psychology toward "disbelief" in the "meta-physical world." Such disbelief, in turn, leads to skepticism about any (conceptual) world beyond physics: concepts are created by man to satisfy his desires and his apparent needs of immanent security and recognition.[34] This translates into disbelief about a world beyond or "above" the senses: disbelief in an "afterworld or heaven." This is the third and final stage of nihilism. The feeling of meaninglessness becomes a critique of metaphysics in all its imagery and transcendental allusions. A full critique: "ontologically," at the level of images, and at the level of "correct of opinion." Everything supersensuous becomes questionable: "becoming" is thereby experienced as the ultimate reality, as perhaps the "one authentic (*eigentlich*) 'true' world" (34).[35]

The result of this threefold process of psychological disorientation, systemic obsolescence, and a monistic disenchantment is a "period of transition."[36] The period of transition, in turn, is also characterized by three "forms" that together "constitute a particular movement or history" (35). The three forms of the period of transition are: (1) the world of becoming "can no longer be denied as unreal"; (2) the real world of becoming has "at the outset no aims and values," and as such could not be endured; and (3) a feeling of both valuelessness and helplessness at the lack of purpose of the real world of becoming.

At this stage, Heidegger claims, what is missing is "an insight into the grounds for the predicament and the possibility of overcoming it" (35). There are two kinds of question during the period of transition: one pertaining the "what" of the problem (a "believable" ontology or non-arbitrary "should" grounded in the "could" seems to be lacking), and the other about the "how" (a "way" to live meaningfully and therefore wholeheartedly through the impasse).

To recapitulate: Heidegger notes that Nietzsche analyzes a conceptual decay or disbelief in the uppermost values which has emotional and historical manifestations. In our transitional period we seem to be "drifting toward an unequivocal historical state." Heidegger claims that we seem to "withdraw again" the *categories*—"purpose" (*Zweck*), "unity" (*Einheit*), "Being" (*Sein*), which used to give value to the world, and "now the world seems valueless" (35). This last remark implies that the process of nihilistic disorientation might be distinct in contemporary European culture, but may not be an unprecedented predicament.

THE UPPERMOST VALUES AS CATEGORIES

Heidegger brings to our attention the opening line of subsection B of *Will to Power* aphorism 12, where Nietzsche "abruptly calls the uppermost values *categories*" (36). There is no overt explanation in Nietzsche's aphorism as to what the relation between "uppermost values" and "categories" would be. Heidegger likens the notion of categories to the "Romanic" (i.e., non-Germanic, Latin-derived) notions of "class" or "sort." These are expressions of classification used to "delineate a region, schema, or pigeonhole into which something is deposited or classified." Heidegger seems to liken "categories" with expressions of "accountability" of imperial power, or of Roman civil law.

According to Heidegger, the expression "category" has deeper sources in the Greek language: *Kategoria* and *Kategorein* are a composite of *kata* ("go-

ing down"; going below; the opening word of Plato's *Republic* is *katabaino*)
and *agoreuein* (from agora or public place, open market, or "public sphere"
of open deliberation as opposed to closed-door council meetings). *Agoreuein*
in Heidegger's interpretation means open communication, announcement,
transparency, revelation. *Kategorein* thereby seems to mean that "in an explicit view on something, we reveal what it is and render it open."[37] Such
disclosure appears primarily through speech, in so far as it has the indexical
quality of pointing to an actual "thing," or to "any being at all" rendering as it
is, addressing it as a distinct being. This kind of public address is most salient
in courts of law.

Heidegger associates such judicial proceedings with the problem of as-
signing "guilt."[38] *Kategorein* in this interpretation conveys the meaning of
"laying charges" into the openness (*Öffentlichkeit*) of publicity. It seems to
imply a revelation of some being in its "thereness," both in terms of "how it
looks and is." Such disclosure of how a being is according to "how a being
shows itself as what it is" is called in Greek, according to Heidegger, *to eidos*
or *idea*. A category reveals the "looks" of how a being both appears and is:
such a being is addressed in its singularity through its "proper name" (37).

At this juncture, Heidegger refers the reader to Aristotle *Physics* B1
192b17. In this passage, Aristotle points to the "nature" of a thing in terms of
the combination of its composing elements (earth, fire, air, water). A natural
thing, as opposed to an artifact, has a "principle" of motion or "stationari-
ness" (not only in terms of locomotion, but also of "growth," decrease,
alteration) within itself. Artifacts have no innate principle of change per se,
but in fact do change, as long as their composite elements (e.g., stone, earth,
etc.) themselves undergo change. Why does Heidegger point to this section
of Aristotle's *Physics*? In that specific passage Aristotle makes a distinction
between nature and art. Nature has a principle of motion or rest within itself,
art produces composites that as such have an extrinsic principle of motion or
rest. The implied question seems to be whether categories (and therefore
"ideas") are a product of "nature" or of "art." If the "uppermost values" refer
to what "matters to us," how does Nietzsche think of categories and ideas? If
values seem to be a product of "art," are "categories" and "ideas" to be
conceived in the same manner? If that were the case, then ideas would be
composites, and as such could not be "eternal," and would be subject to
change. If ideas are according to "nature," that is, if they are "natural kinds,"
then they could be apprehended by the mind everywhere and always and
would not in principle be subject to change. If, on the other hand, ideas were
not by nature but by "art," then they would be a product not of *theoria* but of
praxis. As products of praxis, they would be subject to a practical reason of
some sort, and therefore would seem to be a product of human "willing." If
the ideas were a subset of "willing," they could be disputed at will. The
problem with this line of reasoning, subsuming the ideas under "art," is that it

makes willing and practical reason, and therefore history, the "highest court of appeal." It thereby politicizes the human mind.[39]

Now, Heidegger emphasizes that a *kategoria* is the indexical quality of a "thing." It also seems to indicate the "justness" of something: it is a "word in which a thing is 'indicted' as what it is" (37). A *kategoria* stems from common experience and is not a "lifeless and superficial" conceptual apparatus. Heidegger claims the Greek, Sanskrit, and German languages capture this ordinary nature of the use of words. On the other hand, Heidegger contrasts this profoundly ordinary origin of "categories" with the sophisticated Kantian version, particularly that of the *Critique of Pure Reason*. There the "table of categories" are "derived and deduced from the table of judgments" (37). Heidegger calls the Aristotelian "ordinary" perspective on the word *kategoria* "pre-philosophical," in *apparent* contrast to what he takes to be "philosophy as metaphysics" in the Kantian abstract conceptual apparatus. Heidegger contends that there are instances of categories such as "door" or "window," which are distinct in their particularity, and yet belong to a more fundamental or original category of "thing." These categories are "claim(s) that state in what mode of Being a designated being shows itself" (38). The implication is that in contrast to the Kantian dualistic perspective of seemingly incommensurate *noumena* and *phenomena,* categories point to what "things" show themselves to be in their particularity and in their "thingness." Such particularities are also encompassed in a thing's attributes or qualities such as size, color, durability, etc. Heidegger equates the category of "quality" with a thing's "constitution" (*poiotés*)—the attributes that make or compose a thing as to how it appears constitutively. Quality is a subsidiary category, preceded by a more fundamental category that "grounds" it (a quality is a quality of something). The "underlying ground" of quality is the "*hypokeimenon, subiectum, substantia.*"[40]

From a "metaphysical" perspective, categories are the basic words, expressing "fundamental philosophical concepts." These modes of being delineate pre-existent "things" giving them an essential quality that, in turn, would make it possible to modify and handle them into distinct shapes. Heidegger at this juncture associates *all metaphysics* with the apparently "essential" articulation of how things show themselves to us. This makes possible our subsequent "*poietic*" handling of entities that is at the root of "techno-logy" (in the Greek sense of *techné* art/craft, and *logos* reason or "to give an account"). At some level, technology would encompass the artifacts of our making about which we can give an account. Technology seems to presuppose a "metaphysics" of some sort (39).

In this context, Heidegger identifies "exactly" technology—the arts or crafts about which we can give an account—with "culture" in its contemporary mode. Heidegger claims that, from an Aristotelian perspective, an assertion (*enuntiatio*) implies a "category," but not in a systematic sense. A category is a tacit manifestation of an assertion which, in turn, is a product of "various modes of judgment" (40). Heidegger now claims that this Aristotelian perspective might after all not be altogether at odds with the Kantian account in the *Critique of Pure Reason,* where categories are said to derive from judgments. When Nietzsche says, apparently in passing, that "the highest values are 'categories of reason,'" he seems to be in some measure of consonance with both Aristotle and Kant. But this kind of "judgmental thinking" is not identical in the case of the three thinkers, Heidegger adds. The analytical distinction depends on how they grasp "the essence of 'reason'" and *logos* (which for Heidegger is indistinguishable from the "essence of man").

In this Aristotelian-Kantian-Nietzschean (and non-Platonic?) line of inquiry, there appears to be a "comprehension" of the "Being of beings" on the basis of thinking as assertive judgment. This, in turn, implies a way of "defining the truth of beings as a whole, a metaphysics [that] thinks beings by means of categories" (41). Heidegger seems to mean here a conception that thinks of beings by means of their "most universal element": turning to "Being as beingness," making thereby "thinking" not a direct encounter but reflective "assertory speech." Heidegger therefore comes to the preliminary estimation that Nietzsche, appearances to the contrary, is a metaphysical "reflective" thinker. What this seems to mean is that Heidegger's Nietzsche assimilates the uppermost values not only with "cosmological values," but also with the "categories of reason," which for Heidegger are somehow in line with Aristotelian "physics" and Kant's critical judgment.

Heidegger's presentation, however, is still underway as to whether Nietzsche "strays from the path of metaphysics" (41). Because if Nietzsche conceived categories as values, that would make him an "anti-metaphysician." On the other hand, if instead he makes a (qualified) distinction that would bring "metaphysics to its ultimate end," then perhaps that would make Nietzsche the "last metaphysician." It is unclear in Heidegger's presentation, however, why Nietzsche has to be the *last* metaphysician and not yet another practitioner of perennial philosophy. Be that as it may, Heidegger concludes that the question of whether Nietzsche is a metaphysician is inextricably linked with the account of Nietzsche's concept of nihilism. Heidegger points to the expressions through which Nietzsche, without further elaboration, refers to the ultimate categories that have grounded the interpretation of beings as a whole: instead of "meaning" (*Sinn*) now he says "purpose," or "aim" (*Zweck*). Instead of "totality or system" Nietzsche says "unity," and instead of "truth" he uses the expression "Being."

Prima facie, Heidegger attributes this lack of consistency to the fact that this passage (*Will to Power* 12A) was not prepared for publication by Nietzsche. Rather, this is a text where we see a "thinker in dialogue with himself" (42). A dialogue, Heidegger adds, not in terms of Nietzsche and his "ego" nor with his "person," but with "the Being of beings as a whole" partaking in the realm of the history of metaphysics. For Heidegger what is key to keep in mind here is that Nietzsche apparently "grasps 'truth' as a category of reason and equates 'truth' with 'Being.'" Heidegger suggests that the perspective of taking Being as *alpha and omega*[41] and not as a geometric neutral abstraction offers something essential to explore Nietzsche's "basic metaphysical position, in which the experience of nihilism has its roots."

Nihilism appears now to be the non-essential "grounding" of values (geometrically abstract neutral categories) as if they were in Being. At this point of Heidegger's reading, understanding nihilism implies a recognition of the difference between the rhetoric of values and apparently lacking substantive categories. In this nominalist rendition, values as categories are abstract and non-substantive. Among other things, there appears to be missing a sense of genuine "singularity" in this "categorical" account.

NIHILISM AND THE MAN OF WESTERN HISTORY

Heidegger refers the reader back to the seminal last line of *Will to Power* 12A. Nietzsche references the key categories of "purpose," "unity," and "Being," which have "invested a value in the 'world'" (43). With the specter of nihilism these categories appear to wane, however, and thus the world "now" appears "valueless." Heidegger notes Nietzsche's reference to the "now" implies a historical indication, not a final or definitive claim.

This development can be encapsulated in three moments: (1) the obsolescence of the categories of "purpose," "unity," and "Being" in the landscape of "values" (i.e., categories that matter to us in a given historical epoch); (2) the period of transition this "withdrawal" entails; and subsequently, (3) the prospects for the positing of the new valuation. To posit and to retract values (note that Nietzsche doesn't use the language of "constructivism" and "deconstruction" here) is a characteristic of western history. The positing and retracting of values seems to refer to the "horizon of significance" that organizes and gives "meaning" and therefore purpose(s) for the development of the human condition. The period of transition between two "horizons of significance" implies for Heidegger an act of "perception" with the "greatest possible awareness."[42]

Heidegger notes again that the nihilistic period of transition is an "intermediate state." The "decisive will to overcome it" presupposes an awareness of its existence. Why does Heidegger want to overcome the period of transition instead of envisioning it as a "crystalized *aporia*"? Because he has in mind the fulfilment of the "essence of man," for which a horizon is a *sine qua non.*[43] The period of transition appears to lack a genuine horizon, thereby preventing this fulfilment.

Heidegger rather forcefully claims Nietzsche's exposition is a "declaration" of what we are acting out: in fact, of what we "must act out." This is a declaration that is both descriptive and prescriptive. In other words, there is no "fact/value" distinction in this declaration: "something imminent is at stake, something barely underway, involving decisions and tasks whose transitional character is interpreted as investing values in and withdrawing values from the world" (44). But nihilism is not a monolithic phenomenon. It goes beyond the withdrawal of obsolescent values—*the very language of values is already nihilistic.* From an ontological perspective, what is nihilistic would be the claim that the uppermost categories are the product of human willing and representation, and therefore of the primacy of human practical judgment of some sort.[44] Nihilism is the movement that conceives the categories of "purpose," "unity," and "Being" as products of human making, and that, as such, can be manipulated, disputed, posited and retracted—compromised at will.

Heidegger points out that Nietzsche, in the manner of nineteenth-century Russian dramatists, makes the claim that nihilism "will have to enter the scene" psychologically (45).[45] Again, this is expressed in three stages: lack of meaning or purpose, disjuncture between individual aspiration and a credible system of ends, and its "third and final form," which is two-fold: the positing of a world beyond ("idealism"), followed by a non-dualistic retraction that merely affirms earthly life ("naturalism" or "environmentalism"). The final stage of nihilism seems to have the unintended consequence that we immanentize "the world" as "the environment," we therefore also, unawares, become "geocentric" again, and as such appear to undermine from a practical and therefore *possibly* from a moral and political stance the Copernican revolution. Since the Copernican revolution is a key milestone of modernity, the third stage of nihilism appears to be in "structural contradiction" with a key premise of the modern project.

These three stages, according to Heidegger, portray the "fundamental condition," followed by the "actual beginning," and culminating in the period of transition that conveys "the necessary fulfilment of the essence" of the *history* of contemporary nihilism. When Heidegger says the fulfilment of nihilism may be "necessary," he implies that it appears to be largely outside our control: this seems reminiscent of the image of *fortuna* in Ch. XXV of Machiavelli's *Prince*. The "fulfilment" of nihilism would be both "necessary" and "historical," perhaps because it also extrapolates the consequences of taking the categories of "purpose," "unity," and "Being" as products posited by our own making. If we take "purpose," "unity," and "Being" to be products of practical reason (as impositions of the human mind onto phenomena), then the distinction between history and "necessity" would arguably make no sense: history is necessity in so far as it is "created" and determined by the categories of practical reason. What falls outside such determination would fall outside what counts within the realm of "historical reality." Heidegger, however, takes a step back from unyielding fatalistic conclusions: he acknowledges that "everything is indeterminate here." Since we are referring to human "action," no *necessary* determination appears to be there in the last analysis.[46] Nevertheless he tells us that this line of reasoning implies the need for a fateful "decision" of some sort.[47]

The problem at this juncture seems to be the basis of such decisions. Heidegger points to Nietzsche's distinction between the "true world" and the "illusory world." Heidegger refers to this distinction as "Platonism." Platonism—notice that the discussion all along is not about "Plato" but about the historical appropriation and legacy of Plato's writings—distinguishes the "true" supersensuous world of Being from the apparent mutable world of becoming. Platonism therefore implies the identification of "truth" and "Being," as opposed to the world of the here and now. Heidegger adds that for Nietzsche Christianity is "Platonism for the people" (*BGE*, Preface). Thus, the claim that this apparent world is a "vale of tears," and a pilgrimage toward an eternal world beyond, is prefigured by a doctrine of two worlds that would follow from a dualistic interpretation of Plato's philosophy. For millennia our fundamental "decisions" have been made on the basis of the horizon made possible by a form of Platonism. Since nihilism implies that Platonism ceases to have a hold on European culture, Heidegger contends we must search for "pre-Platonic" "historical forms" of philosophy, in order to try to come to terms with its "foundational" essence (46). Heidegger notes that the positing of "unity" for being as a whole (*das Seiende im Ganzen*) was prefigured by Parmenides, from whom only fragmentary texts remain.

THE NEW VALUATION

Heidegger points out that there is a shift in nihilism taken under psychological and historicist conditions. The movement occurs from psychology and history (both of which for Heidegger would be modes of Being, "sounded through" by logos) to the need for "results" of some sort. Results are a product of calculation or "reckoning."[48] Nietzsche's "reckoning" takes its measure of value from the "will to power." The standard of evaluation becomes quanta of power. For Heidegger, however, this is also a nihilistic "train of thought" (48). There is a double movement from a "conscious" devaluation of the highest values and a "simultaneous" "staying in front of the lack" that, as we have noted, results in a historical period of transition. Our era becomes defined by nihilism: nihilism becomes our historical "element" (like water to fish), not something that lies separate from our condition. Nihilism in this manner "imposes its own effective limits on the age." If we conceive of "time as history,"[49] time would not be an absolute dimension separate from consciousness from which we may or may not exercise cool neutrality, but rather, it would seem to encompass our own timeliness as the non-uniform unfolding of our self-consciousness.

Heidegger again notes the fundamental problem of not having a genuinely shared "Archimedean point": "we do not stand in this history as in some uniform space in which any stand point or position can be assumed at will" (48). The period of transition seems to be characterized by the obsolescence of the highest values hitherto—and this deposition is "needful" for the appearance of the new values: a new genesis. The question still seems to be, however, whether the new values will be a negation of the old values (and thereby will be anchored in them), or whether the "new affirmation" will stem from a "clean start" that is not determined by its reaction to the old.

As the old values rendered a distinction between the non-earthly and the earthly world, now, in the period of transition, the new experimental perspective tries to grapple with the earth trying to limit non-earthly considerations. Since the non-earthly was identified with metaphysics, and metaphysics with the "Being of beings," the apparent obsolescence of the non-earthly leads to questioning our ability to speak at all of beings and Being. Otherwise put: we seem to have difficulty disentangling metaphysics from religion. Since we are critical of religion, as a matter of course we are also critical of metaphysics. The conundrum of the period or transition is that we don't just want to replace the highest values with new ones relying on the same structure: we desire a world that does not posit a separate structure "above" or in the "beyond" (49). This would imply a transformation in the "essence of values," so a "new principle of valuation becomes necessary." This is a consciously analytical process—a process of reckoning—that aims to have better historical conditions. The new valuation wants to have its origin in "new and enhanced conditions."

We become aware that values are reckoned by human consciousness. Since there appears to be no "beyond," such consciousness becomes self-reflective and conceives itself as "psychological reckoning": perhaps some kind of indistinct "intuition" or "instinct." Instinct may not only be mere "bestial impulse," but also constitute a complex process of feral consciousness that drives us to make values now in a conscious way—our way. But for what purpose? At the outset, apparently for the (circular) purpose of making possible a new valuation. "Classical nihilism" comes to completion when being as a whole is "newly reckoned and knowledge of the essence of values and of valuation is expressed without obfuscation" (50).

Heidegger seems to associate "classical nihilism" with a consummated "fact-value" distinction whereby we suspend identification with "being as a whole," and measure it anew on the basis of unspecified conditional attributes. We seem to realize that the *source* of values is speculative. Values themselves are speculative, or non-categorical, or merely conditional imperatives. Values "matter" to us, however, and as such they would seem to be necessarily political. But they are not given: for Heidegger they are "constructs of domination." Values result from and are a means of power. The period of transition makes us aware that, despite rhetorical appearances, values are a manifestation of power: values essentially depend on power. Values don't exist in themselves but depend essentially on a "will to power" that sustains them: values are made and sustained by political struggle. [50]

From a more fundamental level, Nietzsche's *"overall insight"* (51) at this point is that the period of transition is definitely not a neutral "time out." It is a moment of opportunity perhaps not unlike Hölderlin's "where danger is, grows the saving power also."[51] So-called "pessimism," or the proud non-reliance on a world "beyond," seems to combine suffering and the possibility of some kind of "growth." Heidegger notes that pessimism is not the final word for Nietzsche—pessimism is *transitional pessimism*. He seems to be saying that unless pessimism be experienced thoroughly by some unspecified "nihilistic movement," the overman, "the meaning of the earth," cannot become an essentially historical possibility. [52]

NIHILISM AS HISTORY

Heidegger offers two distinct renditions of the concept "European nihilism." First, nihilism is a "history" (*Geschichte*) that develops in three stages of devaluation, transition, and non-categorical new valuation brought forth by will to power. Second, the entire process remains within the sphere of "valuative thought": both the critical phase and the attempt at an overcoming occur within the plane of values. Heidegger calls Nietzsche's new valuation "metaphysics of will to power" (52). Heidegger seems to be assimilating Plato's "eidetic metaphysics" and the "metaphysics of values" which is, presumably, a metaphysics that matters particularly in our historical epoch.

The liaison between these two possible kinds of "metaphysics" implies that the "ideas" taken as "values" would not be perennially transcendental entities but would turn out to be results of human reckoning: a political fact of a (particular) historical will to power. Whether this characterization does justice to the Platonic enlightenment where the ideas are coeval with philosophical wonder, allowing us therefore not to politicize the mind, seems to be a different issue altogether. Heidegger is not primarily interested in understanding classical authors as they understood themselves. Neither Heidegger nor Nietzsche seem to give Plato his interpretative due (though Nietzsche is probably more ambivalent[53]). Although Heidegger and Nietzsche usually distinguish Plato from Platonism, at times they seem to be inconsistent in this key distinction. Part of the critique of Leo Strauss, to the problem of "radical historicism" and his reappraisal of "classical political rationalism," stems

from taking a distinction between Plato and Platonism more consistently [54]—
going back to the ancients to read firsthand *sine ira et studio* what the classics said and could have meant, on the basis of primary sources.

Now, according to Heidegger, Nietzsche's metaphysics takes "will to
power as the truth of being" (52). Being is active under this principle of
valuative thought, defining the whole of beings, including man, as will to
power. This is what makes nihilism a history. More specifically: as an essential attribute of will to power, "nihilism *is* history." Heidegger claims this
would in itself even be "world history," but he takes a step back, saying it is
in the province of western history. Nihilism, "in Nietzsche's sense," is essential to western history because it "co-determines the lawfulness of the fundamental metaphysical positions and their relationships." Heidegger seems to
waver with regards to the "historicity" (*Geschichtlichkeit*) of western history
and world history. In order to grasp the "essence of nihilism," it is not
necessary to rely on contextual historical particulars "depicting its various
forms" (53). Although for Heidegger Being has a history, the "thinking of
Being" (*Seinsdenken* [55]) recurs eternally amongst thoughtful people in a variety of contexts. [56] Nihilism, however, seems to be a "law of history": a
positing of values that become devalued and are subsequently and "inevitably" revalued. The devaluation of values is correlated with the experience of
"pessimism": the melancholic and unsettling mood that our world may not be
the best of possible worlds.

Nihilism and pessimism are therefore ambiguous. [57] "Pessimism of
strength" analyzes the given conditions as they are in an attempt to "establish
control over things." Pessimism of strength is analytical or positivist thought
for the instrumental motive of exercising power over the given. "Pessimism
of weakness," on the other hand, is "existentialist" in the gloomy or dark
meaning of the term—seeing the glass half empty as its fundamental and
perhaps only "realistic" outlook. At the level of understanding, the "nihilism
of weakness" explains events as products of historical forces, granting impli-
citly that they are what they are, although perhaps they could have been
different. The pessimism of strength is "analytical," drawing distinctions to
mark and influence events in factual terms; the pessimism of weakness is
more heavily "historicist" (53): the movement of events holds sway and
ultimately determines the historical record. In that manner, although these
two kinds of pessimism share the same origin, they oppose one another "in
the most extreme way." This polarization signals two kinds of nihilistic
pessimism that come to characterize the period of transition: analytical "philosophy," and existentialist historicism or so-called theory of practice. [58]

Heidegger claims that during the period of transition, the process of "incomplete nihilism" fills the void slates of the old categories with new "doctrines," some of which Nietzsche enumerates as: "universal happiness," or
"socialism," "Wagnerian music," or the "Christian ideal." These seem to be

expressions of different kinds of "fideism," in a variety of manifestations: utilitarian, artistic (*l'art pour l'art*), and religious. This unstable "wealth of shapes" in cultural transition seems to make the problem more acute. Why? Because it seems to foster cynicism and hypocrisy, what Nietzsche calls "histrionism," from people who behave under structures and for "causes" they don't believe in, that they couldn't *truly* believe in, because the very structure of the endeavor is merely conditional and ultimately not "needful."

In the period of transition the urge toward revaluation is "preceded and accompanied" by a state of uncertainty. The uncertainty is a product of the contradiction between the wish of living in truth and the realization that actuality seems to block such aspiration. This contradiction points to an apparent re-definition of truth (54). From an analytical "active" perspective, this leads to the association of truth with power. But this is a temporary association: in "extreme nihilism" truth itself becomes questionable. As a result, extreme nihilism becomes reflexively "passive," or apparently more "meditative": instead of identifying truth with power, it challenges all truth and therefore all power as well.

Active nihilism structures a "configuration of will to power" within a conventionally determined rank-order. This could take an ample variety of shapes, some of them politically desirable (based on a reasonable consensus of some sort) some of them very undesirable (for instance, fascism in all its modes). Such shapes of historicity seem to assume a conventional framework for political action believing history per se "proves" it is "right." Historical right becomes thereby a "legitimation" of will to power. The process seems to complete itself when "extreme nihilism," as product of active analytical pessimism, transforms itself into "classical nihilism" looking back on itself as an accomplished fact—its retrospective actuality enforces its historical recognition (55). Classical nihilism consummates an act of power, not through supra-historical contemplation, but by an active reckoning of past deeds apparently vindicated by, and interpreted from, a given present. Here Plato and Machiavelli differ markedly—while Plato takes Socrates as his philosophical hero, cross-examining the train of reasoning of his interlocutors under the premises that "virtue is knowledge," "no one does wrong knowingly" and "it is preferable to suffer injustice than to commit it," Machiavelli on the other hand shifts the focus of virtue to convey the "effectual truth of the thing." Such effectual truth shapes historical conditions, apparently leading to the timely expectation that "what is rational is actual, and what is actual is rational."[59]

Heidegger tells us that from "classical nihilism" now characterized by historicist reckoning, a distinct and "ecstatic" kind of nihilism becomes possible—with complete lack of measure, it opens up space for "ecstatic-classical nihilism": presumably the liaison of measurelessness and form, the "fullness of nihilism," which might be a "divine way of thinking."[60]

To recapitulate: at this juncture Heidegger reports Nietzsche's view that there are several "interwoven" modes of nihilism: an early form of "pessimism" that is therefore incomplete, followed by extreme nihilism, that in turn can be either active/analytical or passive/historicist, culminating in the paradoxical "epiphany" of ecstatic-classical nihilism where nothingness is transfigured and presumably finds a "new name" (56).[61] This is a process of which Nietzsche seems to have been a personal or inner "witness." It doesn't seem, however, to have been merely a process "'contemporary' to Nietzsche's time." At this point of the analysis nihilism appears to be a constitutive feature of "time as history." Heidegger notes that the "name *nihilism* points toward a historical movement that extends far behind us and reaches forward far beyond us" (57).

VALUATION AND WILL TO POWER

Heidegger steps up from historical experience in the direction of thought. Even if we take nihilism as the "history of valuations," understanding it would still depend on grasping its "essence." By "essence" Heidegger here means "metaphysical necessity." There appears to be the need for some kind of interplay between the realm of historical valuations on the one hand, and of "metaphysical necessity" on the other, in order to understand nihilism.

We may ask, however: why is this necessary? Because, according to Heidegger, Nietzsche thinks the origin, unfolding, and fulfilment of nihilism in terms of "valuative thought." Valuative thought is a "necessary constituent of the metaphysics of the will to power" (58). Thinking in terms of values is derivative of a conceptual configuration whose first principle is thinking in terms of volition, and therefore action, and thus power. But Heidegger still poses the question as to how the arena of history and the sphere of thought can be juxtaposed. It is an "interpretation" of beings that claims to be correct, and as such would have to aim to be necessary or substantive or somewhat non-accidental. Perhaps "valuative thought" could, at some level, echo a kind of "correct opinion" (somewhere between sensible imagination and intellection of the ideas in Plato's *Republic* 509d-511e).

If this interpretation carries some weight, the perspective of correct opinion would be grounded on the metaphysics of the will to power—that is, a species of action that is valuable because it matters to us. Thus, values express an opinion that is not merely any opinion, but a kind of opinion that claims to be "correct," or perhaps "useful." Valuative thought would therefore be somewhat "flexible" but not in itself relativistic. But that would also mean that "values" (qua correct opinion) would be distinct from the "ideas." This claim to correctness seems to establish a significant link between values and the metaphysical realm as a stable, or at least more definable standard.

Strictly speaking what is in motion cannot be defined (think of Heraclitus' river): since definition is a necessary characteristic of a thing's substance, what is in motion appears to be lacking in substance, unless it be somehow defined "metaphysically." "Valuative thought" seems to supply that function: it makes things in motion matter meaningfully through a kind of opinion obliquely informed by "metaphysical substance." Heidegger notes that correct opinion understood as valuative thought appears to be a function of (willful) "action," therefore partaking in the "metaphysics of the will to power."[62]

The question for Heidegger at this point is whether Nietzsche's metaphysics is the "fulfilment of western metaphysics" (59). Heidegger makes the explicit remark that he is engaging in thoughtful "confrontation" (*Aus-ei-nander-setzung*) with the thinker Nietzsche; he follows up, however, with the remark that he is not trying to be merely "polemical" or to engage in "vain critique" (59). His attempt is to "meditate on the truth that is up for decision." This seems to involve a kind of "active meditation," that somehow will lead to a further decisive (i.e., possibly non-necessary?) practical act and commitment. Heidegger qualifies this statement claiming that this is not "our decision," but a dispensation made by Being, or by the *Seinsgeschichte*, which will have an impact on our history. In this apparently all-encompassing process there seem to be no "standpoints" outside the history of Being. Being unfolds (qualifiedly?) through time. Our human perspective seems to be necessarily in time.

"Valuative thought" is also an act of human humility. We become ontologically meek, as it were. The predominance of the language of values "partly as a result of Nietzsche's influence" is a recent turn, which appears to be coeval with the fulfilment of the essence of nihilism. Values, moreover, appeared to be amenable to systematic arrangement, giving rise to a "philosophy of value" of a Neo-Kantian sort (Heidegger mentions Windelband, Rickert, Herman Cohen, etc.). However, the "philosophy of value" does not take nihilism seriously. In its pretention that it is possible to speak of epistemology and ethics without dealing with the problem of ontology, it becomes in Heidegger's dramatic depiction merely a retreat and "a refusal to look into the abyss" (60).[63]

What is the essence of valuative thought? What is its origin? Heidegger refers back to *Will to Power* 12B, to go over Nietzsche's view of the origin of cosmological values. The origin of our belief in cosmological values is "the will of man to secure a value for himself" (61). At some level, cosmological values appear to have an anthropocentric source. Such anthropocentric origin of cosmological values seems to offer an "ideal," articulated in terms of "meaning," "purpose," "unity," and "*truth*" (61 Heidegger's emphasis). At this juncture valuative thought relies on interpreting will to power as (cosmological) truth, which as such offers meaning, purpose, and unity. Values articulate aspirations of power. Values are posited by power.

Heidegger follows up with *Will to Power* 715: "The view point of 'value' is the view point of the *conditions of preservation* and *enhancement* with regard to complex constructs of relative life-duration within becoming" (62). What Heidegger omits is that in *Will to Power* 715 Nietzsche imagines a perspective with no "durable ultimate units, no atoms, no monads," where only "multiplicities" and no "unities" take place in the realm of becoming. Even the will itself in this passage becomes questionable: "there is no will: there are punctuated alliances of willing (*Willens-Punktationen*) that are constantly increasing or losing their power."

From Nietzsche's perspective, "value" is therefore a "viewpoint" from the dynamic perspective of power. It is a reckoning in terms of "quanta of power." It implies a quantitative measure in order to gauge its (constant) increase or decrease. Values suppose punctuated seeing-grasping. This makes valuative thought self-referential: values give value because they are valued. From this derives their validity, and therefore their power. In other words, the distinction between reality and appearance becomes attenuated. The medium seems to increasingly become the message.

Values are not self-subsistent entities but presuppose a particular viewpoint: a punctuated atmosphere of reckoning. The viewpoint of values takes into account the "conditions of preservation and enhancement" (63). What we "reckon with," according to Heidegger's Nietzsche, is not an inchoate natural realm, but rather "something that conditions."[64] "Values" are the conditions to reckon power. From this Machiavellian (and possibly Arendtian) perspective, the essence of power is never stable, it always either increases or decreases. Values are the conditions to measure or to reckon the increase (enhancement or self-overpowering) or decrease (apparent "preservation") of power. Will to power is never at a standstill. Heidegger concludes that in Nietzsche's metaphysics "will to power is a richer name for the overused and vacuous term *becoming*" (63).

The unfolding of the will to power is not one-dimensional. Overpowering presupposes some kind of preservation or endurance in order to make enhancement possible: "only what already has stability and a firm footing can 'think' about enhancement." Heidegger now moves to a spatial metaphor: "a stage must first be secured in itself before it can be used as a staging area." This process of fulfilment is not undifferentiated but appears to be a distinct kind of what Heidegger calls "the real" or "what is living" (64). Both preservation and enhancement have in view increasing power. Even to preserve is to secure with the prospect of enhancement. Preservation and enhancement ground the "perspectival character" of the will to power. As "perspectives" they would be particular optics. But this particularity, although it is "a single and individual" perspective, is not idiosyncratic but seems to express the "metaphysical" view that *"beings as such are perspectival."*

Quite unexpectedly, Heidegger claims that "Nietzsche's metaphysics" is in line with the thought of Leibniz. Leibniz, Heidegger notes, affirms that every being (*jedes Seiende*) is defined by two attributes: *"perceptio* and *appetitus"* (65).[65] Perception and appetite are "urges" or drives that claim "representation of the whole of beings." Such representation is a view-point or perspective. Every "center of force," which seems to mean every animate being, as constituted by perception and appetite represents or "construes the world from its viewpoint." It is constitutive of power to make the world into its own image. Heidegger notes, however, that *for Leibniz viewpoints are not values*, presumably because values have to "matter," and Leibniz's monadology is a species of transcendental or dualistic thought, and as such it seems to be species of Platonism. For Heidegger, Nietzsche remains within the orbit of Platonism, but brings its metaphysics to fulfilment. The reality of the "interweaving of perspectives and valuations" is a construct of a "complex kind," it is not "simple," and therefore it is bound to have contradictions.

The will to power implies both preservation and enhancement. It is a complex reality of permanence and impermanence: rest and motion appear to be "relative," and are reckoned by whether they make configurations of power for the overpowering of power possible. Such platforms are "forms of domination." Value would thereby "essentially" be the condition for "the viewpoint for the increase or decrease of these centers of domination" (66). Values are subsidiary of the will to power, their "essence" and even their "possibility" depends on a prior condition: the measurement of increase or decrease of power. At another level, power here appears to be measured in terms of "utility and use." Value is "essentially use-value." Values are conditional on their utility and are therefore never absolute (there seems to be therefore a politically relevant distinction between "valuative thought" and "absolutism"). Even the constructs of domination that harbor values are themselves conditional. From this monistic perspective "becoming itself—that is, reality as a whole—'has no value at all.'" Hence becoming itself cannot be measured.

Heidegger refers us to *Will to Power* 708: *"the overall value of the world cannot be evaluated;* consequently, philosophical pessimism belongs among comical things" (66-67). This passage is embedded in an extensive discussion on whether the world of "becoming" can reach a final state. If it could, presumably it would have reached it already. But Nietzsche asserts the non-mechanistic "fundamental fact" that the motion of the world does not aim at a final state. Can becoming be explained without final intention(s)? If we needed Being to explain becoming, then "becoming would lose its value and actually appear meaningless and superfluous" (this would probably take us back to Pascal's wager). Being, for Nietzsche, would thereby be "world-defamation." Conversely, perhaps becoming is reality and Being is appearance (i.e., inverted Platonism). But then how are we to interpret becoming, without the "tools" of being, that is, without number and measure? Becoming would be "of equivalent value every moment": there would be no all-encompassing value to reckon within becoming. In other words: there would be neither knowledge of the whole, nor partial knowledge of parts. This realization leads Nietzsche to conclude that "philosophical pessimism," that is, radical analytical reason, left to its own devices has no genuine final-point: it can go on and on without end, therefore it "belongs among comical things."

Paradoxically therefore, in Heidegger's account Nietzsche's claim that "being as a whole" (*das Seiende im Ganzen*) has no value is not meant to be a disparaging remark. It is also a way to demarcate the sphere of values as distinct from the essence of Being. Values are "essentially conditioned conditions," dependent on will to power which encompasses, uses, and supersedes them for its "conscious efforts." Heidegger now attributes agency to the "will to power" as the being that conditions values: "values, as conditions of the enhancement and preservation of power, are essentially related to man." They are "essentially" "human perspectives." Heidegger however immediately follows up with a quote from *Will to Power* 713, where Nietzsche qualifies that values are used by "a man" (*der Mensch*) and *not* by "mankind" (*die Menshcheit*).[66] "Man," as a conscious manifestation of will to power, appears to be the agent that "shapes" or gives form to the "matter" of humankind, in view of its preservation and enhancement. Heidegger concludes that from the (human, non-absolute) perspective of preservation and change "will to power and value-positing are the same" (68).

SUBJECTIVITY IN NIETZSCHE'S INTERPRETATION OF HISTORY

Heidegger begins this section exploring the implications of "valuative thought" apparently taking over metaphysics. This gives the impression that all prior "metaphysics" has been a species of a metaphysics of will to power. From this interpretation even the "Being of beings" seems to be interpreted as will to power. Heidegger notes, however, this is not merely a "historiological" (*historisch*) interpretation. Rather, it is a "revaluative" thought: both descriptive and prescriptive of previous metaphysics. The metaphysics of the will to power seems to affect the "very essence of history," which becomes redefined in a new way as "eternal recurrence of the same" (70). This redefinition appears to be a foundational act of the highest sort. The appearance of the descriptive/interpretative prescription of "eternal recurrence of the same" is a consequence of the obsolescence of the "values" of "unity," "totality," and "truth" (*Wahrheit*). The origin of the revaluation would seem to depend decisively on grasping the "values" of "Being," "purpose," and "truth" as products of valuative thought. We note in passing that at this juncture Heidegger seems to use "Being" and "unity," "purpose" and "totality" interchangeably. But, as Heidegger previously noted, "purpose," "totality," "truth," and "Being" are also referred by Nietzsche (*WP* 12) as "categories of reason" (*Vernunft-Kategorien*), perhaps in the spirit of post-Kantian "German idealism" (Heidegger mentions Kant and Fichte, Schelling and Hegel). Heidegger adds that Aristotle also makes use of "categories," though in a different sense from German idealism: instead of subjectivity Aristotle relies on *nous*, which is essentially trans-subjective.[67]

According to Heidegger, in his analysis of "cosmological values" Nietzsche appears to take his bearings from the "transcendental subjectivity" of German idealism. This would be a modern or non-Aristotelian perspective, which also makes the categories of reason appear as "uppermost values." But, Heidegger tells us, Nietzsche extrapolates this modern conception onto Aristotelian metaphysics because his interpretation of the metaphysics of the will to power as the "history of valuations" seems to presuppose it (71). Nietzsche thereby re-interprets Aristotle under the prism of the metaphysics of the will to power: Nietzsche therefore doesn't aim to understand Aristotle as Aristotle understood himself. Nietzsche's interpretation of "all metaphysics in terms of valuative thought" is "rooted" on the basic definition of the whole as will to power. According to Heidegger, Nietzsche's interpretation of all prior philosophy as will to power includes modern (Hegel, Kant, Leibniz, Descartes), medieval, and ancient philosophy (Aristotle, Plato, Parmenides, Heraclitus) even though none of them "knew of will to power as the fundamental character of things." If this interpretative *Blitzkrieg* holds, then Nietzsche's historiological contention that all prior philosophy is will to power would be self-referential, and therefore would not seek to stay true to the distinctive character of past philosophers. To address this concern, Heidegger raises the question: are not all historical interpretations historically conditioned by their times? After all, Nietzsche made the claim in his second *Untimely Meditation* that the ultimate purpose of history is to "serve life."[68]

Heidegger, however, seems to raise questions about historical revisionism. The issue then becomes what would prove Nietzsche's "image of history" correct. Although Heidegger seems to be saying that Nietzsche's interpretation of the history of metaphysics disregards and therefore possibly distorts authorial intent, he seems to be saying that that would not be sufficient grounds to reject it. Why? Because Nietzsche is not after the "illusion of a supposed 'historiological objectivity in itself'" (72). In other words, if the essence of history is "becoming," and therefore will to power, then any interpretative "act" would necessarily be a species of will to power. Hence a claim to historical objectivity would have rhetorical but not necessarily substantive grounds. All history is *political* history. History told by the winners is likely to look quite different from history told by the losers.[69] The quandary, however, seems to be whether we can make a distinction between political and *politicized* history, and if so, whether such distinction would be of degree or kind.

Perhaps valuative thought was alien to earlier metaphysics because "they could not yet conceive of the being as will to power" (72-73). Heidegger seems to be implying that Aristotle was unaware of the God of Thomas Aquinas that is active in its essence, and therefore could presumably be likened to (providential) "will to power." The source of valuative thought appears to be an active or "willful" "fundamental fact," that manifests itself in time through the metaphysics of valuations. Heidegger notes that this *factum* seems certain to Nietzsche but is questionable to us. But if we take the source as questionable, then *a fortiori* what follows has to also be found wanting.

This takes us to the question of the essential source of will to power. For Heidegger, we are now "for the first time" thinking about "the roots of the origin of valuation within metaphysics" (73). Valuation "within metaphysics" is a consequence of the apparent fact that metaphysics is "rooted" on the will to power. But presumably will to power is will to power *always*, therefore the understanding of early metaphysics can "legitimately" be interpreted under this rubric, despite the fact that that does not appear to have been the explicit authorial understanding of previous philosophers. Heidegger makes the historicist assertion, itself derivative from Nietzsche's "projection of beings as a whole" as the will to power that "roots" valuative thought, that "we too must observe and interpret past thought within the horizon of a particular thinking: that is to say, our own" (73). From this perspective, apparently, we cannot step out of history onto some "absolute standpoint" to observe "what has been in-itself."

From a classical Aristotelian sense, Heidegger's radically historicist thought would seem to pose serious problems. It would be very difficult to engage in prudent political deliberation when all limits are ultimately a product of willing. Aristotle uses the image of the "physician" to account for the kind of learning and informed practice that would seek to know why, how, to whom, and to what extent a specific political measure would need to be applied.[70] For Heidegger limits are more fluid, however, and thus the question of the "truth" of "the image of history" seems to take us to a "circle of genuine decisions." For Heidegger, the essence of European nihilism is co-eval with how the "historicity of human *Dasein* is determined for us." European nihilism is a manifestation of an experience of "being-there," partaking in the historical business of a "community of fate" that seems to be constantly in motion. But such fate would not be strict necessity. Heidegger notes: "a meditation on that theme can go in several directions." Heidegger chooses to explore the perspective of the philosophy of history, thinking about the form of history, which, if conceived as a species of fate would "perhaps" become superfluous (74).

Heidegger's question now seems to be the extent to which metaphysics prior to Nietzsche may have decisively prepared the ground for valuative thought. Heidegger notes the risk of turning Nietzsche's conception of history—the history of metaphysics as will to power—into a commonplace of paradoxical subjectivism or relativism. Heidegger closes the section noting that in Nietzsche's "opinion" a definite will to power must have been operative since the beginning of metaphysics: since the first projection of the values of "purpose," "unity," and "truth" into the "essence of things" (75). Apparently, it is Nietzsche's belief or opinion that such categories are always posited as values by a configuration of the will to power at work in every context.

NIETZSCHE'S "MORAL" INTERPRETATION OF METAPHYSICS

Heidegger makes the conditional assertion that if "the truth" (*Wahrheit*) were posited onto the beyond, then presumably human life would have to be subordinated to it. By the "truth" here Heidegger means that which is "inherently desired, what ought to be" (76). Heidegger asserts that such "ought" would command human desire, thereby becoming our "ideal." Heidegger in this passage seems to equate what truly ought to be desired by human beings with "correct virtues" (*rechte Tugenden*) and with "ideals" (*den Idealen*). The man "humbled" by such "ideals" strives, according Heidegger, to become "virtuous" and a "good man" (*gute Mensch*).[71]

Granted, this line of reasoning seems too compact, especially because Heidegger does not mention what he means here by virtue. A series of questions come to mind, for instance: why does Heidegger call "correct virtues" "ideals"?[72] If there are "correct" virtues that would presumably mean that there could also be "incorrect" ones. Can there be "incorrect virtues"? On what basis do virtues become correct or incorrect in Heidegger's thought? So far, the indication seems to be that correct virtues guide the "good man"—they are a human referent that is beneficial to human beings. As such, correct virtues ought to be sincerely desired. But Heidegger continues: correct virtues are not only objects of "desire" but also of "will." Humans beings seem to have no autonomous power over such correct virtues or ideals: they exist in themselves and the "good man" ought to willingly submit to them, in so far as he wills to be good. Although the good man wills the ideals, the ideals themselves don't appear to be subject to his will or to his power. To put it somewhat unfairly but perhaps not altogether wrongly: ideals seem to be coeval with the impotence of the good man's will to manipulate them. The will of the good human being fuses "will" and "good":

it is a moral will. From the perspective of will, "truth" becomes "moral truth." The "good man" is after moral truth.[73]

Heidegger now sweepingly equates "correct virtues," "ideals," and the "highest values hitherto." These are all manifestations of transcendent "Being" that inform willing as to what it ought to be—they align desire and will morally. Presumably, "willing" here means "rational desire," that is, desire that aims at some good, especially to becoming a good or moral man. Heidegger elaborates on what he takes Nietzsche to "usually" mean by morality: "a system of valuations in which a transcendent world is posited as an idealized standard of measure." According to Heidegger, there is a consistent understanding of morality in terms of metaphysics in Nietzsche's thinking. Morality does not aim to decide particular moral facts, but tends to be a rubric encompassing the "whole of beings." In Heidegger's formulation, in the history of Platonism the good or the moral is the true transcendent "Being": the world of "ideals" or what ought to be, contrasted with the "sensible world" of unending labor and submission that "conditions everything" (77).

Heidegger elaborates on this point with a series of passages from Nietzsche. According to *Will to Power* 400, the projection of a dual world expresses a separate true "other" reality, whereby "slaves, and the oppressed, and then misfits and those who suffer from themselves, and then the mediocre attempt to make those value judgments prevail that are favorable to them." Heidegger adds to this characterization the following remark from *Will to Power* 356: "modest, industrious, benevolent, temperate: is that how you would have men? *Good men?* But to me that seems only the ideal slave, the slave of the future."[74]

In *Will to Power* 358 Nietzsche adds: the "ideal slave" or *so-called* "good man," tends to instinctively honor "selflessness," because presumably he cannot posit goals for himself, let alone posit himself as a goal. The "selfless" man lacks the capacity to posit himself as a goal, to "command," because of impotence of power. In this provocative account, Nietzsche concludes in *Will to Power* 898 that it is the man that experiences impotence of power who posits a "transcendent world" in itself, thereby "dwarfing man" in return. The dualism of "Being" and appearance is a consequence of a moralization of reality. Any metaphysics that posits a "true" world above the sensible world is a product of a moral interpretation of reality. Heidegger quotes *Beyond Good and Evil* 34: "it is no more than a moral prejudice that truth is worth more than semblance." "Truth" (*Wahrheit*) here is understood as the moral positing of "ideals" in a world beyond, where "morality" is a product of earthly misfortune, and prima facie seems to be a sort of "prejudice."

However, there appears to be more than one kind of morality. Morality in the "broadest formal sense" entails "every system" that makes possible in a generic way the basic conditions for living. On the other hand, and "as a rule," there is the morality of the "good man" which Heidegger associates with "Platonism and Christianity," in "opposition to evil." Such morality therefore does not take itself to be "beyond good and evil."[75] To be "beyond good and evil," however, seems to be a key characteristic of the period of transition. In the period of transition a critique of moral universalism seems to draw the mind toward mere particulars: from good and evil universals to good and bad "things." Hence "beyond good and evil" does not mean "beyond good and bad." It also does not mean "outside all law and order, but rather within the necessity of a *new* positing of a different order against chaos" (78).

The morality of the "good man," not in the Aristotelian sense, but understood as the man who posits another world out of being-himself overpowered in the here and now, is the "origin of the highest values hitherto." For such man the highest values, the conditions for "his life," are "unconditioned." Yet, such man does not suspect the origin of values to be a sort of humble powerlessness. Lack of self-awareness does not make "transcendent" values less dependent on a kind of will to power. Such an apparently naïve man "takes values (purpose, unity, totality, truth) as if they had descended to him from elsewhere, from heaven" (79). The values conditioned by the humble man become imperative demands—a kind of "hyperbolic naiveté" occurs when the "selfless" man loses his innocence about being the source of values that have hitherto unconditionally burdened him: man now posits "himself as the meaning and standard of value for things."[76]

But man seems to remain "naïve" because he still posits values as the "essence of things." He still lacks awareness that such positing is a kind of will to power. The fault of such naiveté, Heidegger claims, is not derived from lack of anthropocentrism—on the contrary, the fault is that the "humanization is not *consciously* carried out" (80). Human will to power remains naïve and is therefore still deficient. The decisive shaping of the world in the human image requires that human naiveté about the origin of values be dispelled. The positing of highest values is an imposition of values from a human perspective.

The "humanization of beings" is still "innocent." However, as human self-consciousness about value-positing moves forward, the increasing awareness of the subjunctive conditionality of values also tends to make the world "valueless." This valueless "void" is a necessary precondition for the poetic or *poietic* self-awareness of man as creator of values. Heidegger draws the conclusion that, at this stage, the world becomes radically a product of human making: time *qua* human consciousness becomes the conceptual creator of worlds. This is both a historical description and a normative prescription for man as "unconditioned will to power" (81). Time becomes coeval with will to power, which as such is not only a "means," but also the "essence" and "standard," for the appraisal of values. The real and the actual seem to become identical: the essence of will to power is to believe that it progressively creates the "best of possible worlds" through its unfolding as time.[77]

In its essence, however, power seems to be "aimless" beyond its own power-enhancement. If there were an aim to (anthropic) power it would be somehow "man's absolute dominion of the earth." Heidegger seems to associate this eerie predicament with the appearance of the "overman." Heidegger, however, grants that the overman is "usually" interpreted as an indeterminate character, which would be, as such, possibly incomprehensible. It would be incomprehensible presumably because it might not be possible to subsume the overman within a hitherto known category of person. The enigmatic figure of the overman would have to be "grasped" in his singularity: a unique manifestation and "essential determinateness of absolute power." At the same time, Heidegger seems to interpret Nietzsche's musings on the overhuman to be some kind of overcoming of the personhood of the past, shifting emphasis from the "idealization" of the "beyond."

In the closing remarks of this section, Heidegger reminds us that, in his reading, Nietzsche's metaphysics is a philosophical anthropology of the will to power in tandem with the "doctrines of nihilism, overman, and above all the eternal recurrence of the same." The constellation of such parts would constitute the core of Nietzsche's "thought within the history of the essence of western metaphysics" (83).

For Heidegger the identification of metaphysics with "anthropomorphism" implies shaping and grasping the world in the image of human beings. Nietzsche's teaching seems to affirm a decisive (moral) role within the whole for the cultivation and reception of the overman, as "unique measure of all things" (84). Heidegger, however, links the image of the overman with his view that Nietzsche identifies the history of metaphysics with anthropocentric valuation. But such valuation, as seemingly limited to the anthropological sphere appears to be a moral and presumably non-metaphysical teaching. This leads Heidegger to assert that a "more original" look at the source of metaphysics is warranted.

NOTES

1. Ivan Turgenev *Fathers and Sons* Ed. and Trans M. Katz. (New York: Norton 2009 [first published in 1862]).

2. Nietzsche *Gay Science*, 125.

3. Nietzsche *Beyond Good and Evil*, 53. Michel Haar *Nietzsche and Metaphysics*. Trans. and ed. Michael Gendre. (Albany: SUNY Press, 1996), p. 133, analyzes this image from Christian confessional religion to nineteenth-century positivism. Haar notes that "the centuries-old religious practice of the examination of conscience gave birth to a spirit of scientific scruple, which itself engendered a methodological atheism, forbidding appeals to ´hidden causes´ to explain phenomena, requiring adherence to facts." For an exploration of this theme in terms of the apparent death of the "Godhead," see Heidegger "The Word of Nietzsche: God

is Dead," in *The Question Concerning Technology*, p. 53-112. Also, *Contributions to Philosophy*, Sections 57-58.

4. Nietzsche also uses the image of the star, but for a different effect, in *Gay Science*, Prelude, 63.

5. Besides "determination," the German word *Bestimmung* can also be rendered as "vocation," "calling," "provision," "definition." Cf. Heidegger's use of the expression in the *Introduction to Metaphysics*, p. 41.

6. Nietzsche *Ecce Homo* "Why I am Destiny," 1.

7. Eli Friedland "Not to Destroy, but to Fulfill," in Horst Hutter and Eli Friedland eds. *Nietzsche's Therapeutic Teaching* (London: Bloomsbury, 2013), p. 235-245. Heidegger composed the *Contributions to Philosophy* on the basis of six "joinings" to describe how this transition or crossing (*Übergang*) might be characterized. The joinings of "echo," "playing fort," "leap," "grounding," "the ones to come," and "the last god" trace, according to Heidegger, the space-time in which the transition toward the "new beginning" in western history is reservedly occurring. Cf. Heidegger *Contributions to Philosophy*, Section 3.

8. Heidegger seems to associate the process of "classical nihilism" with the image of the "lion" in "On the Three Metamorphoses of the Spirit" in *Thus Spoke Zarathustra*, I.1. The "lion" stage denotes freedom from the old valuation, but also the affirmative capacity to procure the conditions for a "revaluation of values." The *thumotic* lion, however, is not a creator.

9. Cf. Augustine *City of God against the Pagans* (London: Penguin, 2003). Augustine's magnum opus encompasses an "architectonic" ontological shift from Roman paganism toward the nascent hegemonic establishment of the Christian dispensation. Some of the relevant passages can be found in: bk. 1 (on how the pagan gods didn't protect Rome), bk. 2 (on examples of how the pagan gods offer no moral teaching), bk. 4 (on the plurality and subsequent contradictory futility of Roman "polytheism"), bk. 5 (on the monotheistic critique of the notions of fatality and destiny), bk. 8 (on the rejection of "demonology," and the contrast between the pagan cult of the dead and the Christian cult of martyrs), bk. 10 (a critique of Platonists who don't acknowledge Christ as the universal way of salvation), bks. 11 and 12 (on "divine creation," the non-eternity of the world, and the non-existence of evil), bks. 14 and 18 (on the distinction between the earthly city and the city of God), bk. 19 (on peace as man's supreme good), bk. 22 (creation and resurrection, and the "vision of God"). Augustine also seems to have been the first "philosopher of the will." Hannah Arendt emphasizes this point in *The Life of the Mind* (New York: Harcourt, 1978), p. 84-110. Contrast with Jan Assman *The Price of Monotheism* (Stanford: Stanford University Press, 2010), Ch. 2.

10. Nietzsche *Thus Spoke Zarathustra*, III.12 "On Old and New Tablets"; *Beyond Good and Evil* 194-195; *GM* I: 7-10; Heidegger *Nietzsche* Vol. II, part 2, "Who is Nietzsche's Zarathustra?" p. 215. Machiavelli *Discourses* III.30.1; *Prince* Chs. 6; 26.

11. Hannah Arendt notes that "we, who are earth-bound creatures have begun to act as though we were dwellers of the universe." *The Human Condition* (Chicago: University of Chicago Press, 1958), p. 3; cf. also 1-11; 257-273. Another possibility is that the earth seems to become the "Archimedean point" anew (that might be the meaning of globalization). But if the Copernican revolution was the undoing of the geocentric perspective, the return to "the earth" as central point of reference could mean the epistemological (and thus political?) undoing of the Copernican revolution. For an extensive historical analysis from the philosophy of science cf. Thomas Kuhn *The Copernican Revolution: Planetary Astronomy in the Development of Western Thought* (Cambridge: Harvard University Press, 1985). For a literary depiction of the intellectual climate of Copernicus' time see John Banville *Doctor Copernicus* (New York: Vintage, 1993).

12. Heidegger *Nietzsche* Vol. II, "Who is Nietzsche's Zarathustra?", p. 226-27. Consider Horst Hutter's interpretation of the *Übermensch* as *Hyperanthropos*, that is to say, a man or woman who has healed within what Nietzsche calls "the spirit of revenge." Horst Hutter and Eli Friedland eds. *Nietzsche's Therapeutic Teaching: For Individuals and for Culture*, p. 11, footnote 9. Contrast with Heidegger *What is Called Thinking?*, p. 86-87. To reiterate, in the German language *Mensch* can mean either man or woman.

13. Eric Blondel *Nietzsche: The Body and Culture*, p. 261, footnote 17, notes that "genealogy" is not part of Heidegger's "five rubrics."

14. In "The Will to Power as Metaphysics" (Volume III, Section 3, p. 187-251) Heidegger offers an analysis of some of these categories. Heidegger begins with "will to power," followed by "nihilism," "eternal return of the same," "the overman," and ends with a section on "justice." By way of preliminary speculation perhaps we could highlight two points: First, the central section here, "eternal return of the same," uses the expression "eternal return" *(die ewige Widerkunft)* instead of "eternal recurrence" *(die ewige Widerkehr)*. The expression "eternal return" seems to have an "alethic" resonance (perhaps akin to the notion of "moksha" in Hinduism, that is, the serene "release" from the karmic cycle of cause and effect), while the expression "eternal recurrence" seems to be a "form of time," that is, a continuum where life-and-death appear to be "natural kinds" rather than strict opposites (i.e., life and death are natural: both seem to be species of the genus "nature"); as such, the "not-yet" and the "no-longer" appear to be "experienced" simultaneously with the living "now" (cf. Plotinus *Enneads* IV.3.27; Nietzsche *Beyond Good and Evil*, 193; Heidegger *Nietzsche* Vol. II, Part 1 "Eternal Recurrence of the Same," sections 8 and 12, p. 57; 84-85; consider also Arendt *The Human Condition*, p. 46-48, which likens "eternal recurrence" to cyclical "labor").

Second, Heidegger's line of analysis here begins with "will to power" and culminates in "justice." "Justification" would be rooted in some form of "action" and thus on "will to power." By the time Heidegger lectures on "European nihilism," however, there seems to be a conceptual shift. Nihilism appears to take away the conditions of possibility for action, thus negating the "will to power" that could be the efficient cause of "justice." In the context of the overcoming of "nihilism" the "overman" appears to be a *deus ex machina* of sorts, an agent who embodies a new efficient and formal causation, so as to make liberation or "justice" understood as "love with open eyes," a species of actuality. Krell attempts to capture the "rhythm" of this discussion in his analytical essay to Volume III of Heidegger's *Nietzsche*, p. 262. Contrast with Nietzsche *Thus Spoke Zarathustra* I. 19 "On the Adder's Bite"; *Uses and Disadvantages of History for Life*, p. 89-90.

15. Nietzsche *Beyond Good and Evil*, 31; 198. This is reminiscent of Machiavelli's advice to the *giovanissimi* to conquer *fortuna* in *Prince*, Ch. 25. Aristotle, on the other hand, thinks the young are mostly swayed by feeling *(pathos)*, hence from his perspective they are not yet apt for deliberate political action *N.E.* I.3.6-7. Cf. Gadamer *Truth and Method*, p. 520, footnote 108.

16. Contrasting references to the notion of "value" *(der Wert)* are discussed by Hobbes and Aristotle. Aristotle speaks of *axia* or "worth" denoting a claim to "goods external to oneself" in *N.E.* IV.3.10; Thomas Hobbes discusses the "value or worth of man" as a non-absolute measure of judgment dependent on another's need in *Leviathan* Bk. I. Ch. 10. 16. In a post-Nietzschean manner, Max Weber distinguishes *Wertrationalität* or value/belief oriented-action from *Zweckrationalität* purposive instrumental calculation, and from affective and traditional considerations. On the apparent "irreconcilability of facts and values" cf. Max Weber "Science as a Vocation" in *From Max Weber: Essays in Sociology* trans. and ed. H. Gerth and C. Wright Mills. (New York: Oxford University Press, 1946), p. 147.

17. Cf. Leo Strauss' remark that "all 'isms' are a species of monism" in *Studies in Platonic Political Philosophy* (Chicago: University of Chicago Press, 1983), p. 36.

18. Heidegger *Letter on Humanism*, p. 265.

19. It seems fitting to pose the question: wouldn't it better to refer to the "freedom of a people" as a *virtue*? Otherwise put: can there be an epistemic account of the freedom or emancipation of a collective body? Nietzsche acknowledges the languages of values and of virtues. In *Beyond Good and Evil* aphorism 284 Nietzsche declares that his cardinal virtues are: "courage, insight, sympathy and solitude" *(Mut, Einsicht, Mitgefühls, Einsamkeit)*. Perhaps the language of "values" denotes in Nietzsche's thinking a kind of "correct opinion" that would seem to allow a free exercise of presumably higher kinds of virtue.

20. Heidegger *Being and Time* II.4.68d, p. 401; II.4.69b, p. 408.

21. Cf. Desmond Paul Henry *The Logic of Saint Anselm* (Oxford: Oxford University Press, 1967), p. 207-219.

22. The young Nietzsche discusses the distinction between "nature" and "nothingness" in *Wagner in Bayreuth,* Section 11.

23. Nietzsche *Ecce Homo* "Why I Write such Good Books" 4.

24. Cf. "On the Essence and Concept of Phusis in Aristotle's Physics B, 1" in *Pathmarks* Trans. Thomas Sheehan, p. 183-230, where Heidegger hears echoes of *aletheia* in the word *phusis.*

25. The work of Karl Löwith is arguably situated at the interstice of "cosmology" and "revelation." Löwith finds that a return to a classical Aristotelian sense of wonder at natural recurrence can perhaps approximate again the notions of "cosmos" (wholesome order) and "logos" (giving an account) which would presumably assuage our modern theologically de-rived feverishness for historical movement. *Meaning in History*, p. 1-19. Cf. Ronald Beiner *Political Philosophy: What it is Why it Matters* (Cambridge: Cambridge University Press, 2015), p, 71.

26. Nietzsche *Beyond Good and Evil,* 71. Consider Moses Maimonides "Letter on Astrolo-gy," in Ralph Lerner and Muhsin Mahdi eds. *Medieval Political Philosophy* (Ithaca: Cornell University Press, 1972), p. 227-236. Joseph Ratzinger *Jesus von Nazareth. Prolog. Die Kind-heistgeschichten.* Spanish Trans. J. Fernando del Rio (Barcelona: Planeta, 2012), Ch. 4.

27. Nietzsche *Will to Power,* I: 55. Gianni Vattimo *Nietzsche: An Introduction* (London: Continuum, 2002), p. 120-133.

28. Heidegger *What is Called Thinking?*, p. 155; 200; 238.

29. Cf. Nietzsche *Beyond Good and Evil,* 265; 269-70, with Beatrice Han-Pile "Nietzsche and the 'Masters of Truth': the Pre-Socratics and Christ" in Mark A Wrathall and Jeff Malpas, eds. *Heidegger, Authenticity and Modernity: Essays in Honor of Hubert Dreyfus,* Volume I. (Cambridge: MIT Press, 2000) p. 165-86.

30. Consider Nietzsche's thoughts on Vedanta philosophy in *Beyond Good and Evil,* 54, together with Chs. 4-7 in Graham Parkes ed. *Nietzsche and Asian Thought* (Chicago: Univer-sity of Chicago Press, 1996).

31. Cf. Michel Foucault "Nietzsche, Genealogy, History" in *The Foucault Reader.* Pail Rabinow ed. (New York: Vintage Books, 2010), p. 76-100.

32. What Heidegger fails to mention is that the notion of "will" as *voluntas* seems to be inexistent in Aristotle, and perhaps does not originate until Augustine. Aristotle uses instead expressions such as "choice" (*boulé*) or "deliberate choice" (*prohairesis*). The notion of "will" as a distinct faculty independent of determination or fate appears to have its origin in patristic Christianity. On the distinction between strong and weak wills cf. *Beyond Good and Evil,* 21. For an extensive analysis in both Greek and Early Christian thought see Albrecht Dihle *The Theory of Will in Classical Antiquity* (Berkeley: University of California Press, 1982).

33. This seems to be the root of Zarathustra's critique of the last men who "blink" (*Thus Spoke Zarathustra* I Prologue, 5). "Blinking" in Heidegger's interpretation means to live pre-tending that principles are substantive when in fact they are merely conditional, and could therefore be otherwise. *What is Called Thinking?*, p. 74-75; 82-85.

34. Richard Schacht offers a persuasive account of Nietzsche's view of "concepts" in rela-tion to the solid sense of touch in *Nietzsche*, p. 80. See also *Gay Science,* 373.

35. Heidegger discusses "authenticity" (*eigentlichkeit*) at length in *Being and Time.* Divi-sion II, Parts 2-3. Cf. the penetrating analysis by Magda King *A Guide to Heidegger's Being and Time*, Chs. 11-12. Also, Rüdiger Safranski Martin *Heidegger: Between Good and Evil*, p. 163 ff.

36. On the notion of the period of transition toward new "forms of time," see Nietzsche *Gay Science,* 356; 377. *Dawn,* 164, 171, 453. Heidegger, *What is Called Thinking?,* p. 51; *Contribu-tions to Philosophy,* Sections 5; 40. Hegel *Phenomenology of Spirit,* Preface, Section 11. Also, Jürgen Habermas *The Philosophical Discourse of Modernity*, p. 5-7; Leo Strauss "Note on the Plan of Nietzsche's Beyond Good and Evil", in Laurence Lampert *Leo Strauss and Nietzsche* (Chicago: Chicago University Press, 1996), p. 188-205. Michel Haar *Nietzsche and Metaphys-ics*, p. 131-149. Hannah Arendt *Between Past and Future* (New York: Penguin, 1972), p. 3-16; Eugenio Trías *La Edad del Espíritu* (Barcelona: Penguin, 2014), p. 525 ff.

37. This is a key topic of Ch. 2 in Hannah Arendt *The Human Condition,* "The Public and Private Realm," p. 22-78.

38. Contrast with Nietzsche *Dawn* 208. In the second essay of the *Genealogy of Morals* Nietzsche makes "guilt" (*Schuld*) synonomous with "promise-making" and "debt." It is an internalized memory of reciprocity (which can be either positive or negative). For an extensive analysis of the differences between extrinsic "shame culture" and inner oriented "guilt culture" for the ancient Greeks, cf. E. R. Dodds *The Greeks and the Irrational* (Berkeley: University of California Press, 1951), p. 28-63. Dodds also analyzes the Greek "social" and psychological experiences of *aischune* and *aidos* (p. 18; 26). Heidegger discusses the notion of "Being-guilty" (*Schuldigsein*), which he takes to be akin to "responsibility," as one of the "modes of concern" (*Besorgen*) characteristic of Dasein in *Being and Time*, Section 57, p. 326-29. Other renditions in Heidegger that offer a lighter connotation are "voice," "care," "calling," "conscience." These ontological possibilities are also based on the existential structure of the Being of Dasein, but don't seem to carry the punitive heaviness of *Schuld.* I expand on this theme in Part IV "Hermeneutics and Political Philosophy."

39. This seems to be a major problem of the "Cambridge school" of contextualism or historicism. Thought, as by-product of will, becomes an expression of its times, thus making all thought potentially subject to dispute: if "categories" of thought are expressions of will then thought would be inherently polemical, and (from a human perspective) indistinguishable from ideology. For an account of Cambridge school methodology, cf. Quentin Skinner "Meaning and Understanding in the History of Ideas," *Visions of Politics Vol.* I (Cambridge: Cambridge University Press, 2002).

40. For Aristotle *to hypokeimenon* means "that which underlies" and is variously translated as "substance," "substrate," "subiectium," or "ultimate ground." Cf. Aristotle *Metaphysics* Z3 (1029a2-3). If nihilism is a manifestation of skepticism about ultimate grounds, then one corollary would be skepticism about substantive qualities. This seems to be the main premise of Robert Musil's monumental novel *The Man without Qualities* 2 Vols. Trans. Sophie Wilkins. (New York: Vintage, 1996).

41. An expression Nietzsche uses in *Thus Spoke Zarathustra* III "The Seven Seals," 6.

42. Nietzsche *Beyond Good and Evil,* 203; 210-213; *Human all too Human,* II Preface, 5; *Dawn,* 575. Leo Strauss points out Nietzsche's distinction between the "free spirits" who live in the period of transition, and the "philosophers of the future" who presumably will inhabit some future non-transitional horizon. In that sense, Strauss notes, the "free spirits may be freer than the philosophers of the future." Cf. "Note on the Plan of Nietzsche's Beyond Good and Evil," in Laurence Lampert *Leo Strauss and Nietzsche*, p. 189-190. On the other hand, Nietzsche's "philosopher" also differs from the Hegelian "wise man." The Hegelian "wise man" is a "son of his times," as such belongs and is therefore aligned with his times. Nietzsche's philosophers are "stepsons" of their times, always in potentially critical relation to their present (cf. *BGE* 212). This is due to the possibility of them having other interests in contradiction to the modes of the times (p. 201). I expand on the distinction between free spirits and philosophers of the future in "'Who Educates the Educators?' Nietzsche's Philosophical Therapy in the Age of Nihilism," in Hutter and Friedland eds. *Nietzsche's Therapeutic Teaching*, Ch. 5.

43. According to Nietzsche, the need for overarching references seems to be essential for individuals and cultures at large: "a living thing can be healthy, strong and fruitful only when bounded by a horizon," *Uses and Disadvantages of History for Life*, Section 1, p. 63; *Beyond Good and Evil,* 188.

44. Cf. Heidegger *What is Called Thinking?*, p. 159. This signals echoes of a possible contradiction between Aristotelian *phronesis* and Heideggerian "fundamental ontology." Hans-Georg Gadamer *Truth and Method*, p. 489-90, in the context of a response to Leo Strauss' critique of historicism, suggests the two could be approximated on the plane of historical hermeneutics; but there seems to be a "determination" or at any rate an urgency in Heidegger's critique of the primacy of human reflection that would situate him closer to Kierkegaard's *Either/Or* and *Fear and Trembling* than to Aristotelian prudence or practical judgment. George Steiner discusses this point in *Martin Heidegger* (Chicago: University of Chicago Press, 1989), p. 147. Consider also *Being and Time* II.2. Section 56 ff.

45. Cf. Nietzsche's closing lines of *Beyond Good and Evil,* 23 where he remarks that the return to psychology as the "queen of the sciences" is by no means a "*sacrifizio dell' intelleto,* on the contrary! [. . .] psychology is now again the path to the fundamental problems."

46. Contrast with Heidegger's discussion of the relation between singular "fate" (*Schicksel*) and communal "destiny" (*Geschick*) in *Being and Time*, II.5. Section 74, p. 434-39.

47. This ambivalence about the consequences of Heideggerian "communities of fate" are critically explored by Hannah Arendt in *The Human Condition*, p. 248-325; Eric Voegelin *New Science of Politics*, p. 162 ff. Leo Strauss *What is Political Philosophy? and Other Studies* (Chicago: University of Chicago Press 1988), p. 9-55. Leszek Kolakowski *Modernity on Endless Trial* (Chicago: University of Chicago Press, 1990). Czeslaw Milosz *Native Realm: A Search for Self-Definition.* (New York: Farrar, 2002), p. 91-147. Many European *émigré* political philosophers took their theoretical bearings from the problem of radical historicity in twentieth century Germany and Russia, with its subsequent total politization, expansionism, and ruthless ideological and technologically driven elimination of non-conforming peoples.

48. There are at least two paradigms of reason as "reckoning" in this context: the skeptical version of Thomas Hobbes' *Leviathan* Bk. I Ch. 5.2 where reason is taken to be the "reckoning" or addition and subtraction of conventional names, and Pascal's "wager" where he calculates that even if eternal life seems to be improbable, it is in principle not impossible, and given the infinite distinction between salvation and damnation it would be reasonable to opt for faith in salvation. Cf. the insightful comparative analysis in Leszek Kolakowski *God Owes Us Nothing: A Brief Remark in Pascal's Religion and on the Spirit of Salvation* (Chicago: University of Chicago Press, 1996).

49. George Grant argues that coming to terms with Nietzsche's thought is key in order to understand the modern world: "the thought of Nietzsche is the fate of modern man." *George Grant: A Reader*, p, 281. For Grant the modern project is coeval with taking "time as history," that is, taking thought as subset of will, which in his view undermines (Christian) and philosophical (Platonic) "forms of reverence" (p. 287). Modernity turns upside down the classical distinction between contemplation and action: since all events are taken to be a species of action, and therefore of "will," the modern predicament is constitutively incapable of finding rest of any sort.

50. Cf. Nietzsche *Genealogy of Morals*, II, 18.

51. Heidegger *Contributions to Philosophy*, Section 23. *The Question Concerning Technology* p. 28. Cf. also "What are Poets for?" in *Poetry, Language, Thought*, p. 89-139. Dallmayr *The Other Heidegger*, p. 132-148.

52. There might be echoes in this passage of ascetic communities, perhaps in some ways not unlike the ancient Essenes or the Therapeutae. Contrast with Nietzsche *Will to Power*, 112; *Uses and Disadvantages of History for Life,* Section 2, p. 70; Plato *Republic* 600 a7-b5; Cicero *Republic* I.16. Gadamer *Truth and Method*, p. 436; Arendt *Lectures on Kant's Political Philosophy*, p. 55.

53. Contrast, for instance, *Beyond Good and Evil* (Preface) on Plato as inventor of "the pure spirit," and the "most beautiful growth of antiquity," possibly corrupted by Socrates. Nietzsche here is ambivalent as to whether his quarrel is with Plato or with "Platonism for the people;" also, *BGE* 14 on the Platonic "noble way of thinking" (*eine vornehme Denkweise*), resisting sensualism in a hyper-sensual epoch; *BGE* 28 on Plato keeping the comedies of Aristophanes under his pillow; *BGE* 190 on Plato as "the most audacious of all interpreters," shaping the figure of Socrates "into his own masks and multiplicities;" *Genealogy of Morals,* III, 25 on "Plato versus Homer" as the "complete, genuine antagonism"; *Twilight of the Idols* "What I Owe to the Ancients," 2 on Plato/Platonism in opposition to Machiavelli and Thucydides.

54. Cf. Heidegger *Nietzsche* "The Will to Power as Art," Section 20. Gadamer also insists on making a distinction between Plato and "Platonism." Cf. Gadamer's intellectual memoir *Philosophical Apprenticeships* (Cambridge: MIT Press, 1985), p. 193.

55. Thomas Sheehan translates *Seinsdenken* as *alethic* "thinking the clearing," which, he gathers, saves the phenomena in the ontological search for the "truth of Being" [*die Wahrheit des Seins*], in a way that the "ontology of primordialism" does not. *Making Sense of Heidegger*, p. 218. Contrast with *Being and Time* II.3. Section 65.

56. Cf. Hans Jonas "Heidegger and Theology" *The Review of Metaphysics,* Vol. 18, No.2 (Dec., 1964), p. 216 ff.

57. Nietzsche *Will to Power,* 22. The classic study of "active and reactive" nihilism is Giles Deleuze *Nietzsche and Philosophy* (London: Continuum, 1983), p. 39-72.

58. E.g., Pierre Bordieu *Outline of a Theory of Practice* (Cambridge: Cambridge University Press, 2006). Strictly speaking, the expression "theory of practice" belongs to the category of the "squared circle" or "dry water." Practically and more loosely speaking, however, since all human theory might necessarily be an act of some sort, paradoxically, at some level it seems to make sense to put forth theorizing as a form of "practice." Cf. *Being and Time* II.4, Section 69b, p. 409; 412. In the language of the ancients: after his/her ascent to the idea of the good, the Platonic philosopher returns to the cave (*Republic* 516aff). Does this mean that perhaps Plato doesn't make a categorical distinction between theory and practice? This question seems to be analogous to the problem of dualism. Contrast with *Zarathustra* I, Prologue, where Nietzsche's Zarathustra, after ten years of enjoying his spirit in solitude up in his cave, experiences a "change of heart," and "overburdened by his wisdom" "goes under" becoming human again. Nietzsche's Zarathustra seems to be offering here a distinct turn from the theory/practice dichotomy: bringing together *theoria* and "freedom of willing" understood as freedom from the "spirit of revenge." Cf. *Thus Spoke Zarathustra* II "On Redemption." This section is at the center of the text.

Politically speaking, a possible middle ground regarding these symbolic allusions in Plato and Nietzsche may be found in Aristotle's discussion of *phronesis* in Bk. VI of the *Nicomachean Ethics*. Aristotle discusses practical wisdom leading to a "nomothetic" kind of architectonic legislation that establishes constitutional limits for subsequent political action or *politiké* (*N.E.* VI.7.7; VI.2.8). Cf. also the Athenian Stranger's proposal for a *sophronisterion* in-sync with the nocturnal council to help steer the ship of state in Plato's *Laws* 908a ff.; 957c1.

59. Machiavelli *Prince*, Ch. 15. Hegel *Philosophy of Right*, Preface. There might be, however, from the perspective of the "life of the mind" an area of *tentative* convergence between Plato and Machiavelli: "divine mania." This question seems to imply two levels of analysis: whether Machiavelli is a philosopher, as well as how to interpret the historical emphasis the Platonic teaching ought to have depending on time and place. If this question carries some weight, what it seems to imply is that perhaps the cleft between ancients and moderns might not be as stark as Leo Strauss argues. Strauss takes the Platonic ideas to be "permanent problems" of thought rather than ideals of will; this seems to be why Plato would reason differently than the more historically-minded Machiavelli: the "wonder" elicited by the ideas would lead to Socratic rather than historical dialectic à la Hegel. The difference, in other words, would hinge on the meaning of virtue: Platonic virtue, in Strauss' view, seeks to philosophically draw the *psyche* away from unnecessary entanglements (political or otherwise), while Machiavelli's spirited *virtù* appears to take the city to be higher than his soul (cf. Letter to Vettori, April 16, 1527). There are therefore echoes already in Machiavelli of Hegel's critical view of the "beautiful soul." Nietzsche, on the other hand, seems to signal a closer association between Plato and Machiavelli in *Beyond Good and Evil*, 28. Maurizio Viroli *Niccolo's Smile: A Biography of Machiavelli* (New York: Farrar, 2002) also offers references in that direction. Gadamer, in a critique of Eugen Fink's *Vom Wesen des Enthusiasmus*, puts forth a distinction between the power of 'purely human rapture,' and the *anamnetic* evocation of Platonic "divine mania" in *Truth and Method*, p. 512, footnote 35. Strangely enough, Gadamer's Plato is akin to Hegel, but seems to be far apart from Machiavelli. Cf. *Dialogue and Dialectic Eight Hermeneutical Studies on Plato* (New Heaven: Yale University Press, 1980), p. 73. On the other hand, in *Truth and Method*, p. 271-74, Gadamer explores the notion of "horizon" in relation to Nietzsche and Husserl. The "fusion of horizons" for Gadamer is an interpretative act that partakes in "the task of the effective-historical consciousness." This expression seems to resonate with Machiavelli's reference to *la verità effettuale della cosa* in Ch. 15 of *The Prince*. Gadamer, however, apparently gives it an Aristotelian turn by way of a hermeneutic application of *phronesis* (p. 278-89). Contrast with Strauss' opening line in *Thoughts on Machiavelli* (Chicago University of Chicago Press, 1978), p. 9. Further on, in footnote 151, Strauss points out that Machiavelli distinguishes between "goodness and virtue" (*Discourses* III.1), and "the wise and the good" in *Florentine Stories* IV.1 and VII.23. For Strauss, Machiavelli is a "teacher of evil" primarily for "ontological" reasons: the major premise in Machiavelli's mind is not "goodness" or "fittingness" but "the effectual truth of the matter." One of the reasons for Strauss' critical stance toward modernity is that Socratic virtue mistakenly seems to become assimilated with Machia-

velli's history-making *virtù*. Strauss takes modernity to be a philosophical trajectory that goes from Machiavelli to Heidegger.

60. Nietzsche *Will to Power*, 15. Cf. Heidegger *Being and Time*, II.3. Section 65; contrast with Plato's *Phaedrus* 244a ff. In the philosophical imagery of the *Phaedrus* the mythical allusion is meant to speak of the recollection of the erotic "ascent of the soul." From this Platonic perspective, however, it would seem unlikely that the language, mood, and state of mind of nihilism would resonate with such "ascent." Heidegger seems aware of this difficulty in *Nietzsche* "The Will to Power as Art," Section 23.

61. Nietzsche *Beyond Good and Evil*, 295.

62. This train of reasoning is also reminiscent of the discussion between Socrates, Thrasymachus, and Cleitophon in Bk. 1 of the *Republic* (335b-354c). This is a complex, potentially *aporetic* section, in which Cleitophon only makes a pithy seven-line interpretation of Thrasymachus' position: "the advantage of the stronger is what the stronger believes to be his advantage" (340a-b). Thrasymachus' disagreement with Cleitophon is what makes him amenable to be refuted by Socrates' *techné* analogy.

63. Nietzsche *Beyond Good and Evil*, 146. Cf. Martin Heidegger "The Anaximander Fragment" in *Early Greek Thinking* (New York: Harper, 1975), p. 13-58. Despite the dramatic rendition as "abyss," I take the notion of "a-peiron" in Heidegger as a quality of mind. It may symbolize the "boundless" lack of limit ("a-peras,") which in Heidegger is no mere lack of "measure," but may perhaps be the beginning of true thinking, open-mindedness bodied-forth in a culturally rooted *Dasein*. Such view of *Dasein* seems to square the circle between the singular thinker in a particular time and place, ontologically open and attuned to the call of universal thought. The rhetoric of the "abyss," however, seems to imply that the "clearing" of thinking is not a matter of course but would imply a kind of spiritual "leap" of some sort.

64. Cf. Krell's footnote, p. 63: "To condition" (*bedingen*) means literally to make something into a "thing" (*Ding*). Things, as opposed to natural entities, become things by that which conditions or establishes limits on them: this active capacity in turn appears to be a result of will to power. For a poetic account, however, where Heidegger takes the word "thing" in relation to "gathering" and "dwelling" cf. *Poetry, Language, Thought*, p. 151.

65. Leibniz's monad seems to have only two attributes, unlike the depiction of the tri-partite Platonic psyche. As such, Leibniz's monad apparently lacks distinct spiritedness. Cf. Nietzsche *Beyond Good and Evil*, Preface.

66. Nietzsche *Beyond Good and Evil*, 126; 268.

67. Cf. Aristotle *N.E.* Bk. VI.6.2; Plato *Phaedrus* 247 c-e. See also Stephen Menn *Plato on God as Nous*, Ch.6.

68. Nietzsche *Uses and Disadvantages of History for Life*, p. 63.

69. On reading Nietzsche "like a looser," that is, not naively identifying his rhetoric with the perspective of "master morality," see Malcolm Bull's discussion in *Anti-Nietzsche*, p. 36 ff. Bull persuasively puts Nietzsche in dialogue with the likes of Heidegger, Antonio Gramsci, and Simone Weil.

70. Aristotle *Nicomachean Ethics* V.11.15; contrast with Nietzsche *Gay Science*, 326.

71. Cf. Aristotle *Politics* III. Ch. 4 ff. In the context of his discussion of the possibility of the "just city" in speech Leo Strauss points out that "'ideal' is not a Platonic term." *City and Man*, p. 121. Contrast with Nietzsche *Will to Power*, 889: "*How can something disagreeable become agreeable?* . . . That one should like to do disagreeable things—that is the object of ideals." *Ecce Homo*, Preface, sec 2: "*Overthrowing idols* (my word for "ideals")—that comes closer to being part of my craft" (Nietzsche's italics).

72. Cf. Kant *Critique of Pure Reason* A805 / B 833.

73. Contrast, however, with *Beyond Good and Evil*, 153, where Nietzsche seems to befriend Thomas Hobbes.

74. This theme is explored by Alexandre Kojève *Introduction to the Reading of Hegel* (Ithaca: Cornell University Press, 1980). In his Heideggerian and Marxist interpretation of Hegel, Kojève argues that the modern technological world is a product of the slave's thoughtful labor. In the "dialectic of recognition," the master preserves the vanquished slave and makes him work for his (the master's) interests. The slave is forced to labor in exchange for his life. The slave prefers to labor for someone else's interests instead of fighting, and in that way he

preserves his life; the master prefers to fight rather than labor. Labor, however, gives the slave the ability to learn how to manipulate tools: over time the laborer becomes a "worker" with an intelligent grasp of technique. Meanwhile, the master either fights or remains at leisure. The master lacks incentive to learn a *techné* (hence the master would also seem to lack motive to learn Socratic justice). As the slave's world of technique expands, the bodily self-assertion of the master seems to become anachronistic (eventually drones replace hoplites and centurions). In other words, the masters are increasingly overpowered by technological machinery. At a structural political level, technology becomes the basis (the efficient cause) of the modern state. The modern state, constitutionally crafted by the more intelligent "slaves" puts forth the conditions to make everybody an equal modern subject, and eventually a modern citizen. The slaves gain civic equality for all and the masters are forced to join the social contract to avoid becoming outlaws. Since this is a rational process which is in principle universal, Kojève claims it should eventually lead to the formation of a world state.

75. Nietzsche seems to take the historical Zoroaster/Zarathustra as the founder of moral dualism. For an account of the sources of Zoroastrianism in ancient Persia and India and its possible influences on the Abrahamic religions cf. S.A. Nigiosian *The Zoroastrian Faith: Tradition and Modern Research* (Montreal & Kingston: McGill-Queen's University Press, 1993). Nietzsche's goal in *Thus Spoke Zarathustra*, however, is to reconfigure Zoroaster in a new and different light. Cf. Hans-Georg Gadamer "The Drama of Zarathustra" in Michael Allen Gillespie, and Tracy Strong eds. *Nietzsche's New Seas*, p. 220-231. Gadamer's reading of Nietzsche's *Zarathustra* takes the teaching of living wisely in the "mediated immediacy" of the "child" as the key goal for the human spirit. Zarathustra's vision of eternal return is not to be understood conceptually: it cannot be spoken but "sung" (*Thus Spoke Zarathustra,* III.13 "The Convalescent"). In Gadamer's take, "wisely innocent" eternal return, and not metaphysical will to power, is the ultimate teaching of Nietzsche's Zarathustra (16). For an extensive reading centered on the interplay of will to power and eternal recurrence in the drama of Zarathustra cf. Laurence Lampert *Nietzsche's Teaching: An Interpretation of Thus Spoke Zarathustra* (New Haven: Yale University Press, 1986). Lampert, however, does not focus sufficiently on the third (possibly Messianic) angle of "Nietzsche's trinity"—the *Übermensch or Hyperanthropos.* In this speculative reading of Nietzsche's *Zarathustra,* the "overman" could be interpreted as a redeeming "mediator," coeval with eternal return and will to power. The figure of the overman might offer a "trinitarian" way to overcome the antinomy of freedom: the overman "freely" wills the essential needfulness of eternal return. Differently put: the overhuman "goes under" to teach us how to "become who we are," healing the "spirit of revenge," by compassionately and mindfully embodying the eternal return (cf. *Beyond Good and Evil,* 56; *Thus Spoke Zarathustra,* I Preface; II. 20 "On Redemption"; II.21 "On Human Prudence"; II.22 "The Stillest Hour"; III.2 "On the Vision and the Riddle"; *Gay Science,* Preface to the Second Edition, Sections 1-4; Heidegger *Nietzsche* Vol. II, part 2, "Who is Nietzsche's Zarathustra?" p. 211-233). Heidegger points out that Nietzsche's Zarathustra "knows that what he is teaching remains a vision and a riddle . . . what we envisage thereby always appears as worthy of question" (Vol. II, p. 227; see also Heidegger's note, p. 232-33).

For contrasting accounts in ancient philosophy and the Bible, consider: Plato *Phaedo* 71d14-73a-3; Matt 2: 1-12; 1 John 5:7-12. From contemporary perspectives: Jürgen Habermas discusses the notion of "Dionysian Messianism" in relation to Nietzsche in *The Philosophical Discourse of Modernity,* p. 91-92; 97. Tom Darby highlights the notion of "panentheism . . . a mediating position between pantheism with its extreme immanence and theism of the type which tends to extreme transcendence" in *The Feast: Meditations on Time* (Toronto: University of Toronto Press, 1990), p. 75, footnote 54. Etienne Gilson, on the other hand, in *The Philosophy of Thomas Aquinas* (New York: Barnes and Noble, 1993) grants that, as an apparent challenge to the principle of non-contradiction "the trinity . . . is not an object falling within the purview of the philosopher as such" (p. 98). Thomas Aquinas discusses the trinity in "Exposition of Boethius' *On the Trinity*" in *Selected Writings of Thomas Aquinas* (London: Penguin, 1998), p. 109-141; *Shorter Summa* (Manchester: Sophia Institute Press 2002), p. 35-62. The dispute between Trinitarian and Arian interpretations of Christianity, before and after the council of Nicea, is explored by Richard Rubenstein *When Jesus became God: The Struggle to Define Christianity during the Last Days of Rome* (New York: Harcourt, 1999). Trinitarians see "the Son" as co-eternal with the God-head and the Holy Spirit. This theological assertion became dogma in the Christian West for a thousand years until the Reformation. Arians, on the other hand, thought Jesus was not necessarily co-substantial with the God-head: he was a creature, a highly admirable, but still human man. The "Arian heresy," came to define historically Eastern Orthodox Christianity, and through Socinianism, it appears to have influenced the thought of Hobbes, Locke, and Newton. Eric Voegelin links the end of "political theology" in the late Roman Empire, with the de-divinization of political power concomitant with the symbol of the trinity, and which, in his account, eventually led to the (Augustinian) distinction between the monastic *vita contemplativa* and the feudal society of the Middle Ages. Such bifurcation of the sacred and the profane was undermined, according to Voegelin, by the revivalist, "gnostic," re-immanentized speculations of the Franciscan monk Joachim of Fiore in the twelfth century. Apparently, Joachim was the first to immanentize the symbol of the trinity onto three ascendant millenarian historical epochs (which eventually became Bossuet's ancient, medieval, and modern eras). Voegelin interprets this as an "immanentization of the eschaton," a process of politicized secularization that he takes to be at the origin of the radical totalitarian movements of twentieth century Europe. *New Science of Politics*, p. 106-110; 162-189. Hannah Arendt *The Life of the Mind* Vol. I, p. 212, remarks that "historically speaking, what actually has broken down is the Roman trinity that for thousands of years united religion, authority, and tradition."

76. Nietzsche *Gay Science*, 9; *Thus Spoke Zarathustra*, I.1 "On the three metamorphoses of the Spirit," particularly the shift from humble and cunning "camel," to fierce and imposing "lion."

77. Grant *Time as History*, p. 17.

Cartesian Re-Founding

METAPHYSICS AND ANTHROPOMORPHISM[1]

Heidegger takes us now to *Beyond Good and Evil,* aphorism 36. In that aphorism, Nietzsche emphasizes the will to power as standard for human experience of itself and of its interpretation of the world. Will to power seems to be a psychological and epistemological "fact." Aphorism 36 begins with a conditional "suppose" that nothing else were "given" to our world except our "desires and passions." The world of will to power seems to presuppose a Hobbesian anthropology where thought appears to be subsidiary, and appetites and "spiritedness" or passion try to affirm themselves as a "*pre-form* of life." The passions and desires have been understood as "mechanistic" in modernity and Nietzsche poses the question of whether that should be granted as "given." To what measure can we posit the "will" as "efficient cause"? There appears to be a contradiction between causality and willing because "will of course could only affect will—and not matter."[2] Heidegger gathers from *Beyond Good and Evil* 36 that Nietzsche interprets the "metaphysics of the will to power" anthropomorphically: the world as will to power is the world not only interpreted but "fulfilled" through man. But, upon closer inspection, anthropocentrism might appear superficial. Hence Heidegger ponders the need to probe "into more primordial regions," apparently hitherto known in prior metaphysics. This leads him back to Descartes.

Heidegger claims that Cartesian metaphysics is at the origin of modernity. The Cartesian proposition *Ego cogito, ergo sum* seeks to establish the know-

ing human "subject" as the "unshakeable ground of all certainty" (86).[3] The
ego becomes the standard of the "real." What this seems to mean is that the
Cartesian ego conceptualizes a distinct series of "objects," against which the
"representing subject" knows the world. Heidegger sees Nietzsche's thought
in continuity with this Cartesian postulate. From Heidegger's perspective
both seem to offer a metaphysics of subjectivity.[4]

Heidegger adds, however, that this teaching is not new: it draws back to
the ancient sophist Protagoras who famously taught that "man is the measure
of all things." It appears "as if all metaphysics" of subjectivity could be
drawn back to Protagoras. The apparent implication for contemporary
thought could be the association of "metaphysics" with anthropology: the
"interpretation of the world in accordance with the image of man." But this
interpretation, in Heidegger's estimation, implies a "decision" not only about
man, but also about "beings as a whole" (*das Seiende im Ganzen*). What
gives man the right to assume he is the measure of all things? Is this a proud
assertion or perhaps a sensible recognition? Heidegger ponders whether the
link Protagoras-Descartes-Nietzsche might be an "exaggeration," rather than
"the temperate and well-balanced thoughts of an authentic knowing" (87).
What seems to be taking place is the reappearance of a teaching or "doctrine," which in distinct historical shapes attempts to make the world in the
image of man. Heidegger wonders whether the identification of metaphysics
with "anthropomorphism" is warranted. Heidegger hesitates to grant that
their non-identification would be a "primitive," "animistic," or simply naïve
view of the world.

Heidegger calls the identification of metaphysics and anthropomorphism
an "opinion" (*eine Meinung*). This is an opinion that expresses the "guiding
question of all metaphysics," from which Heidegger is trying to explore a
more "original" inquiry that might convey the "truth concerning beings as a
whole." However, such inquiry has a specific name: it is "first philosophy"
(*proté philosophia*). The "all-pervasive question" about "the being as a being," is for Heidegger the central focus of Descartes' *Meditations on First
Philosophy*. Heidegger notes that first philosophy was first systematically
expressed in Aristotle's *Metaphysics*.

Before dwelling on the Cartesian *Meditations*, Heidegger asserts some
preliminary reflections on the structural movement from the medieval to the
modern world. Aside from ancient and modern philosophy, from the perspective of Christian medieval Europe the question of "what the being is" appears
to have been "conclusively answered by Christianity." The answer was so
conclusive that the question appears to have ceased to be a question: Biblical
doctrine asserts that being was "created" and is continuously sustained by a
"personal creator God." In the Christian account the creator God creates *ex-
nihilo* and is therefore a creator of being. The question of "the Being of a
being" becomes part of doctrinal teaching, transmitted by revelation, and

subsequently codified and interpreted by the doctors of the church. The truth about being becomes thereby revealed "doctrine" (*der "Doktrin"*) which, as such, can only be appropriately conveyed in the form of a theological "summa" (88). A summa encompasses a series of propositions, possible rhetorical refutations, and conclusions in conformity with church doctrine. Thought about beings becomes a species of revelation to be received by means of organized tradition.[5]

The study of beings as a species of revelation becomes the purview not of philosophers but of theologians. "Christian philosophy," from Heidegger's perspective here, would be a contradiction in terms: philosophy inquires through the understanding into the "primary, unshakeable truth" of being, which as such presumably is always, while theology relies on revealed doctrine of beings as created *ex nihilo* by a personal creator God: creation as such need *not* be always. Even if both philosophy and theology were in search of truth, truth in each case would have to mean something "utterly divergent." The truth sought after by philosophy pertains to a meditation on "what is the being," while the truth of Christianity is essentially "practical": its truth is the "truth of salvation." More specifically, it pertains to the salvation of individual immortal souls in the hope of resurrection. All knowledge in the Christian dispensation is thereby subsidiary to this soteriological aim, which as such becomes the truth of man and therefore of history. In this way history becomes the "history of salvation." The categories "creation," "fall," "redemption," and "final judgment" become standards to "know" the historical truth of the Christian teaching (89). Such teaching, moreover, is studied through *schola* or *doctrina*: those who study and teach such doctrine of "faith and salvation" become school-men or "scholastics."[6]

For Heidegger what makes the modern period distinct from the medieval world is the attempt of man to become "certain" and distinct as a human being "in the midst of beings as a whole." The question of salvation abandons the realm of faith and becomes immanentized as "knowledge" sought for the "free development of all creative powers of man."[7] While in the medieval period the way to salvation shaped and made "firmly established" the "modes and orders" for the transmission of this "truth," now, in the modern period, "the quest for new paths—a question of method—becomes decisive" (89).[8]

What was previously grasped as revealed doctrine for eternal salvation becomes reformulated at the origins of modernity as a metaphysical question of "method." Metaphysics still seems to be understood under the species of revelation or the search for some kind of "way," but now apparently without the transcendental eschatological goal. Modern method seeks a way to define the "essence of truth" that could be "grounded only through man's efforts." The question of philosophy is no longer about the meaning of being itself: from the impassioned motive of emancipation from medieval doctrine, it becomes the experimental search for a way to attain unshakeable, methodically attainable, human facts. According to Heidegger, a negation of medieval scholasticism apparently under its own "historicist" premises (i.e., conceiving being as created either by God or by the "certainty" of the human ego) constitutes the origin of Cartesian modern philosophy.[9]

THE SAYING OF PROTAGORAS

Heidegger takes a comparative look at Protagoras and Descartes. The purpose is to contrast a series of apparently similar statements in their possible ancient and modern meanings.[10] Protagoras' fragment, as transmitted by Sextus Empiricus, reads: "Man is the measure of all things, of things that are that they are, of things that are not, that they are not" (*Panton chrematon metron estin anthropos, ton men onto hos esti, ton de me onton hos ouk estin*). Heidegger offers the following rendition (which he claims that, "of course," is also an interpretation):

> Of all "things" [of those "things," namely, which man has about him for use, customarily and even continually—*chrémata, chréstai*], the [respective] man is the measure, of things that are present, that they are *thus* present as they come to presence, but of those things to which coming to presence is denied, that they do not come to presence (91).[11]

For Heidegger, what is talked about here is the "beings and their Being," or "the being that comes to presence of itself in the purview of man." Heidegger notes that "man" in the fragment is referred to as "*anthropos*" (not "*aner*"[12]): the reference is apparently about man in the broadest sense, perhaps also in terms of the "human ego." Having said that, however, Heidegger insists it would be a "fatal illusion" if we were to identify the metaphysical positions of Protagoras and Descartes on the knowing "subject." How to distinguish between "Protagoras' saying" and "Descartes' principle"? Heidegger offers four interdependent guidelines to "determine" a metaphysical position:

1. The "selfhood of man": the gathered self-knowledge of the speaker.
2. The "concept of Being": "projection of beings on Being" (from below, as it were).
3. The "essence of truth": the establishment of the sphere of "the essence of the truth of beings" (this may be akin to the problem of the "hermeneutic circle").[13]
4. The "manner of standard-giving": the "way" of the singular man to take and give measure for the truth of beings ("each respective man" would have a non-idiosyncratic and distinct measure, presumably in accordance with his attunement to the whole).[14]

Now, Heidegger offers a word of caution: these standards cannot in themselves be determined or called for "metaphysically" (92). Although from Protagoras' fragment "man" is the "measure for the Being of beings," we, according to Heidegger, are trying to interpret him in a classical Greek way. In Protagoras' saying the "ego" of "man" is not the fundamental knowing ground in the manner of Descartes. In Heidegger's interpretation man is a sensible being who "perceives" what is "unconcealed" around him from a humanly accessible realm. This appears to mean a realm of non-representational sense: the "natural cave" as it were, which Heidegger refers to as "the realm of the unconcealment of beings" (93). Such realm of unconcealment we seem to take for granted today, although in Heidegger's estimation it has been forgotten for "many generations before us."

Cartesian modernity takes for granted a subject-object distinction. Such distinction makes the object dependent on the positing subject. The "I," or "ego," seems to become the measure of objects through a cognitive act: the "world" becomes thereby a product made and objectified by the categories of cognition. Heidegger's attempt at this juncture is to try to go back to a Greek sense of the mystery of "unconcealment," in which "being comes to presence" and which "the being brings in tow, as it were" (93). Heidegger, one may say, wants to make possible again the original expression of "wonder" of the Greek philosophers, unburdened by patristic and scholastic accretions, and pose the *Seinsfrage* again.[15] Such attention and recollection to the realm of unconcealment, even without necessarily thinking in the Greek way, is for Heidegger a search for an experience where "our human being has its sojourn."

The "I" of man in the experience of unconcealment becomes the radius of belonging within and around which the "being-oneself of man" is "co-constituted."[16] Thus, the man who participates in tandem with the radius of unconcealment, and not the abstract Cartesian ego, is what the Greeks seem to mean by the experience of the human "I" as "measure." Wonder about unconcealment also implies "the recognition of a concealment of beings and the admission of an inability to decide about presence and absence, about the outward aspect of beings pure and simple" (94). We may take Heidegger to mean here that the Kantian distinction between *noumena* and *phenomena*, itself a development of the Cartesian demarcation between subject and object, doesn't account for the "Greek experience" of qualified non-duality, which, at a human level, seems to lead to what Levinas calls "ethics as first philosophy."[17]

Heidegger continues with Protagoras' fragment B4:
Peri men theon ouk echo eidenai, outh' hos eisin, outh' hos ouk eisin outh' hopoioi tines idean, which he renders as: "To know [in a Greek sense this means to "face" what is unconcealed] something about the gods I am of

course unable, neither that they are, nor that they are not, nor how they are in their outward aspect." Heidegger translates "idea" as "the outward aspect" of what is perceived. For Protagoras, therefore, there cannot be an "idea" of the gods in so far as we do not "face them."[18]

Parmenides' passage continues: *Polla gar ta koluonta eidenai he t'adelotes kai brachys on ho bois tou anthropou.* In Heidegger's rendition: "For many are the things which prevent beings as such from being perceived; both the not-openness [that is, the concealment] of beings and also the brevity of the history of man." Heidegger here chooses to interpret what Protagoras may mean by the brevity of human "life" apparently in terms of all historical human knowing. Heidegger illustrates referring to Plato's *Theaetetus* 152b where Socrates reacts to the (ontological) "prudence" of Protagoras, whom therefore presumably does not talk "foolishly" (contrast with *Republic* 605c2-3). Protagoras' prudence "presupposes that the unconcealment of beings reigns," and was as such assumed as the basic character of beings, but was interpreted in different manners at the beginning of western philosophy by such thinkers as Anaximander, Heraclitus, and Parmenides.

"Sophistic thought," exemplified in this case by Protagoras, is apparently based on the primordial experience of "sophia." Heidegger takes this to mean "the Greek interpretation of Being as presence," and the definition of the "essence of truth as *aletheia* (unconcealment)" (95). To become a wise source of "measure" would therefore become possible while remaining aware of (that is, without forcing a decision on) the all-encompassing unconcealment, and, without the "subjectivity" of man becoming a judge of beings, let alone of Being. According to Heidegger, in contrast to the Cartesian positing of God as an ontological *sine qua non*, the essence of Protagorean metaphysics is characterized by four interdependent "moments": (1) the experiential relation with unconcealment or "post-critical" wonder, which, (2) finds its manifestation in one's "presence"; (3) it is claimed as "truth experienced as unconcealment," that is, facing the non-categorical distinction between *noumena* and *phenomena*, and, (4) finding its "measure" by our authentic "self-remembering" in wondrous "sense of the measuredness of unconcealment."[19]

Now, for Descartes these four steps of relation, presence, experience, and intuitive measuredness would have to be separated analytically, and would thereby each have to have a different—distinct and clear—meaning. For Protagoras and for Greek thought in general, on the other hand, they seem to crystalize a comprehensive (silent) incorporation. Heidegger tells us it would be inappropriate to speak of Protagoras as the Greek Descartes, as it would be to make parallels between Plato and Kant, or Aristotle and Thomas Aquinas.

THE DOMINANCE OF THE SUBJECT IN MODERNITY

We enter now the central section of Heidegger's text on "European Nihilism." Heidegger is concerned here with the meaning of "subjectivity": particularly how the conception of subjectivity has become dominant to guide "modern humanity and its understanding of the world" (96). Heidegger, as we have noted, situates the Latin "sub-iectum" as interpretation of the Greek "*to hypokeimenon*"—that which "under-lies" and "lies-at-the base-of," or is the fundamental ground of all "wholesome" experience. Since Descartes and by means of Descartes a transformation has taken place whereby this overarching ground has come to be interpreted as the human "I," becoming thereby the "'subject' in metaphysics." Man becomes the "one and only subject proper" and subjectivity becomes co-terminus with "I-ness" (97).

In other words: the Cartesian "*ego cogito*" comes to mean the "ground." Heidegger, however, finds this identification unwarranted. He proposes to distinguish between the "concept man" from the "concept of the essence of *subiectum.*" What this seems to mean is that, besides man, all other natural entities such as stones, plants, and animals are also "subjects," in the sense of being "something lying-before of itself." If "subjectivity" is inherent to all given entities, then that would seem to undermine the fundamental (dualistic) premise of Cartesian philosophy. To address the original question of metaphysics—"what is the being?"—Cartesian philosophy proceeds from radical doubt to a distinct kind of "method" based on the "subjective" absolute certainty of the ego cogito. Perhaps Descartes did not have a "Pyrrhonic" aim of endless skepticism: his method attempts to secure a path through which man as man could circumscribe "the essence of truth" (97).[20]

With Descartes' method grounded on the "certainty" of the *cogito* we enter the modern age. This contraction of the horizon posed by philosophy turned into method is the beginning of the "new thinking," at the core of the epochal change effected by Descartes. This appears to have been experienced as "liberation" from the old medieval Christian order. Heidegger notes that every "authentic liberation" is not only a setting free, but is also mainly a new "determination of the essence of freedom."[21] The "certitude of salvation" ceases to be the goal and standard of all truth, and now man is "transformed" and becomes the center of his autonomous existence. Heidegger notes that if this movement of emancipation is experienced as "self-legislation," then we can already see the movement from Cartesian "subjectivity" to Kantian "autonomy." In this framework the key building block appears to be "freedom" that wants to give itself its own law. Such "freedom" seems distinct by being neither subservient to divine and natural laws, nor by falling into "arbitrariness and license" (98).

Modern freedom is thus Cartesian in origin. Heidegger, however, does not seem to elaborate further, and refers the reader to Descartes' *Meditations*

IV. What specific kind of freedom would Descartes have in mind, and how does it fit with his metaphysical assumptions? At this point it might be fitting to look in some detail at Descartes' fourth meditation, "Of the True and the False," to gain some clarity as to what Heidegger might have had in mind with this reference.

Descartes "Of the True and the False"

Descartes begins his fourth meditation distancing himself from the sway of the senses and "corporeal things." His claim is that we can know more about the human mind, "and still more about God," without reliance on the senses. Descartes' view of the human mind as "non-extension," seems to allow him to distinguish it completely from everything corporeal. His experience of doubt, and therefore of incompleteness, is contrasted with his ability to think of a complete "being" (in a non-Heideggerian sense) distinct from himself, which as "perfect and independent" must be God, or at any rate an "idea of God." [22]

If Descartes in his imperfection happens to exist (which his thought seems to make indubitable), this leads him to think that perfection can exist as well. His existence as an imperfect being is dependent on perfection. The imperfect (the non-perfect) can only exist if there is an idea of perfection: since Descartes is certain that he in his imperfection exists, he also has to be certain that at least the idea of perfection exists. If God, or the idea of God, is perfection then God or the idea of God exists. Such contemplation of God, which Descartes associates with "perfect wisdom and science," leads him to the possibility of knowledge of "all other beings in the universe." [23] Descartes claims that, in its perfection, it would be impossible for God to deceive him: the grounding of the mind on an undeceiving God seems to give Descartes the ability to trust his mind in the making of judgments regarding the true and false.

In contrast to a perfect and infallible God, Descartes realizes that as part of his imperfection he is also liable to makes mistakes. Although he is distinct from such perfect God, he is also distinct from "nothingness," which he assumes means "not-being," or what is "infinitely removed from every kind of perfection." Descartes thinks himself as the "mean" between God and nothingness. [24] Unlike Plato's Socrates, for whom error or *hamartia* is to miss the mark in knowing, Descartes seems to take a different angle: following Augustine's categorical demarcation between willing the will of God and falling into vain error. [25] Error on this account "is not something real which depends on God, but [is] only a deficiency." But if God is an "artisan," and given that he "always wills what is best," shouldn't we expect the products of his making to be perfect? Descartes enjoins greater humility: it would be preposterous for an imperfect creature to claim to understand the "purposes" of a perfect God.

Now, all created objects should also be considered together. Something that in itself may appear imperfect, given a larger perspective, might show its perfection. Descartes follows up with an acknowledgment that since he undertook to "doubt everything," he has only come to be certain about his existence and the existence of an omnipotent God. [26] From the experience of his existence it seems to follow that he has two faculties: understanding and free will. The understanding finds its limits regarding that which is infinite (the understanding has "no idea" of the infinite because ideas imply limits, and the infinite by definition is limitless). Descartes appears to grant a subdivision of the capacity of understanding which he calls his capacity of "conceiving." He says that such capacity appears to be of "very small extent," and is "greatly limited." The capacity of free will, on the other hand, being limitless, seems to Descartes to be an indication of his being made "in the image of God." It is the capacity of willing which renders to his mind a likeness to an incomparably greater (omnipotent) God. Free will, however, is characterized by "choice": "the fact of affirming or denying," on the basis of the understanding of "goodness and truth." Such understanding, Descartes reassures us, strengthens his freedom. [27]

This is the specific kind of "freedom" that Heidegger appears to have had in mind in this context—neither necessarily subservient to divine and natural laws, nor a kind of "arbitrariness and license." More generally speaking, Heidegger is thus exploring the link between Descartes and Nietzsche in relation to "willing." In this account, the source of error is not in the "power of willing" itself, nor in the faculty of understanding, nor in the capacity for conceiving. What is the source of potential error then? It lies in the mismatch of the limited understanding and limitless willing: mistakes are made when willing "encompasses" more than is permitted by the limits of truth and goodness as conceived by the understanding. [28]

Descartes touches now on the problem of mind-body dualism. By way of conjecture, Descartes claims he is unable to make a judgment on the question. To make a proper decision, the understanding would have to inform the will on a topic made "clearly and distinctly" evident for such choice. But it would be an imperfection and an improper use of the capacity of willing to make a "rash" decision based on conjectures. Being perfect, it would have been easy for God to have made us error-free. But perhaps the heterogeneity of the world is part of its perfection, and therefore some degree of defect seems to be a constitutive aspect of such heterogeneous perfection. [29]

Even within his imperfection Descartes finds reason to be grateful for the "few perfections that he has." His conviction to deliberate on the basis of "clear and evident knowledge" is the basis of a method distinctly within his power to "firmly adhere to the resolution never to pass judgment upon things whose truth is not clearly known to me."[30] Making such method a habitual disposition, keeping infinite volition within "clear and distinct" bounds of understanding (i.e., "the truth and the good"), Descartes concludes, can help him avoid "error." True judgment is therefore supported by perfection, while error is an absence of perfection and relapse in the "confusion and obscurity" of nothingness or non-being.[31]

Heidegger and Modern Freedom

To return to the text: Heidegger claims that "for us" it remains significant to see that the origin of modern freedom lies in non-reliance on faith. It is the non-reliance on faith that makes man "free" to conceive "independently" the content of the "necessary and binding" for his freedom. This subjectivity of freedom, with the corollary of man's explicit self-mastery, his power over himself and over mankind, lies at the source of the modern age. In contrast to Leo Strauss' claim that modernity originates with Machiavelli's distinction between real and imaginary republics, Heidegger points to the origins of modernity in a metaphysics of will to power and Cartesian subjectivism. The hegemony of Cartesian subjectivism, in turn, tends to limit our historical awareness of how the "subject" would have been experienced in the "natural" milieu of classical Greek sensibility (*aisthesis*).

At another level, however, Heidegger claims that Christianity continues to make its presence felt in the "development of modern history." In Heidegger's estimation Protestantism has furthered that development, which, in turn, has found metaphysical expression in German idealism and romanticism. Protestant Christianity has sought to adapt itself to the spirit of the times, aligning "modern accomplishments" with "ecclesiastical ends" (99).[32] For Heidegger this is a disclosure of the lessening of power, and the subsequent need for accommodation and compromise Christianity has undergone in modern times. Christianity no longer "shapes history" the way it did in the Middle Ages. Christianity has become that which is negated by modern freedom: this implies two interrelated kinds of "liberation"—from the hope of the salvation of the soul, to the apparent "certitude [that] man can by himself be sure of his own definition and task" (99).

This change of direction implies a new focus of dominion. Man's immanent goal in this period appears to be his dominion over the entire earth.[33] The positing of this "binding" doesn't appear to be monolithic, however. Heidegger offers at least ten possible lines of development for the "consciously posited binding" of the dominion of the earth including: enlightened global law; positivist institutionalism; neo-classicism and the re-birth or re-configuration of an appreciation of "the beautiful" ("the human ideal of classicism"); power-politics in nationalistic form; the affirmation of the international labor movement and the triumph of the proletariat; the progress of human rationality presumably through the rule of modern science; the un-specified development of "the seeds of each individual age," or the distinc-tiveness of individuals through some unspecified cultural shape (by way of the "organization of the masses"); or, last but not least, a kind of human organization reliant neither on individualism nor on the organization of "mass," but rather on the affirmation of "types." The notion of human "types," according to Heidegger, would transform the "uniqueness previous-ly claimed by individuality" and the "similarity and universality" that the nascent global community demands.[34]

The notion of "types," according to Heidegger, has the characteristic of expressing the "same coinage" as class or sort without suffering the problem of homogeneity. It would therefore imply a qualified set of distinctions. To speak of "types" would imply distinctive kinds of men and women who can become sources of aspiration for human self-modeling (Heidegger tellingly gives the examples of Prussian soldiery and the Jesuit order). Heidegger associates this line of inquiry with Nietzsche's thought of the "overman," who would be in this light a "mediator," or a source of mimetic "measure" for the essential transformation of a differentiated, yet interwoven, human-kind.[35]

In the spirit of Nietzsche's qualified pluralism, this could be interpreted in the form of distinct kinds of *askeses* or exercises for "self-shaping" in philo-sophical schools of diverse orders depending on specific human "types."[36] However, from the perspective of modern mankind at large, for Heidegger the route toward self-preservation appears more dim: unfolding as a process of dominance toward "absolute serviceability" (100). The globe turning into the Egypt of the book of *Genesis*, it would seem.[37]

Now, as the history of modern mankind turns away from the Biblical aim of salvation, it still receives echoes of the "*certitude*" of that orientation, but now in a secularized or "worldly" fashion. Although such modern seculariza-tion appears to have left Christianity behind, and as such conceives itself as "post-metaphysical," for Heidegger this is not quite so. The decisive begin-ning of the modern age lies in a kind of metaphysics: it is not only a subsidi-ary development of Christian (Augustinian) soteriology, but also a historical development of Cartesian metaphysics in the quest for freedom through self-legislation. Otherwise put: Descartes not only anticipates but also encom-passes Kant. Cartesian dualism is the subjective-ground of Kantian critical philosophy.

Heidegger ends this section on a somewhat cryptic note. He asserts that philosophy is not a conceptualization or a systematization of the present. Modern (Cartesian/Kantian) positivism in Heidegger's estimation is "below" Hegelian philosophy "which in some sense was its fulfillment." Even as Hegelian philosophy stood against Kantianism, as a sort of negation, it was dependent on what it negated. It was the rift between Kantian dualism and

Hegel's philosophy of history that created the positivist intellectual climate of the late nineteenth century. Such positivism, Heidegger gathers, was subsequently transformed by Nietzsche into a "new liberation" (101).

THE CARTESIAN *COGITO AS COGITO ME COGITARE*

Although Descartes, according to Heidegger, "anticipates" modern philosophy, modern philosophy is not simply Cartesian. Heidegger's question at this juncture is the relation between Cartesian philosophy and modern "freedom."[38] Does Cartesianism provide the "ground" for it? Cartesianism would give modern man the method for self-reliance with regards to "intentions" (willing) and "representations" (conceptualization of objects). Cartesian methodical intention and representation depend on the certainty of being grounded on human subjectivity. The new freedom established by human conceptualizing and human willing is based on the apparent certainty that both intentions and representations are grounded on and posited by the human "I."

The new certitude is based on the "*ego cogito (ergo) sum*" (102). This is the first axiomatic "truth," the indubitable basis of all subsequent knowledge. Heidegger, however, offers a note of reservation stating that the indubitable character of the Cartesian *cogito* has made some conclude that it "must be clear to everyone." In the Preface to the *Meditations*, Descartes points out that although in principle his line of reasoning should be clear and distinct to those who follow it closely, most human minds tend to find it difficult to follow a long chain of reasoning, and waver, losing the thread of the argument, thereby failing to be truly persuaded. Cartesian philosophy is therefore in principle available to anyone willing to "meditate seriously along with [Descartes to] free the mind from attachment to the senses and clearing it entirely of all sorts of prejudices." Descartes also claims his *Meditations* are a "treatise," and not a dialogue. [39] The implication seems to be that treatises "dictate" teachings on which the writer seems to have certainty, partaking apparently in the realm of settled wisdom. In contrast to the treatise mode, the dialogue form appears to be a species of philosophy or non-wise love of wisdom, which in turn is of two kinds: *aporetic,* leading to perplexity, or "ironic," with a higher pedagogical aim. [40]

The new "ground," and guiding principle for "truth," becomes a "certitude" derived from radical doubt. The "I" becomes the certain, necessary condition for "truth." Heidegger however notes that this process also lends itself to "every possible misinterpretation" (103). The problem presumably is that it opens the door for radical subjectivism and thereby relativism. [41]

Heidegger's speculative premise is that Nietzsche's thought is derivative from Cartesian metaphysics. On the other hand, Heidegger also "believes" there are differences: their teachings, he thinks, are aligned but are not identical. Heidegger contends that the link between Descartes and Nietzsche lies in the claim that they are both thinking "the selfsame" (*das Selbe*) in the "historical fulfilment of its essence."[42] Although the process of the historical fulfilment of modernity begins with Descartes and culminates in Nietzsche, these two moments "differ in the extreme." The modern age for Heidegger "originates" with Descartes and "expires" with Nietzsche. The expiration is also an acceleration and a further transformation: "the most modern times begin with Nietzsche" (103).[43] Even if it brings about the fulfilment of Cartesian philosophy, Nietzsche's position is also "against" Descartes. The line of continuity between Descartes and Nietzsche is the history of the metaphysics of "valuative thought." Valuative thought was prepared metaphysically by Descartes on the certitude of the *ego cogito (ergo) sum*, and is accelerated, critiqued, and "fulfilled" by Nietzsche.

"I think"—the "fact" of the thinking ego—is the basis for the logical deduction of the "certainty," or "proof," of the ego's existence. Heidegger ponders what Descartes might have understood by "thinking," *cogito, cogitare*. What does Descartes understand by "thinking" (*denken*)?[44] Heidegger notes that in "important passages," Descartes uses interchangeably the words *cogitare* and *percipere* "to take possession of a thing, to seize something"; this intellectual-grasping Heidegger further associates with the notion of "representing" (104). Heidegger claims that if we understand the "Cartesian concept of *cogitation*" as *perceptio*, we then come to take this in two "ambiguous" meanings: "in the sense of 'representing,' and in the sense of 'something that is represented'" (105). The implication appears to be a subject/object distinction mediated or "grounded" by thinking as representation. For the word *perceptio* Descartes often uses the word "idea," in at least three possible meanings:

1. *Ideae adventitiae*—as a representation of that which is impressed onto the senses.
2. *Ideae a me ipso factae*—akin to "phantasy," or a sort of "arbitrary," and therefore illusory representation that does not have a substantive referent.
3. *Ideae innatae*—as essentially inborn or intrinsic representation, given to the structure of the human mind.

In the act of cogitation there appears to be not only a distinct and clear designation of the idea as "pre-given," but also as something that would be *within our reach*. This second connotation means for Heidegger that cogitation as representation can reach out and appropriate: it is akin to a will to "mastery," a "thinking over," based on the certitude of the "I." *Cogitare* implies a kind of deliberation based on representation. All representation, however, is also "doubtful": *cogitare* is *dubitare.*" Heidegger urges us to not take the always possible Pyrrhonian road of endless "anti-foundational" skepticism at this point: Cartesian radical doubt precedes the certitude of *cogitare*. Deliberation here would imply a "securing," and a "reckoning of power" within the circle of an indubitable "I." "Deliberative doubting" in terms of "representation" means to "secure" or to "seize," which conceptualizes an account that claims to be non-doubtful. But to what purpose? For further representing taken to mean "further securement" (106).

This (circular) process appears to be modeled on efficient representation (the "how"), but leaves unanswered the question of the "final cause" (the "what for").[45] What is this process of never-ending securing *for?*[46] However this may be, under the Cartesian concept of *cogitatio*, representation of outward "things" or objects occurs in tandem with the representation of the "subject" or the "ego." The role of the "ego," or "I," is not just incidental in this process of representation. When I say "I represent," the grasp of the subjecting "I" is more essential than the act of representation which is subsidiary on the certitude of the "I" (107). Although the representation of "objects" occurs "to me," the ego takes the representation also to be "intersubjective," or perhaps "transcendentally intersubjective." All representation is thereby the apparent recognition of "co-representation" of object along with subject. The subject presupposes the represented object, not incidentally, but "essentially."

Heidegger continues: since "human consciousness is essentially self-consciousness," under the Cartesian framework human consciousness becomes individuated as "sub-iectum," or as self-referential "ground." Therefore, the structure of representation acquires a transversal or intersubjective import: "Being-alongside of beings characteristic of *Dasein* as 'falling'" in the act of "knowing."[47] From cogitation Heidegger focuses now on the other faculties of the Cartesian ego: "willing and asserting, all 'affects,' 'feelings,' and 'sensations.'" The representing and self-represented "I" relates not only the faculties of "knowing and thinking," but also all capacities of comportment and action, including "willing, imagining, and also sensing." All these derive their essence from cognitive representation (109).

Heidegger, however, does not mean to say that for Descartes all manifestations of human behavior are forms of thinking. Rather, he seems to be implying that all kinds of behavior presuppose the certainty of the representing subject, and are therefore "relational" and dependent on thought as long as they are the subject of representation. This sounds complex, but Heidegger assures us that it isn't. The point seems to be that *cogitatio* assures the apparent simplicity of the "unitary essence of representation" (109). I think therefore I am (with all my affections).

Man becomes the self-conscious representing animal. Representation always implies co-representation of the cognitive subject. Since the "I" is the basis of all human representation, all else being uncertain, then in principle the "I" or "ego" has the capacity to choose in advance what will accept as object of "re-cognition" endowed with "place and permanence." The human cognitive subject becomes the "ground" of representation, and thereby posits itself as the standard for the "essence of truth" (110).[48] Since Heidegger interprets Descartes to mean "representation" by "thinking," *ego cogito, ergo sum* would therefore mean "I represent, therefore I am." This Heidegger takes to be the "essence" and "first principle," the presumably "unshakeable ground," of metaphysical thinking inaugurated by Descartes in its presumably intersubjective form, accelerated and brought to completion by Nietzsche.

DESCARTES' *COGITO SUM*

Heidegger takes Descartes to task. He first provides a recapitulation on the three possible meanings of Cartesian *cogitare*: *per-cipere* (perception), *dubitare* (doubt), and *cogito me cogitare* (self-consciousness). Heidegger finds troublesome the syllogistic deduction from cogitation to existence, particularly the conjunctive "ergo." He finds the syllogism: "he who thinks exists" (major premise), "I think" (minor premise), ergo "I am" "gratuitous" and inconclusive. Instead of a deductive logical process, this appears to be an "elucidation" on the part of Descartes expressed in syllogistic form. If the Cartesian *cogito* is taken to be a "first principle" as such it would not be "transparent"; it seems to lack further proof beyond itself (111). Heidegger wonders: if the cogito were self-evident, why would it need rational elucidation? Why is argument necessary to posit this "supreme certitude"?

Heidegger's point is that despite the myriad of erudite commentaries *pro* and *con* Cartesian philosophy, there has been lacking an essential understanding of its fundamental presupposition. This presupposition is taken to have the geometrical, "eternally valid," quality of "axiom" (112). Heidegger does not mention Euclid explicitly, but he brings up the distinct implications that axioms seem to have in many thinkers, such as Aristotle (epistemic axioms apparently reached by inductive-deduction), Leibniz ("monadology" as axiom), Hegel (Spirit-in-time as axiom), and Nietzsche (will to power as axiomatic "fundamental fact").

Heidegger remarks that *cogitatio* in Descartes points to the "I am." But again, if the "I am," understood as the "ego," is certain as a kind of representation, why is deductive logic needed to prove it? The act of "representing" should make the representing "I" self-evident as both representing subject and self-representing object. No syllogism could make more evident to the "I" its own existence than its own self-representation. Hence the "ergo" seems to be a rhetorical trope rather than a meaningful signifier. The "I am" is already presupposed in the "I think," but it seems that for Heidegger the apparent process of thinking cannot be taken as a given presupposition of the "I's" existence.

Now, if "I think" is taken to mean "I represent," then the thinking subject's being is not just a product of "thinking" per se, but of the reflective process of "representation," or distinguishing subject from object on the basis of a representing "I." The "ergo" is not a conclusive conjunctive, but a "joining together" of the "I" and its capacity of "representation," that is, the "ego" and its capacity to distinguish subject ("I") and object ("other"). The essence of *cogito me cogitare* is the ego's representing itself as "being." The ego "is" a thinking/representing being—such "ego" translates into the axiomatic principle "*cogito sum*" (113).

Heidegger warns us not to make this definition a "mathematical" equation of commensurate parts. Heidegger seems to be saying that we cannot assume a unit of counting, and therefore mathematics, unless the first principle of the "I" as *subiectum* (which for Heidegger, to repeat, is the Latinized translation of *hypokeimenon*, the "groundless ground" or foundational "stepping stone") be established. Why? Because the positing of the cogito as *subiectum* is not only an idiosyncratic affirmation, but the ground of everything that "is" (including numbers), which is derivative from the knowing/representing subject. For Heidegger this implies that "representation, which is essentially represented to itself, posits Being as representedness and truth as certitude." But if Being and truth are products of representation,[49] then, since man performs the act of representation, both Being and truth would be products of human "thinking." Man would become the "definitive standard" of Being and truth. The principle *cogito sum* identifies cogitation with the *subiectum*. Thereby the ultimate "ground" becomes the "thinking I" (114). This act of representation gives identity to the "I" as a thinking "thing" (*res cogitans*). The subject thereby also becomes an object of reflection, of which "thinking is its distinctive property" (115).

Heidegger complains that Descartes makes the "superficial and inadequate interpretation of *res cogitans*," by "dividing being as a whole" in scholastic categories of infinite and finite substances. In other words, Heidegger finds the key premise of Cartesian dualism, the distinction of infinite immaterial substance and finite *res extensa*, incongruent with the positing of the "representing" subject. Heidegger notes the "conventional and predominant" translation of *hypokeimenon* as *substantia,* which, if taken "metaphysically" also means *subiectum*. The scholastic distinction between infinite substance (the creator God) and finite substance (creation) becomes in Descartes *res cogitantes* and *res extensa.* The "old framework" is reconceived in terms of human metaphysical "subjectivity": man replaces God through the cognitive and therefore "creative" act of (self) representation.[50]

Heidegger offers a hermeneutic disclaimer: he is performing a "historical meditation" on Descartes: "striv[ing] to think Descartes' principles and concepts in the sense he himself wanted them to have, even if in so doing it should prove necessary to translate his assertions into a different 'language'" (115). But we may well wonder: how does Heidegger know Descartes' intent? Why is he certain that Descartes wants to "overcome" and anthropomorphize the scholastic framework? Presumably, since from Heidegger's perspective the actualization of metaphysics takes place through history, then it would be possible to understand a thinker better than he understood himself, on the basis of a previous thinker's historically actualized thought. Heidegger seems to be giving us a Kantian Descartes, on Kantian premises.[51] Be that as it may, Heidegger interprets the Cartesian *sum res cogitans* not only as a "thing" with the quality of thinking, but rather as a "being whose mode to be consists in representing." Thought as representation gives definition to the Cartesian "ego" as a constant process of certain self-referential subject/I-and-object/other representation. This yields a spiral of "representing that represents into representedness" (115).

The "I" that represents becomes the "self," whose essence is to be the apparent "measure" of Being and truth, in so far as they are products of its representedness. This process determines the essence of "all knowledge and everything knowable." The certitude of the subject gives unity to knowledge or *mathesis*, thus all knowledge becomes potentially "mathematical." Mathematics is thereby the measure for reckoning "lifeless nature," "all that man is not," in other words all *res extensa*. Descartes, however, equates extension with *spatium*. Lifeless "nature" becomes equated with the "empty" category of homogeneous "space." The stark contrast occurs between non-extensive *res cogitans* or "humanity," and non-human objectifiable, measurable, *res extensa*.

The ground of this distinction is "Being as representedness" (116). The metaphysical representation of "nature" as mathematically quantifiable *res extensa*, according to Heidegger, is the prelude to the unfolding of "modern machine technology" and by implication of "modern mankind." In Heidegger's historical analysis of nihilism, however, we are experiencing the "mysterious law of history," when a people "no longer measures up to the metaphysics that arose from its own history." Heidegger thereby reveals the unexpected proposition that "metaphysics" would be a subset of history, and therefore of "time."[52] The completion of "a metaphysics" occurs when it is "transformed into its absolute." Heidegger seems to be saying that both Marx and Nietzsche share a similar analysis of our historical situation: the "absolute form" of modern "machine economy," the "reckoning of all activity and planning," changes the material conditions upon which a "new kind of man" not only is a possibility but also becomes a "demand."

For Heidegger the "essence of modern technology" apparently makes a new form of mankind "needful," in order to match the metaphysical truth of this historical dispensation.[53] A new kind of person is needed, "precisely to steer and deploy individual technological processes and possibilities" (117). The "machine economy," left to its own devices, aims at turning into a ship of state the "entire earth." For Heidegger such state of affairs, the apparently intractable problem of "complex sovereignty," and the "institution of the absolute dominion of the earth," would seem to be the material or necessary condition for the "overman" to appear on the world scene.[54]

Politically speaking, Heidegger is critical of this development mainly because it would entail the application of representational subjectivity or "enframing" upon all of nature, including human nature. Here Heidegger and Nietzsche differ in their political focus: Heidegger affirms a sense of rootedness to the land of origin as grounding the source or aspiration to a human "abode"; Nietzsche, on the other hand, seems to poetically envision the "free spirits" becoming the future "good Europeans."[55] Nietzsche, we might say, is a qualified wandering European cosmopolitan, and thus on this question closer to Descartes than to Heidegger. Although Nietzsche is highly critical of democratic sensibilities, in my reading his prognosis of nineteenth-century Europe conveys certain parallels with Tocqueville's *Democracy in America.*[56]

Now, the Cartesian principle of subjectivity is based on "self-representing representation." Subjectivity becomes axiomatic representation. Heidegger claims that, "of course, Descartes was not explicitly committed" to the development of his philosophy into our modern metaphysics of subjectivity.[57] Nevertheless, Heidegger claims Descartes had "lucid knowledge of its uniqueness" (118). For Heidegger, Descartes' thought is a negation (which as such remains wedded to that which is negated) of the scholastic distinction between essence and existence—now turning existence into *res extensa*, or "space," and essence into the metaphysics of intersubjective representation or anthropomorphic time.[58]

THE FUNDAMENTAL METAPHYSICAL POSITIONS
OF DESCARTES AND PROTAGORAS

Heidegger takes Protagoras and Descartes as archetypes for his comparative analysis of ancients and moderns. In order to elaborate on that comparison, Heidegger goes back to the typology he offered in the section on "The Saying of Protagoras." Now in this particular segment, Heidegger will discuss on the one hand the metaphysical position of Descartes, and on the other, how it contrasts with the stance of Protagoras.

Heidegger divides Descartes' metaphysical position in four points:

First, for Descartes man is the *subiectum* understood as a subjectivized *hypokeimenon*. The notion of "subject" comes to define the essence of man—man is identified with the notion "subject"; "object" therefore becomes all that is distinct from subjectivized man. The subjectivized version of *to hypokeimenon* or ground is not attuned any longer to the "natural whole": it does not encompass other "natural kinds" such as animals, plants, and minerals (not to mention higher possible kinds). Man as subject appears to be other than *res extensa* or "physical nature."

Second, the definition of the "beingness [*die Seiendheit*] of beings" comes to lie on representation. More specifically: on the representing *subiectum*, Heidegger is cautious to point out that this does not imply that the actuality of objects be compromised. For both Descartes and Kant the actuality of beings is never denied. But, according to Heidegger, the key question here lies in the relation of beings with Being, and how it comes to be reckoned and conceptualized from the perspective of Cartesian subjectivity. This is not a passive act of representation, but implies an active grasping and "proceeding in the midst of beings, as well as the scrutiny, conquest, mastery" on part of man, on his own terms (119).

Third, this kind of metaphysics seems to give the essence of truth a particular shape. For Heidegger *every metaphysics* aims at matching knowledge with beings, giving them "definition," by means of a distinct delineation. Cartesian metaphysics subsumes knowledge under *percipere* and *cogitare* and thereby makes the sphere of objects of knowledge a subset of products of subjective representation. Otherwise put: "positivism" begins with Descartes.[59] For Descartes knowledge is knowledge of some "being": beings need to be encapsulated by an act of representation in order to be "known." Therefore, the true becomes "the secure, the certain." "Truth" becomes a sphere of certitude dependent on the self-certitude of the representing subject.

In order to communicate his findings "intersubjectively," the representing subject needs to objectify "itself" by means of "method." Method thereby becomes impersonal and virtually "metaphysical": a kind of disembodied essence of subjectivity that can be applied anytime, anywhere, apparently by anyone. Methodology suffers a shift from the inductive-deduction (perception, principled abstraction, and universal deduction on the basis of given particulars) of Aristotelian philosophy and scholasticism, becoming now a means to change the given "securing, conquering, proceeding against beings, in order to capture them as objects for the subject" (120). At another level, there seems to be an emotional shift from the experience of wonder of classical philosophy or of providential natural order in Thomism, to a perception of underlying anxiety of the separate ego, that therefore uses his conceptual apparatus to try to make himself secure in the world. The certitude of the need to control the world of objects is a by-product of the certitude of the vulnerable Cartesian ego in need of protection from "nature."

Fourth, and this builds on the previous point: man becomes the source of measure of other (objectified) "beings." "Truth" becomes the methodological certitude of subjective representation: what partakes or not in the status of "beings" becomes a human "decision." This mapping out of entities becomes in principle co-extensive with the entire world. Man's representative subjectivity "dominates" the world conceptually: it claims to have "the world" in its representational grasp, from which it derives its measure.

Discovery becomes conquest. What counts as (a) being or not becomes apparently subject to human decision. (Hamlet's tragically subjective "to be or not to be?" would have been either comical or incomprehensible for an ancient: what Socrates has to say in perhaps similar circumstances is that "we owe a cock to Asclepius.") Heidegger, however, also seems to see redeeming qualities in relation to modern subjectivity: this might be the purview of "exceptional individuals," whom Heidegger, inline with Nietzsche, associates with the type "genius" (121). Genius-types, according to Heidegger, presuppose a distinct version of the individual as *subiectum*. The conception of man as "genius" is a modern "Cartesian" phenomenon, which presupposes the essence of man as subject. Heidegger declares that for the Greeks it would have been "inconceivable" to have thought a man as genius. The notion of "genius" is dependent on a conception of human subjectivity that "creates" by means of subjective representation. [60]

Cartesian Method and Protagorean Horizon

In sum, Heidegger seeks to establish a possible parallel between his four Cartesian metaphysical positions and the classical Greek thought of the sophist Protagoras. His analysis goes as follows:

First, while the Cartesian subject appears to be the object-creating "ground," for Protagoras man is situated within a "hermeneutic circle," whereby his selfhood is defined by his "belonging to the radius of the unconcealed" (122). For Protagoras man comes into a world that is not of his own making, which Heidegger takes to mean that the distinction between "subject and object" might be one of qualified degree and not of kind. Second, for Protagoras the unconcealed "transpires" onto beings giving them their "beingness" (*die Seiendheit*). For Descartes the beingness of beings is a result of the representational subject. Third, for Protagoras "unconcealment" itself sheds truth on the actual. For Descartes "truth" is a subset of securing representation. Fourth, for Protagoras "man is the measure of all things" in the qualified sense that such measure is subservient to the constitutive realm of unconcealment, which would encompass the grounds of the concealed. Here there appears to be a receptive and possibly vivid "horizon" that gives measure and orientation to beings and that is not a product of human making. For Heidegger's Descartes, on the other hand, "man is the measure of all things" as he delineates and therefore objectifies beings with a view of securing and reckoning a methodically certain representation.

Heidegger reiterates that although the metaphysical positions of Protagoras and Descartes appear to be "the same" in so far as they proclaim man as the measure of all things, they are by no means identical. We now learn that Heidegger's motive to draw a contrast between Protagoras and Descartes is to adumbrate another, "more *original*" (*ursprünglicheren*) metaphysics distinct from Descartes and therefore, apparently, distinct also from Nietzsche's "moral interpretation" of metaphysics "determined by valuative thought" (122). In the next section Heidegger recapitulates: before expanding on his rendering of this more original version of metaphysics, he offers some remarks on the "historical liaison" (*geschichtliche Zusammenhang*) between Descartes and Nietzsche.

NIETZSCHE'S POSITION VIS-À-VIS DESCARTES

Heidegger says that there are two questions about Nietzsche's "essential" relation to Descartes. Heidegger not only wants to see the relation of their two metaphysical positions, but also "why and how" Nietzsche rejects Descartes' position. The "intrinsic presuppositions" of the metaphysis of the will to power seem to be determined by this complex relationship (123). Nietzsche appears to radicalize the Cartesian *cogito*, undermining it under its own subjectivizing assumptions. Nietzsche subverts Descartes' key analytical division, pointing out that, if the *hypokeimenon* and the subject are identical, and if the "essence" of the dividing subject is its cognitive or analytical capacity of thinking "clearly and distinctly," then it seems to follow that analytical thought would have to apply to the subject itself, making it thereby infinitely divisible. The problem therefore is the limit or purpose of such fragmentation.

Heidegger intimates that the aim of studies in the history of philosophy is to grasp and question what is essential in a thinker's thought. The point for Heidegger is not to mirror or paraphrase systematically a given set of propositions but to engage with a thinker's text through a potential "mixture of mistaken interpretations and essential insights." This, he tells us, is how Nietzsche approaches Cartesian thought: indeed, this is how Heidegger approaches Nietzsche. At this juncture, Heidegger grants conditionally the familiar interpretation of "I think, therefore I am" as a logical deduction. He notices that the key motivation of this inference is to prove that the "I" is or exists. The proposition *ego cogito ergo sum*, encompasses a series of presuppositions on the meaning of "cogitare," "esse," "ergo," and "subject" (124).

Heidegger notes that "according to Nietzsche and others," what may or may not be presupposed by such notions is what subsequently grounds the "certitude" Descartes claims to have found. In fairness to Heidegger, he acknowledges that Descartes anticipated the objection to the problem of presuppositions and granted that these are the "simplest concepts" (*simplicissimae notiones*) "which alone provide knowledge" (125). The "certitude" of the Cartesian subject presupposes that the notions "thinking" (*cogitatio*), "existence" (*existentia*), and "certitude" (*certitudo*) be assumed before-hand.

Descartes therefore concedes that his radical doubt is only possible on the basis of selective non-doubt. Heidegger interprets these presuppositions geometrically as "axioms," or "primal certitudes," that nonetheless remain representations: coeval essential representations of "being, certitude, and thinking" that are assumed as the "*notissimum*" or that which is most recognizable and noteworthy (126). This set of assumptions precede logical distinctions and are meant to recognize the most simple presuppositions, prior to conceptual analysis. Heidegger refers us to Aristotle *Physics* B1 (perhaps specifically to 193a 1-5), where Aristotle claims that there are "things" that are self-evident, such as the existence of nature: it seems unnecessary to prove the obvious. To illustrate what he means, Aristotle gives an example: a blind man from birth might reason about colors, but someone who has perception of color does not need to doubt whether color is there.[61]

Heidegger draws the conclusion that, should one criticize all presuppositions, then out of consistency "every fundamental metaphysical position" would also be questionable. Heidegger, however, claims that "metaphysics" may at least have two sources: certitude of knowledge of the essence of Being, and, (presumably) from the counter-side of that certitude. Heidegger interprets Descartes to be making a self-referential division between "being" and "conceptual truth": conceptual "truth" gives being its determination, making it an "axiom." Moreover, Descartes makes the axioms of "Being, truth and thinking" conceptual touchstones not subject to further questioning; he takes them to be the *fundamentum absolutum inconcussum veritatis* under the assumption that what is certain is what is from a philosophically ordinary perspective "most known" (127).

According to Heidegger, Nietzsche's critique of Descartes hinges on his critique of the sources or motives of such presuppositions. He offers at least two kinds of objection: one foundational, the other logical. Nietzsche's foundational objection questions the equation of "first principles" with axiomatic certitudes. His logical objection follows from this: the process of deductive logic, the "ergo," becomes questionable once the set of presuppositions ceases to be taken for granted as self-evident.

Heidegger, however, charges Nietzsche with obscuring his analysis of Cartesian rationality by making it "psychological."[62] This appears to be the motive that makes Nietzsche interpret Cartesian metaphysics in terms of "will to power." Heidegger wishes to disentangle the discussion of subjectivity from the psychological self-references of Nietzsche, because, Heidegger claims, *"everything depends on conceiving Nietzsche's philosophy as metaphysics."* Unless Nietzsche's philosophy is metaphysically grounded, Heidegger seems to be saying, it would be idiosyncratic, and therefore of no interest to us.

Heidegger contrasts the Cartesian method with British empiricism. If the experience of "thought" antecedes the "subject," as the "skeptical trend" of British empiricism claims—Heidegger mentions Locke and Hume here—in response to Cartesian rationalism, then the subject would not necessarily be a "substance," but rather a "habit of thought" (128). But perhaps Locke and Hume failed to get Descartes right: Descartes' point appears to be that the attainment of the "most universal and most known concepts" are not only grasped through thinking. Rather, they are coeval with awareness of "truth as certainty," in the establishment of representation. Cartesian thought is coeval with the representing or reflective subject (the *ego cogitans*). Nietzsche, however, apparently following the critique of the British empiricists, shifts the focus from thinking to psychology or "affect": making the process of subjectivity primarily a matter of motion and "time," and not of axiomatic forms of reflective consciousness. [63]

Heidegger claims the key aspect of Cartesian "modern thought" is the subjective certitude of representation. In so far as Nietzsche seems to share this assumption, he follows Descartes and his thought is thereby "thoroughly modern." However, Nietzsche also "believes" he is contesting Cartesian rationalism, which he interprets as "will to truth," itself a subset of "will to power" (129). Differently put: Nietzsche's thought undergoes a shift of focus from cognition to volition. From the thinking ego, he moves to the volitional "I," which, as partaker of the "basic character of beings," wills the "will to power."

Heidegger argues that the shift from "thought" to "willing" becomes the "self-mistaking of metaphysics," at the stage of its completion in the philosophy of Nietzsche. Heidegger cites *Will to Power* aphorism 485, where Nietzsche correlates the notion of substance with the notion of (modern) subjectivity. The aphorism conveys that the "concept substance" is posited by the "concept subject." Since there is no substance prior to this positing, at the outset the subject lacks substance. The subject that posits substance is insubstantial, but only what is substantive can posit substance. Since there can be no substance without the positing subject, and the subject is insubstantial, both subject and "substance" necessarily lack substantiality.

Heidegger, however, goes on to qualify his critique of Nietzsche's "belief" that the "concept of substance" is a consequence of the "concept of subject." To expand on what he has in mind, Heidegger references the ancient Greeks. The classical Greek understanding equates the "subject" as *subiectum* with *to hypokeimenon* and *ousia*, but the new interpretation that extends from Descartes to Nietzsche substitutes *to hypokeimenon* for the human *cogito*. Nietzsche is mistaken about the origin of the "concept of substance" because he appears to take for granted the priority of "man as subject" of Cartesian metaphysics (130). It follows from Nietzsche's interpretation that such subject, and thus the essence of its thought, becomes a manifestation of will to power. Thought becomes a subset of willing: the conundrum at the source of the modern project from Descartes to Nietzsche is that "theory" seems to become a kind of *praxis.* [64]

Cartesian certainty becomes a subset of the will to power. Heidegger references Nietzsche's remark that "thinking is for us a means not of 'knowing' but of describing an event, ordering it, making it available for our use: that is what we think today about thinking. Tomorrow perhaps something else" (130). Thinking at this juncture seems to become part of the province of political economy, by which Heidegger would mean that thought seems to become subservient to the standard of "preservation of will to power." It is on the basis of this train of reasoning that, Heidegger notes, Nietzsche came to the critique of the presuppositions of Cartesian subjectivity. Such presuppositions become "hypotheses," not derived from thought but from "feeling," from "the greatest feeling of power and security." The assertion of "valuative thought" follows from the primacy of willing over thought: the "feeling" of will to power posits that which is valuable to itself as "true." The reckoning of Cartesian subjectivity becomes thereby "psychological" in Nietzsche: subjectivity becomes a "form of man's self-securing that arises from will to power" (131).[65]

Nietzsche goes further, claiming the *hypokeimenon* itself is will to power. This is a "fundamental fact" that seems to follow from taking Cartesian subjectivity "hypothetically," making it questionable, and thus realizing that the *cogito* is an epiphenomenon of a yet deeper substratum that Nietzsche identifies with the "feeling of will to power" or "life."[66] If "will to power" is the fundamental fact, then "Being and truth" would not be the "highest values." Instead, the highest values would be posited by the exigencies of the "preservation" of will to power. Since "Being and truth" are species of willing (and therefore of "time"), it is "doubtful" whether their representations account for actually real "things." Everything is in motion: representational truth attempts to offer "snap shots" that may depict and shape "objects," but don't really define them in their essence. Since representations are static, and becoming is fundamentally dynamic, all representation seems to define what becoming "'is' not." Representation therefore is "essentially an error," in so far as it encapsulates becoming conceptually. Since conceptual representation is taken to be "truth," therefore "truth" would also be a kind of error.[67]

Although the "truth" of the representation of becoming is an "error," nevertheless it appears to be a useful one. Will to power or "life" becomes therefore the decisive standard for which the representational error of "truth" becomes "needful."[68] From Nietzsche's "vitalistic" study of "psychology" as will to power Heidegger draws two interrelated conclusions: (1) will to truth becomes a means of "will to power" or "life," and, (2) the "concept of subject" is critiqued by Nietzsche taking it to be an invention of "logic."

"Obviously," Heidegger continues, the follow-up question would be: "what is logic?" (132). Logic is an "imperative," a "form of command," or an "instrument" of life/will to power. Logic is not a disinterested set of propositions seeking to provide knowledge of the true: "logic does not stem from the will to truth." Rather, it is an instrument of "life," which takes its "truth" to be to live (well) always. Heidegger notes a problem, however. By forgoing the correspondence between "truth" and the fact of mortality, truth becomes a semblance, or a "semblance of a semblance": wishful thinking that seems to imagine away the question of whether securing the value of living always is actually possible. Nietzsche's voluntaristic use of thought, taking "thinking" as a species of "will to power," and therefore as a kind of *praxis* of "life," appears to lead to "its own dissolution." However, if "will to power" is the *hypokeimenon*, and if "truth" is a means of the will to power, then perhaps "semblance" might not necessarily be an error and could perhaps be taken to be a "value." The correlation of "semblance" and valuative thought is a "function" of the will to power that disassembles the primacy of "Being and truth" (133). The primacy of semblance, or "phenomena," makes "aesthetic judgment" the non-contemplative historical criterion of valuative thought.[69]

Now, Heidegger points out an apparent contradiction in Nietzsche's thinking. Nietzsche dissolves the Cartesian subject, but still seems to affirm or "presuppose" some sort of subjectivity in the "metaphysical sense of subiectum." In other words, Nietzsche also claims that not the "I," nor the "soul," but the "great reason" of the "body" (*Leib*) becomes in our time the situated signal of human measure.[70] Nietzsche appears, therefore, to mirror the Cartesian method replacing the *cogito* by the *Leib*. The shift from Cartesian dualism to some kind of embodied "qualified non-dualism" at first glance appears to lead to sheer becoming, and therefore possibly to meaninglessness. But if becoming is "true," then so-called meaninglessness would not necessarily be an objection, provided that becoming be grounded and sustained by "will to power." In the midst of this apparently nihilistic "labyrinth of becoming," the body becomes "Ariadne's thread."[71]

Heidegger interprets Nietzsche's view on the *Leib* in terms of the primacy of passions and desires. Specifically, Heidegger refers to *Beyond Good and Evil* aphorism 36. In that passage, Nietzsche develops a line of argument to the effect that "desires and passions" seem to constitute "reality" (134). Perhaps unexpectedly, Nietzsche seems to become indistinguishable from Hobbes. In Heidegger's reading, Nietzsche effects a movement from the

Cartesian emphasis on "representation and consciousness" (*perception*) to the realm of "affect," appetites and drives, and thus to a "physiology of will to power." Heidegger appears to wonder, however, whether Pascal rather than Hobbes would shed more light in order to understand the "bodying-forth" (*das Leibende*) of Nietzsche's thought.[72]

Understanding Descartes in a "truly *metaphysical* way"—in its "*inner* scope"[73]—Heidegger claims would lead to Pascal, who "sought to save man's Christianity," while being "essentially determined" by a Cartesian way of thinking. Heidegger takes this to mean the following. Since Christianity is a kind of "civilization" and apparently not a "culture," for Pascal Cartesian thought contributes to the civilizational role of Christianity rather than to the growth of "culture" in terms of the cultivation of "natural" reason. Heidegger thinks, however, that Cartesian philosophy is a rather essential critique of the "realm of speculative thought of faith for Christian man," in terms of a subject that abstracts itself from all received "prejudices,"[74] from all past "opinion." Cartesian man grounds its newly found instrument of subjective cognition on the capacity to represent and give "reality" shape, extension, motion. This newly found *res extensa* becomes a "predictable and controllable" intersubjective product of the human "mind" (134). The Cartesian way of structuring "reality" makes nature a representation of cognition. In *The Discourse on Method*,[75] Descartes contrasts scholastic speculative philosophy with his new "practical" philosophy. Cartesian "philosophy of practice" issues forth from the critique of scholasticism: both, however, appear to be species of willing. Scholasticism reasons systematically on the doctrine(s) revealed by the providential will of God; Cartesianism, for Heidegger, reasons to methodically affirm human willing. As a species of willing, Cartesianism aims to be "useful for [human] life" (135): giving applied form to nature (including human nature), eventually giving shape to the modern age.

THE INNER LIAISON BETWEEN THE FUNDAMENTAL POSITIONS OF DESCARTES AND NIETZSCHE

Heidegger asserts now that Nietzsche misread Descartes. Nietzsche fails to see the "historically essential inner connection" between Descartes' metaphysical position, and his own. For Heidegger this is a "necessary misapprehension," in so far as Nietzsche shifts the source from the subject/cogito to an underlying will to power as ultimate ground.

To explain what he means, Heidegger offers four guidelines to contrast Descartes' and Nietzsche's metaphysical stances:

1. For Descartes the subject represents "I-ness" (the "I" conceived as an "essential" entity). For Nietzsche, on the other hand, the subject is a "mask"[76] behind which there are "drives and affects" that constitute actual "reality."[77] For Nietzsche, the body (*Leib*) is a "metaphysical guideline" (Ariadne's thread) from which "world interpretation" in the midst of Dionysian cyclical motion could be undergone.

2. For Descartes the "beingness of beings" is coeval with the subject's act of representation. Subjectivity makes a conception of objective "reality" possible, but only as a result of a subjective representation. Nietzsche also seems to share the notion of "Being as represented-ness," but, if "Being" is conceived as permanence, then apparently it could not account for the dynamism of "beings" (136). "Being" would become a "semblance of becoming," a by-product or practical postulate in the interests of beings. Being therefore would cease to be "transhistorical" and presumably would turn into a subset of becoming or will to power. For Heidegger it remains unclear the extent to which this process is in turn rooted both on the primacy of the subjectivity of drives and affects, and "at the same time it is essentially co-determined through the projection of beingness as representedness" (137).

3. For Descartes truth is a correlate of "self-representing representation." Practically speaking, the Cartesian cogito has to become of relative substance: otherwise it would be mired in an infinite regress of never-ending semblances. From the perspective of the (conditionally substantive) Cartesian cogito "truth is certitude." For Nietzsche, on the other hand, "truth" is a process, a subset of the will to power: therefore "truth" is apparently a kind of human "making." Such making encapsulates all "objects" of representation, including being(s), in the interests of the "enhancement of power" or "life." "Truth," therefore, becomes a projection of the post-Cartesian subject now grounded in the *Leib's* interests in the realm of "life" (137).

4. The Cartesian attempt to make man the measure is dependent on the methodological certitude made possible by geometric delineation of "objects." Such activity of delineation, of shaping and establishing bounds and limits, is for Nietzsche a capacity of human mastery. As such, it is a manifestation of will to power.[78]

Heidegger turns to *The Genealogy of Morals* III 12. He wants to illustrate that for Nietzsche "objectivity" is not an act of disinterested contemplation. In an act of rhetorical rejection of classical *theoria*, Nietzsche polemically calls contemplation a "nonsensical absurdity," because apparently the "eye is turned in no particular direction." For Nietzsche human "objectivity" involves an interplay of forces, perspectives, and "affective interpretations" (Goethe's *Elective Affinities* comes to mind here). Nietzsche's point is not that "objectivity" is hopeless, but that in order to "truly" grasp a given "thing," the knower should use a plethora of perspectives, "more eyes, many different eyes," to shed conceptual light on a given "thing."[79] The preponderance of "affect" in the period of nihilism translates into the primacy of "need and utility," as the appropriate categories to plan and reckon. Heidegger notes that it would be erroneous to assume that the shift from Cartesian to Nietzschean "subjectivity" should be a mere anthropological turn.[80]

Heidegger seems to pause here, bringing to a close this part of the analysis. He ends this section with two assertions:

First, so far his analysis has tried to indicate "provisionally" the "essential ground of the historicity of metaphysics as a history of the truth of Being." The crux of the "matter" is that such "historicity" (*Geschichtlichkeit*) is a subset of an apparently unfathomable body/soul "qualified non-dualism" that represents will to power or "life." It would seem to follow that Being and becoming ultimately do not partake in altogether separate realms. This for Heidegger seems to be reflective of two kinds of "subjectivity": "conditioned" (in the context of western history) and "absolute" (with regards to the end of metaphysics as such).

Second, and more specifically, Heidegger sees an essential continuity in all western metaphysics that ties "subjectivity" in both its "conditioned" and "absolute" meanings. In this light, Heidegger, through his reading of Nietzsche, seeks to bring all metaphysics to "fulfillment" (*Vollendung*) (138).[81]

Heidegger's next step is to see the fulfilment of metaphysics as a new dispensation of the "question of Being." What this seems to mean is that the essential ground (will to power/"life"), the *hypokeimenon*, which is (unfathomably) both substantive and in apparent motion, is itself indicative of the way historical man could understand himself metaphysically, perhaps "making" possible the clearing of unconcealment—from Being, and back toward Being, by way of consciously willed time.[82]

NOTES

1. *Metaphysik und Anthropomorphie*. Heidegger's focus seems to be both on the "form" as well as the self-representation of the human being (*anthropos*).

2. *Beyond Good and Evil* 36 is a central aphorism to understand Nietzsche's view on the will. In a nutshell, he finds the dualistic relation between "will" and "matter" intractable; thus, he "risks the hypothesis" that either there is no "will" (which he also finds implausible), or, perhaps *everything* is will: "the world viewed from inside, the world determined and characterized according to its 'intelligible character,'" Nietzsche gathers, would be a manifestation of will to power. In this aphorism Nietzsche's view on the "will" appears to be a reversal of *der Wille* in Schopenhauer that to some extent seems to draw from Augustinian *voluntas* (cf. the following aphorism 37: "'What? Doesn't this mean . . . God is refuted but the devil is not?' On the contrary! On the contrary my friends").

3. Harry Bracken *Descartes* (Oxford: Oxford University Press, 2002) argues that Cartesian philosophy sought to make use of "methodical doubt" in order to overcome Pyrrhonian skepticism, which Descartes apparently took as one of the main theoretical sources that fueled the

theological disputes of the early sixteenth century. According to Bracken, Descartes relied on the principles of "distinctness and clarity" (40) to meditate upon and seek what could be known indubitably, with the motive of undermining the skeptic modes of Montaigne on the one hand, and of the Reformation on the other (14). Alexandre Koyré, on the other hand, argues that *au coeur* Descartes fell in line with Montaigne. For Koyré, Montaigne was Descartes' "opponent and master." *Entretiens sur Descartes* (Paris: Gallimard, 1962), p. 182-83. For an extensive discussion on the theological and theoretical sources of this period cf. Michael Allen Gillespie *The Theological Origins of Modernity* (Chicago: University of Chicago Press, 2009). Gillespie argues that perhaps *the* starting point of modernity lies in the nominalism of Ockham.

4. The problem of subjectivity as opposed to authentic singularity seems to lie at the root of the German critique of modernity. Consider Goethe's remarks to Eckermann: "I will now tell you something you will often find confirmed in your experience. All eras in a state of decline and dissolution are subjective; on the other hand, all progressive eras have an objective tendency. Our present time is retrograde, for it is subjective: we see this not merely in poetry, but also in painting, and much besides. Every healthy effort, on the contrary, is directed from the inward to the outward world; as you see in all great eras, which were really in a state of progression and were all of an objective nature" (Sunday evening, January 29, 1826). *Conversations of Goethe with Johann Peter Eckermann* (London: Da Capo Press, 1998), p. 126. The young Nietzsche was an avid reader of this text.

5. I have found the following commentaries particularly useful to grasp, *grosso modo,* at a structural level the Protestant and Catholic traditions. For a Protestant (Lutheran) critique of Catholic "structure," see Karl Heim *Spirit and Truth: The Nature of Evangelical Christianity* Trans. Edgar P. Dickie. (London: Lutterworth, 1929). Heim enumerates the Catholic modes of objectivist "realism," *unio mystica* and the immediacy of personal experience, liturgical form, style, and universalist syncretism incorporating the wisdom of all ages (26-27). Heim is critical, however, of the apparent Catholic fixation on worldly power, scholastic systems of thought grounded on ineffable mysticism, the emphasis on works as opposed to divine grace (128), of priestly mediation through confessional methods of "inquisition" and "absolution" (140). Heim also notes the seemingly uncritical temper of Catholic practices: the expectation that the laity need only believe and not understand—understanding being the role of theologians and erudite scholars; he finds especially questionable the Jesuit vow of obedience or *excaecatio* (108-112). For Heim, the solitary experience of conscience—*sola fide justificamur* (116)—epitomized by the young Luther, in addition to evangelical morality and scriptural self-reliability, is the ground of Protestant spirituality. On the other hand, for a ("post-Cartesian") take on Catholic Thomism, see Etienne Gilson *The Philosophy of Thomas Aquinas* (Op. cit.). Gilson offers a compact and accessible account of the Thomistic synthesis: from metaphysical principles rooted in theological apprehension to a philosophical anthropology that aims to account for the inner structure of man and the moral consequences that would follow. Thomas Aquinas, according to Gilson, was an innovator attempting a synthesis of "Athens . . . Bethlehem and Rome," for the purposes of the "perfect development of man and of reason in the name of the supernatural and of revelation" (p. x). See also Leo Strauss' review of Heinrich Rommen *The State in Catholic Thought: A Treatise in Political Philosophy* (St. Louis: Herder, 1945), in *What is Political Philosophy?,* p. 281-284. Strauss points specially to the distinction between the Protestant emphasis on "rights," in contrast to the Catholic focus on "duties." On what would perhaps be a possible middle ground in the liberal catholicism of Tocqueville, see Ronald Beiner *Civil Religion: A Dialogue in the History of Political Philosophy* (Cambridge: Cambridge University Press, 2011), Ch. 20. Keith Ansell-Pearson sketches a parallel between Nietzsche and Tocqueville in *An Introduction to Nietzsche as Political Thinker* (Cambridge: Cambridge University Press, 1999), p. 6-8.

6. In the Latin translation of *Leviathan* (Bk. IV. Ch. XLVI. Sec. 21) Hobbes muses about the apparent lack of scholastic consensus on whether "eternity is not a succession of time without beginning or end but a *nunc stans,*" which as such would apparently contradict the Christian doctrine of sequential time. For an account stretching from Jacob Burckhardt back to the Hebrew-Christian understanding of history by faith, see Karl Löwith *Meaning in History* (Op cit.). Cf. also Löwith's letter to Strauss (April 15th, 1935) *Independent Journal of Philosophy* Vol 5/6 (1988), p. 181: "your solution . . . radical critique of '*modern*' *presuppositions* lies

for me historically as well as substantively in the "progressive" direction of Nietzsche: that is, in thinking to the end until modern nihilism." From that point on, Löwith's approach to the problem of nihilism is neither Kierkegaard's "leap of faith," nor Nietzsche's "eternal return," but "in good late ancient fashion (Stoic—Epicurean—Skeptic—Cynic) to arrive at the really practicable wisdom of life—at the 'nearest things' and not at the furthest ones." Löwith laments, however, that "the Germans as much as the Jews lack the sense for the present—for the *nunc stans* of Noon and Eternity." Löwith's appraisal of Hellenistic philosophies of consolation, particularly his embrace of "neo-stoicism," was possibly reinforced after he took over a teaching position in Japan. Considerations of this sort are what seem to drive Habermas to call Löwith a "stoic [in] retreat from historical consciousness." At this point of their correspondence, Strauss and Löwith were fleeing from Nazi Germany with bleak prospects of finding teaching posts. They were in their mid-thirties.

7. Michael Haar defines this reversal of perspective: "as if everything were conceived in order to lead to the salvation of the soul: this is what has come to an end" *Nietzsche and Metaphysics*, p. 14. Cf. Nietzsche *Genealogy of Morals, III. 27.*

8. Contrast with Nietzsche *Thus Spoke Zarathustra*, III.11 "On the Spirit of Heaviness," Section 2. Also, *Beyond Good and Evil*, 191.

9. Although Heidegger does not elaborate at this point on what he takes to be the difference between Descartes and Protagoras, Krell (p. 90) references Heidegger's essay "The Age of the World Picture" in *Question Concerning Technology*, p. 143-47 (cf. also Plato *Theaetetus* 152). While for Descartes human cogitation becomes the *subiectum* or the fundamental "ground," for Protagoras "Being is presencing and truth is unconcealment" (p. 147). What this appears to mean is that the *hypokeimenon* or "groundless ground" may be distinctly experienced by man in his singularity but is not a product of his own cognition. Heidegger is saying that for the Greek sophist there would be no subject-object duality *à la* Descartes: the *subiectum* is itself the *hypokeimenon*, which, although open to self-overcoming within holistic recurrence, cannot be imagined away by man.

10. Cf. Plato *Laws* 716c-d.

11. (Passages in Greek-to-English of Protagoras in this section are from the Krell/Capuzzi translation). Heidegger references Plato's *Theaetetus* 152a2-4 where Protagoras' saying also appears. A few lines later in that dialogue, at 152e5-6 Socrates adds: "let us take it as a fact that all the wise men of the past [i.e., Protagoras, Heraclitus, Empedocles . . . and Homer], with the exception of Parmenides, stand together."

12. On the difference between *anthropos* and *aner* cf. Leo Strauss *On Tyranny*: Including the Strauss-Kojève Debate. Gourevich and Roth eds. (Chicago: University of Chicago Press, 2000), p. 110, footnote 35. This seems to mirror the two kinds of *humori* in Machiavelli *Prince*, Ch. IX: the *aner* wants to rule, the *anthropos* doesn't want to be ruled. Nietzsche interprets this dichotomy in *Dawn* 181. It also seems to be the basis for his distinction between "master" and "slave" moralities, which extends from Aristotle to Hegel. Contrast, however, with Nietzsche's comprehensive view in *Beyond Good and Evil*, 260. I discuss the psychological sources and implications of having both tendencies within a single soul in Hutter and Friedland eds. *Nietzsche's Therapeutic Teaching*, p. 50-51.

13. Cf. Gadamer *Truth and Method*, p. 146 ff. Heidegger *Being and Time* Intro. II.7c; I.3.21; II.3.63.

14. This hermeneutic is developed by Beatrice Han-Pile "Nietzsche and the 'Masters of Truth': the Pre-Socratics and Christ" in *Heidegger, Authenticity and Modernity: Essays in Honor of Hubert Dreyfus, Vol. I*; Nishitani *The Self-Overcoming of Nihilism*, offers a series of readings to establish a dialogue between East and West on this light; Graham Parkes interprets the figure of the *Übermensch* in terms of the "bodhisattva ideal" of Mahayana Buddhism in *Nietzsche and Asian Thought*, p. 18. Carl Jung in his seminar on Nietzsche's *Thus Spoke Zarathustra*, in the opening lecture of May 2nd 1934, also alludes to the Hindu figure of the returning bodhisattva. Cf. *Jung's Seminar On Nietzsche's Zarathustra* (Abridged version). James Jarrett ed. (Princeton: Princeton University Press, 1998), p. 13. Well into the seminar, Jung makes the following remark: "perhaps I am the only one who takes the trouble to go so much into the detail of *Zarathustra*—far too much, some people may think. So nobody actually

realizes to what extent he was connected with the unconscious and therefore with the fate of Europe in general." (p. xviii). Jung, like Heidegger, lectured on Nietzsche during the 1930s.

15. Cf. Heidegger *Being and Time* Intro. II.7b.

16. One is tempted to say that at this point Heidegger sides with Vico in his critique of the Cartesian subject-object distinction. But this does not seem quite the proper interpretation: Heidegger, unlike Vico, also wants to go behind *Genesis*, as it were. See Martin Heidegger *Basic Concepts* (Indianapolis: Indiana University Press, 1989), p. 97 ff.

17. Emmanuel Levinas *Ethics and Infinity* (Pittsburg: Duquesne University Press, 1985), p. 77.

18. Cf. Exodus 20:19: "And they said unto Moses, speak thou with us, and we will hear: but let not God speak with us, lest we die." For an interpretation of this passage in terms of the political theology of early modernity, see Joshua Mitchel *Not By Reason Alone: Religion, History, and Identity in Early Modern Political Thought* (Chicago: University of Chicago Press, 1996), p. 12; 161, footnote 49. Cf. Joseph Ratzinger *Einfürhrung in das Christentum* (München: Kösel-Verlag, 2000), ch. 2, Section 1.

19. See the discussion of Safranski *Heidegger*, p. 286 ff. Cf. Plato *Phaedo* 84d ff.

20. Laurence Lampert in *Nietzsche and Modern Times* (New Haven: Yale University Press, 1993), p. 145-271, develops an analysis of Cartesian philosophy in line with Baconian modern science in "perennial" continuity with the philosophy of Plato and Nietzsche. Lampert therefore seems to agree with Heidegger's thesis on the history of Platonism stretching from Plato to Nietzsche, but he does so on Strauss' premises (i.e., the relative stability of the philosopher's way of life across time).

21. Nietzsche *Will to Power*, I: 23; Contrast with Aristotle *Physics* IV: 6-9: "nature abhors a vacuum."

22. René Descartes *Meditations on First Philosophy*. Trans. with and Introduction by Laurence J. Lafleur (New York: Library of Liberal Arts, 1951), p. 50-51. I rely mostly on Lafleur's translation, with some amends.

23. Ibid. 50. This cognitive "ascent" might not be unrelated to the dialectical ascent from *doxa* to *episteme* in the "analogy of the Line" in Plato *Republic* (509d1-511e). Descartes, however, makes a more categorical distinction between the "visible" and the "intelligible" than Plato's Socrates seems to depict in that passage.

24. Ibid. p. 52. Michael Gillespie *Nihilism before Nietzsche*, p. 33 likens this distinction from both "nothingness" (taken to mean non-being) and from God's perfection, with Descartes' grasp of the "absolute I" as the "Archimedean point."

25. Charles Taylor interprets the link between Descartes and Augustine in terms of "inwardness," with a radical twist in Cartesian "disengaged reason," that seemingly moves from "substance to procedure." *The Sources of the Self: The Making of Modern Identity* (Cambridge: Harvard University Press, 1989), p. 143; 156. Hannah Arendt takes her bearings from this Augustinian/Cartesian view of reality when she put forth the expression "the banality of evil."

26. Descartes *Meditations on First Philosophy*, p. 53-54.

27. Ibid. p. 55.

28. Ibid. p. 56.

29. Ibid., p. 57-59.

30. Ibid., p. 59.

31. Ibid., p. 60

32. In terms of his philosophical biography Heidegger's thought seems to have moved in three phases: from a Catholic upbringing in Messkirch, to a perhaps more Protestant sort of philosophizing crystalized in *Being and Time*, to his late thinking on "poetic" creation, Orphic song, and *a-lethic* disclosure. (Heidegger, for instance, muses on Aristotle's view that poetry is higher than history in the *Letter on Humanism*, p. 275.) For a probing engagement with the political philosophy of Heidegger in response to Nietzsche around the problem of religion, see Beiner *Civil Religion*, p. 400-408. From a biographical angle, Safranski, *Heidegger*, p. 15 notes that on September 30th 1909, at age twenty, Heidegger joined the Society of Jesus as a novice, but "a mere two weeks later, however, on expiry of his probationary period, he was dismissed." Safranski reports that Heidegger complained of "heart trouble," which prevented him from

continuing his training as a Jesuit priest. Cf. John Macquarrie *Heidegger and Christianity* (New York: Continuum, 1994), p. 13-15.

33. The foreseeable end point of this train of "practical reason," as species of willing, seems to be a sort of Global *Leviathan* framing and enforcing international development, social security, and (procedural) international "law," apparently on the epistemological basis of Cartesian inter-subjectivity. Contrast with Nietzsche *Will to Power*, 890; 898; 888; *Human all too Human*, I. 481. Heidegger *What is Called Thinking?*, p, 57.

34. Consider Taylor *Malaise of Modernity*, Ch. IX. "An Iron Cage?" and Ch. X. "Against Fragmentation" (p. 93-121). For a "naturalistic" (Hippocratic) interpretation of "types," cf. Anthony Parel *The Machiavellian Cosmos* (New Haven: Yale University Press, 1992), p. 101-112.

35. Karl Löwith *Nietzsche's Philosophy of the Eternal Recurrence of the Same* (Berkeley: University of California Press, 1997), p. 108.

36. For instance, in the context of the late Middle Ages "contemplative types" would join a Benedictine order, while more "active types" would join a Dominican (half-way between contemplation and action) or a Franciscan order, etc. For a synthetic take describing the links between the religious orders with the emerging European universities, see Bernard Guillemain *The Later Middle Ages* (London: Burns, 1960), p. 12 ff., with Richard Rubenstein's more extensive and comparative account *Aristotle's Children: How Christians, Muslims and Jews Rediscovered Ancient Wisdom and Illuminated the Middle Ages* (Op cit.). Cf. Nietzsche *Dawn* sec. 174, together with his letter to Erwin Rohde, December 15th 1870. A novel exploring this theme in the spirit of Nietzsche is Herman Hesse *Magister Ludi* (London: Penguin, 1975). For Nietzsche's disclaimer: *Ecce Homo* "Why I Write such Good Books," 1, with Preface, 4. Recent explorations of philosophical *askesis* can be found in Michel Foucault *The Hermeneutics of the Subject* Ed. Frédéric Gross. Trans. Graham Burchel. Intro. By Arnold I. Davidson. (New York: Picador, 2004), *The Care of the Self: The History of Sexuality Vol. 3.* (New York: Vintage, 1986); Pierre Hadot *Exercises Spirituels et Philosophie Antique*. Préface d'Arnold I. Davidson. (Paris: Albin Michel, 2002); Horst Hutter *Shaping the Future: Nietzsche's New Regime of the Soul and Its Ascetic Practices* (New York: Lexington, 2006), with "Philosophie et religions comme gymnastiques de la volonté dans la pensée Nietzschéenne," *Conjonctures, (2008)*, No.45/46, Èté-Automne, 2008, p. 89-120. Note, however, Heidegger's more critical view of "schools" or "orders" in the *Letter on Humanism*, p. 269: "Along with 'logic' and 'physics,' 'ethics' appeared for the first time in the school of Plato. These disciplines arose at a time when thinking was becoming 'philosophy,' philosophy *episteme* (science), and science itself a matter for schools and academic pursuits. In the course of a philosophy so understood, science waxed and thinking waned. Thinkers prior to this period knew neither a 'logic' nor an 'ethics' nor 'physics.' Yet their thinking was neither illogical nor immoral. But they did think *phusis* in a depth and breadth that no subsequent 'physics' was ever again able to attain." Heidegger goes on to mention Sophocles to substantiate this assertion. We may well wonder: how was Sophocles educated?

37. Cf. Heidegger *Nietzsche*, Vol. 1 "The Will to Power as Art," Section 4, p. 22. Nietzsche *Dawn*, 174.

38. In his study of the nascent American republic this influence was also key for Alexis de Tocqueville. Cf. *Democracy in America* Vol. II.1.1 "On the Philosophic Method of the Americans." Cf. Steven B. Smith "An Exemplary Life: The Case of René Descartes." *Review of Metaphysics,* Vol. 57, No. 3 (March 2004), p. 571-97.

39. Descartes *Meditations on First Philosophy*, p. 10.

40. Nietzsche *Beyond Good and Evil*, 63; the distinction between Aristotelian "treatise," and Platonic "dialogue," is discussed in Strauss *The City and Man*, p. 50-62. On Socratic irony in light of the Platonic dialogue form, cf. Jacob Klein *A Commentary on Plato's Meno* (Chicago: University of Chicago Press, 1989), p. 1-31; Gadamer discusses Plato's "unwritten dialectic" in *Dialogue and Dialectic*, p. 124-155.

41. Cf. Habermas *The Philosophical Discourse of Modernity*, Ch. 4. Richard Bernstein *Beyond Objectivism and Relativism: Science, Hermeneutics and Praxis* (Pennsylvania: University of Pennsylvania Press, 1991), p. 16-18; 34-45.

42. Heidegger's expression of the "selfsame" appears to mean thinking in terms of Being as the (metaphysical) "One." The question from the perspective of western history appears to be whether this notion is metaphysically extant in itself, or, whether it implies an ontological derivation from some kind of "monotheism." On the implications of this ambiguity cf. Nietzsche *Dawn*, 139; *Genealogy of Morals* II: 20; Heidegger, "Anaximander's Fragment," p. 13-58; R.J. Hollingdale *Nietzsche* (London: Routledge, 1939), p. 39-40; Hannah Arendt *The Life of the Mind, Vol. 2 Willing*, p. 189-194.

43. Unlike Löwith, who thinks that Nietzsche can infuse a measure of classical thought "at the peak of modernity," Heidegger makes the more radical claim that, not only the modern period that originates in the seventeenth-century Enlightenment, but the entire epoch stretching from Plato to Nietzsche encompasses a metaphysical view of the world that occludes the "question of Being," and as such, needs to be "cleared" anew. Cf. Sheehan *Making Sense of Heidegger*, Ch. 9; Appendix II. Note, however, that the expression "clearing" (*die Lichtung*) in Heidegger seems to aim at transforming the distinct "clarity" of the Cartesian method in favor of a manner of reasoning that sheds light (*die Licht / Lumen*) on sensible and thoughtful experience. Another possible allusion to "the clearing" might be as in being-there finding a "clear" in the midst of a forest: perhaps a metaphor for another way of thinking not reducible to the *either/or* of "universal" (the forest) and particulars (the "trees"). With these allusions Heidegger seems to be pursuing a new kind of "enlightenment" or perhaps an "enlightenment of the enlightenment."

44. In a footnote (p. 104) Krell refers us here to Heidegger's *What is Called Thinking?*. This text is an extensive meditation on the resonances Heidegger hears in the words *denken* and *danke* as echoes of "taking to heart" [*noeîn*, p. 207] and thinking the "eternal return." This was the first lecture course Heidegger taught at Freiburg University after his prohibition from teaching was lifted in 1951. The lecture course "Der Europäische Nihilismus" was delivered about a decade earlier, during the Winter of 1940.

45. Cf. Heidegger *What is Called Thinking?*, p. 94-95.

46. Nietzsche *Beyond Good and Evil*, 201-202. On modernity as a "reflexive" process of social structures in an apparently never-ending search for security or non-risk, Ulrich Beck *Risk Society, Towards a New Modernity*. (London: Sage Publications, 1992).

47. Heidegger *Being and Time*, Sections 12 and 41, referenced by Krell (p. 108). The notion of "falling" or "thrownness" seems to be analogous to the Hobbesian state of nature in *Leviathan* Ch. XIII. Whereas for Hobbes the nature of subjectivity is based on thoughts being "scouts of desires" (VIII.16), for Descartes, in the ultimate analysis, the distinction between sense and cogitation is not of degree but of kind; therefore, the thinking "I" becomes a distinct entity of cognitive consciousness based on the deductive "certainty" of non-bodily existence. Hobbesian man, on the other hand, appears to be a more idiosyncratic locus of desires whose thoughts are instrumental to avoid the *summum malum* (politically) and to aim at some pleasurable good (privately).

48. A number of questions come to mind: don't the Cartesian *Meditations* depend essentially on the anchoring of the "I" on the "idea of God"? Why does Heidegger choose to read Descartes anthropocentrically, as if Descartes hadn't explicitly argued in the "fourth meditation" that what gives substance to the human "I" and distinguishes it from nothingness is the "idea of perfection," that he likens to God? Presumably for Heidegger to encapsulate God within the limits of an idea, even through a likeness, would perhaps imply a negation of its infinite essence, and would then turn into a kind of atheism. In *The Theological Origins of Modernity*, p. 171, Michael Gillespie argues that the aim of Descartes was to "construct a bastion of reason against the God of nominalism." Gillespie defines the three key aspects of nominalism as: the omnipotence of God, singularity of individuals, and conventionality of words (p. 228; cf. Nietzsche *Beyond Good and Evil*, 231 with 268). There are two main versions of the nominalist God: Ockham's (radical) and Duns Scotus' (moderate). An extensive comparative analysis in contrast to Latin Averroism and Thomism is offered by Armand Maurer *Medieval Philosophy: An Introduction*. Preface by Etienne Gilson. (Toronto PIMS, 1982), p. 163-237; 265-287. Heidegger completed his "Habilitation" (1916) with a dissertation on "Duns Scotus' Doctrine of Categories and Meaning."

49. What Descartes seems to be doing, however, is subsuming the knowing subject, and thus the subject's knowledge of geometry and arithmetic, under the "idea of God." Cf. the Synopsis of the *Meditations*, p. 13-16.

50. Cf. Alain Finkielkraut *Nous Autres, Modernes* (Paris: Gallimard, 2005). In reference to Hans Jonas (and Tocqueville) Finkielkraut notes that "Descartes non lu nous détermine que nous le voulions ou non" (p. 12). Hans Jonas offers a critique of Cartesian dualism, taking the concept of "responsibility" to mediate between human "life" and modern technology, with the aim of preventing the problem of utopianism. See Hans Jonas *The Imperative of Responsibility: In Search of an Ethics for the Technological Age* (Chicago University of Chicago Press, 1985). Leszek Kolakowski makes a distinction between utopia as "regulative idea" and anti-human *kakotopia* in *Modernity on Endless Trial* (Chicago: University of Chicago Press, 1990), ch. 12: "The Death of Utopia Reconsidered."

51. Kant *Critique of Pure Reason* A314-B370; Rosen *Hermeneutics as Politics*, p. 19-49. Gadamer *Truth and Method*, p. 484.

52. Heidegger's point seems to be that there is a distinction between the ontological *Grundfrage*, the question of Being coeval with but not reducible to time, and the *Leitfrage* of the "metaphysics" of representation which "blocks out the clearing" of Being. Cf. Sheehan, *Making Sense of Heidegger*, 255-268. There also seem to be echoes of Augustine's *Confessions* (Bk. XI) in Heidegger's meditation on "time." In other words, unlike Kant for whom time is a category of human understanding (analogous to space and causation), for Heidegger "time" is a mystery (*Geheimnis*), perhaps to be understood in relation to "music" (as in musical tempo, harmony/soundmindedness, tone, or rhythm). *Geheimnis* is also etymologically related to the notion of the uncanny (*unheimlich*) and to not-being-at-home (*unheimlichkeit*).

53. Heidegger *Nietzsche* Vol. II, part 2, "Who is Nietzsche's Zarathustra?", p. 215.

54. Nietzsche *Will to Power*, 128, 131; *Beyond Good and Evil*, 46; 150; 242; *Gay Science*, 353. The analogy is the historical correlation between the Roman Empire and the rise of "primitive Christianity." On the world-wide levelling generated by the Roman Empire cf. Hegel *Philosophy of Right* (London: Oxford University Press, 1967), Preface, p. 9. From the perspectives of the Abrahamic faiths, Ralph Lerner and Muhsin Mahdi offer the following analysis. They note that in Islam and Judaism the law is considered all-embracing, comprehensive, and supreme: hence theology is subordinate to jurisprudence. The Christian community, on the other hand, was not constituted by a "single divine law that comprehensively prescribed opinions and actions of every kind," but rather by a "sacred doctrine or teaching" (12). The Christian "good news" prescribes "beliefs that complement rather than supplant the civil and public law of the Caesar" (e.g., Romans 13). The implication seems to have been that primitive Christianity was coeval with (Roman) imperial power structure, which as such appears to be unassailable, and could therefore afford to be tolerant of robust social difference. This development, in turn, gives rise to two kinds of law: civil (political law) and canonical (trans-political law). For "structural" reasons such distinction appears to be inexistent in mainstream Judaism and Islam.

Despite their similarities, the "Abrahamic faiths" (at least in their systematized articulation) have significant underlying distinctions. On the one hand, Judaism and Islam are rooted on "revelations" of "prophet-legislators," which have the "all-inclusive character of religious law." What this means is that the architectonic structure of the legal frameworks of Jewish and Islamic cultures encompass a "divine" and therefore unquestionable quality: to question or challenge the law is to question or challenge the word of God. Since faith and the law are indistinguishable, critical thought at the legal level would be akin to impiety; since the law and morality are also identical, the critique of divine law would therefore be immoral. In contrast to Islamic and Jewish frameworks, Christianity introduces a new distinction between human or civil law on the one hand, and divine law on the other. While the human law is pertinent to the civil or imperial power (e.g., "render unto Caesar the things that are Caesar's" [Matthew 22:21]), the divine law applies to the legal framework of the Christian church. What this seems to mean is that, structurally speaking, it is in principle possible to have a critical stance toward the civil law without being "impious" or unduly critical of the sphere of revelation. Since the main source of Christian morality lies in revelation, being critical of civic law does not compromise the realm of Christian moral teaching. This distinctly Christian separation of spheres, further developed by the Augustinian demarcation between the "city of man" and the "city of God," may be taken to be at the historical origin of the secular distinction between church and state in modern liberal culture. See Lerner and Mahdi's introduction to their edited volume *Medieval Political Philosophy* (Ithaca: Cornell University Press, 1963), p. 1-20.

55. Nietzsche *Beyond Good and Evil*, 241-42; *Gay Science*, 377.

56. Cf. Alexis de Tocqueville *Democracy in America* Vol. II. Part 1, Chs. 1-7. In Ch. 8 Tocqueville focuses his attention on the themes of "equality" and the "perfectibility" of man, noting that "aristocratic nations are naturally brought to contract the limits of human perfectibility too much, and democratic nations sometimes extend them beyond measure." In my reading Nietzsche would not have disagreed altogether with that statement (cf. *Beyond Good and Evil*, 253-256). His reasoning, however, seems to have been that our historical epoch was to be as a matter of course democratic (if ontology is occluded, all our standards become conditional, originating in and leading to political "struggle": struggle where the strong presumably prevail; but since the *demos* are in the majority everywhere, the *demos* are quantitatively speaking the strongest. Democracy would therefore be politically speaking the rule of the strongest). In the historical shape of a people the *demos* becomes "sovereign," that is to say, becomes in principle the ultimate source of authority, above the law. Generally speaking, this appears to be the "post-metaphysical" source of "legitimation" of modern democracy. In this state of affairs, Nietzsche seems to have thought that for the sake of higher culture, and particularly to save the "free spirits" from feeling compelled to become technicians or gray functionaries of some sort (Nietzsche is perhaps not unlike Franz Kafka here), a philosophical exhortation of high intensity seemed needed to counter-balance the intellectual and cultural levelling tendency of the democratic consensus. Note, however, that Nietzsche is a philosopher of power, therefore it seems to follow that he would not be against democracy per se. Nietzsche's philosophy is a spiritual war-cry for the love of what is sublime in man. Tocqueville, a man of the world, struck a more measured note. By way of musical analogy perhaps we could say that in their interpretation of the human situation Nietzsche is akin to Wagner, while Tocqueville sounds more like Chopin.

57. This would presumably encompass the metaphysics of inter-subjectivity as well, in so far as it takes the *cogito* as the source of meaning. Inter-subjectivity would be a relation between or among Cartesian subjectivities. This is what would make Habermas' "communicative action" problematic from Heidegger's perspective. Dallmayr offers an interesting dialogue between Habermas and Heidegger in *The Other Heidegger*, ch. 2.

58. Contrast with Heidegger *Being and Time* II. 4. Section 70, pp. 418-21.

59. Leo Strauss and Eric Voegelin identify positivism with the "fact/value distinction" of Weberian social science. They fear that this kind of social science lies at the origin of scientism applied in the political sphere. Cf. Strauss *Natural Right and History*, p. 35-80; Voegelin *The New Science of Politics*, p. 1-26. Michael Oakeshott shares a similar concern in "Rationalism in Politics," *Rationalism in Politics and Other Essays.* (Indianapolis: Liberty Press, 1991), p. 5-42. Nasser Behnegar *Leo Strauss, Max Weber and the Scientific Study of Politics* (Chicago University of Chicago Press, 2003) draws a parallel between the fact/value distinction and nihilism with two possible political problems: activist "fanatical resoluteness," and passive conformism/philistinism (p. 65-87). Behnegar's point is that the fact/value distinction institutionalized in the political sphere lessens the legitimacy of Aristotelian prudence and discretionary judgment (which tends to become associated with lack of transparency and possible prejudice). Arendt discusses the Kantian emphasis on "publicity," or "being fit to be seen," as perhaps the key principle of public action in her *Lectures on Kant's Political Philosophy*, pp. 48-49; Habermas defends Weber's "differentiation of value spheres," arguing that it is an advantage of modernity to separate the logics of "truth," "justice," and "taste." *The Philosophical Discourse of Modernity*, p. 112. Habermas' distinction is based on Kant's three *Critiques* of pure reason, practical reason, and (aesthetic) judgment. Leszek Kolakowski, on the other hand, traces the origin of positivism back to Humean skepticism in *The Alienation of Reason: A History of Positivist Thought* (New York: Double Day, 1968), pp. 11-46.

60. Kant *Critique of Judgment* I, 46 ff. Gadamer *Truth and Method*, p. 51-55.

61. Cf. Nietzsche *Dawn* 426.

62. Heidegger here seems to echo Edmund Husserl's critique of psychologism, in "Philosophy as Rigorous Science," in *Phenomenology and the Crisis of Philosophy* (New York: Harper, 1965), p. 98 ff. Contrast with accounts on the vital link between psychology and philosophy in Nietzsche, especially Hollingdale *Nietzsche*, p. 43-46; Strauss "Note on the Plan of Nietzsche's Beyond Good and Evil", p. 188; Rüdiger Safranski *Nietzsche: A Philosophical Biography* (New York: Norton, 2003), p. 300. For Nietzsche's statement that in the philosopher "nothing whatever is impersonal," cf. *Beyond Good and Evil*, 6; *Ecce Homo*, Preface.

63. Cf. George Grant *English Speaking Justice* (Toronto: Anansi, 1974), p. 50.

64. Nicolas Lobkowicz *Theory and Praxis* (South Bend: Notre Dame University Press, 1968). As Hannah Arendt puts it: "where formerly the truth had resided in the kind of "theory" that since the Greeks had meant the contemplative glance of the beholder who was concerned with, and received, the reality opening up before him, the question of success took over and the test of theory became a "practical" one—whether or not it will work. Theory became hypothesis, and the success of the hypothesis became truth." *The Human Condition*, p. 278. Consider also Eugenio Trías *El Artista y la Ciudad* (Anagrama: Barcelona, 1997).

65. At least to some extent, a sense of ambivalence between human cognition and affect (affect becomes will once it assumes the form of rationality) also seems to be present in Descartes, if we complement the *Meditations* and the *Discourse on Method*, with his final publication, the *Passions of the Soul* (1649). Heidegger discusses "affect" as a possible attribute of "will" in *Nietzsche* Vol. I "Will to Power as Art," Sections 8 and 10.

66. Nietzsche *Thus Spoke Zarathustra* III. 15 "On the Other Dance Song."

67. This is the main theme of part 1 of *Beyond Good and Evil*, "On the Prejudices of Philosophers."

68. Heidegger references Pascal's *Pensées*, note 18. Heidegger takes Pascal's "thoughts" on what we do and do not know, and the relative "utility" of certain "errors" to combat the restless curiosity of man trying for no purpose to grasp what he cannot understand, to be the model for Nietzsche's interpretation of representational "truth." Cf. Blaise Pascal *Pensées and the Provincial Letters* (New York: Modern Library, 1941), p. 9. (Referenced by Krell, p. 132). For Nietzsche on Pascal: *Beyond Good and Evil*, 45-46; 62; 229.

69. Cf. Arendt *Lectures on Kant's Political Philosophy*, especially p. 128-130.

70. In *Shaping the Future: Nietzsche's New Regime of the Soul and its Ascetic Practices*, Horst Hutter notes that in Nietzsche "the mysterious entity called body" may be understood as *Leib* and not as *Körper*, which would be akin to the Paulinian notion of "flesh" (*Gay Science*, 139) and eventually the dead "corpse" (26). Hutter contends that "belief in the *Leib* is the new article of faith advocated by Nietzsche. According to this new faith, soul, ego, spirit, mind, and self are all to be 'read' as subsidiary functions of the 'great reason' of the body" (133). Hutter claims that we may think of the "whole human that is the *Leib* as a hierarchically structured aggregate of wills to power. *Leib* is a name for the visible individual that encompasses all "biological" and "cultural," "bodily" and "spiritual," as well as all aspects of the old "soul" (27). Hutter notes this interpretation seems to fall in line with the philosophy of Epicurus. Hutter, however, offers a *historically conditioned* Epicurean reading of Nietzsche (i.e., non-final, and apparently determined by the exigencies of the times), which also could give way to a Platonic interpretation in due course (13-14; Nietzsche *Beyond Good and Evil*, 200). David Konstan discusses Epicurean psychology in *A Life Worthy of the Gods: The Materialist Psychology of Epicurus*. (Athens: Parmenides, 2008). Konstan argues that the Epicurean notion of *pathé* is a distinctly non-rational or *a-logon* part of the soul: as such it would seem to be the locus of pleasure and pain, as opposed to the rational responses of "fear," "desire," and "joy" (p. ix-xvi). Konstan's Epicurus separates apparently rational "fear," "joy," and "desire" from non-rational sensations of "pleasure and pain" (p. ix). For two starkly distinct positions on the implications of human belief on the ultimate status of the body contrast Augustine *City of God* (bks. XIX-XXII), with the "Melian dialogue" in Thucydides' *History of the Peloponnesian War* (V. 84-116). In his commentary on Thucydides' *History* (*City and Man*, p. 208, footnote 70; cf. Nietzsche *Dawn*, 168) Leo Strauss claims that Socrates, like the ambassadors at Melos, doesn't appear to believe in the permanence of the body beyond "earthly life." Therefore, on those grounds, for Socrates there would seem to be no reason to fear "punishment" or "retribution" in a world beyond, because regardless of whether the "soul" is immortal or not it would

have no body to sense any pain. From a "Nietzschean" perspective the follow-up question seems to be whether the "eternity" of the "*Leib*" is a kind of "experience," and if so, then in what form and to what purpose (cf. *Genealogy of Morals,* III. 1; *Beyond Good and Evil,* 12; 295; *Dawn* 574-575; *Thus Spoke Zarathustra* III. 15. "The Other Dance Song").

At a historical level, Michel Foucault focuses on a "genealogical" angle whose aim is to expose the structures of power-relations that shape our self-understandings. Foucault is a sympathetic interpreter of the "nay-saying" side of Nietzsche, who wants to alert the reader about the process of historicist "determination" as product of contingent institutional arrangements— one of many "possible worlds" posing to represent "the nature of things" in a given culture. Genealogical thought, "situated within the articulation of body and history," contends that we are not just "suprahistorical" minds with inalienable rights by virtue of our human existence, but rather, Foucault argues, our human relations vitally involve power, contingent struggle, resistance. In Foucault's account, the process of "effective history" molds our dispositions and tends to take a momentum of its own, overriding our sense of agency. Hence Foucault's interest in the "ethical formation of the self," and the exploration of "ascetic practices" to overcome and reconfigure past conditionings. Michel Foucault "Nietzsche, Genealogy, History" in *The Foucault Reader,* p. 76-100. The late Foucault draws from Heidegger, Nietzsche, and classical culture to attempt to figure out a "care of self" for individuals in the midst of contemporary nihilism. *The History of Sexuality* Vol. 3 (New York: Vintage, 1988).

71. Cf. Nietzsche *Beyond Good and Evil,* 295. Karl Reinhardt, "Nietzsche's Lament of Ariadne" Interpretation 6 (1977): 204-24; Lampert *Nietzsche's Teaching,* p. 346, footnote 133, notes all the references, excluding the correspondence, where Nietzsche mentions Ariadne. Henry Staten discusses the relation between Ariadne and Zarathustra in *Nietzsche's Voice* (Ithaca: Cornell University Press; 1990), p. 156-169. Pierre Klossowski signals Nietzsche's illness as the primary motive for his focus on the "body." The "body" becomes "Ariadne's thread through the labyrinth of the impulses." *Nietzsche and the Vicious Circle.* Trans. Daniel Smith. (Chicago: University of Chicago Press, 1997), p. 30. Cf. Nietzsche *Dawn,* 169.

72. Nietzsche *Beyond Good and Evil,* 45; 36-37.

73. Heidegger uses italics for the words "metaphysical" and "inner" in this line, suggesting synonimity.

74. Cf. Gadamer's discussion of prejudice as "prejudgment," "fore-having," and ontological "fore-structure of understanding" that makes a tradition intelligible in *Truth and Method,* p. 235 ff. Gadamer also contends that "the fundamental prejudice of the enlightenment is the prejudice against prejudice itself," which, in his view, "deprives tradition of its power" (239-40).

75. René Descartes *Discourse on Method* (London: Penguin, 2006), Part VI, p. 44. Heidegger seems to be working with the Gilson (1925) edition.

76. Nietzsche *Beyond Good and Evil,* 30; 260; 239.

77. Nietzsche *Gay Science,* Preface, secs. 3-4. *Beyond Good and Evil,* 260; 239.

78. Cf. Nietzsche *Beyond Good and Evil,* 22.

79. This is reminiscent of the story of the blind men and the elephant shared by Jain, Hindu, Buddhist, and Sufi lore. Curiously, as far as I know, it is not part of the Judeo-Christian tradition.

80. Aristotle *NE* bk. III. 1 ff. draws a distinction between human deliberate actions (involving virtue/agency/knowledge), and "non-deliberate" behavior (implying necessity/compulsion/ ignorance). Affect according to Aristotle partakes in the "involuntary" realm: it is a kind of compulsion potentially suffered by most (or all) living entities. Since it is not voluntary, "affect" should therefore evoke some kind of sympathy, or compassion, or pity. Anger is an inappropriate reaction toward what apparently cannot be otherwise, or is a consequence of ignorance. For an extensive analysis on variations of Nietzschean compassion see Michael Frazer "The Compassion of Zarathustra: Nietzsche on Sympathy and Strength," *Review of Politics* 68 (2006), p. 49-78. Frazer points out a key etymological distinction between pity as derived from the Latin *pietas,* and the German word *Mit-leid,* literally "suffering-with," more akin to compassion, or sympathy (p. 60). Nietzsche himself was troubled by the simplicity of the German language to account for this drive (see for instance *Dawn,* 133). On *passio* as "suffering of spirit" contrasted to "pain of body" cf. Ficino *Platonic Theology* VII.6.1. Ficino asserts that "spirit" is what links body to rational form. From a contemporary perspective,

Michael Ure contrasts Nietzsche's epistemic "view from above" or the Olympian "vice of laughter," and his "temptation" of compassion, in Hutter and Friedland eds. *Nietzsche's Therapeutic Teaching*, p. 131.

81. Thomas Sheehan reads *die Vollendung* as *telos* in *Making Sense of Heidegger*, p. 51. Krell/Capuzzi also render it as "perfection."

82. Nietzsche *Thus Spoke Zarathustra* II.20; *Beyond Good and Evil, 2.*

III

Metaphysics to the *Seinsfrage*

THE ESSENTIAL DETERMINATION OF MAN, AND THE ESSENCE OF TRUTH[1]

Heidegger opens with a meditation on the uses and disadvantages of "metaphysics" for us. According to Heidegger, there are two "fundamental positions" (*Grundstellungen*) of metaphysics. Each would have an essential quality in terms of their specific essence of truth and their essential "interpretation" of the "Being of beings." Metaphysics would have a double role: it encompasses the truth of beings in their *singularity* and in their open *comprehensiveness*.

Modern metaphysics, within which our thinking "seems to stand," takes for granted that these two roles of metaphysics are "determined" by human subjectivity. Modern metaphysics is mainly self-referential: subjectivity itself is determined by the "certitude" of representation and from "Being as representedness." Only what is subject to representation "exists" (139). Taking representation as its starting point, modern metaphysics transforms and narrows the subject into the human "I." Man seems to become indistinguishable from subjectivity—man becomes its "bearer and owner"—but upon closer analysis, the identification between man and *subiectum* or the "essential ground of subjectivity" is asserted rather than proven.

In his "reflection" on the "origins of subjectivity," Heidegger historicizes the "essence of man" and thus questions whether and how the interpretation of such essence is a consequence of the "essence" of Being and the "essence" of truth. What this obscure passage seems to mean is that, for Heidegger, the traditional Aristotelian understanding of man as rational animal might not be decisive, but would apparently be a conditioned manifestation of how the essence of "Being and truth" project themselves onto the human rational subject "co-determining" his existence.

To expand on this point, Heidegger refers us to *Being and Time*[2] where, Heidegger claims, he attempted to enquire into the truth of Being no longer for "the question of the truth of beings" but to explore the link between the essence of man in terms of his "relationship to Being."[3] For Heidegger this means that the essence of man in relationship to the question of Being is *Dasein,* "being-there," which at some level seems to be akin to *Anwesen* "coming to presence," "being essentially there in the present." This perspective is misunderstood when it is taken to mean some kind of mere anthropological description, which in turn assumes some sort of modern subjective represent-edness (141-142).[4] It would imply a subject/object distinction unfaithful to the reality of the singular situation while the *Seinsfrage* as such remains unaddressed.

The Aristotelian interpretation of man as "rational animal" (*zoon politikon*) implies a primary emphasis on man as living or animalistic creature. *Zoa* is taken to be primary, and *ratio* or *logos* is the main attribute that distinguishes that living form "as opposed to mere animals." From *logos,* Heidegger continues, arises the "relation to beings" because the categories are a product of *logos.* The capacity to attain categories by means of *logos* is used thereby to establish a difference between man (who has *logos*) and other animals that are inarticulate and are therefore "*a-loga.*" For Heidegger, this distinction is a categorical imposition that sheds light on the *logos* itself, but not on the "essence of truth and of Being," which shows that both rational and irrational animals partake in the realm of "living creatures" (142). Heidegger is trying to establish a qualified measure for living creatures in their singularity and comprehensiveness.

Heidegger takes us from Aristotle to Descartes. As we saw previously, in the fourth *Meditation* Descartes offers his analysis on the distinction between "truth and falsehood." Descartes claims that since the senses appear to be unreliable, then we ought to use the analytical criteria of "clarity and distinctness" to establish conditions of certitude. The essence of man from the perspective of the fourth *Meditation* appears to become an "in-between" or "*metaxy*": man is neither God nor nothingness. This status of being "in-between" is linked in Heidegger's estimation with human freedom. Freedom, however, from a Cartesian perspective seems to mean human self-making. From a Cartesian perspective to "err" is a "needful" lack, if man's self-representation is to be free. Error is constitutive of subjectivity: freedom "not to err" (which presupposes the possibility of error, and therefore of non-necessity) appears to be more essential than the "inability to err." Only the non-free are unable not to err. The possibility to "err," to "miss the mark," is essential for human freedom. From a "subjective" perspective, not "reason" but "freedom" to possibly err is what seems to make us human.

To illustrate this point, Heidegger offers a counter-alternative where no possibility for error is foreseen: "the case of a stone," apparently an instance of Newtonian "gravity," which for Heidegger has "no relation to truth at all," presumably because it is governed or rather compelled by inertial movement.[5] At another level of interpretation, however, even "rocks" seem to partake in the realm of being: what Heidegger calls the "essence that is absolutely knowing and creative" bound trans-subjectively by "pure truth" (143).[6]

Now, "non-necessity," as the "possibility and capacity of not erring," has for Heidegger a qualified condition. It is related to truth in so far as it avoids error, but it also is "error-capable" in so far as it is "entangled with untruth." Both seem to be required for the possibility of human freedom. Untruth is significant because—with Hegel—it appears as a set of contradictions that can and therefore presumably ought to be negated. The conditioning and finitude of untruth becomes subject to negation which asserts "spirit" for the sake of the "positivity of absolute representation." "Spirit" becomes "absolute" when its subjectivity masters all representations significant for what appears to partake in the human condition. For Nietzsche, Heidegger argues, subjectivity is also absolute, but its "determination" stems from a different essential "truth": "truth" as a kind of error, which is therefore untrue, thus the distinction between truth and untruth apparently ceases to be significant in itself. What determines truth is will to power or "life": truth is "life." Therefore, from the perspective of the "spirit," everything that negates the continuation and self-overcoming of "life" would seem to become ultimately untrue.

Both "truth" and "untruth" appear to be subsets—"perspectives"—of will to power.[7] Since will to power is ultimately will to "life," the "justification"[8] of truth and error and all shades of semblance in between occur on the basis of the protection, enhancement and "representation" of "life" itself. Heidegger now makes a sweeping claim: Nietzsche's notion of "justification" would be distinct from "Christian, humanistic, enlightenment, bourgeois and socialist" kinds of morality. The standard of "justification" in will to power/"life" appears to be the chain of living creatures that aim at self-overcoming naturally and transcendentally in a variety of embodied shapes (144).[9] Now, this kind of spirited "realism" (which, if interpreted ontologically, would perhaps be analogous to the "great chain of Being"), if reduced to a mere geopolitical interpretation (Heidegger after all is lecturing during WWII, in the year 1940), might seem to tragically associate "justification" with merely ontic "enhancement of power."[10] It is therefore troublesome that neither Heidegger nor Nietzsche seem to offer even a hint towards a theory of "just war" (beyond what might perhaps be taken to be the "just war" of conquest).

Prima facie the dire political problem of this line of interpretation appears to be the lack of genuine justification for political action: every power (at all levels: individual, local, national, supranational) would seem to be "compelled," as far as it is capable, to exercise its "right" to expand so as to maximize its power. This is the natural state of Hobbes, but with a caveat: it occurs not only among but also *within* "individuals" (whom as such seem to become "dividuals"), and also among groups of all sorts.

Heidegger at this point of the text in other words seems to echo Carl Schmitt's critique of liberal "neutralization and depolitization"[11]: from the perspective of "metaphysical tactics," each "power" uses the rhetorical standard of universal human morality to undermine the counterpart that appears to block its preservation and enhancement of power. Perhaps at some level not unlike Schmitt, in this particular passage Heidegger seems to also allude to the "political" perspective as the "essence of truth as justification," which in times of emergency represents itself as "absolute." Whereas for Hegel untruth was a transitional state to be *sublated* by "spirit," Heidegger remarks that in Nietzsche's metaphysics "untruth in the sense of error" is posited as part of "the essence of truth." At this juncture, Heidegger appears to enlist Nietzsche in his critique of liberalism: if interpreted ontically, the passage seems to overlook nuances that would favor a more ontological accent. Although my own reading of this section would veer toward an ontological direction, it seems adequate to signal its ontic reverberations. It is also the case that many parts of Nietzsche's rhetoric[12] easily lend themselves for misappropriation.

From a cultural perspective, the problem would be as follows: will to power as the underlying source of "subjective" delimitation makes "the true and the false" in its own interests, thereby apparently configuring the "truth" of beings in its own image. From an "epistemological" view-point this appears to become a process of technical problem-solving (145) that has come to define large segments of public discourse and the modern research-university. Heidegger, however, worries deeply that the equation of power and knowledge (Foucault's power/knowledge) might be in truth a sort of dominion (*Herrschaft*) that conceptualizes the world as homogeneous *res extensa*—flattening phenomena in a self-referential intersubjective domain of appearances.

THE END OF METAPHYSICS

Heidegger characterizes Nietzsche's philosophy as "the metaphysics of subjectivity." Heidegger also claims "subjectivity" is interchangeable with "the metaphysics of will to power." Nietzsche's philosophy is the philosophy of the metaphysics of will to power. In the transitional epoch of nihilism, the metaphysics of subjectivity seems to be accelerated toward either progress or return.

In Heidegger's reading of Nietzsche, "classical nihilism" (the nay-saying part of Nietzsche's teaching) may be characterized as a "metaphysics of the absolute subjectivity of will to power." This absolute subjectivity is a subjectivity of the "body," of "desires and affects," which Heidegger subsumes under the rubric of "will to power" (147). Heidegger contrasts this kind of subjectivity with another kind of rationalistic subjectivity: Hegelian "spirit." Hegelian spirit absolutizes reason as the "dialectical" unity of knowing-and-willing working itself out in history.[13] Hegelian rationalism therefore requires "time" to be understood: it cannot be a rationalism of "pure understanding," because it seems to involve thoughtful-willing.[14] Heidegger asserts that the essence of man "always enters into these two kinds of absolute subjectivity"—"body" and "spirit"—but in different ways. In Heidegger's Hegel, the Aristotelian definition of man as "rational animal" becomes "animate reason": reason determines "dialectically," and therefore "historically," the animal in man. In Nietzsche's metaphysics the opposite occurs: the metamorphosis of natural *animalitas* becomes the guide.[15] For Nietzsche, in the expression "rational animal" *animalitas* is the genitive and "rational" seems to be a subsidiary attribute. In his contrast of Hegel and Nietzsche, Heidegger "transfigures" the Latin distinction between *anima* ("soul") and *animo* ("spirit"), taking them to mean *Leib* and *Geist.*

Heidegger, however, pushes what he takes to be Nietzschean "subjectivity" to a limit conclusion: at the end of metaphysics *"homo est brutum bestiale."* Metaphysics heretofore has been the means by which the concept "humankind" has arisen in contrast to more situated bodily configurations— for example, the "nation"—apparently "determined" or "fated" by its surrounding and constitutive elements (148).[16] The problem of forgoing non-bodily (Cartesian) metaphysics and Hegelian "spirit" is that there appears to be a contraction from the concept "human-kind" toward more particular natural kinds. A possible consequence is that the form of humanity ceases to be abstract and becomes embodied in particular body-types genealogically shaped by history.

Heidegger feels the need to emphasize the following assertion: all this talk of the end of metaphysics does not mean that metaphysical systems will cease to exist. Heidegger does not even "intend to say that in the future mankind will no longer 'live' on the basis of metaphysics." Heidegger emphasizes the *fulfilment* of an apparently overripe kind of metaphysics and its "resurrection" in "altered forms." From Heidegger's perspective this is effectively the transformation of an old framework into a "new world."[17] The problem then is: why talk about the "end of metaphysics" at all? Heidegger responds: because there is a current exhaustion of the "essential possibilities of metaphysics." All "modes and orders" seem to be have been tried out, and therefore, in the period of transition it would seem more authentic to have a "politics without vision." For Heidegger, however, grand "visions" are not a mere product of the imagination: they are dispensations and echoes of "thinking." But what characterizes the period of transition is that we have forgotten the experience of thought.[18]

This realization leads to a reversal: the "conscious" search for "origins" (148). The return to understand the origins, Heidegger continues, does not have to cancel-out the existence of previous metaphysical positions which continue to have a hold on the present. What this seems to imply from the perspective of representational thought is a kind of "syncretism" or at least a "pluralism" of world-systems tentatively cohabitating during the fulfilment of western metaphysics. This leads to a "reckoning" that need not be indiscriminate: it seems to become a mere "anthropological mode of thinking," that no longer grasps the essence of the metaphysics of subjectivity and therefore is inclined to disdain it (149). Anthropology, however, increasingly becomes systemic "metaphysics" giving rise to the modern perspective of *Weltanschauung* ("world view").[19] But apparently we are still unaware of new kinds of genuinely historical metaphysics. For Heidegger there is no "transhistorical" perspective. Metaphysical configurations are products of history: "overarching metaphors" that metaphysically roof the human condition.

Now, in Heidegger's rendition of Nietzsche, history is coeval with "time." Hence time cannot be a "thing." If history is time, we cannot stand above history. If time is history, if history is not a "thing" subject to the material law of non-contradiction, then somehow time would seem to encompass boundless possibilities. This proposition for Heidegger seems to presuppose a "decision": we decide whether to live time as history, or, whether to make time a subset of space.[20] This is a momentous decision, akin to Kierkegaard's *either/or*. If space precedes time then, indeed, the second law of thermodynamics is a quite dire prospect. If, on the other hand, time precedes space, then space would be a subset of time: there could not be space without time, but perhaps there could be time without space or "extension." These two speculative possibilities, which perhaps could also be characterized as the tension between "reason" (positivism) and "revelation" (historicism) present themselves starkly at the end of western metaphysics, offering an insight into how "European nihilism essentially unfolds in the history of Being."

RELATIONS WITH BEINGS AND THE RELATIONSHIP WITH BEING: THE ONTOLOGICAL DIFFERENCE

The dichotomy between pluralistic relations of beings, and the "indicative" (*Weisende*) relationship with Being,[21] brings Heidegger to address a fundamental *question*: the question of the "selfsame" (*das Selbe*). The question of the "selfsame" links the three metaphysical positions of Protagoras, Descartes, and Nietzsche. The selfsame is what "everywhere sustains," is "indicative," and is "one-and-the-same" despite the transformations of bodies and the fluctuations of history. The selfsame makes possible to establish the fourfold criteria to compare the metaphysical stances of Protagoras, Descartes, and Nietzsche:

1. The "way" of man himself.
2. The "projection" of the "Being of beings."
3. The "essence" of the truth of beings.
4. The "manner" in which man becomes the "measure" of the rest of beings.[22]

Heidegger wonders whether there is a link, an "inner connection," between these four guidelines. If they are indeed connected, then the next question would be how such unifying thread would connect with the apparent intersubjective set of relations of "man with beings" (150).

The first guideline, the "way" in which man distinguishes himself from the rest of beings, implies a conscious formal demarcation. This is the "truth" of man as a "type," distinct from other beings: the relation of the "way" and "type" therefore links the first and third criteria. The second and third criteria are also mutually inclusive: the "projection of the Being of beings" is a manifestation of their "essence," or distinct "type" (the question seems to be whether types are universal or "singular," or, perhaps what might be more likely some combination of the universality of the *logos* and the singularity of the *psyche*). The fourth criterion is linked as follows: the self-consciousness of being, a projection of the Being of beings and of being an actual "type," also informs the "manner" through which man takes and gives measure over himself and over the rest of beings. The *way* of man is the *manner* through which he *projects* himself as the *measure* on the basis of his mindfulness (*Besinnung*) concerning the Being of beings. For us the configuration of these four guidelines seems to remain "nameless," however (151).[23]

Heidegger notes that such character stands in two kinds of relation: vertical and horizontal. A vertical relationship with Being, and horizontal relations with beings. Heidegger is trying to gather these two kinds of crucial references in a "non-modern" manner, that is, without assuming a Cartesian subject-object distinction. To explore such a possibility, to find the primordial essence of metaphysics, it may be necessary to go back to the beginning of western metaphysics, to the Greek world, "specifically to Plato."[24] The manner in which man is to be understood in this dispensation is not as a separate "self," but as someone who is perhaps not unrelated to the "remaining beings (earth, stars, plants, animals, fellow men, works, facilities, gods)" (151). The horizontal relationship between man and the rest of beings, "to this or that thing," is coeval with his careful relation to the Being of beings.[25]

The crux of "metaphysical thought" is the "justification" that man's relationship to the Being of beings (in tandem with the "selfsame"[26]) provides for his relations with beings. In Heidegger's view, because the relationship with the selfsame seems to be taken for granted, man's relation with other beings appears to be clear-cut. But if the relationship to the selfsame becomes problematic, that is, if man thinks he lives in a "postmetaphysical" world with no apparent need for the metaphysical principle of "self-sameness,"[27] then the question becomes on what grounds he can claim to be the measure with regards to himself and to the rest of beings. Without the "selfsame," the *logos* becomes indistinguishable from chatter. If the *logos* lacks unity or "substance" in the ultimate analysis, then it necessarily ceases to be "reason." If man is the political animal because he is the rational animal, without *logos*, man ceases to be political. Heidegger wants to draw our attention to the centrality of man's relationship to Being. This is the "unitary" essence that structures man's self-understanding, as well as his subsequent relations, including political life.[28]

The relationship with the Being of beings might not be static, however. It reveals itself differently, radiating in accordance with its own essence, related to but seemingly "other" from beings. Heidegger wonders whether, so far, there has been a definition of the essence of man in terms of the "relationship with Being" (*der Bezug zum Sein*). Here he seems to draw a clear-cut distinction between Being and history: the former is the source of "wonder" (in the classical world), the latter is a "matter" to be investigated as it unfolds. Perhaps our "horizontal" focus on particular beings leads us to forget the question of Being. Or perhaps it is metaphysics, interpreted as species of power, that occludes and "enshrouds" what might be called, at some level, the scintillating boundlessness of Being.[29]

For Heidegger the relationship of man to the *Seinsfrage* appears to be obscure (153). Despite that obscurity, the question is essentially unavoidable, determining our comportment with ourselves and with the rest of beings. We somehow "stand" metaphysically "in-between" beings as a whole (*das Seiende im Ganzen*) and Being. Our relationship with Being is fundamental even if we are unaware of it: it establishes our set of existential and proportional distinctions, otherwise the entire world would be undifferentiated and we (all-beings as a whole), would be a seemingly condensed, fluid, "inconceivable" mass—surrealist overlapping images in shapeless contortion.[30]

Being makes possible the differentiation between what is and what is not. It is still ambiguous, however, what the relationship, and therefore the contrast, between Being and beings might be. Metaphysics seeks to explore and perhaps "clarify" that distinction. According to Heidegger, "metaphysics" draws from the "selfsame" and moves on to structure its own domain, taking "Being" as a basic presupposition. From this follows everything that metaphysics makes possible: "conceiving," "experiencing," "naming" beings as such.

In Greek the combination of "the being," "*to on,*" and its articulation or "*logos,*" comprise what we might call "ontology," namely the "essence of metaphysics" (154). The expression "ontology" stems from Greek terms, but it is a modern neologism apparently coined in the early seventeenth century.[31] By "ontology" Heidegger wants to convey its "simplest application," as "addressing and grasping the Being of beings." For Heidegger ontology is meant to be taken in the broadest sense as a gathering "event" (*das Ereignis*).[32] In its authentic sense ontology is an "event" (a *periagoge*) in which "being is addressed . . . in its Being" (155).

"Ontology" perhaps is not impossible because Being and beings are both the "same" and "different." The possibility of ontology does not make it actual, however: the dual condition of the relationship and difference between Being and beings is nevertheless "questionable."[33] Such ontological pondering is a fundamental questioning of the ground of metaphysics. In *Being and Time* Heidegger refers to this as the question of "fundamental ontology." What is the primordial source of ontology? What is its fulfillment? Heidegger signals a "return" to the origins of metaphysical thought to pose the question of *ta onta* anew. Why and how did beings become differentiated from Being? This differentiation of Being and beings has become a presupposition and seems to be the "ungrounded ground of all metaphysics" (155). Since such ungrounded ground is fundamentally "unknown," all "metaphysical" systems, all subsequent ontologies have been for Heidegger a "flight" from such "open question."

From this seems to follow that any designation of the "selfsame" is already an "interpretation." Such interpretation indicates not some "neutral quality," however, but rather the "decisive ground that historically guides and shapes every metaphysical inquiry." Metaphysics takes Being to be constant: since Plato beings interpret Being as "*ousia,*" substance, or, as Heidegger puts it "being*ness,*" signifying "the universal in beings." By "beingness" (*das Seiendheit*) Heidegger designates the ultimate "genitive," the "*koinotaton,*" the synoptic and common genitive that makes universals universal (156).[34] Such designation makes it possible for being to distinguish itself from other distinct points of particularity and specificity. Being seems to be the ultimate universal "abstraction." Taken as an abstraction, however, it would seem to tell us nothing about its essential soundness.

Being, as universal abstraction, seems to become what is most distinct from particular beings. Being appears to be lacking in attributes: nothing can be predicated of an abstract Being. Since Being is taken to be the ultimate universal, and its predicates (beings) are also taken to be universals, nothing can be predicated of Being without turning the predicate into yet another universal "genitive" (157). This would contradict Being's essence of ultimate universality. However, since in this passage for Heidegger universality is equivalent to "abstraction" (i.e., "form" apparently distinct from "substance"[35]), then the sole invocation of universality would fail to consider the essence of Being, and thereby of beings as well. As universal abstraction, Being becomes the "emptiest concept," giving the impression that qua ultimate formal generality its interpretation "requires no further grounding." The metaphysical conception of Being suggests an abstract grasp, but says nothing about Being itself. Hence, for Heidegger a thoughtful meditation (*Besinnung*) on the essence of Being is distinct from the metaphysical conceptualization of Being as the ultimate *a priori*. To conceptualize Being as the ultimate *a priori* means for Heidegger to make it into an "older being": a concept of historical recollection. But the question of the differentiation between Being and beings may not be a question of mere temporal succession. The question of the "all-too-near" is mistakenly abstracted into the metaphysical postulate of an *a priori* (158). This is therefore an ontological critique of abstraction and of conceptual temporality.

BEING AS *A PRIORI*

In order to address the abstraction of the *a priori*, Heidegger reformulates the problem of "primary" and "secondary" qualities. Heidegger makes a distinction between an apparent by-product of sense perception (color) and "measurement." If color is enmeshed with the process of perception, each particular grasp of color would have to be unique. Although supposing the equal tonality of two similarly colored objects for the purposes of "everyday cognition" seems sufficient, upon closer inspection, "likeness" and "equality" differ significantly.[36] Hence Heidegger turns now to the question of "likeness." In order to know whether colors are alike, we need to have a prior notion of likeness (e.g., crimson and scarlet are different kinds of red, etc.). Heidegger seems to approximate "likeness" with the representation of "equality": the notion of likeness makes it possible to perceive "similar things" (159). A conception of likeness and similarity would appear to precede our perception of what is alike.

The question Heidegger might be trying to pose is whether the notion of likeness is *a priori*, prior to experience, and whether "equality" or the grasp of "equal things" might be a "consequence" of such an assumption. The popular or "superficial" explanation is that perception comes first and reflection of likeness follows. But Heidegger seems to be saying that we may with "greater justice" consider that likeness and equality are "given beforehand," and only in light of these notions is it possible then to make distinctions of what something is like or unlike (160).

Heidegger invokes some unspecified "Greek thinkers," for whom "colored existing things" were viewed in reference to the "everyday" perspective of those who observe them. This, Heidegger claims, would have been a process of revealing prior to the operation of notions such as likeness or equality. Apparently, from the perspective of such Greek thinkers, observation precedes likeness and equality: their relation would be possible but by no means necessary. It would be a perceptual, not a causal relation. Hence the notions of likeness, equality, and—Heidegger adds, in what seems to be a brisk *non sequitur*—"even Being" would follow "afterward" from the perception of beings and are not *a priori*.[37] For instance, from an Aristotelian perspective, "natural" perception precedes conceptual distinctions. The unexpressed political problem for Heidegger at this juncture seems to be whether Aristotle and Kant can be somehow compatible in their own terms.[38]

Excursus: Strauss' Political Philosophy

The inductive process that Heidegger is describing metaphysically, from ontic perception of beings to an elusive gathering of the ontological question, could be compared with Leo Strauss' critique of *doxa*, and the Socratic pursuit of "political philosophy." Indeed, the contrast between Heidegger and Strauss lies deep, and it is not my intent to minimize their differences.[39] There does seem to be, however, some degree of approximation with regards to a key problem: how to interpret the non-identity of ontology and history. Both Heidegger and Strauss thought that the impasse of European nihilism required a qualified return to the ancient Greeks. Their respective approaches to the ancients were distinct, but nevertheless both share a rejection of "positivism": while Heidegger opted for a "historicist" path, Strauss seems to have sought a *sotto voce* rebirth of perennial philosophy.

What I propose to do in this excursus is to offer some preliminary remarks that might begin to prepare a dialogue between Strauss and Heidegger. Unlike Gadamer, Arendt, Levinas, *and* Strauss, Heidegger's thought, particularly his "fundamental ontology," seems to be at an altogether different plane from "ethics."[40] Ontologically speaking, Heidegger appears to have an underlying intent of giving uncompromising priority to "thinking" in a radical manner independent of the more sophisticated opinions of his contemporaries.[41] Naturally, from a political standpoint, this can be deeply problematic, and in some instances altogether disastrous ("dynamite," in Nietzsche's words[42]). It was Strauss' project to re-establish a distinction between thought and action, to insulate and protect genuine uncompromising thinking, while at the same endorsing an Aristotelian politics of prudence. Unlike Heidegger, Strauss thought it was prudent to theoretically forestall the consequences of what he calls "radical historicism" in the politics of liberal democracies.[43] That is to say: Strauss sought to conserve and uplift the constitutional form of liberal democracy, because in his lifetime it was the political regime most conducive to the life of philosophy.[44]

In what follows, I offer a brief interpretation of Strauss' answer to Heidegger in the form of Platonic political philosophy. Although they offered different alternatives to the problem of nihilism, both were concerned, to use again the medical analogy, with its diagnosis and "treatment."[45] My aim in this excursus is therefore not to forcefully align Strauss and Heidegger, but to signal a contrasting account, to consider how certain aspects of Strauss' thought resonate in relation to Heidegger's interpretation of Nietzsche. Strauss' political philosophy is a response to Heidegger and Nietzsche.

What Is Political Philosophy?

According to Strauss, it is only when the "here and now" ceases to be the sole focus of reflection that a philosophic or scientific approach to politics can begin.[46] Knowledge of political things implies a non-accidental or non-contingent sense of the "nature," or the different levels of possible causation in political things. Strauss observes that all political claims link particular perceptions to universal aspirations. However, public perceptions and aspirations driving political action have the character of opinion: only when they are made the theme of critical and coherent analysis does a scientific or philosophical approach to politics begin to emerge.[47]

All political action seeks "preservation" of what is good or advantageous, or "change" of what is not deemed good or advantageous.[48] Political action is guided by some standard of better or worse and thus presupposes awareness of some understanding of what may or may not be "good." Pre-philosophical awareness of the good manifests itself in the "surface of things": that is, sense perception that, as such, has the character of opinion. Is our opinion of the good *true*? For Strauss, the questioning of opinion seeks to investigate the analytical relations (i.e., identities, similarities, differences, oppositions, contradictions) between the given and the good, the given and the true. The emergence of political philosophy has an explicit directedness to acquire knowledge of the "good life" and the kind of society that can make it possible. Political philosophy is a branch of philosophy: in the expression "political philosophy," "philosophy" indicates an exploration of formal and final causes, and "political" indicates the subject matter and function (i.e., material and efficient causes). In this preliminary definition, political philosophy deals with political matters in a manner meant to be relevant for political life.[49]

However, from a more comprehensive level, philosophy apparently ceases to be political and is primarily the realization of wisdom. By "wisdom," Strauss seems to mean universal knowledge, knowledge of the trans-political "whole." Politics being a particular realm, strictly speaking philosophical knowledge would seem to be necessarily unpolitical.[50] Strauss, however, notes that the quest for universal philosophical knowledge would not be necessary if such knowledge were immediately or spontaneously available. In our human experience, knowledge of the whole is preceded by (political) experience expressed in opinions about the whole. Opinion (*doxa*) can take a variety of shapes: religious, ideological, patriotic, civilizational, etc. Philosophy is the attempt to replace opinions about the whole by knowledge about the whole. What does Strauss mean by "the whole"? He defines it as "all things," or as "natures in their totality." Strauss' idea of the whole, one might say, is both "nominal" and "structural": the whole is composed of heterogeneous parts. Though we seem to have awareness of the whole, in fact we have only partial knowledge of parts. From this seems to follow that philosophy is not possession of truth but quest for truth. For Strauss the philosopher knows that he "knows nothing"—his knowledge of ignorance about the most important things induces him to see that "the one thing needful"[51] is striving to have an informed awareness of our situation, both particular and universal.

Critics might note that this line of reasoning leads to an infinite regress. If philosophy is knowledge of ignorance, what is the link, if any, between action and thought? Strauss goes to Plato's Socrates, to classical dialectic, to begin addressing the impasse. In Strauss' "Socratic" judgment, "nothing which is practically false can be theoretically true." It seems that in Strauss' account political philosophy has the character of a *chiaroscuro*: political philosophy finds manifestation at the interstice between (contingent/historical) opinion about political things and epistemic (necessary/perennial) knowledge about the nature of political things.

Political things, however, presuppose freedom or agency: they are subject to approval and disapproval, choice and rejection, praise and blame. They are characterized by not being neutral, raising a claim to our duty, allegiance, decision, judgment.[52] Understanding political things as they are entails finding out whether they are fitting according to some standard of goodness or justice. Strauss claims that political philosophy, which is set in motion by the presumed awareness of the fundamental difference between opinion or belief and knowledge, ought to be distinguished from *political thought* which apparently identifies political right with positive law. "Political thought" seems to be a subset of political philosophy: it delineates public activity, exposing what it deems to be legitimate courses of action, assuming the validity of its normative presuppositions, which it defines as settled constitutional "first principles" or as established consensual norms. The political philosopher, however, tends to reflect on first principles as "permanent problems": why have this and not *that* set of first principles? Are all "first principles" equally valid? Strauss' skepticism at this point appears to be qualified: there are degrees of political knowledge—its highest degree being "political science" (*politiké episteme*).[53]

From the perspective of *politiké* it would seem possible to square the circle as it were, and have "epistemic" or "scientific" understanding of the substance or at least of the limits of "the political." We may wonder, however: why can't epistemic knowledge of cause and effect completely explain political "facts"? Because, Strauss points out, political knowledge tends to be enclosed by political *doxa* (i.e., opinion, errors, guesses, prejudices, forecasts, beliefs) and is "interspersed" with it.

Since the essence of epistemic understanding is causal or at least "logographic" *necessity* (which by definition apparently cannot be otherwise), and the "element" of political action is *freedom* (which can therefore be this or that), then the direct or non-oblique political application of epistemic understanding would be antithetical to the "element" of political life.[54] Now, some degree of relation between epistemic political knowledge and political life seems to be necessary to grasp and reform unjust contradictions or prejudices, but epistemic knowledge would also have to remain relatively set apart from political action—their full identity would negate political freedom and would therefore appear to do injustice to the phenomena.

How to estimate the right measure of *politiké*? Strauss makes the Burkean observation that in former times aspiring statesmen acquired political skill by sharing in the company of "wise old men," or by reading political historians, as well as by judicious apprenticeships and involvement in public affairs. This had an intellectual and practical component: learning both by study to figure out the craft of statesmanship, and by practice, to acquire a clear-eyed, soundminded, and tactful disposition.[55] Today, however, these ways of gradually acquiring political knowledge and experience seem to no longer be sufficient because we live in "dynamic mass societies" of immense complexity and rapid change.

At a more general philosophical level, this complex social dynamism appears to be the political result of conceiving the Platonic "ideas" as if they were a subset of "time." Since time implies motion, then apparently the "ideas" cease to be "perennial" problems or intuitions, and as such would therefore be subject to change. This seems to lead to confusing the "ideas" with conceptual "*ideals.*" If ideas become practical "ideals," the account or *logos* of such ideals seems to turn into ideology. Ideologies are not metaphysically self-evident: they are primarily a matter of political "decision" and "commitment." Depending on shifting passions and interests such decisions can always be otherwise: therefore, in order to be relatively stable, they need to be sustained by "political will." Political will, in turn, needs to be cogently theorized in order to make itself a credible political "cause." Reason therefore becomes an instrument of (political) willing, with the consequence that the mind seems to become increasingly politicized. Contemporary political science tends to overlook the qualified distinction between (scientific, universal, necessary) "thought," and (contingent, particular, contextual) "action." This seems to take two forms: it either separates the two following a "fact/value" distinction at the origin of cultural relativism, or, it integrates them non-distinctly producing different sorts of social engineering.

Strauss, on the other hand, apparently in line with medieval Islamic and Jewish political philosophers, sees the perennial discussion of the relationship between the philosopher and the political community in *The Laws* of Plato. In Plato's *Laws,* the philosopher becomes an "Athenian stranger" (an *emigré* intellectual, as it were), whom, perhaps by force of circumstances, does not exercise direct political rule. Rather, he seems to become an educator of statesmen, particularly in their capacity as potential "founding fathers" of political regimes. Once the law is constitutionally codified, political action becomes for the most part procedural business circumscribed by the architectonic limits laid out by the founding-legislators. Strauss is critical of the utopian interpretation of Plato's *Republic* whereby the "philosopher-king" would assume directly the reins of power. The reason for this is strategic: the philosopher's highest calling is contemplation, not action—political *praxis* is a necessary but insufficient condition for the "good life" as the Platonic philosopher sees it. The political philosopher only partakes in political life qualifiedly: his true interests lie elsewhere. Strauss' response to Heidegger begins with a return to Socrates.[56]

Heidegger's Being: from Socrates back to Anaximander

To return to the text: Heidegger claims that the sequence of *"our knowing"* presumably unfolds in an ontological direction, from beings to Being. But Heidegger also notes the *a priori* is supposed to carry a "distinctive determination of *Being.*" What this seems to mean is that Being in its perfection is supposed to be independent of our perception and our (limited) comprehension. The issue, however, is how Being and beings come to *"essentially unfold of themselves"* in time, through the fact of history. Heidegger wonders how this unfolding would be possible in so far as Being "is," which presumably would imply that it could suffer no change or motion.

In order to clarify, Heidegger evokes the Greek notion of *"phusis"* as that which primordially issues-forth from itself. *Phusis* is "essentially self-preserving in upsurgence, self-revealing in the open region," prior to human convention (what might be called *nomos*). Heidegger seems to be saying that *phusis* could be akin to Being: in so far as Being "is," it antecedes beings (beings as such would be subsequent to Being). *Phusis* understood as *"proteron,"* or primordial "upsurge" (*Aufgehen*), has two senses for Heidegger: it is prior to our articulate "grasp" of beings and Being in terms of temporal sequence, and it is also an essential foreground through which "Being essentially unfolds and beings 'are'" (161). All this sounds rather obscure. In order to make sense of it, Heidegger tells us that it is indispensable to think in a "Greek fashion." Thinking in a Greek fashion here apparently means for Heidegger to think along the lines of Plato and Aristotle (161).[57] Plato and Aristotle understand Being as *"ousia,"* which Heidegger defines as "the presence of what endures in the unconcealed." In this passage Heidegger seems to be saying that *"ousia,"* "Being," and *"phusis"* are possibly "the same."

From the perspective of the "unconcealedness of Being," notions like "equality" or "likeness" stand essentially in open view. This, in Heidegger's reading of Plato, issues forth by means of their "visibleness" (*die Sichtsamkeit*) or "eidos."[58] For Heidegger, Plato interprets Being as "idea": the "presence of what endures in the unconcealed." This would differ from conceptual representations in the consciousness of the "I." In Heidegger's account in this particular passage, the ideas are "given by nature" in the sense that they are an upsurge of unconcealedness that happen to be there (162). Their intellection would therefore be distinct from the Cartesian conception of "subject." The "recollection" of the Platonic idea takes place as an *eidos*, "the outward appearance" of a being, how it comes to "presence" with respect to Being. Heidegger assures us that this is different from how modern sense would take "outward appearance" as a superficial "aspect" of a thing.

The Platonic idea sheds light on how a particular being turns out to be universal. By "universal" Heidegger understands what has endurance by partaking in a common definition that encompasses essentially many particulars. The Platonic idea confers "proper being" (*ontos on*) on particulars. The "idea" gives "substance" to what comes to presence, thereby apparently becoming an *"a priori,"* but as it manifests "toward us into the open" (163). The implication for us seems to be that beings can "become who they are" as their timely appearance intimates an essential *a priori*.[59]

The *a priori* becomes the "pre-vious" (*Vor-herige*). Heidegger associates this with the "timely" relation of "Being and Time," essentially mediated by *eide*. In Heidegger's view, this original gathering of the ideas is not understood by modern consciousness because of its Cartesian structures of thought and a series of subsequent apparently unsound cognitive habits. We would need to return in thought to "primitive Platonism," to contrast ancient and modern metaphysics, to see how the problem of foundations unfolds from Plato through Descartes till today. According to Heidegger, in his identification of Being with idea, Plato was the first to equate Being with the *a priori*. Being would therefore be by "nature" and would essentially precede beings, "reigning" above them. The knowledge of such Being would be necessary or "epistemic," and as such it would be more adequate than mere opinion. Since Being is "above" or "beyond" the beings, it would have the character of the "*meta*"; since the beings are the "physical," then the epistemic knowledge of Being over beings would therefore be "metaphysics" (164).

We come to learn that "the matter" in consideration is the Platonic identification of the knowledge of Being with metaphysics, which for Plato is envisioned as idea. This, Heidegger claims, is the starting point of Platonism, shaping subsequent western metaphysics "historically" all the way to Nietzsche. Heidegger takes this to mean that all metaphysical philosophy has been some sort of "idealism," from that point on: "all western philosophy," including Nietzsche's, would be Platonism. Heidegger equates the notions "metaphysics," "idealism," and "Platonism" in the history of the west. Heidegger points out that Nietzsche's philosophy is both in quarrel and in epic dialogue with the legacy of Platonic philosophy at the level of "foundational" thought.[60]

Plato, in other words, is the key turning point of the western metaphysical tradition. All prior philosophy according to Heidegger is called "pre-Platonic philosophy" (although it is common usage to refer to it as "pre-Socratic," still, we know mostly about Socrates from Plato's dialogues).[61] Nietzsche's early works on the pre-Platonic philosophers as well as the *Birth of Tragedy* according to Heidegger refer to these philosophers as "personalities." Heidegger, however, notes that Nietzsche makes a distinction between the Greeks and the Romans: Nietzsche's metaphysics of the "will to power" appears to be in line with his conception of "Roman culture and Machiavelli's *Prince*" (165).[62] Heidegger notes that Nietzsche also sees an "essential" link between Machiavelli and Thucydides, both of whom he takes to be his "cure" for "Platonism" (165).[63] The main point seems to be a contraction in perspective: from "formal and final causes" (Platonism) to more explicit emphasis on "efficient and material causes" (Machiavelli and Thucydides).

Heidegger notes that Nietzsche, at the end of the history of Platonism, and therefore at the end of metaphysics, appears to stand in between these two sets of causation. Here is where the notion of "values" comes to the fore as the "conditioned conditioning of beings" (165). This development, according to Heidegger, seems to have been prefigured since the beginning of metaphysics with the identification of the highest idea with the "*agathon.*" Heidegger at this juncture doesn't interpret the *agathon* as "the good," but takes it to mean the "fitting" for a being in order to make it what it is.

If Being is taken to be a "condition of possibility," then Being becomes a "value."[64] This apparent *non-sequitur*[65] is of course not what Plato had in mind: Heidegger knows Plato didn't think in terms of values. But, independent of his intention, Plato's interpretation of Being as "idea and *agathon,*" Heidegger claims, became the starting point of an unfolding in the history of metaphysics culminating in Nietzsche's "transvaluation" (*Umwertung*) of will to power. Our mental landscape "extends" between Platonic "ideas" and Nietzschean "values" (166). Heidegger criticizes *both*. "Ideas" and "values" are two distinct kinds of delineation that for Heidegger seem to assume the "givenness" or the "whatness" of Being, instead of considering the question. Heidegger's concern is whether Being can be subject to the bounds of metaphysical *eide* and historicist value.

Indeed, Heidegger is here deliberately polemical. Nietzsche seems to have thought of values as "perspectival appearance" and not in terms of metaphysics. Heidegger also fails to mention that Plato's Socrates is of the "opinion" that "being" (*ousía*) and "the good" are distinct. Socrates takes the good to be "beyond being" (*epekeina tes ousias*, in *Republic* 509b). But Heidegger may wonder: if the good is beyond being, it seems paradoxical that there could be an "idea" of the good.

BEING AS IDEA, AS *AGATHON*, AS CONDITION

Being, according to Heidegger, has been interpreted in three different "modes": as "*eide*," as the "good," and as the shaping and tending of possibilities. Plato's interpretation of *eidetic* metaphysics establishes a "compelling analogy," between mindfulness and "vision" (*thea*). The expression "theory" and "theatre" (Heidegger doesn't mention "*theos*") stem from *thea* or "seeing."[66] "Seeing," in this context, showcases what "is present and is permanent" (167). The experience of Being as "seeing" gave the Greeks their character as a "visual people," experiencing the Being of beings as "presence and permanence."

Heidegger, however, asserts that no especial organ, taken separately, has reason to have exceptional preeminence in the experience of beings. The experience of "being as being" is not a product of a sense-organ. To explain this point, Heidegger cites the end of Plato's *Republic* Bk. VI, the "allegory of the sun," to discuss the analogical correspondence between "seeing" and "being." In Plato's allegory the organ of vision and the object of sight are conjoined—"illuminated"—through the scintillation of the sun. Being as idea performs an analogous function: it is a mediator that makes contact possible between the eye of the mind, and that which is known. In Plato the "idea" grants "unconcealment" (*Unverborgenheit*) to what knows and to what is known.

The Platonic "idea" seems to have a moral effect: it is ultimately the "idea of the good" (*Republic* 509b), which, again, Plato's Socrates depicts allegorically through the image of the sun. The sun grants a complementary effect: it provides light illuminating all that is beneath it, and also emanates "warmth." By means of these, beings become beings, coming to presence under the unconcealed. The idea of the good therefore makes unconcealment possible, grants being to the knower, to the known, sheds "light" and "warmth" on "beings as beings," thereby letting them "grow."

Now, the idea of the good in the Platonic account is "beyond being." If "the Good" is beyond being what could Plato possibly mean by "the Good"? Heidegger notes that there has been extensive disagreement on the part of classical commentators about this seminal passage. In the "Christian era," the Good was equated to the *summum bomum* and the "creator God," whose goodness is coeval with his omnipotence and omniscience. But Plato takes the idea of the good as the *agathon*[67] understood as "the idea of ideas." For Plato the idea of the good is not a theological notion but apparently signals the name of a poet.

Heidegger notes the main difficulty: the idea of the good, as its name indicates, is an "idea," but at the same time it is beyond ideas, beyond "beingness." For Heidegger this means that the *agathon* "remains rooted in the basic character of idea" as the essence of "beingness." The Platonic essence of being is that it is "good." However, Heidegger claims there is a possible bifurcation of the meaning of the good in both Christian and Platonic senses. According to Heidegger, in the "Christian-moral" interpretation "good" has become synonymous with "well-behaved, decent, in keeping with law and order" (169). In the Platonic sense *agathon* means "the fitting": that which "makes something worthwhile," what makes a being the being that it is. The good for Heidegger's Plato is what fittingly "conditions" a being in its essence.

Nietzsche, on the other hand, uses the primordial "prism" of "will to power" to explain the origin of valuations, and thus the "basic character of beings" (169). Nietzsche is also concerned with the "conditioning" of beings, that is, how beings become suitable or habituated on the grounds of what they are. Although Nietzsche claims to be a critic of Platonism, Heidegger maintains that both Plato and Nietzsche rely on the notion of the *agathon* understood as "the fitting" for the "conditioning" of beings. For Heidegger, Nietzsche thinks Platonically, that is, "metaphysically," even if he declares himself to be an anti-metaphysician.[68]

For Heidegger the Platonic "ideas" and Nietzschean "values" are not to be made indistinct. The ideas configure a "metaphysics of presence" of the unconcealed, and values are a configuration of the will to power. Heidegger acknowledges that *agathon* and *bonum* are not values in the ultimate analysis. To illustrate this point Heidegger refers us to his own *Habilitationsschrift*, "Duns Scotus' Doctrine of Categories and Meaning" (1916).[69]

For Heidegger a key link between Plato's "ideas" and Nietzsche's "values" seems to be the notion of "condition."[70] To condition means to condition *something*: apparently only "beings" can be conditioned as subsets of the "actual" or "becoming." Heidegger's Plato originates "metaphysics" by interpreting Being as *idea of the good*. Such foundational "interpretation," in turn, established the "conditions" to explain "the possible" in terms of whether it is good. For Heidegger, Plato's metaphysical claim that only the good or the "worthy" is possible seems to culminate in Nietzsche's "valuative thought." In fairness, Heidegger notes that neither this process, nor the reduction of noetic vision to a facet of inter-subjective representation and reckoning was intended by Plato (170).

Heidegger seems to be saying that the notion of the *a priori* is not necessarily an attribute of Being. In order to grasp the truth or essence of Being (*aletheia*), Being needs to be thought "in its own terms." Before Plato, Parmenides and Heraclitus associated *aletheia* with *nous*. *A-letheia* (alpha privative of "*lethe,*" which Heidegger takes to mean "un-hiddenness": the un-concealed, or revealed, in other words *revelation*) seems to shift its meaning from non-forgetfulness of the river of forgetfulness to a matter of "perception." Once this shift is made, Being seems to become *ontos on*, and "beings" *me on*. Being seems to become a subject of "possession," a "property" or "*ousia.*" However, the realization of Being as the "alethic" unfolding of *phusis* also becomes obscured—fading into the background behind the light of the "ideas" (171). At some level, the ideas therefore would seem to structure the conditioning of beings. From a more fundamental perspective, however, the unfolding of *phusis* issues forth from the emanation of light toward nascent man.[71] Birth seems to be a miracle, or at least a deep mystery. Apparently, the emanation of birth is not only subject to the sequential "history" of metaphysics that structures genealogical extension. Every being is born authentically singular.

To conclude this section, Heidegger signals a possible difference between the metaphysical positions of Plato and Aristotle. Whereas Plato makes "being" (*ousía*) a subset of the Good, Aristotle seems to have taken a "step back" before such "moral" or formal identification, in order to see the efficient origin of "being" in *dynamis*. Heidegger links Aristotle to Nietzsche, distinguishing them from Plato and from Thomas Aquinas. It merits reflection for Heidegger why Nietzsche dedicated so much attention to Plato while apparently neglecting the thought of Aristotle.[72]

THE INTERPRETATION OF BEING AS *IDEA*
AND VALUATIVE THOUGHT

Heidegger takes the equation of Being with "idea" to be "Plato's teaching."[73] Heidegger takes the Platonic idea to denote "vision," "visuality," "outward appearance," "presence." This is not only a visual set of "structures": it is also a moral interpretation of Being. For Heidegger's Plato, Being is the *agathon*, the idea of the good (173). This, apparently, is a "decisive interpretation": Being as *"agathoeides"* a composite idea of Being taken to be "the fitting," what makes or shapes a being into the kind of being it is. "What fits" (*was tauglich*) establishes the conditions of possibility for beings. As such, it would seem to presuppose necessary conditions. A being cannot rationally fulfill its possibilities unless it satisfies its necessary conditions. But are "beings" at some level independent from necessity? On the relation between necessary conditions and conditions of possibility for beings, Heidegger's Plato seems to remain silent.

For Heidegger's Plato, Being comes to entail two conditions: "presence" (*Anwesenheit*) and "possibility" (*Möglichkeit*). "Presence" therefore seems to replace "necessity." Being seems to be interpreted as an *a priori* "horizon of significance," that fades as beings posit themselves as the center of attention. As beings become more self-centered, the *a priori* is interpreted as an "addendum": the hegemony of beings tends to make them oblivious of the horizon that makes their condition possible. The ambiguity of Being as "idea" seems to emphasize the role of "seeing" as knowing in terms of presence and in terms of the question of possibility. What cannot be "seen" appears to lack "presence," hence falling from the realm of possibility to the realm of apparent impossibility (i.e., positivism). As an apparent "impossibility," the "unseen" becomes subject to negation, phantasy, and "forgetting."[74]

At another level, Heidegger now reiterates that the history of metaphysics unfolds from Plato to Nietzsche via Descartes. The structure of the ideas turns into a conceptual act of representation derived from subjective cognition. Only what is subject to representation is taken as a possible being or entity. This change of focus from self-sustaining ideas to subjective categories of representation leads to the centrality of "reckoning," which, in Heidegger's estimation, reaches its end in valuative thought. Heidegger claims the process of "transformation" from *eidetic* metaphysics into a kind of valid *"perceptio"* is "decisive" (174). The post-Platonic interpretation of "Being" as what establishes "conditions of possibility" (an "if—then" structure) for beings, once it is circumscribed by human cogitation, becomes an enframing *Gestalt* that determines all what counts as objects of experience.

The reference to "conditions of possibility," what might be rendered as our cognitive conditionality on the possible, appears to be an allusion to the philosophy of Kant. In the Kantian account,[75] the categories of thought become the conditions of possibility for experience per se, and for experience of "phenomena." Kant for Heidegger appears to bring together Descartes and Leibniz: the cogito and "pre-established harmony" rendered possible by the "synthesis" of Newtonian physics of "pure" (mechanical) reason, and the *noumenal* moral "categorical imperative" of practical reason. Now, Heidegger adds that for both Aristotle and Kant the conditions of possibility are "categories." For Heidegger's Plato, categories are indistinguishable from the "ideas" (175). Kant Platonizes in so far as he assumes the (noumenal) "apperception" of Being as the beingness of rational beings. In the Kantian framework, Being becomes representedness in so far as it is subject to *moral* reason or the "practical" use of "logos." This is both categorical and conditional: hence not ontologically inherent in the structure of reality. Kantian man "is" insofar as he is a "creature of reason" that guarantees his categorical and conditional possibility of moral representation.

For Heidegger, Kant "clears the way for Nietzsche's value thinking," because Kant's interpretation of Cartesian representation makes cogitation the ground of all conditions of possibility and not only of subjective representation. Kant seems to be at a crossroads where "Being" is no longer an "idea" (the noumenal order cannot be known), but it is not yet a "value" posited by the will to power. Nietzsche's project—following the Hegelian critique of Kantian "asymptotic dualism"—is to complete this process of "metaphysical" transvaluation. It seems that not unlike Hegel, Heidegger's Nietzsche tries to close the gap between *noumena* and *phenomena*. In contrast to Hegel, however, Nietzsche very much feels the disparity between the rational and the timely. [76]

As we have seen, for Nietzsche values are a projection of the will to power. The aim of values is "preservation and enhancement" of will to power. This would seem to make the character of the "Being of beings" an apparent part of "all-encompassing becoming." [77] According to Heidegger, the interpretation of Being as ("epistemic" and moral) "condition of possibility" leads to "valuative thought." Heidegger claims this unfolding was prepared by Plato's "vision" of Being as idea (encompassing *ousia* and the *agathon*), conceptualized by Descartes as subjective representation, and made the "condition of possibility" for all objects by Kant. In other words, Heidegger outlines the history of western metaphysics from Plato to Nietzsche mediated by Cartesian rationalism and Kantian compartmentalized critical philosophy. In Kant, "objects" are "made possible" through the "categories of understanding": if "time," "space," and "number" don't have objective referents but are only products of the subjective mind, then the "world" would only be what we make of it. This, however, seems to open the door for intersubjective "constructivism" of all sorts.

According to Heidegger, Nietzsche "interprets the essence of value as a *condition.*" Nietzsche seems to identify "values" with "conditions of possibility" (176). In Heidegger's interpretation of the metaphysical history of valuative thought, the link between Kantianism and Plato in Nietzsche seems to stem from the "conditional" ground of values in the "*agathon.*" Nietzsche seems to take the meaning of "condition," as "conditional," or "non-categorical" possibility for some *agathon*. This seems to make Heidegger's Nietzsche a moral philosopher. [78]

Now, to think in terms of values can also mean to "estimate" on the basis of assessment and comparison. "Estimation," according to Heidegger, is more than an approximate relational measure: "essential estimating is reckoning" (*wesentliche Schätzen ist das Rechnen*) revealing a fundamental kind of behavior, as when we say that we can "count on a man."[79] From a Kantian perspective, "estimation" appears to be based on an essential reckoning of beings grounded on Being as their categorical "condition of possibility" (177). In the realm of estimation as "essential reckoning," valuative thought seems to provide the articulation of possible "conditions." The self-referential "essential" representation of Being makes possible the equation of values with conditions of possibility as if they were the conditions of Being. Values become conditions of possibility, and in this context conceptual representation seems to become all-encompassing at will.

For Heidegger's Nietzsche, representation is a subset of "will to power." It would seem to follow that all representation, including the "reckoning" of the Being of beings, becomes a species of will to power. Will to power is the "essence of willing." All willing requires "estimation" as reckoning: nobody wills the incommensurate. The incommensurate cannot be reckoned and as such could not be a source of "estimation," let alone "trustworthiness." The estimation that makes willing possible is performed by means of valuative thought. Values are a subset of willing, and therefore of will to power. As the source of the highest values and of highest estimation, "Being" seems to become inseparable from will to power.[80]

THE PROJECTION OF BEING AS WILL TO POWER

Heidegger wonders how Being as will to power eventually comes to historical "projection." Heidegger says that in the era of nihilism we are "ill-prepared" for the experience of the "most concealed history of Being." Perhaps we can attain a "historiological report" (*historischen Bericht*),[81] but this would be far from a "historical meditation" (*geschichtliche Besinnung*) that might intimate the "history of the truth of beings" (178).

In fairness to classical authors, specifically Plato, Heidegger reiterates that there is no textual evidence to claim from Plato's perspective that the "ideas" were to be grasped as correlates of "will to power." Also, in Descartes where "eidetic vision" becomes the representation of the *sub-iectum,* it would still be an incorrect interpretation to claim that such representation was conceived by Descartes as will to power. In Kant too, for whom the act of representation becomes the condition of possibility of all intersubjective representation, there is still no mention of the will to power.[82] But this does not seem to be a hermeneutic problem in Heidegger's reading of Nietzsche: *the self-interpretation of the will to power can will and therefore interpret itself backwards.*[83]

According to Heidegger, the basis of Nietzsche's metaphysics of "absolute subjectivity" through history is an expansion of Kantian transcendental inter-subjectivity. The "post-Kantian" question at this point is: on what basis does Nietzsche, the last heir and consummator of the "metaphysics of presence," come to associate the essence of metaphysics with "will to power"? Heidegger notes that in Nietzsche's interpretation the will to truth is a subset of the will to power—will is will, and truth is, apparently, a species of power. In its search for "truth," Kantian inter-subjectivity expands on Cartesian metaphysics ultimately and perhaps "unwittingly" for power.

However, strictly speaking, the notions of "idea," "representedness," and "objectivity" in themselves seem to be independent of the will to power. If they hold "ontologically," perhaps they ought not to be subject to an act of willing. If they were subject to an act of willing, that would make them subject to constant "disputation" (at will), thereby possibly negating their essence. "Representedness," however, implies an *act* of representation. Representation implies something that is outwardly and "objectively" represented (otherwise it could be a mis-representation, or distortion), presumably by some subject that performs or actualizes such an "act." According to Heidegger, the "actuality" of representation establishes the connection of representation with the "essence" of will to power (179). The "beingness" (*die Seiendheit*) of representation (all representation is representation of something by "someone") links subjectivity (the Cartesian "ground") with will to power ("act").

At some level, for Heidegger this could be a substantive unfolding of both distinctiveness and "harmonious development": willing as will to power aspiring to make the "best of possible worlds." Heidegger's thinking here seems to approximate Leibniz.[84] The distinct, singular being of every *subiectum* becomes a "monad." The "monad" is both *subiectum* and *obiectum.* This produces an ambiguity that would be resolved in action. It seems to imply an "objective," that is, "actual" or "effective" representation of a monadic "substantive" subjectivity. The "actual" monad becomes "effective" in deed. Since "effectiveness" is "*vis primitiva activa,*" the "effective" monad makes *potentia* and *actus* simultaneous, and therefore, in its unity of perception (representation) and appetite (motion for some good) the monad "lives."

Further, Heidegger links Aristotle and Leibniz. Heidegger understands *potentia* as *dynamis,* and *actus* as *energeia.* The "entelechy" of power as *potentia/dynamis* is to become "energy" or "act" (180).[85] But this development for Heidegger is perhaps only a "historiological" account of how beings come to be projected as will to power. If Heidegger interprets Aristotle's notion of "*energeia*" as "energy" or "*ergon,*" it would seem to follow that energy itself is akin to some form of power.[86] The mediating thought between Aristotle and Nietzsche at this juncture appears to be Leibniz, who approximates Aristotelian *energeia* with *vis* (life) in the Cartesian direction of modern subjectivity. This interpretation seems to depend on the medieval notion of *"actus"* or act that is a consequence of intrinsic foreseen volition. The link between Aristotelian *energeia* and Nietzschean "will to power" is, in other words, steeped in a history of metaphysical palimpsests where "potency" is taken to mean "volition," that in turn becomes the substrate of all subjective representation. In Heidegger's sweeping account, "humanism" and "idealism," representing the vitality or potency of "transcendental subjectivity," are products of (inter)subjective representation. [87]

Transcendental (inter)subjectivity is grounded on the "rational will": the liaison of "reason" and "will" or "spirit." This Heidegger takes Nietzsche to have interpreted and "incorporated" in the sense that, in order to be grasped, such "transcendental subjectivity" has to be "lived." Nietzschean philosophy is essentially historical, anthropological, and psychological autobiography. It is an autobiography of a "monadic" or singular projection of "Being" as will to power. Nietzsche's "life" is a transformation of will to power from "beingness into subjectivity."

Heidegger then poses the question: is "absolute subjectivity" the basis for the interpretation of beingness as will to power? Or rather: is will to power the ground for the crystallization of the "absolute subjectivity of the body"? Heidegger is dissatisfied with this *either/or*. Both miss the essential unfolding of "Being" that projects itself "essentially" in the history of metaphysics as its own "historicity" (*Geschichtlichkeit*). If the unfolding of "Being" as will to power is fundamental, then "thinking" has to establish its "measure" or its capacity to "reckon" in accordance with that essential (speculative) "fact" (182). Differently put: thought taken as subset of willing becomes the origin of historical "values." "Values" are "conditions of possibility" of historical representation. If willing were primary, the unfolding of history in its differentiation between Being and beings would make thinking, and therefore the structure of metaphysics, an apparent subset of essentially historical will.

THE DIFFERENTIATION BETWEEN BEING AND BEINGS, AND THE NATURE OF MAN

The path of differentiation between Being and beings seems to go in two directions: from Being to beings and from beings to Being. This oscillation for Heidegger is *to some extent* mirrored by Kantian metaphysics: "unknowable" noumenal Being, apparently "other" than categories of space, time, motion, number, and phenomenal "beings" apparently subject to laws of necessity but ultimately derived from the thing-in-itself that governs their dynamic "historical" movement with a universal intent (i.e., return to Being). For Kant, speculative metaphysical awareness is a "ripening" of human maturity.[88] This maturing of metaphysical reason remains for Kant speculative, a subset of Cartesian representation (itself a product of the categorical distinction between *res cogitans* and *res extensa*).[89]

The Kantian language of metaphysical speculation as a "ripening" entails an organic analogy that accounts for a "natural disposition."[90] The "natural disposition" of metaphysical thought seems to ground the differentiation (*Unterscheidung*) between Being and beings (183). However, if that holds, the relationship of Being and beings would be dependent on man. Heidegger seems to be concerned about the anthropocentric presuppositions of Cartesian-Kantian philosophy leading to "valuative thought" in Nietzsche: not only in terms of social relations, but, more fundamentally, regarding the relationship of Being and beings and the overall ontological "conditions of possibility."[91]

Heidegger, in other words, wants to reform our grasp of "metaphysics." If we assume that there is a "natural metaphysical predisposition in man" which grounds the differentiation between Being and beings, then, Heidegger claims, focusing on the differentiation per se seems to offer a more "original" or fundamental (*urspünglich*) "concept" of metaphysics. Man's relations with beings seem to mirror this differentiation from Being on the basis of man's "natural" metaphysical disposition (which for Heidegger, at least at this juncture, is also expressed in the cognitive language of "concepts"). The differentiation between man and beings is dependent on man's differentiation from Being. Man's differentiation from Being sustains his (distinct) relations with beings: man's relation to beings is "determined and defined by metaphysics" (184).

Heidegger, however, wonders whether the differentiation between Being and beings is a "natural disposition" in man. To verify such assertion, we would need to know what man is: we would need to have a definition of human "nature." Heidegger's question at this point is what the words "human" and "nature" mean, and whether they can be conjoined significantly. "Delineating" the "essence of man's nature," would be key in order to "prove" man's disposition toward metaphysics. This would be the prerequisite in order to "identify" the differentiation of Being and beings "as the very core of that disposition" (184).

Now, the problem with this reasoning is that it appears to be circular. The differentiation between Being and beings seems to be a given condition to determine the "essence of man" or "his nature." If the differentiation between Being and beings is primary, then it would be independent of human "action." Man's role would be to preserve and to sustain (but mostly to acknowledge) the given differentiation of Being and beings. For Heidegger, however, the origin of this differentiation is puzzling. To begin with: "why are there beings at all instead of nothing?"[92] Heidegger's inference is that whether the differentiation of Being and beings is primary, or a product of a human "act," is a "decisive" philosophical question. Instead of "necessity," Heidegger takes his bearings from will and therefore not only "choice" between given alternatives, but from "decision"[93] where time and creation would presumably be coeval.

To illustrate this point, Heidegger poses a series of follow-up questions: (i) whether "all metaphysics" are grounded on the differentiation of Being and beings; (ii) what "differentiation" itself means; (iii) the order of essential sequence between differentiation and "human nature"; (iv) whether this is an *"either/or"* essential situation, or a developing continuum; (v) what the ground itself would mean if instead of a binary logic we assumed an infinite regress, and if an infinite regress/continuum were unsound, then what we could understand by "the ground"; (vi) finally, whether "the ground" would be Being itself, or an (essential) attribute thereof.

At this point, Heidegger takes a step back. In the midst of these foundational questions, Heidegger notes that we are also "immediately forced to take man as given, as a nature at hand on which we then impose the relation to Being" (185). This makes anthropomorphism "inevitable," apparently justified by a metaphysics of subjectivity. Heidegger notes the political fact that once we assume a metaphysics of subjectivity, genuine philosophical dialogue seems to be foreclosed, unless one shares the historicist consensus of the metaphysics of (inter) subjectivity. But inter-subjectivity seems to drive us into collective "inter-solipsism," or ideology.

This problem leads Heidegger back to Kant. Kant links the human natural disposition for metaphysics to his conception of "human nature." This, in turn, seems to imply a necessary development, as if the "nature of man [were] unequivocally determined: as if the truth of that determination and the grounding of the truth were utterly unquestionable!" (185; Heidegger's emphasis). Heidegger finds the notion of a fixed human nature highly questionable.[94]

Naturally, this leads to the question "what is man?" Kant seems to assume the "inner" essence of man in light of a given differentiation between (noumenal) Being and (phenomenal) beings, "essentially" grounded on the categories of human understanding. Kant assumes that the categories of understanding are *a priori*, a "fact" of human reason and therefore a by-product of human "nature." Man for Kant is the "rational animal," not in an Aristotelian but rather in a *Cartesian* interpretation of that expression.[95] Man therefore is the rational or representational animal who represents the differentiation between Being and beings: such faculty of differentiation represents the "essence of man."

The faculty of representation "grounds" the character of modern thought. The subjective representation of the differentiation between Being and beings becomes "the basic constituent of subjectivity" (186). For Heidegger, however, whether such act of subjective representation is "true," and therefore whether from an *ontological* perspective modernity represents "progress," is still an undecided question. What comes essentially first: the differentiation of Being and beings (ancients), or the human representation of such differentiation (moderns)? If the nature of man were "grounded" on subjective representation, then representation or cognition would itself be a product of representation or cognition *ad infinitum.* [96] Representation seems to be an attribute of infinity.

The cultural quarrel between ancients and moderns is an expression of the contrast between cosmos and infinity. But the fundamental question of metaphysics for Heidegger is not in itself the goal. The heart of the question is to understand what sort of metaphysics can help us "experience" the differentiation between Being and beings, particularly but not only the relationship between Being and man.

BEING AS THE VOID AND AS ABUNDANCE

In this concluding section, the key proposition seems to be that Being is coeval with eternity. This means that the oscillating cycle of differentiation seems to return eternally: "at all times and places" from Being to beings and from beings to Being. [97] Heidegger notes that this "image" makes us imagine a differentiation of beings and Being as if they partook in different "ontic shores" (two "cities," to use Augustine's imagery). The question therefore is whether there can be an image mediating or tracing the "flow" between Being and beings. [98] But all images remain wanting in Heidegger's thinking for the essence of this "differentiation."

Heidegger wonders how these series of deliberations have taken us from "nihilism" to the problem of how to mediate ontological differentiation (188). This leads him again, in full circle, back to the word "Being" (das *Sein*). From the perspective of speech, Being is a "substantive formed by making the verb *Sein* into a noun, placing *das* before it." Being as *das Sein* is thereby "grasped" as an active verb (*Sein*), and "is" turned into a "neutral" substantive "*das* Sein." The word "is" (*ist*), which "sustains all saying," appears to be "most familiar to us," and as such is interpreted in a variety of ways.

Heidegger's point is that we "comport" ourselves as if the verb "is" were self-evident. This has a pragmatic aspect: it makes possible our employment of notions such as place, belonging, (dis)location, signification, presence, prevalence, prediction, rootedness, resting, holding sway (189). But Heidegger here wants to move from a pragmatic to an essential use of language. To that effect he considers a passage from Goethe: "Above all peaks / is repose," [99] in search of an explanation of "is," in its uttermost simplicity. [100] The simplicity of "is" in Goethe's poem is a simplicity of "rare abundance" far removed from a "void of indeterminacy" (190).

From a logical perspective we tend to characterize the "sayability of Being" in terms of "multivalence." Heidegger is concerned with the indexical quality of the word "is," and of the expression "to be" as they point toward Being. Even if Being were made "indefinite and trivialized," it might still be possible to countenance its "echo," still perhaps claiming something essential. Given that the word "is" seems to imply a variety of transitive "contextual" meanings, can we still ponder the verb "is" in its simplicity? From a literal meaning the word "is" and the expression "to be" (which appear to be indistinct at this point of the text) offer a kind of "univocity that itself permits a transformation into manifoldness" (191). All analytical division into parts presupposes the synthetic capacity of recollection into simple meaning: gathering what something "is." However, this oscillation of simplicity and manifoldness does not imply that the simplicity of "is" should be interpreted as an "empty receptacle" and concept of universal determination.

Heidegger, instead of focusing on Being as universal and empty abstraction of determination, wishes to focus on Being and the "is" in a "Janus-faced" relationship of "peculiar indeterminacy" and "fullness." Being as "Janus-faced" figure implies simultaneous looking-forth and a looking-back.[101] The "trail of Being's essence," in other words, is "transitive" in the sense of being "transitional" without being "dialectical": in its simplicity Being encompasses no contradiction within itself, therefore no dialectic is really possible as far as Being as concerned.[102] Being appears to be "emptiness" (unfathomably, as in some sort of substantive void—Heidegger, rather dramatically, calls the underlying side of Being "the abyss": Heidegger seems concerned that we may, foolishly, fall off unnecessarily) but also "abundance," potentially giving each of the beings past, present, and future their "essential form" and singularity (192).[103]

Being, as encountered in every being, is experienced as most universal as well as most common. Yet, it is not possessed by any being: Being itself is "most singular," unique, without counter-part. The main contrast of Being is "the nothing," and even the nothing, Heidegger suggests, may "perhaps" essentially partake in the realm of Being. Being is also "most intelligible" yet apparently incomprehensible: how could it be comprehended?[104] Heidegger also notes that Being is "most in use." Every action, from every standpoint, presupposes the "is." As it is most in use, Being also remains assumed, not subject to doubt, therefore remaining unthought and "forgotten" as *the* question.

We take the "is-ness" of Being as most reliable, not unsettling us with doubt. We may wonder about particular entities, but for the most part the ground of their is-ness does not seem to be in question. Yet, from Heidegger's perspective, if we take "das Sein" as an "infinitive verb" the stability and permanence of the "is" would have to become questionable. In taking for granted Being we forget to wonder about it, and seem to become fixated on "beings" instead. But without Being our historical "hastening" toward beings cannot be understood beyond fleeting impressions (193). All words presuppose Being: in our use of speech the essence of Being remains in silence. [105] The oceanic "silence" of Being essentially permeates all "non-coincidental" differences between universality and uniqueness, stability and motion, limits and boundlessness.

The question remains, however: not only how the representation of essential differences and oppositions is made possible on the grounds of being, nor how we relate to beings, but, essentially, whether and how being relates to Being. In other words: "viewed with respect to matters as they stand, is our relation to Being a discordant one?" (194). [106] The "decisive" question for Heidegger, however, is whether the relation of beings to Being is not the other way around: emanation, or "flow," or perhaps "trace" from Being to beings. Heidegger wonders whether the relationship of beings to Being may be discordant. If there is discord between beings and Being, that would also seem to "determine" or produce a discordant tone in our comportment toward beings as a whole. But we take for granted our relation to Being, we take it as neutral, and therefore don't see a problem in our comportment toward beings (194). Since we assume Being is neutral, there appears to be no reason to focus on the differentiation between Being and beings. We take both for granted. For Heidegger, however, taking for granted the relation of Being and beings is the key aspect of metaphysical thought. According to Heidegger, in the history of metaphysics from Plato to Nietzsche, from *eidetic* metaphysics to valuative thought, Being is taken as a "self-evident" *a priori*.

Metaphysics takes for granted the distinction between Being and beings. "Today," which for Heidegger means the historical period determined by Nietzsche's valuative thought, [107] we take the relation of Being and beings for granted. We bracket it out "as if" it does not matter, and on that basis distinguish between "matters of fact" and (ideal) "values." But if Being does not matter, both "ideas" and "values" would seem to lose the essential ground or experience from which they derive their metaphysical "sense." [108] Ideas and values become intersubjective "conceptual frameworks," indifferent or "agnostic" with regards to Being. Yet, the passionate reactions that determine the assertions of distinct *Weltanschauungen* imply that there are metaphysical presuppositions underlying our conceptual constructs which, as objects of passion, we take to be "right" (195).

In the midst of European and what seems now global nihilism, that is, philosophically in our identification of Plato and Nietzsche, of "idea" and "value," we make the mistake of believing that all metaphysics is a product of willing, at least overtly for willing's sake. Nihilism is the assumption that the will is primary or "sovereign," that therefore reason is a mere instrument of our willing.[109] The implication seems to be that the Platonic "idea" loses its supra-political essence: its standards become subject to practical reason that as such can be disputed at will. Platonic metaphysics apparently ceases to convey essential virtues, becoming instead the subject of the configuration of rights-discourses framed by particular historical *Weltanschauungen*. Heidegger seems to omit, however, that Platonic political philosophy is about the recollection of the *psyche* and is therefore only tangentially concerned with history.[110]

The belief that there are distinct, potentially incommensurable *Weltanschauungen*, assumes, in turn, an unquestioned attitude regarding the differentiation between Being and beings. From the (corollary) perspective of the metaphysics of inter-subjectivity, this seems to make "complete, absolute, undisturbed, and undistracted dominion over beings" an apparently reasonable and commonsensical technological project of extensive development (196).[111] The metaphysics of inter-subjectivity believes itself to be self-evidently pragmatic because it assumes Being and the possible form and manner of its relation to beings is a non-question. As such, it structures its intersubjective consensus in terms of normative and empirical measures that seem to mirror a fact/value distinction.[112] "European nihilism" in Heidegger's reading of Nietzsche represents the "age of the fulfilment of metaphysics," not independent of Being, but essentially released by it thereby revealing an epochal course for human learning.

NOTES

1. *Die Wesensbestimmung des Menschen und das Wesen der Wahrheit.* Capuzzi translates *Bestimmung* here as "determination," but note that for Heidegger *die Wesensbestimmung* also resonates as an essential "attunement," or "calling" or "vocation."

2. Krell notes that this passage was not part of the original lecture Heidegger delivered in 1940, and was added in the 1953 version (cf. Krell's footnote, p. 140-141).

3. Perhaps a parallel could be drawn here between "the question of the truth of beings" as *nomos/Geschichtlichkeit,* and the attunement of the essence of man in terms of Being as a rather antinomian *phusis/aletheia.*

4. Contrast with Heidegger *The Question Concerning Technology*, p. 3-35.

5. Michael Gillespie *The Theological Origins of Modernity*, p. 41-42, suggests a link between Newton and Hobbes by way of "religious passion" and physical "determination" manifested in the form of human momentum. Contrast with Simone Weil *Gravity and Grace* (London: Routledge, 1999), p. 104-106.

6. Graham Parkes in his essay "Nietzsche's Care for Stone" in Hutter and Friedland eds. *Nietzsche's Therapeutic Teaching*, Ch. 13, points out that "rock" is the "hardest, heaviest part of the earth" and a "witness of prehistory." According to Parkes, Nietzsche takes rock to be one of his natural "friends" (some of his "enemies" being "mosquitoes, cloudy skies, and warm damp air") (176). Parkes notes that thinkers such as Emerson, Schopenhauer, and Goethe were also philosophically interested in rocks. Emerson for instance speaks of "how much firmness the sea-beaten rock has taught the fisherman" (189). Parkes claims that Zarathustra combats his "arch-enemy," the "spirit of gravity," making use of (and taking off from) the "philosopher's stone." Cf. Matt 16:16-20. Heidegger *Nietzsche* Vol. II "The Eternal Recurrence of the Same,"

Section 2, dwells on the "genuine action" of the creator who is liberated from the "petty ego," standing firm on "the bedrock of essential thought."

7. Nietzsche *Will to Power*, I: 15. Contrast with Plato *Republic* 412e4-413c5; 427b1-c2; *Timaeus* 29c-d.

8. *Gerechtigkeit*, "justice" or "righteousness," an attribute of the Abrahamic God that Nietzsche takes to be the historical source of our "intellectual probity" (*Beyond Good and Evil*, 213; *Genealogy of Morals*, II: 21).

9. From this perspective the human being for Heidegger becomes the "shepherd of Being . . . finding what is fitting in [his/her] essence that corresponds to such destiny; for in accord with this destiny the human being as ek-sisting has to guard the truth of Being." *Letter on Humanism*, p. 252. cf. Karl Löwith *Martin Heidegger and European Nihilism* (New York: Columbia University Press, 1995), p. 63. Contrast with Plato *Statesman* 275 c1-5. Cornelius Castoriadis *On Plato's Statesman* (Stanford: Stanford University Press, 2002) interprets this Platonic passage distinguishing the philosopher/statesman/shepherd, from the "sophist," or "trafficker in non-being" who as such tends to become a shadow-maker or "maker of false images" (p. 22).

10. It might be significant to keep in mind here the famous Heidegger-Cassirer debate that took place in Davos, Switzerland, in 1929. Cassirer, a Neo-Kantian liberal constitutionalist, was an outspoken defender of the Weimar republic, who argued that constitutional democracy was part of the German philosophical tradition going back to Leibniz, Wolf, and Kant. Heidegger, on the other hand, was concerned that Cassirer was too keen on circumscribing the freedom of spirit in reified and therefore rigidified (political) "forms," "making matters too easy for himself in the dwellings of the spirit." Safranski *Heidegger*, p. 184-188. For Heidegger political forms are a subset of willing. It seems noteworthy that Leo Strauss chose the liberal Cassirer to supervise his doctoral dissertation on Jacobi at the University of Hamburg (defended in 1921). David Janssens *Between Athens and Jerusalem: Philosophy, Prophecy, and Politics in Leo Strauss' Early Thought* (New York: SUNY Press, 2008), p. 77-90 offers an analysis of Strauss' dissertation. The thesis was titled: "The Problem of Knowledge in the Philosophical Doctrine of Friedrich Heinrich Jacobi." Subsequently, Strauss worked as coeditor to the jubilee edition of the collected works of the Jewish thinker Moses Mendelssohn, a representative of the modern enlightenment. The "pantheism controversy," over the philosophy of Spinoza, took place between Mendelssohn and Jacobi. As Janssens notes, in his dissertation Strauss takes Jacobi to be attacking enlightenment rationalism on two separate but not unrelated grounds: knowledge, and morality/politics.

At the level of epistemology, Jacobi's critique went against Cartesian rationalism and its method of universal doubt (the resolutive-composite-method of radical doubt leading to the *ego* as ultimate *factum* of existence, and recognizing only "clear and distinct" knowledge resulting from it). But this development, according to Jacobi, appears to reduce Being to non-being, to "nothing," in so far as it could not be independent of the thinking subject. Methodical radical doubt, in Jacobi's estimation, is akin to "nihilism." The "pure thinking subject" becomes the only source of knowledge and of reality. From this seems to follow that we, as thinking subjects, can only know those aspects of reality amenable to rationalistic deduction: everything else becomes "irrational" or "suprarational." But, for Jacobi, there are "intuitive" aspects of experience that are not amenable to Cartesian reductionism, that cannot be "proven," such as the experience of "I am," or that "there is a God" (78-79). For Jacobi, Descartes didn't go far enough: the cogito is not a fact, but rather a kind of "intuition," a species of "faith" (*Glaube*), not unlike the experience of God. Jacobi apparently associates nihilism with the (Cartesian) enlightenment, and tries to make the case for *Glaube* and "atomistic individualism" in light of the whole (perhaps à la Goethe). Jacobi rejects Cartesian rationalism, and as a corollary also rejects Kant's notion of "God as regulative idea of reason," which is ultimately based on the Cartesian "autonomous" subject (79). Because Cartesian rationalism negates the "natural limits of knowledge," it is hardly more than the "organization of ignorance" (79).

The subsequent problem, at the level of politics and morals, would be that since the notion of Kantian "autonomism" presupposes the soundness of radical doubt, Kantian philosophy would also have to be radically doubtful about moral norms presumably inherent in reality. Any moral postulate on those grounds would also have to be a kind of "organized ignorance."

Jacobi, on the other hand, claims that habituation and therefore a given tradition precedes insight. Following moral obedience leads to moral insight; radical doubt prevents the experience of moral insight which has as its necessary condition some form of moral obedience. Strictly speaking radical doubt prevents morality. Spinoza, according to Jacobi, "exemplifies the defiance of Cartesian rationalism in the face of transcendence" (80). If one were to take the radical position of accepting nothing as given without giving up the mind (as epistemic grasp of cause and effect), this would ultimately lead to atheism, and subsequently "fatalism." The motive behind enlightenment reason is to liberate man from the authority of transcendence. For Jacobi, however, this motive proves to be as tyrannical as its opponent. Descartes and Spinoza unleash a new tyranny of "autonomous demonstrative reason," apparently finding its political complement in Hobbes' *Leviathan* (80).

Jacobi finds the roots of nihilism in Cartesian doubt, but his attempt to resolve the problem of nihilism makes use of a similar method: pursue rationalism all the way to atheism, fatalism, and, ultimately nihilism (the "irrationality" or "suprarationality" of reason itself). This leads to the realization of the rootedness of reason itself is a kind of ignorance about its genitive source. This experience of utter ignorance prepares the ground for the "leap" to faith, motivated by taking the choice of believing in reality rather than doubting it. In Jacobi such faith or belief takes a "Humean" meaning (80), based on the recognition that human knowledge depends on indemonstrable beliefs (cause and effect appear to be a speculative correlation and presumably not a species of necessity). The sun may well not rise tomorrow for Jacobi and Hume. The choice of enlightenment rationalism, like the choice of revelation, apparently depends on a foundational act of faith.

Now, Jacobi's understanding of faith is not primarily an epistemological but an ethical claim, upon which "true virtue" would be founded. Jacobi equates virtue with knowledge: both of them are grounded on the "recognition of heteronomy," that is the basis of our experience of "reality." Jacobi equates this with a Platonic attitude of high aspirations, contrasted to a non-Platonic "Epicurean" attitude of apprehension and distrust exemplified by enlightenment rationalism, and animated by Cartesian fear of "the immediacy of transcendent reality" (81). Spinoza has the "Epicurean" motive of liberating man from fear of the gods (82). For Jacobi, "the enlightenment's revolutionary antitheism animated by proud human reason is self-postulating, and therefore is deeply problematic" (83).

The young Strauss seems to not have been ultimately satisfied by Jacobi's "leap of faith" or "decisionism" (89). For Strauss, Jacobi seems to do injustice to Descartes' "profound practical legitimacy" (83). Jacobi's thinking is ultimately rooted on "historicism" (90) and as such, from Strauss' perspective, Jacobi appears to not have gone far enough in his critique of modern philosophy. In addition to Janssen's account on the intellectual development of the early Strauss, cf. also Daniel Tanguay *Leo Strauss: An Intellectual Biography* (New Haven: Yale University Press, 2007).

11. For Karl Löwith's critical reading of Schmitt's *Concept of the Political* see "The Occasional Decisionism of Carl Schmitt," in *Martin Heidegger and European Nihilism*, p. 137-169. Cf. Beiner *Civil Religion*, Ch. 28, for a contrast between Schmitt and Hobbes. On Heidegger's critique of liberalism see Fred Dallmayr "Heidegger on *Macht* and *Machenschaft*" *Continental Philosophy Review* 34 (3), September 2001, p. 261-263.

12. Contrast with Gadamer's characterization of Hegel as having a deliberate passion for shocking effect, cited in Donald Phillip Verne "Metaphysics of Folly" in *Philosophy and the Return to Self-Knowledge* (New Haven: Yale University Press, 1997), p. 97. Nietzsche, indeed, manages to out-shock the shocking Hegel. I tend to see the purpose of Nietzsche's rhetoric to be deliberately provocative with a "proleptic" intent: beneath the stormy vortex of apparent contradictions and stark paradoxes rests a constant aim to awake the reader from intellectual slumber so he can begin to think for himself. Gadamer, Adorno, and Horkheimer discuss the "ironic" quality of Nietzsche's writings, which makes it difficult to analyze them conceptually unless one is attuned to the rhythmical tone of the texts and their oft-indirect but intended allusions and omissions. "Nietzsche et Nous" entretien entre Theodor W. Adorno, Max Horkheimer et Hans-Georg Gadamer, in *Nietzsche L'Antipode: Le Drame de Zarathoustra*. Trad. Christophe David. (Paris: Éditions Allia, 2000), p. 51-68. Heidegger discusses the relation

between "tone" "melody" and thought in *What is Called Thinking?*, p. 37. See especially Nietzsche *Dawn* Preface, sec. 5.

13. Heidegger discusses "Hegel's interpretation of the connection between time and spirit," in *Being and Time* II.6.82b, p. 484-86. In this section, Heidegger also marks a distinction between the Hegelian "concept" and the Platonic "idea."

14. Hegel *Phenomenology of Spirit*, Preface, sec 38. Heidegger *Being and Time*, II.6.78, p. 457, towards the end.

15. Nietzsche therefore seems to be offering echoes of a kind of poetic thought that, in a way, stretches from Ovid to Kafka. Contrast with Arendt *The Life of the Mind* Vol. I, p. 202-212.

16. Contrast with Nietzsche *Beyond Good and Evil*, 256.

17. Nietzsche *Will to Power*, I, 23; *Genealogy of Morals*, II: 16.

18. Cf. Heidegger *What is Called Thinking?*, p. 8; 30-31; 135-37. *Contributions to Philosophy*, Section 44.

19. Cf. Heidegger "Comments on Karl Jasper's Psychology of Worldviews." Trans. John van Buren, in *Pathmarks*. William McNeill ed. (Cambridge: Cambridge University Press, 1999), p. 1-38; also, Heidegger's critical remarks on worldviews/ideologies in *The Question Concerning Technology*, p. 115-54.

20. Cf. Plato *Laws* 891c-892c; 896a-897e.

21. Perhaps one way to interpret this "relationship" could be what Michael Oakeshott calls the "pursuit of intimations." In *Contributions to Philosophy*, Sections 5-6, Heidegger discusses the notion of "intimation" (*Anklang*) as a historically situated attunement that, he thinks, conveys echoes toward the "other beginning" that is unfolding in contemporary western history. The notion of "wonder" was indicative of the "first beginning" in Greek culture, and now, in the period of transition there seems to be a sense of silent "startled dismay" (*Erschrenken*) at the question of how to hold fast to *Da-sein* in our time.

22. These four criteria might be reminiscent of the four Aristotelian kinds of causation. Aristotle *Physics* II 3; *Metaphysics* V 2.

23. In the *Letter on Humanism*, p. 276, Heidegger elaborates on what he means by the "fittingness of thought on the history of Being." He lists three "laws": rigor of meditation (*die Strenge der Besinnung*), carefulness of saying (*die Sorgfalt des Sagens*), frugality of words (*die Sparsamkeit des Wortes*).

24. Plato *Timaeus* 81a3-5. *Phaedrus* 246a-247e5. See Heidegger's discussion in *Nietzsche* Vol. I "The Will to Power as Art," Section 23: "Plato's *Phaedrus*: Beauty and Truth in Uplifting Quarrel" (*Platons Phaidros: Schönheit und Wahrheit in einem beglückenden Zwiespalt*). In the opening line of Section 20, in Volume I, Heidegger makes an explicit distinction between Plato and Platonism: "*Wir sagen Platonismus und nicht Platon*" (151). In Heidegger's reading of Plato's *Phaedrus* (which he calls "the *akmé* of Plato's creative life"), there is no *either/or* between beauty (*die Schönheit*) and truth (*aletheia*).

25. Contrast with Heidegger's later articulation of the "thing" (*das Ding*) as the unitary "fourfold" that gathers "sky and earth, mortals and divinities, which is stayed in the thinging [that is to say, the carrying out] of things, we call—the world." *Poetry, Language, Thought*, p. 197. This is also Heidegger's "sensible" response to the Kantian *das Ding an sich*.

26. Note that Heidegger does not use the expression "I am that I am" (*Exodus* 3:14). This shift seems to be at the core of the ontological movement from "identity" to "difference" which, to this day, governs post-Heideggerian philosophy. Now, Heidegger associates the "Being of beings" with Leibniz's *Natura*: "nature in a broad and essential sense . . . gathering everything to itself, which in this manner releases every being to its own self." *Poetry, Language, Thought*, p. 98. Other words that resonate with the "Being of beings" for Heidegger in this text are "*phusis*," "*zoe*," "the will," "the venture," "the widest orbit," "the other side of life," "the Open."

27. In other words, there seems to be a significant distinction here between geometrically fixed "identity" (A = A) and dynamic yet steadfast "self-sameness." But we may wonder: is this a virtuous circle?

28. It seems quite likely that a man who lacked some sense of "transcendental unity" would be in a state of "conflictual multiplicity," lacking a center of psychological "gravity." Such man

would kaleidoscopically swirl continuously into something-other than he appears to be or not to be. In limit conditions from a human perspective this would probably mean some kind of "madness." Notice that it is "the mad man" (*der tolle Mensch*) in *Gay Science* 125 who announces that "God is dead. God remains dead. And we have killed him." Nietzsche self-consciously seems to link the lack of "transcendental unity" with some kind of madness. The dead God seems to reflect, from a historical perspective, the obsolescent identity of transcendental unity and monotheism. Unlike Judaism and Islam, Christian monotheism gives transcendental unity a "Son": God becomes Christ to feed our divine hunger. On the other hand, during the transitional period of nihilism transcendence apparently ceases to have a "face." In *Gay Science* aphorism 143 Nietzsche discusses "the plurality of norms" that follow, which he also calls "polytheism." This seems to imply that God is dead but perhaps theism is not. Cf. *Genealogy of Morals,* II 19-22; Jan Assman *The Price of Monotheism*, p. 31-84; see also Alasdair Macintyre's lecture "On Being a Theistic Philosopher in a Secularized Culture," available at https://www.youtube.com/watch?v=0tm-5JXRXkM . On configurations of madness or "mania" in the European enlightenment consider Michel Foucault *Madness and Civilization: A History of Insanity in the Age of Reason* (London: Routledge, 2005). See especially Foucault's Hippocratic analysis in Ch. V.I "Mania and Melancholia."

29. Cf. Heidegger *Nietzsche* Vol. 1 "The Will to Power as Art," Section 23. Also, *Contributions to Philosophy*, Section 70.

30. Nietzsche *Will to Power*, 617.

31. In a helpful footnote Krell (p. 154) notes that the expression "ontology" seems to have been coined by a Cartesian philosopher, taken up in German thought through the legacy of Leibniz, falling then into oblivion as a result of Kantianism (if *noumena* is unknowable then ontology is necessarily nonsensical), and then taken up again in the 20th century in the works of Heidegger and Nicolai Hartmann. For a contrast between ontology-and-art and religion, cf. Eugenio Trías *Filosofía del Futuro* (Barcelona: Ariel, 1983), p. 116-117.

32. Martin Heidegger *The Event*. Trans. Richard Rojcewicz. (Indianapolis: Indiana University Press, 2009). Cf. Gadamer *Truth and Method*, p. 419: the hermeneutical event "is made possible only because the word that has come down to us as tradition and to which we are to listen really encounters us and does so in such a way that it addresses us and is concerned with us."

33. Jacques Derrida takes his bearings from this ambiguity. Derrida uses the expression *différance*—to be different (distinct) and to differ (endless transitivity)—to claim that language is a game of signifiers signifying other signifiers ad infinitum. Derrida thereby separates "literature from truth." See Jacques Derrida *Dissemination* (Chicago: University of Chicago Press, 1981). For a "reconstructive" critique of Derrida on the basis of an *eidetic* reading of Plato's *Phaedrus* in terms of "vision" and mindful silence, cf. Rosen *Hermeneutics as Politics*, p. 50-86.

34. Contrast with Etienne Gilson's discussion on "divine attributes," in *The Philosophy of Thomas Aquinas*: "The Divine Being is neither *genus*, nor *difference*, nor *species*. This is a conclusion of the greatest importance . . . if God falls outside the range of *genus* and *difference*, it is evident that He cannot be defined, since all definitions are reached by way of *genus* and *differences*. It is also evident that no proof of God can be given, except from His effects," p. 103. Cf. Thomas Aquinas *On Being and Essence*. Trans. with and intro. by Armand Maurer. (Toronto: PIMS, 1968), p. 45-50. Magda King *A Guide to Heidegger's Being and Time*, p. 256 (toward the end).

35. "Form," in other words, seems to be akin to immaterial "vision," while "substance" would be closer to the senses of touch, scent, and taste. For Heidegger "hearing" echoes the soundness of a given "substance" and "form," gathering as well as releasing the two. Perhaps this is not meant to be a mystifying remark: Heidegger's thinking tries to be attuned to the soundness and meaning of *logos,* as when we use the expression "I hear you." Cf. *Being and Time*, I.5.31, p. 186-88, I.5.36, p. 214-16, and II.4.68c, p. 396-400 for Heidegger's discussion on "vision," and I.5.34, p. 204-208, for his analysis of hearing and keeping silent as "modes of understanding." In *Being and Time* II.2.54, p. 313-14, "hearing" is taken to mean *Stimme des Gewissens*. Gadamer, on the other hand, associates the sense of hearing with hermeneutic interpretation in *Truth and Method*, p. 420. Gadamer also cites Aristotle's *De sensu* 437a;

87. For a counter-narrative, situating Italian Renaissance humanism in the context of Marsilio Ficino's Neo-Platonic reading of Plato, see Ernesto Grassi *Heidegger and the Question of Renaissance Humanism* (New York: Medieval and Renaissance Texts & Studies, 1983), p. 9 ff.

88. Kant *Critique of Pure Reason* B, 21; cf. "An Answer to the Question: What is Enlightenment?" in *Perpetual Peace and other Essays* , p. 41-48.

89. Kant "Idea for a Universal History with a Cosmopolitan Intent," Ibid., p. 29-40.

90. Kant *Critique of Pure Reason* B, 22.

91. Cf. Nietzsche *Beyond Good and Evil*, 285.

92. For Heidegger (following Leibniz) this is the fundamental question of metaphysics. *Introduction to Metaphysics* (New Haven: Yale University Press, 2000), p. 1

93. Heidegger *What is Called Thinking?*, p. 8. In my reading, this is not the "decisionism" of Carl Schmitt, but rather a movement in the spirit of Pascal and Kierkegaard. Heidegger, however, offers a more historically-situated account of the "essence of decision" in *Contributions to Philosophy*, Sections 43-49.

94. Nietzsche is also puzzled by the question of human nature, see for instance *Beyond Good and Evil*, 9.

95. We might consider that, if Kantian philosophy is derived from Descartes, and Descartes' philosophical anthropology can be traced back in relation to Hobbes (both seem to rely on the resolutive-composite method), then Kant would be a Hobbesian of some sort. Nietzsche seems to anticipate this English-French-German intellectual "development" in *Beyond Good and Evil*, 252-53. In the following aphorism, however, Nietzsche disentangles this intellectual history and conveys his preference for the French: "the French character contains a halfway successful synthesis of the north and the south which allows them to comprehend many things and to do things which an Englishman [or a German] would never understand." Nietzsche, who claims to be "a southerner, not by descent but by faith" (*BGE* 255), gives the example of the Provençal poets who symbolize the "good Europeans," those "rare and rarely contended human beings who are too comprehensive to find satisfaction in any fatherlandishness and know how to love the south in the north and the north in the south" (*BGE* 254). Culturally speaking, it is probably no exaggeration to say that Nietzsche is the philosophical herald of the European Union (*BGE* 256).

96. See Nietzsche *Beyond Good and Evil*, 15-17. For some of Nietzsche's thoughts on Kant: *Beyond Good and Evil*, 11, *Gay Science*, 335, *Dawn*, 481. Gianni Vattimo *Dialogue with Nietzsche*, p.103, notes the Kantian influence on the early Nietzsche, especially in the *Birth of Tragedy*, through the philosophy of Schopenhauer. Perhaps the Kantian influence on the young Nietzsche could also be traced back to Luther. It was his strict Lutheran upbringing what he was trying to overcome in his positivistic "middle period," with an increased focus on the body forced upon him by his chronic dis-eases. Cf. Stefan Zweig's biographical portrait *Nietzsche* (London: Hesperus P, 2013), p. 15-26; Safranski *Nietzsche*, p. 179 ff.

97. Nietzsche *Will to Power*, 617. Cf. Heidegger *Nietzsche* Vol. II, part 2, "Who is Nietzsche's Zarathustra?", p. 211-233; *What is Called Thinking?*, p. 103-109.

98. Cf. Heidegger *Being and Time*, II.1. Section 49, p. 292.

99. Goethe's poem "Wanderer's Nocturne" (Capuzzi trans.) reads:

Above all peaks,
Is repose,
In the treetops
You trace
Scarcely a breath;
The song birds are silent in the wood.
Only wait, soon
You too will repose.

100. Cf. Pierre Hadot *Plotin ou la Simplicité du Regard* (Paris: Folio-Essai, 1997).

101. Walter Benjamin "Theses on the Philosophy of History" in *Illuminations*. Trans. Harry Zohn. Ed. and Intro. by Hannah Arendt (New York: Shocken, 1969), p. 253-264, notes that only from the perspective of the victors, history appears to have a unitary, sequential, and

Metaphysics A 1, and 980b 23-25, to propose that "the primacy of hearing over seeing is something that is due to the universality of the *logos,* which does not contradict the specific primacy of sight over all the other senses, as Aristotle emphasizes" (p. 531, footnote 94). Contrast with Leo Strauss *The Rebirth of Classical Political Rationalism* (Chicago: University of Chicago Press, 1989), p. 95. Cf. also Hans Jonas "Heidegger and Theology," p. 207 ff., for a characterization in favor of "vision" over "hearing" in the thought of Philo of Alexandria.

36. In reference to this allusion Krell cites Plato *Meno* 74-76. Jacob Klein *A Commentary on Plato's Meno* (Chicago: University of Chicago Press, 1989.), p. 55-63 interprets *Meno* 74-76 in terms of the problem of the "unity of virtue": how are virtues as distinct as "courage," "wisdom," "moderation," "munificence" related to one another? Their "unity" is important because otherwise they could possibly be in contradiction. In the *Nicomachean Ethics* bk. I. vii.16 Aristotle claims that happiness is an "activity of the soul in accordance with virtue, and if there are many virtues then according to the highest virtue"; Plato's *Gorgias* dramatizes Callicles' inner conflict between "wisdom" and courage in the form of outspokenness (*parrhesia*) on the one hand, and the limits of justice and moderation on the other (516b5-7; 492a-d); Hobbes *Leviathan* Ch. XXI.16 points out the possible contradiction between the soldier's "courage" and his self-interest in not risking life and limb. According to Klein's reading of Plato's *Meno,* the distinction between the "one" and the "many" virtues can be mediated by a genuine grasp of geometry. All geometrical shapes, all "shaped surfaces" (56), are unique particulars that instantiate universal forms: "what is the same about all those surfaces" (58). All color is also color of a shaped surface: color seems to be a necessary attribute of our vision of surface: "color" and "surface" are "co-extensive" (59). They are "under all circumstances mutually complementary," as far as we can see. Socrates uses the example of the complementarity of color and surface as an analogy to account for the complementarity of the virtues. Socrates associates the question of human "excellence" with the phenomenon of "shaped surfaces" and "color." Color can be seen by anyone who is not color-blind: the same appears to apply to human virtue. If virtue is knowledge and knowledge comes to be instantiated through "shaped surfaces," and all shaped surfaces are a product of some kind of "making" (*poiesis*), then knowledge and making appear to be complementary. The proposition "virtue is knowledge" would therefore be akin to the proposition "knowledge is shaping." All shaping, however, seems to be a shaping of surfaces. Virtue therefore would be (auto) *poietic* or a kind of (self) shaping. Apparently, this would be as self-evident as the grasp of color(s) for the non-color-blind. Kinds of color, in turn, are distinguished by different "names." General or universal names delineate the specific or particular kinds of color coeval with shaped surfaces. Virtues are the general or universal names that delineate and shape a human being, making him/her a distinct "person."

37. For Kant, on the other hand, the categorical imperative is the quintessential *a priori.* Cf. Nietzsche *Genealogy of Morals,* II, 6.

38. Gadamer proposes a "fusion of horizons," encompassing the "subjectivisation of aesthetics" in Kant, in dialogue with a hermeneutical "ontological shift" to be sought on the basis of Aristotelian ethics centered on practical wisdom (*phronesis* or *prudentia*). *Truth and Method*, p. 278 ff. There are elements in Hannah Arendt's notion of "action" that can also be interpreted as a kind of synthesis between Aristotle and Kant. Cf. *The Human Condition*, Ch. 5. However, as Ronald Beiner remarks, one of the difficulties in Arendt's account lies in her claim that "action" and purpose or *telos* seem to remain distinct. Purpose pertains to "work" and not to "action." Arendt makes this distinction in order to associate action with freedom or spontaneity, which, from her perspective, presumably would be compromised if it were taken to be a means (a function of something else) rather than an end-in-itself. But, as Beiner points out, "of course Aristotle would never have claimed (and was right not to claim) that *praxis* is non-teleological." *Political Philosophy*, p. 16, footnote 20. Arendt's view of "action" seems to be an evocation of political freedom and "responsibility" as in the politics of, say, Themistocles, or Demosthenes, or Cato.

39. "Ontology" is the question of Being for Heidegger, and it is arguably the problem of natural right for Strauss. Perhaps we could say that, at some level, Heidegger's expression "Being and Time" is analogous to Strauss' "Natural Right and History." Gadamer's "Truth and Method" might be another interpretative response to Heidegger's formulation.

40. This, of course, needs to be qualified. Heidegger's relation to the ethical realm, taken at a non-political level, in my reading echoes Søren Kierkegaard's "dialectical lyric" in *Fear and Trembling.* In Kierkegaard's interpretation of the experience of Abraham, the spirit undergoes a passionate movement from aesthetics, to the universality of ethics, which, in turn, is overcome by a higher, singular, paradoxical calling in relation to the Absolute. *Fear and Trembling.* Ed. and Trans. with and Intro. and notes by Howard Hong and Edna Hong. (Princeton: Princeton University Press, 1983), p. 48 ff.

41. See Heidegger's discussion of "the They" (*Das Man*), in *Being and Time*, Section 4.

42. Nietzsche *Ecce Homo,* "Why I Am a Destiny," 1. I don't want to suggest, however, that radical thinking is always dualistically separate from political life. Thought and action under proper conditions need to find concord in the political sphere. In fact, it is difficult to see how necessary reforms could be made without such (very uneasy) approximation. Contrast with Foucault's study of the Greek notion of *parrhesia* in the *The Courage of Truth: The Government of Self and Others II.* Trans. Graham Burchell. (New York: Picador, 2012).

43. Here Strauss takes sides with Cassirer against Heidegger, but for non-Kantian reasons. Despite his thoughtful resistance to "historicism" (the view that thought is a subset of history, and therefore of will, or perhaps of "spirit"), Strauss seems to not have been averse to "historical" learning *per se*: see the intriguing image of slightly tilted scales in the dust jacket of the original 1953 edition of *Natural Right and History* (mimeographed in the second page of the U Chicago P 1965 paperback edition). Cf. Pöggeler *The Paths of Heidegger's Life and Thought*, p. 46.

44. See Strauss' autobiographical account in the Preface to the English translation of *Spinoza's Critique of Religion* (Chicago: University of Chicago Press, 1997), p. 1-31. It seems significant that, in 1962, Strauss wished to annex his autobiographical remarks to his book on Spinoza.

45. As we noted previously, Heidegger lectured on "European Nihilism" at the University of Freiburg in the first semester of 1940; Strauss lectured on "German Nihilism" at the New School for Social Research in New York, in February 1941. Part of Strauss' argument is that Heidegger, among others (Strauss mentions Spengler, Moeller van den Bruck, Schmitt, Ernst Junger), paved the way for National Socialism. A movement that Strauss associates with a nihilistic "ardent passion underlying the negation of the present world and its potentialities." Strauss "German Nihilism", p. 362. In *Heidegger, Strauss, and the Premises of Philosophy: On Original Forgetting* (Chicago: University of Chicago Press, 2001), p. 121-132, Richard Velkley argues that Strauss' response to Heidegger (his "unnamed opponent") is *Natural Right and History.* Strauss' *Natural Right and History* begins with a reference to the American Declaration of Independence and ends with an allusion to the "quarrel between ancients and moderns ... on the status of individuality," in the context of Burke's "Ciceronian" critique of Hobbes and Rousseau (p. 1; 295; 323). In the epic spirit of "philosophical legislators" (*Beyond Good and Evil*, 211; *Thus Spoke Zarathustra*, II.22 "The Stillest Hour"; II. 18 "On Great Events") Strauss' project seems to be twofold: steering the new world away from the radical politics of "European nihilism," while preserving the European inheritance of uncompromising thought.

46. Strauss *What is Political Philosophy?*, p. 9-55.

47. Strauss *Natural Right and History,* p. 81.

48. Strauss *What is Political Philosophy?*, p. 10.

49. Ibid. p. 10

50. Plato *Laws* 804b5-c1, cited in Strauss *On Tyranny*, p. 198.

51. Ibid. p. 201.

52. Strauss *What is Political Philosophy?*, p. 12. Cf. Aristotle *NE* Bk. VI.5.1 ff. where he discusses *phronesis* or "practical judgment," a species of action, distinct from *techné* (art/craft) and *episteme* (scientific knowledge of cause and effect).

53. Aristotle *Nicomachean Ethics,* 1179b20-1181b25.

54. Strauss *What is Political Philosophy?*, p. 221.

55. Plato *Statesman* 296e3-297a2.

56. How would Heidegger have responded to Strauss' indictment of "radical historicism"? Consider the following remark from Heidegger's "Der Spruch des Anaximander": Are we the

late-comers that we are? But are we at the same time also the precursors of the dawn of an altogether different age, *which has left behind our present historicist conceptions of history?*" Cited in Dallmayr, *The Other Heidegger*, p. 119 (emphasis added). In their own distinct ways, Strauss and Heidegger make a "historical" return to the classics: both seem to find their way back to "Aristotle," to address the Kantian/Hegelian voluntaristic dualism of late-modern thought. Although their divergent interpretations of the ancients derive from their respective textual approaches (Strauss pursues a rhetoric of close reading, Heidegger assumes a post-Kantian hermeneutics), both seem to take their bearings from Aristotle's *nous* rather than the Cartesian *cogito*. One way to make sense of their fundamental disagreement might be that, while Strauss appears to think *nous* is analogous to "vision," (*On Tyranny*, p. 277-280), Heidegger seems to think it is closer to "hearing" *Letter on Humanism*, p. 241; *Being and Time* I.3.23, p. 141. For an Aristotelian reading of Strauss cf. Thomas Pangle *Leo Strauss: Introduction to his Thought and Intellectual Legacy* (Baltimore: Johns Hopkins UP, 2006), p. 99 ff.; for a study of Heidegger's "Aristotelian beginnings," see Thomas Sheehan *Making Sense of Heidegger*, Part I, Chs. 2-3.

57. Heidegger unfortunately does not elaborate on what specific passages he might have in mind.

58. Cf. Heidegger "Plato's Doctrine of Truth," and "On the Essence of Truth," in *Pathmarks*, p. 155-182; 136-154.

59. Nietzsche *Gay Science*, 270. See also Matt: 7: 20.

60. Nietzsche *Beyond Good and Evil*, Preface; 190-191.

61. Mainly our other ancient sources on Socrates come from Xenophon, Aristophanes, Aristotle, and Diogenes Laertius.

62. Cf. Beiner *Civil Religion*, p. 393.

63. Nietzsche *Twilight of the Idols*, "What I owe to the Ancients" sec. 2. Note that Hobbes was also a translator into English of Homer and Thucydides.

64. Cf. Heidegger *Letter on Humanism*, p. 265.

65. It might be an enthymeme rather than a *non-sequitur*: to reason in terms of Kantian "conditions of possibility" seems to be a consequence of Cartesian representation. Nietzsche's valuation, for Heidegger, also partakes in that way of conceptualizing the mind.

66. Gadamer interprets the relation between *theoria, nous,* and "presence" (*Anwesenheit*) in *Truth and Method*, p. 111.

67. We learn in Plato's *Symposium* (199c4-5) that the poet Agathon is Socrates' friend. They are therefore akin but different: Socrates and "Agathon" are different characters or figures in Plato's mind. In the dialogue, Agathon is a rather passive and dreamy lyrical poet of youthful innovative love. Unlike Socrates, Agathon sings the identity of beauty and love.

68. Derrida makes the same claim about Heidegger; cf. *Of Grammatology*, p. 22.

69. Cf. John Duns Scotus, *A Treatise on God as First Principle* (Chicago: Franciscan Herald Press, 1966), especially section III "The simplicity, infinity and intellectuality of the first Being," p. 73 ff. See Armand Maurer *Medieval Philosophy*, p. 220-241: from Scotus' perspective, the "necessity of revelation" is "proved" first metaphysically (not ascriptively, beginning from experience like Thomas Aquinas). The "proof" goes from consequences back to a first cause, leading up to the "metaphysical truth" of "producibility": "even if God had not willed to create, it would still be eternally true that some being can be produced" (233). Being can be produced by a primary "efficient cause," which is God (224). For Scotus "producibility" is the essential attribute of God. Modern "producibility" appears to take the shape of technology. In *The Question Concerning Technology*, p. 24, Heidegger associates *die Technik* with a certain kind of "destining" (*Geschick*), that issues forth from a "mode of Being." Heidegger is not unaware of the ambivalent—both potentially dangerous but also possibly emancipatory—consequences of technology; toward the end of the essay he quotes twice the lines from Hölderlin: "*Wo aber Gefahr ist, wächst Das Rettende auch*" (p. 34). Heidegger's view on technology might be already prefigured in his *Habilitationsschrift* on Duns Scotus.

70. Heidegger *Being and Time*, I.3. Section 18, p. 115. Cf. *Nietzsche* Vol III. p. 225, where Heidegger associates human conditioning with "creation."

71. Cf. Heidegger "On the Essence and Concept of *phusis* in Aristotle's *Physics* B, I," in *Pathmarks*, p. 183-230. Arendt speaks of "plurality" and "natality" as the fundamental charac-

teristics of the human condition in *The Human Condition*, Ch. V, p. 175 ff. Cf. Heidegger *Being and Time*, II.5. Section 72, p. 425-26.

72. For Alasdair MacIntyre, *After Virtue* (Notre Dame, Indiana: University of Notre Dame Press, 1984), the "decision" between Aristotle and Nietzsche is a stark *either/or* (Ch. IX, p. 109-120). Heidegger, on the other hand, thinks they are not incompatible. Perhaps unexpectedly, John Rawls seems to side with Heidegger on this particular point, associating Nietzsche with Aristotelian "perfectionism." *A Theory of Justice* (Cambridge: Harvard University Press, 1971), p. 25.

73. Capuzzi translates *der Lehre Platons* as "Plato's doctrine."

74. Heidegger links alethic "forgetting" with lack of "thinking." See for instance Heidegger *What is Called Thinking?*, p. 76, 244; Gadamer *Heidegger's Ways* (New York: SUNY P, 1994), p. 61-67, 81-93; Michel Haar *Heidegger and the Essence of Man*, especially the section "Originary Past (Birth and Thrownness), Repetition and Forgetting," p. 41-47; William Richardson *Heidegger: Through Phenomenology to Thought*. With Preface by Martin Heidegger (New York: Fordham, 2003), p. 306-308. Consider also Heidegger's otherwise oblique assertion "questioning is the piety of thought" in *The Question Concerning Technology*, p. 35.

75. Heidegger references Kant's *Critique of Pure Reason* A 158, B197.

76. This might be akin to the young Marx's critique of Hegel. The difference between the young Hegelians and Nietzsche is that while the former embrace forward the philosophy of history, Nietzsche also embodies a desire for eternity. Cf. Löwith *From Hegel to Nietzsche*, p. 175-231. Nietzsche *Schopenhauer as Educator*, p. 191.

77. Paul Catanu *Heidegger's Nietzsche: Being and Becoming* (8th House: Montreal, 2010), takes Heidegger to be the philosopher of Being, and Nietzsche the philosopher of Becoming— each thinking the problem of metaphysics from that respective angle.

78. Contrast with *Beyond Good and Evil*, 32; 188; *Genealogy of Morals*, II: 21; *Dawn* 174; Heidegger *Nietzsche* Vol. I: "The Will to Power as Art," section 20, p. 159-60.

79. Heidegger is here trying to find the origins of "trustworthiness" rather than calculative "valuation." Cf. *Being and Time*, I.4. Section 26, p. 163. Edward Andrew marks a distinction between Nietzsche's language of values and Heidegger's language of "worthiness (*Würdigkeit*) or dignity (*Würde*)" in "The Unworthiness of Nietzschean Values" *Animus* 14 (2010), p. 67-78.

80. Contrast with Etienne Gilson *The Philosophy of Thomas Aquinas*, p. 49; 55 (footnote 20): "Fidelis autem ex causa prima, ut puta quia sic divinitus est traditum, vel quia hoc in gloriam Dei cedit, vel quia Dei potestas est inifinita," *Cont. Gent.*, II.4. Strauss *The City and Man*, p. 240-41.

81. Heidegger discusses the notion of "historiology" in *Being and Time* Intro. I. Section 3. Cf. Nietzsche *Uses and Disadvantages of History for Life*, Sections 1-3.

82. Cf. Nishitani *The Self-Overcoming of Nihilism*, p. 157-172; Habermas *Philosophical Discourse of Modernity*, p. 22.

83. Nietzsche *Uses and Disadvantages of History for Life*, p. 59-71; *Thus Spoke Zarathustra*, II.20 "On Redemption." John Richardson interprets the problem of "willing backwards" in relation to Nietzsche's method of genealogy, liberation, and the thought of eternal return in "Nietzsche's Problem of the Past" in M. Dries (ed.), *Nietzsche on Time and History* (Berlin/New York: Walter de Gruyter, 2008), p. 87-112. Contrast with Aristotle *N.E.* VI.ii.6.

84. Michel Haar raises a series of questions in relation to Leibnizian monads, "theodicy," and the problem of evil in *Heidegger and the Essence of Man*, p. 132; Hannah Arendt *The Human Condition*, p. 281-82, takes Descartes and Leibniz (i.e., Heidegger) to task on the problem of evil. Is it possible, somehow, to reconcile the problem of evil with "pre-established harmony"?

85. Aristotle *Metaphysics* 1047 a30-35.

86. In *Metaphysics* 1050 a21-23 Aristotle associates *energeia* with *ergon* (i.e., action or "works"). One of the aims of Arendt in the *Human Condition* is to make a categorical distinction between "action," organic "labor," and "work[s]." She takes this to be of great importance, to theoretically forestall the Marxist (eschatological) identification of "works" with technological *praxis*. Theologically speaking, Arendt seems to take Marxism to be a reformulation of radical Pelagianism. Cf. Leszek Kolakowski *God Owes Us Nothing*, p. 4-5; 183-85.

rational purpose. The vanquished cannot see history in the same sequential order because their experiences have been curtailed, therefore their account cannot be unitary in a rational-linear way. Hence the "Dionysian" perspective of "rapture" is necessarily the perspective of the vanquished. One of the distinctive features of the modern epoch, however, is that through the Abrahamic faiths "popular culture" shifts from Dionysian lament to (universal) Apollonian emancipation. Generally speaking, monotheistic cultures could be conceived as world-shaping monumental efforts to counter the "idolatrous" fatalism of the vanquished through the psycho-political "gymnastics of willing" of community-forming religion (cf. Aristotle *Politics* 1288b10-38). Nietzsche's critique of "slave morality," on the other hand, stems from his diagnosis that the linear-historical remedy for fatalism seems to have become misbalanced or "nihilistic" in contemporary western culture. The will wills nothing rather than not willing (*Genealogy of Morals*, III: 28); restlessness of willing tends to become increasingly global or "total" in our time. Allegorically speaking, Nietzsche seems to be offering a "shock therapy" in the form of "Dionysian" holistic constitution that may give roundedness to natural destiny, to soothe and mature the emancipatory drive of "Apollonian" linear, individual, and historical agency (*Birth of Tragedy*, Sections 9-12; 21). In my reading, Nietzsche is trying to find a balance between Apollo and Dionysus for individuals and for culture (cf. *Gay Science*, 381-82). Cf. Alex McIntyre *The Sovereignty of Joy: Nietzsche's Vision of Grand Politics* (Toronto: University of Toronto Press, 1997), p. 83. At some level, this question seems to require steering the spiritual reservoir (*BGE*, Preface) of the legacy of European culture in conversation with non-western sources, toward a classically attuned enlightenment in dialogue with the experience of *amor fati*.

102. It would seem, however, that human beings can learn through suffering (*passio*). Compassion is therefore shared learning. Consider, on the other hand, Nietzsche *Beyond Good and Evil*, 96, 153, and 172.

103. Nietzsche *Beyond Good and Evil*, 56-57.

104. Parmenides (Frag. 8).

105. Cf. Heidegger *Being and Time*, II.2. Section 60, p. 342-43; *Letter on Humanism*, p. 262, 276; *Contributions to Philosophy*, Section 13. Nietzsche *Beyond Good and Evil*, 63. Arendt alludes to (silent) "original intuition" preceding, grounding, and guiding explicit knowledge. See Hannah Arendt "Understanding in Politics," *Essays in Understanding 1930-1954*. (New York: Harcourt, 1994), p. 310-11.

106. In this reference to "discordance" Heidegger uses the word *Zwiespältigkeit*, so the implication seems to be a rather intense rift. Heidegger might be associating the "problem of evil" with the book of Job. Contrast with Arendt's discussion of "labor" in *The Human Condition*, p. 79-135. For a classical Greek angle, cf. Sophocles *Oedipus Tyrannos*.

107. Where does modernity begin? Heidegger seems to waver between "Plato" and Descartes. Strauss' critique of Heidegger is that modernity does not begin in Plato or in Descartes. Modernity for Strauss stretches from Machiavelli (*Prince* Ch. 15) to Heidegger's "existentialist" critique of Weberian *Wertrationalität*. *What is Political Philosophy?*, p. 45-46; *Natural Right and History*, p. 35-80; "An Introduction to Heideggerian Existentialism," in *The Rebirth of Classical Political Rationalism*, p. 27-46. Contrast with Arendt *The Human Condition*, p. 77. Waller Newell *Tyranny: A New Interpretation* (Cambridge: Cambridge UP, 2103), p. 68-70, revises Strauss' line of argument, putting him in dialogue with Eric Voegelin. Newell traces the origins of the modern historical unfolding from Machiavelli back to Augustine. Machiavelli drops the city of God, but still wants to shape the city of man by "virtue" of the emancipated Augustinian will. The reference to Augustine seems to establish the divergent pathways of Machiavelli and Luther. Whereas Machiavelli apparently wants to do away with the city of God to be able to freely partake in the city of man, Luther would have the opposite intention. Hobbes would be in-between Machiavelli and Luther.

108. Heidegger *Letter on Humanism*, p. 264 - 265.

109. George Grant *Technology and Justice* (Concord, Ontario: Anansi, 1986), p. 11-34. Consider also Heidegger, *Contributions to Philosophy*, Section 72.

110. Cf. Plato *Gorgias* 521 d7-9; *Apology* 31d-32a3.

111. Heidegger *Question Concerning Technology*, p. 18; *Contributions to Philosophy*, Section 70. Dallmayr *The Other Heidegger*, p. 98-104; Voegelin *New Science of Politics*, Ch. 2, Section 3.

112. Habermas *The Philosophical Discourse of Modernity*, p. 136; Grant *Technology and Empire*, p. 36.

IV

Hermeneutics and Political Philosophy

This final chapter examines Heidegger's treatise "The Determination of Nihilism in Accordance with the History of Being" (*Die Seinsgeschichtliche Bestimmung des Nihilismus*). The text in many ways is a continuation of Heidegger's interpretation of Nietzsche's thoughts on "European nihilism," but now seems to expand upon themes that are more salient in the "later Heidegger": a Heidegger that has become more even-handed with regards to the activity of "willing," and the awareness, in thought, of the human "abode" (*die Unterkunft*). More generally, this chapter offers a hermeneutic "landscape" of the question of Being in modern culture: drawing in large measure from the spirit of Platonic-Aristotelian political psychology, it aims to convey the mystery of the *Seinsfrage* in distinct relation to the character of man.[1]

One

Heidegger starts by asserting Nietzsche's "acknowledgement" of the disjuncture between mere being and the thought of Being. This, of course, is at the core of Heidegger's thesis regarding Nietzsche's alleged "Platonism." Heidegger does not make a simple identification, but goes further: ontology, "thought of Being," is missed when it is conceived in terms of "value," even of "necessary value." Indeed, not even the thought of the "eternal return of the same" (*der "ewigen Wiederkunft des Gleichen"*) conveys the moment of eternal presence that Heidegger associates with the thought of Being. Again, Heidegger's initial remarks seek to signal a cleft between thinking of Being and valuative thought.

The source of "valuative thought" is reasoning derived from "will to power." The "fact" of will to power, the judgment that puts "will to power" under the genus "fact," "blocks the way" to the question of Being (199). In Nietzsche's thinking the question of Being is not even raised because Nietzsche seems to posit Being in terms of "values." Such positing, for Heidegger, "transforms Being" and makes it "lose its name" (199).

Heidegger now seems to move into a more hermeneutic explanation of his reading of Nietzsche: in the present "meditation" (*Besinnung*),[2] Heidegger claims he is not trying to suggest that Nietzsche's thinking is "inadequate," rather, he seems to offer a more nuanced interpretation:

> It is simply a matter of bringing ourselves from our thinking toward the question of truth of Being (*die Frage nach der Wahrheit des Seins*) into proximity to Nietzsche's metaphysics, in order to experience his thought on the basis of the supreme fidelity of his thinking. It is far from the intention of our effort to disseminate a perhaps more correct version of Nietzsche's philosophy (199).

As we have seen throughout the text, this is one of the permanent conundrums of Heidegger's interpretation: Heidegger claims that he remains attentive to Nietzsche's thinking, while apparently working under the historicist assumption that it is possible to understand an author better than he understood himself.[3] But perhaps the underlying premise of this interpretative mode is the assumption that "thought" is a subset of "will": as such the interpreter may remain faithful to the movement of willing while letting reason give an account of what such "thinking in movement" continues to yield.[4] Heidegger discusses the reason for engaging with Nietzsche's thinking as follows: "we are thinking his metaphysics solely in order to be able to inquire into what is worthy of question: *in Nietzsche's metaphysics, which for the first time experiences and thinks nihilism as such, is nihilism overcome [überwunden] or not?*" (Heidegger's italics).

Thus, Heidegger is not pursuing a project in the history of ideas, nor is he engaged in a general exegesis of Nietzsche's thought. Rather, he is mainly concerned with two tasks: first, to clarify Nietzsche's mature thinking, "mapping out" the thoughtful experience of Nietzsche regarding nihilism. Second, once Nietzsche's thinking is organized around the momentous theme of European nihilism, Heidegger draws from Nietzsche's writings pathways to foresee what would be needed to begin addressing the problem (200).

Heidegger's main contention is that Nietzsche is a "metaphysical thinker." "Metaphysics" has traditionally meant the assumption that there is a distinction between "reality" and "appearance" exemplified by the Platonic dichotomy between eternal forms and sensual images, Descartes' distinction between *res cogitans* and *res extensa*, Kant's separation of *noumena* and *phenomena*, and, Heidegger adds, Nietzsche's division between "valuative thought" and the "will to power." Heidegger contends that in Nietzsche this train of dualistic thinking finds its "fulfilment," which Heidegger seems to interpret as the opening toward a new mode of thought that need not assume a *categorical* distinction between thought (*noeîn*) and sensibility (*aisthesis*).[5]

Heidegger claims to be studying the "essence of nihilism" in relation to the status of beings (200). In questioning the "essence" of nihilism Heidegger is pondering whether "there 'is' nothing to beings as such." The question in this passage seems to be whether being is a "no-*thing*" rather than, say, an abstract "subject" or a generic "individual." Nietzsche, on the other hand, also "experiences nihilism as the history of the devaluation of the highest values." Nietzsche takes therefore a "structural" view of the problem of the nothing: the "underlying concern" of beings is for Nietzsche intimately linked with the "overarching metaphor" of "Being," "structured" in terms of "values" and "history." Heidegger takes this dichotomy and phrases it in terms of the "figure" of nothingness: what is the matter expressed in the thought of nihilism and the "nihil"? Heidegger makes the paradoxical claim that "in its own way, the name *nihilism* names the *Being* of beings" (200). There seem to be three levels of analysis in Heidegger's interpretation of the problem of nihilism: (1) the nothing in relation to "being," (2) the structure of thinking, and (3) history.

Nietzsche's "fundamental experience," however, is that being is "will to power in the mode of eternal recurrence of the same" (201).[6] Heidegger seems to have in mind a parallel scenario to the Kantian antinomy of freedom: how to come to terms with the cyclical movement of eternal recurrence of the same as well as the linear affirmation of the will to power? Heidegger seems to think that, for Nietzsche, it was possible to give shape to this apparent contradiction: a being could take the "form" of eternal recurrence experienced as will to power.[7]

But Heidegger notes that a being that bodies-forth the eternal recurrence of the same as the form of the will to power would as such *not* be nothing (201). If valuative thought can give "shape" to the will to power, then it would seem that, normatively speaking, Nietzsche's valuative thinking could overcome nihilism. But Heidegger resists this conclusion: valuative thought brings nihilism to "fulfilment," hence it remains within its sphere of influence. Nietzsche postulated Being "as a value" and therefore "explained it in terms of beings as a condition posited by the will to power" (201). The reason why valuative thought is nihilistic is because Nietzsche does not "recognize" *Being* as such. Values are a mode of subjective cognition that are determined by the pre-eminence of will over thought. Will to power brings about valuation: it gives primacy to "creation" over discovery, of movement over rest, of speech over silence, of action over thinking.

If Being is taken as a subset of will (to power) then it is not "acknowledged" as Being. For Heidegger, however, this is not a dogmatic assertion: it

means that valuative thinking does not persevere in the question of Being
(201). Differently put, Heidegger seems closer than perhaps expected to the
experience of Socratic philosophy at this juncture: valuative thought closes
the mind to the experience of wonder. Since "any discussion of 'Being itself'
always remains interrogative," the experience of wonder is coeval with the
pursuit of questioning. But how to reason if Being itself is in question?
Heidegger's claim is that without the question of Being we have no ground
for confident thought and action. But we forget that we have forgotten the
question.[8]

As opposed to the fact/value distinction of modern positivism, Heidegger
offers a starting aperture that seems to do away with all dualisms of thinking:
"Being—a *nihil*" (201). This assertion challenges the interpretation of phenomena in terms of "facts" that are given to sense experience and "values"
that are dependent on the idiosyncratic judgment of the subject. For Heidegger the "fact/value" distinction is a reflection of the Kantian dichotomy of
speculative *noumena* and extended *phenomena*, in turn a reflection of Cartesian cogitation, which is ultimately a reformulation of the metaphysical distinction between Being and becoming of "Platonism." But, in fairness to
Descartes (et. al), we may ask: why is Heidegger so averse to accepting the
distinction between "is" and "ought" in its different formulations in the history of western thought?

The problem seems to be that the distinction between Being (eternity) and
becoming (genesis) depends on having clarity on the "essence" and the "attributes" of Being. Nihilism, however, means that "the *nihil* concerns Being
itself." The conundrum of the identification of Being and *nihil* is that as
"immaterial substance" Being, like dreams, could possibly at some level not
be subject to the law of non-contradiction. Although Heidegger does not use
the traditional language of the "soul," this same difficulty would apply to the
immaterial soul: an immortal or immaterial soul per se would not be subject
to the law of non-contradiction. Hence the problem of the *nihil* of Being is
not only an ontological speculation but a profound spiritual difficulty about
the relation between the *psyche* and understanding: whether the *psyche* has
being, and if so, what its relation would be to "life."[9] Heidegger, however,
takes "our thinking" as a kind of analytical "reckoning or giving an account"
to be possibly inadequate to meditate on the question of Being: that "perhaps
Being itself does not trouble itself about the contradictions of our thought" is
the problem of nihilism (201).[10]

The pursuit of understanding the essence and attributes of Being has
become an open question. Being—and therefore beings—a *nihil*? Why do
away with the boundaries of the Cartesian self? Didn't Heidegger prior to the
"turn" (*die Kehre*) also partake in the modern tradition of voluntaristic action
over "classical" thought?[11]

Two

Heidegger references two passages from Nietzsche's *The Will to Power,* from aphorisms 14 and 617, one assertion and one "recapitulation": (1) "'Nihilism' as ideal of the *supreme powerfulness* of spirit, of superabundant life—partly destructive, partly ironic"; (2) "To stamp Becoming with the character of Being—that is the supreme will to power." Heidegger interprets Nietzsche to be saying that the idea of "eternal recurrence of the same" is a way of stamping "Being" onto the totality of beings. This seems to be another way to think "will to power in terms of eternal recurrence of the same." Will to power is the "fundamental fact" of beings which, in Nietzsche's thinking, seems to be shaped under the character of Being envisioned as "eternal recurrence of the same." [12] Under this logic Nietzsche seems to be an "ancient" thinker, like Aristotle or Polybius, or even like Machiavelli in the *Discourses on Livy* (II.5), rather than a "modern" in the Cartesian or Kantian sense. The ancients take cyclical nature to be inherent to the experience of political life. The moderns assume that the fate of cyclical natural motion is not inherent to human freedom, which they take to be distinct from circular movement: willing makes possible linear progressive history. But despite this dichotomy, Heidegger claims that Nietzsche's "metaphysics" is in line with "Platonism," and therefore, somehow, Nietzsche would be a classically informed "progressive." In other words, Heidegger's Nietzsche is both ancient and modern. How does Heidegger make sense of this contradiction?

Heidegger calls the stamping of Being (*das Sein*) onto Becoming (*das Werden*) "the supreme form of 'nihilism'" (202). Heidegger, on the other hand, associates thinking in terms of conditional values with an "ironic" mode of thinking. Irony means communicating indirectly or obliquely: expressing one thing while meaning another. Thus, valuative thinking is a conditional or ironic mode of thinking. But the way out of nihilism seems to require that one thinks nihilism to the outmost extreme, at which point "it is no longer even a nihilism" (202). What would this extreme irony or extreme conditionality mean? [13]

Heidegger, however, takes a step back: Nietzsche's metaphysics "is nihilism proper" (203). The proclamation of nihilism is coeval with the expression of Being in terms of values. There is "nothing to Being" under this mode of thinking. Values become historical by-products of the will to power that rise and dwindle depending on their historical effects. From this perspective the "highest values hitherto" are not a permanent feature of reality, but a historical manifestation of the "fundamental fact" of will to power. The "fact" of will to power establishes our relative judgment of conditional valuation.

Heidegger claims that in the historical unfolding of nihilism "valuative thought" is "elevated into a principle," thus occluding the question of Being from our mindful disposition. As a consequence, the mind ceases to be steady, and seems to be ruled by external relations: the *Zeitgeist* rather than clear-eyed epistemic wonder seems to take over the human mind. But if the *Zeitgeist* takes over, how could "an overcoming of nihilism occur here, or even make itself felt?" (203).

Heidegger emphasizes again that nihilism is not an abstract speculation but an embodied experience. There is no "fact/value" distinction in Heidegger's meditation: our thoughts, beginning at the fundamental level of the forgotten question of Being, inform our bodily dispositions. But our bodily dispositions, our "moods," are also profoundly significant to enliven our thinking.[14] Contrary to Descartes and Kant, Heidegger does not make a clear body/mind distinction. Heidegger seems to embody a mode of thinking that complements, and at times challenges, enlightenment thinking with the inner attunement toward the call of conscience.[15]

Hence the heart of the problem: valuative thinking seems to relativize the structure of the human mind, therefore compromising the *thoughtful* experience of inner conscience. The point here seems to be that, in so far as conscience is felt *by man*, it should perhaps be possible to bring it to consciousness by means of thinking.[16] The call of conscience is the call of care, and care is the ontological "Being of Dasein." But nihilism seems to make the call of conscience relative, or a product of mere inter-subjective commitment. If, as Heidegger claims, Nietzsche believes that Being is to be thought of in terms of values, then Nietzsche has not overcome the problem of nihilism. In so far as he uses the language of values, Nietzsche's thinking seems to be "entangled" with nihilism. "Valuative thought" as offshoot of will to power seeks to grasp beings or entities. To think being in terms of value—to think being in terms of the voluntarism of the *ego cogito*—is, for Heidegger, the practical core of the problem of nihilism.

How can we think "Being as Being"? Does nihilism need to be completed or "fulfilled" first in order to open the possibility to meditate on the question? For Heidegger, the "essence of nihilism" seems to be the historical problem of taking Being as nothing, and to conclude from this assumption that our "normative" cues are ultimately indistinguishable from conditional "values," and therefore from inter-subjective "willing." What does nihilism mean? "The uppermost values devalue themselves" as a result of the apparent triumph of 'sovereign' human willing.[17]

Three

The will to power suffers epochal shifts. Heidegger makes the claim that the categories of thinking are coeval with distinct historical epochs that envelope human experience: valuative thought is a mode of nihilistic metaphysics grounded on a historic epochal manifestation of the will to power. Is Nietzsche's interpretation of "will to power" as "permanent fundamental fact" *correct*? Is nihilism a vain anthropocentric confusion or a manifestation of the "history of Being"? In his reading of Nietzsche, Heidegger claims to be pursuing the question of "whether and in what way nihilism is a history that applies to Being itself" (204). The question now is whether "willing" is merely anthropocentric, or, if somehow it has ontological proportions. In other words, Heidegger is asking about the relation between willing and Being (in the sense of *das Sein* and *Dasein*).

In his grasp of the problem of nihilism, Nietzsche does not only negate the given. Nietzsche also negates the negation, and therefore offers a new affirmation: Nietzsche "demands a 'yes.'" Heidegger contends that Nietzsche moves from mere "interpretation" to a "contemplation" of the overcoming of nihilism (204). Such attempt to reach a contemplation or comprehensive "view from above" would not be possible, however, unless "the essence of nihilism" were experienced in its completion. For Heidegger this would be an "essential" confrontation that would presumably lead to the "overcoming" of the problem. But, on Nietzsche's terms, how can human thought participate in this confrontation, which seems to involve Being itself, without falling into the realm of valuative thinking? Apparently, the fulfillment of nihilism begins by experiencing it retrospectively, in a Hegelian mode, as a historiographical phenomenon. Nietzsche's metaphysics of the will to power is the fulfilment of nihilism in so far as it wills the valuation of "Being" in terms of will to power. All valuation is a product of will to power: but what is the ground of all willing? Heidegger claims that such ground precedes the "essence of metaphysics": the "ground" precedes all will.[18]

The return to the experience of the ground, to "fundamental ontology," for Heidegger implies a return to pre-metaphysical thinking. Heidegger tells us that in the tradition of philosophical thinking, going from Descartes to Kant and to Hegel metaphysics is "at bottom experienced as *will*." For Heidegger, unlike Schopenhauer, this primacy of the will "does not mean that the subjective experience of human will is transposed onto beings as a whole" (205). On the contrary, the "unelucidated basis" of nihilism pertains to the realm of thinking: the unruly metaphysics of "willing" seems to be the distinctive symptom of the human malaise of nihilism.

Now, Heidegger claims that it is not only willing but "metaphysics" itself which is nihilism proper. In his polemical characterization: "the metaphysics of Plato is no less nihilistic than that of Nietzsche" (205). Why does Heidegger make this sweeping generalization? For Heidegger the difference is not one of substance but of form: "in the former, the essence of nihilism is merely concealed; in the later, it comes completely to appearance." Heidegger in other words is making a nominalist critique of Plato and Nietzsche on ontological grounds. Heidegger's claim is that both Plato and Nietzsche share a view of reality that abstracts universals and particulars: understanding taken to be the subsumption of a particular case under a universal rule. While Plato takes this mode of reasoning to be based on noetic ideas, Nietzsche takes it to be based on voluntaristic valuation. Although the epistemic status of both categories of thought is indeed distinct (Plato is an "essentialist" and Nietzsche is a voluntaristic "perspectivist") both thinkers, according to Heidegger, share the view that structures the mind in terms of genus and species. What seems to be missing, from Heidegger's perspective, is the experience of "singularity": Plato and Nietzsche deal with the "what," but seem to miss the singular experience of the personal "who."[19] Heidegger, in a way, seems to be putting to Plato and to Nietzsche, at least to some extent, Augustine's qualified critique of the Platonists in the *City of God*.[20] In their concentration on supratemporal "universals" philosophers tend to overlook the embodied dimension of the singular, epitomized not by "natural kinds" or general "types," but by living "persons" who respond to their own "name." But a critic may notice that Plato and Nietzsche attempt to deal with this difficulty in their works: hence instead of writing treatises like Kant or Hegel, Plato wrote dialogues involving distinct characters;[21] and Nietzsche, in his mature thinking, also wrote the story of Zarathustra, and evoked the drama of Dionysus and Ariadne. The question therefore seems to be the extent to which these "masks" depicted by Plato and Nietzsche aim to signal embodied "persons,"[22] or, whether they portray general archetypes that need not refer to a singular "who."[23]

Heidegger is not unaware of the problematic parallel between Plato and Nietzsche. He is not unaware that "these are disturbing statements" that, philosophically speaking, upset the architectonic configuration of the western era: "western humankind, in all its relations with beings, and even to itself, is in every respect sustained and guided by metaphysics" (205). But Heidegger claims that this "thought-provoking" association might "sharpen our thinking as it has scarcely responded to the essence of nihilism proper [. . .] so that afterward we might pass judgment" on it. The equation of Platonic ideas and Nietzsche's valuative thought is not Heidegger's definitive view on metaphysics.

Four

For Heidegger the problem of metaphysics seems to lie in the phenomenon of "representation." Representation seems here associated with the Hegelian notion of boundless or "bad infinity": "metaphysics of metaphysics that never attains to its essence" (206). The rhetoric of representation signals a problem of the ground and of essence (it is unclear whether Heidegger means a simple identity here). What does the word "essence" mean in this context? What would need to be the essence of metaphysics, such that it would be related to the question of Being? This is perhaps *the* central question for

Heidegger. Heidegger's train of reasoning stresses the ontological relationship between the question of *das Seiende* with the ontological question of *das Sein*: "the being as a being *is* such thanks to Being" (206). Plato, according to Heidegger, defines being in terms of "whatness" (*Washeit*) or the "what-being" (*was-sein*) of beings, "*to ti estin.*"

Heidegger claims that the Platonic "whatness" of being comes to be translated as the "essentia of *ens*," that is to say, what we would normally understand as "the essence" of a thing: the "whiteness" of the color white, or the "idea of a table" rather than the potentially infinite number of instantiations of particular tables, etc.[24] The thinking of the "Being of beings" in terms of whatness that seems to follow is for Heidegger "no incidental and harmless identification" (206). It is a "metaphysical interpretation" of essence that focuses on the "what" of beings: to think of beings in terms of "whatness," Heidegger claims, has as a result a mode of thinking in terms of "*genos*": "that from which every being in its being thus-and-so receives the common What" (207). Heidegger's critique of the "metaphysics" of "whatness" is that it overlooks the singular "who" that cannot be subsumed in general terms of genus and species.[25] The metaphysics of "whatness" overlooks the thought of a "peculiar, distinctive, and unique kind." This contrast goes to the heart of Heidegger's thinking with regards to the tension between universality and singularity: it is for this reason that "Being itself remains unthought in metaphysics."

Now, Heidegger grants that it is an "open question" whether metaphysics itself can be appropriately interrogated in terms of singularities. Heidegger uses here the Kantian language of the *a priori* to bring up the possibility that Being be prior to beings: the order of their sequence seems to be at the core of the problem. Thinking of Being of beings as an *a priori*, as a given assumption prior to thoughtful-experience, Heidegger tells us, "prevents any reflection on Being as Being" (208). The *a priori* relation assumes Being, thereby leaving it "unthought." The assumption that this *a priori* is a "first cause," or a "supreme being as the Absolute," or the "condition of possibility of all objectivity" are all manifestation of taking for granted that Being is already there as the metaphysical ground of beings. Heidegger wishes to explore not only the origin but also the purpose of these metaphysical assumptions or events. It is for this reason that he raises again Leibniz's question: "why are there beings at all, and why not rather nothing?"

The first "why question" of metaphysics seems to lead to an inquiry into the first cause and the "highest existent ground of beings," which Heidegger calls the *theion*. Heidegger claims this question is not only endogenous to the Biblical tradition, but is also part of the metaphysics of Plato and Aristotle (209). Metaphysics is taken to mean "thinking the being as such [...] approached by Being" but thought "on the basis of and with reference to beings." Such metaphysics for Heidegger is "inherently theology." As such,

Heidegger adds, ontology would also be "simultaneously and necessarily theology" (209).

The assimilation of ontology, metaphysics, and theology is, according to Heidegger, neither scholastic, nor doctrinal. Heidegger draws from Nietzsche to explain what he means by this assimilation: the ontology of beings in Nietzsche is will to power, it "thinks *essentia* as will to power." It also thinks the *"existentia* of beings as such and as a whole theologically as the eternal recurrence of the same." In the expression "God is dead" there is an onto-theological negation rather than an atheistic affirmation: this negation brings metaphysical nihilism to "fulfilment."[26] In Heidegger's reading of Nietzsche, the "death of God" is an affirmation (a negation of a negation) within the purview of theism.[27]

But still, Heidegger notes that the association of ontology and theology seems to leave the question of Being "unthought." The onto-theological perspective thinks being in terms of *essentia* and *existentia*: ontology takes being in terms of *existentia* and extrapolates from it an essential "Ground" or possible first cause; theology, in turn, takes from ontology the *"essentia* of the being" and makes from it a representation. But Heidegger is uneasy about this formulation: in the traditional account of the history of metaphysics neither ontology nor theology think the question of Being (210). The reason for this apparent oblivion is because, for Heidegger, the question of Being unconceals a "nothingness" independent of the dualism of *essentia* and *existentia*: the question of Being remains unthought by dualistic speculation. Heidegger's sweeping claim is that the independence of the *Seinsfrage* from the *essentia* and *existentia* distinction reveals that the question of Being in the history of metaphysics has remained unthought and without a name.

From another level, Heidegger seems to be making the case for some kind of "qualified non-dualism." He proposes a distinction between two notions: "transcendence" (*die Transzendenz*) and the "transcendental" (*das Transzendentale*). Metaphysics takes the fundamental "attribute" of being to be "transcendence" (*die Transzendenz*), to be "beyond," or "other." The transcendental takes the quality of being to reside in its possible *transition* toward its essence, its "whatness." In Kantian dualism, the critical limit of the entity as an object of experience appears to equate the "transcendental with the objectivity of the object" (211). Transcendence, on the other hand, means not the objectivity of the entity as subject, but the "comprehensive" intuition of the first cause that surpasses the entity, "looming over it in the perfect plenitude of what is essential" (211). Heidegger claims that metaphysical "ontology represents transcendence as the transcendental," that is, it takes a critical stance (a categorical "whatness") to limit entities as objects of experience. It takes therefore metaphysics to define objects in their objective "whatness." Theology, on the other hand, "represents transcendence as the transcendent," that is, takes created entities to participate in a "larger" realm encompassing a first cause, as well as its essential perfect plenitude.

To put it sharply: while theology is after wholesomeness in creation, ontology is after objective "measure." Onto-theology relies on the *essentia/ existentia* distinction. Yet, in Heidegger's thinking, bringing together ontology and theology misses the question of Being because, again, it believes it has already thought Being, which it takes tautologically to be "the being, in so far as the being is" (211). Such metaphysics for Heidegger is "nihilism proper." We would need to re-learn what it means to say that Being remains unthought: "perhaps that is all our thought has to learn in advance." Being (*das Sein*) remains unthought in traditional metaphysics because metaphysics deals with the "whatness" of the being (*das Seiende*) as such. Heidegger, however, introduces a new distinction: "essentially correct" metaphysics which, as opposed to dualistic metaphysics, clears or unconceals the entity: it avoids asking "inadequate questions" that would lead to "searching in vain" (212). The metaphysical problem here is how to distinguish unconcealed "nothingness" from vain "nullity." Cleared metaphysics takes the unconcealment of the entity to be the essence of truth (*das Wesen der Wahrheit*). Heidegger implies that "we have to free ourselves from the customary conception of a merely subjective representation of objects inside our heads" and have to "become engaged in the mode of *Dasein* we already are."[28]

Heidegger in other words is saying, in the language of Nietzsche's *Birth of Tragedy*, that traditional metaphysics gives pre-eminence to Apollonian form and structure, but seems forgetful of the deep solidarity of the Dionysian dimension.[29] In itself, Apollonian form lacks *a-lethic* conscience, thus paradoxically Nietzsche speaks of Apollonian "dream." Apollonian metaphysics, without the Dionysian, "leaves Being itself unthought." What Heidegger seems to be saying is that the "being as a being," the Apollonian in the Dionysian, remains essentially unthought: "but because Being itself remains unthought, the unconcealment of beings too remains unthought" (212).[30]

Heidegger asserts that the "unthought forgetfulness of Being is the self-same" forgetfulness of the entity. The unconcealment of being depends on the unforgetfulness of Being: it is a mutual revelation. Again, using the clarifying imagery of Nietzsche, a dualistic *either/or* between "Apollo" and "Dionysus" prevents the mutual opening of the unconcealment of being and the unforgetfulness of Being. The metaphysical dualism of *essentia* and *existentia* prevents their mutual revelation.

This occluded disclosure appears to be coeval with the unthought question. Metaphysics thinks Being in terms of the *essentia/existentia* distinction. The "concepts" of *essentia* and *existentia* assume metaphysical dualism while "repudiating Being as what is to be thought expressly" (213). Metaphysics takes Being as being within its conceptual domain. Thus, Being itself "stays away" from metaphysics. For metaphysics Being "stands in view," as the self-evident "Being of beings."

Heidegger, at some level, seems to be suggesting that Being itself (in the form of a question) occurs "essentially" when the being "comes to presence."[31] Yet, in this manifestation Being itself "stays away" (*Das Sein selbst bleibt aus*). There is a double concealment of Being—Being conceals its concealment: the "staying away" of Being, its veiling, is the way in which Being occurs in "default" (*Ausbleiben*). It is "the nothing as Being itself" (*das Nichts als das Sein selbst*). Heidegger then poses the question: "do we dare think the possibility that the nothing [*das Nichts*] is infinitely different from vacuous nullity?"

Heidegger therefore wonders and is concerned about how such non-positivist concealing (*Verbergung*) is to be thought. He continues: "is concealing simply a veiling or is it at the same time a storing away and preserving"? Is the "withholding" of Being a "refusal"? (214). Perhaps Being itself "is" in its "default"; but if that is the case, then how does Being "strike our thinking"? Can we foresee features, qualities, or attributes of Being given its "default"?

Even the name "Being" seems inadequate for this exploration. Heidegger claims another "name" might be needed to explore the question; apparently the question resonates in an all-too-human manner when represented under the rubric of "Being" (215). Being would need to be "other than itself, so decisively other that it even 'is' not." Although Heidegger grants this sounds excessively "dialectical," he assures us that "in terms of the matter, it is something other." Still, Hegelian dialectics, in all its willfulness, seems unable to intimate this otherness. Heidegger voices a view of Being as "self-refusing preserving," and "essential self-withdrawal," that somehow remains in view as "the Being of beings." Heidegger, however, finds an "abandonment" of Being toward beings as a whole, and not only toward the being with the "shape of man." Being withdraws from man—Being withdraws from being its truth. This withdrawal has momentous consequences: it is an "event" (*Ereignis*) in the history of Being. This "event" manifests itself as a history in which there is "nothing to Being itself" (215). As a consequence, during this time, "Being itself has remained unthought." This oblivion of Being at the same time seems to be coeval with the unfolding of nihilism.

Hence Heidegger makes the paradoxical claim that the "essence" of nihilism is the "event" that withdraws the unconcealed concealment of Being in the history of metaphysics (216). This double negation of the veiled character of Being is what for Heidegger makes the question resistant to "reification" or graphic depiction. In our epoch Being "is" in its default mode.

The thinking that attunes itself to the *Seinsfrage* may or may not hit the mark or harmonize itself with the question: "thinking is not an independent activity over against Being." Such attunement is not to be grasped in terms of the (inter) subjective ego, nor is it a mere inner feeling—it seems to be embodied in a meditative and affective disposition (*Bestimmung*) that calls man back from self-forgetting in "the They" (*das Man*), towards awareness of his authentic projection—a recollection "with understanding" to thoughtfully become who you are.[32]

Five

Heidegger draws our attention back to Descartes. Heidegger claims that, in contrast to the mode of Cartesian representation, or of Kantian autonomy, "thinking belongs to Being itself." This assertion seems unclear, perhaps because we are used to thinking in terms of a subject and object distinction, so Heidegger tries to describe what mode of thinking he is taking to heart: "Being itself is not something that keeps itself isolated somewhere. From what could it separate itself in any case?" (217). The *ego cogito* assumes a separate or "closed" status that has a hard time understanding the openness of *Da-sein*. The *ego cogito* refrains from dwelling in the opening of Being that "persists in a difference with respect to beings." Heidegger's point seems to be to challenge the notion of the self-enclosed "subject," instead foreseeing a mode of singularity that at the same time would be fundamental openness. From such ontological openness, Heidegger tells us, there "comes to be a relation to something like a place," a "shelter in which the default of unconcealment essentially persists" (217). That "shelter" (*Unterkunft*) or "place" (*Ortschaft*) is the "essence of man" (*das Wesen des Menschen*).

Heidegger's description dwells in the "spirit" of negation: the "shelter" of Being is the "locale of its advent as the abode of the default." It is, he tells us, a localized or specific "where," a "there" that pertains to Being itself: "it 'is' Being itself and is therefore called *being-there (Da-sein)*" (218).[33] But the allusion to the concreteness of *being-there* does imply a sensibility and gratitude to a particular place that is not a generic "space," but a cared-for locale, in time, where *Dasein* can find his or her "voice" and caring "presence."[34] The openness of being to Being heightens and gives meaning to the relation between being and beings, in so far as being is *there*. Differently put, the Aristotelian prospect of "human flourishing" requires a political realm to take place: the point of contention here would be the degree of openness and boundedness required of every particular political "horizon."[35] Aristotle also, correctly in my view, argues that although the political life has a dignity of its own, it is not sufficient for a life of complete realization or happiness (*teleia eudaemonia*). He reserves that prospect to the life of *theoria.*[36]

For Heidegger the truth of *being-there* finds its tone and manner in its attunement to the question. "The *Da-sein* in man" belongs to the essence of Being itself. This belonging is not a product of autonomous self-making: it is a "standing" in the unconcealment of beings as "the concealed locale within which Being essentially occurs in its truth" (218). This opens an *ek-static*

relation in Being, essentially everywhere and always. This stance is for Heidegger the essence of thinking.[37] Heidegger contends that an "experience" of
thinking on the basis of Being does not set off an independent domain from
the experiences of "willing" (*Wollen*) and "feeling" (*Fühlen*). Hence thinking
is not a manifestation of pure theory as contrasted to "practical activity,"
which would limit its "essential importance for the essence of man" (218).
What this meditation (*Besinnung*) seems to imply is that the question of
Being offers an opening for the "post-critical" (that is to say, post-Kantian)
recollection of the "essence of man." In this meditative eventuality in his
thinking man is "approached by Being." The opening of essential possibilities for man's *being-there* is cleared by such thinking; and yet, the opening
also "withdraws," revealing-and-concealing itself in beings, while resting on
Being itself.

This contrast of withdrawal and restfulness of Being is what allows man
to relate meaningfully to beings as such (219). That is why man can become
a poised thoughtful "person" (rather than being possessed or carried away by
some unspecified "obsessive compulsion"). It is the manner in which thinking, and therefore language, "brings Being in the form of a being."[38] At the
same time, however, there seems to be a lack of correspondence between
thinking and the "withdrawal of Being." The problem with *representational
thought* is that it omits this lack of correspondence, dispensing with Being as
such, taking thinking and abstract geometrical deliberation to be identical
(Heidegger seems to evoke here Pascal's distinction between *l'esprit de la
finesse* and *l'esprit de la geometrie*). If Being is taken as "condition of
beings," and as such it is posited—"as if"—by being, then being turns "Being" into a "value" (219).[39] Thus the apparent conditionality of "Being"
"seals" its interpretation as "value." Heidegger is trying to release and therefore open that seal.[40] This interpretation seems coeval with the apparent
"yes-saying" to beings, or to the affirmation of the will to power as the mode
to overcome nihilism. In other words, Heidegger reiterates that Nietzsche's
overcoming "is merely the fulfilment of nihilism." As such, for Heidegger
Nietzsche remains tied to the problem his thinking is trying to overcome.
Nietzsche is not unaware of this problem: hence his mature writings are put
forth only as a "prelude to a philosophy of the future."

The key problem in the nihilistic period of transition, Heidegger contends, is that the default of Being is "authentic" (219).[41] But if the default is
taken only as a metaphysical or abstract phenomenon, then the authenticity
of the event would be missed. Metaphysics, as representational thought,
omits the "default" in the double sense of omitting the omission.

But Heidegger, as usual, introduces a further complication: the apparent
"authenticity" of nihilism is not truly authentic. In so far as nihilism is conceived only metaphysically or "structurally" or "geometrically" it is not experienced in its authentic dimension. Heidegger claims that "the authenticity

of nihilism takes the form of inauthenticity" (220). The default of Being makes beings authentically inauthentic: in a far-reaching lack of self-awareness, sophistication attains the cusp of naiveté. Thereby Heidegger finds that "the full essence of nihilism is the original unity of its authenticity and inauthenticity": an oxymoron, it would seem, in the "form" of a foolish wisdom.

More specifically, what this seems to mean is that inauthenticity attempts to explain nihilism *conceptually*. Nihilism is not experienced as such, it is not "incorporated" and meditated upon as the opening of the question, but is taken as mere psycho-pathology: a type of neurosis to be grasped, articulated, and if necessary pharmacologically normalized, mistaking this kind of undetermined anxiety to be a mere malfunction of human behavior.[42] Now, a caveat is required here: the point of being attuned to the deeper affective dispositions—anxiety, boredom, *Schuld*, etc.—is not to indulge in gloomy romanticism or some kind of dense passive-aggressive *ressentiment*; the understanding of our inner dispositions requires the clarity to discern genuine possibilities, our true "calling" and "voice," such that we may experience an intimation of authentic empowerment (an inner "wake-up call" to pursue what we truly love) and not an excuse for melancholic self-evasion.[43] Freudian psychoanalysis assumes the subject-object distinction of the *ego cogitans*, and as such misses the point of bringing together, in the language of Nietzsche, the Apollonian-and-Dionysian core of human singularity.[44]

Conditional metaphysics—the metaphysics of the "as if"—fails to see that Being "stays away." But for Heidegger even this "inauthenticity" of nihilism, in so far as Being and time are not altogether unrelated, is also somehow "determined" by Being itself. Even the non-essential seems to belong to the essential (221). The inauthenticity of nihilism lies in its inability to experience the "abandonment of beings as such by Being itself." Yet, Heidegger claims that the essence of nihilism is not a product of mere human cognition, nor of mere human willing, but a "matter of Being itself, and therefore also a matter of the *essence* of man" (Heidegger's italics). Heidegger concludes that this is an "originary" relationship that is apparently not to be understood in terms of "mere causal relations."

But is not the absence of the question of nihilism itself a nihilistic "development"? What is the "common root" of nihilism? In this train of reasoning Heidegger seems to be giving some kind of agency to Being: "Being itself has brought it to pass in history that there is nothing to Being itself" (222). It is unclear, however, how Heidegger can justify that Being would have the attribute of agency, when Being remains a question, even "a questionable question."[45]

However this may be, Heidegger notes that the "decline" that seems to be at the core of nihilism is also intimately linked to its opposite: "ascent versus decline, waxing versus waning, exaltation versus degradation, construction versus destruction, all play their roles as counterphenomena in the realm of beings" (222). The "momentum" of nihilism seems to mirror a return to the classical cosmovision of the rise and fall of civilizations. Yet, there still is something distinctly "negative" about contemporary European nihilism; otherwise it would be too general, thereby missing to mean any-thing beyond a historiological extrapolation. The "negative" character of European and now increasingly global nihilism is the negation of authenticity *in the realm of Being* brought to the fore in our time.

Nihilism is the concealed inauthenticity of what seems an authentic realm of beings: the oblivion of self-overcoming. What does "overcoming" (*Überwindung*) mean? Heidegger offers a concise definition: "to bring something under oneself, and at the same time to put what is thus placed under oneself behind one as something that will henceforth have no determining power" (223). Overcoming, however, is not a frictionless exercise: as a mode of affirmation it seems to have the character of passionate self-actualization. In a way, the voluntaristic "overcoming of nihilism" can be an "affront" against Being. Can Being, even in its default mode, be overcome?

Heidegger notes that such overcoming "can never be accomplished" because it would "unhinge the essence of man." Even in its default mode, Being is the "hinge" or "abode" of the essence of man. It is from such abode that Being may proceed with the "advent of unconcealment" (224). Heidegger thinks the overcoming of Being falls in the realm of impossibility: it is no more absurd than to try to deny that there are beings as such.

I take this to be the core of "historicity" (*die Geschichtlichkeit*) for Heidegger: the impossibility of overcoming Being. In a way, our historicity can also be a gift in our pursuit of self-knowledge. But this historicity is by no means "post-metaphysical": the renunciation of Being itself would be coeval with renouncing the spirit of man's "essential possibility." Yet, apparently, despite the logical inconsistency, the renunciation of Being could be "fatefully realized." This statement seems to mirror the Augustinian predicament of human freedom.[46] The impossibility of overcoming Being has, from our human perspective, the character of a free choice: a choice that might well be at the core of the human predicament. Heidegger, however, takes a step back and also seems to be making a "dialectical" distinction between linear "logic" and "cyclical" fate.[47] In his interpretation of Nietzsche's metaphysics, Heidegger claimed that the notions of (linear) will to power and (cyclical) eternal return can be reconciled. How does Heidegger propose to bring about such reconciliation? How are these two notions tied to the problem of European nihilism?

Six

For Heidegger the "essential feature" of nihilism is the omission of Being. The "overcoming" of nihilism, in so far as it appears to overcome the omission of Being, by believing and persevering in the omission, lies in "authentic inauthenticity." In a way, Heidegger seems to associate this paradox with inauthentic "willing." But the omission of Being for Heidegger also seems to take the form of a "metaphysics" of mere "presence," which fails to think being in its "unconcealment." The effort of thinking for Heidegger has a "necessary" character (avoiding *non sequiturs*?) and seems to be manifested in a mode of philosophical anthropology which "implies that man experience the omission" of Being, that is, that man thoughtfully face the inauthenticity of the oblivion as the essence of nihilism (224). "Authentic inauthenticity," our "lost spirit," dwells in an *aporetic*, or "perplexed" mode of reason that nevertheless seems to keep willing for the sake of will.[48]

Now, in order to be "authentic" inauthenticity would presuppose a prior condition of authenticity: to have been "struck . . . by the default of Being in its unconcealment."[49] For Heidegger it is in accord with the "essential relationship of Being to man" that the default of Being be experienced in human *thought.* In terms of human thinking there seems to be a liaison between the default and the advent of the *Seinsfrage.* Heidegger claims the "overcoming" of nihilism is not simply the triumph of a "secular age," which he would perhaps take to be in the mode of a triumph of "sheer willing" (225).[50] Instead of such overcoming, Heidegger seems to be proposing that the "one thing needful" would be to remain steady in the kind of thinking that, "encouraged by Being itself," persists in the simplicity of the encounter with the default of Being. Being withdraws, but such withdrawal is inherent in the relation of Being to the essence of man. Withdrawal and the eventuality of advent find their abode in the unconcealment of Being (225). The unconcealment cannot be willfully controlled or planned by man.[51] Yet, it is also no mere passivity: unconcealment has the character of a thoughtful encounter— thinking begins the encounter by reconsidering the "veiled figure of the *essence* of man."

The unconcealment of Being seems to have the character of an address, an insinuation to the essence of man: Being is "the promise to itself" (226).[52] The encounter with the default of Being is to become aware of the "promise" of Being to itself. By way of the promise Being itself "is." The concealment of Being is the history of this promise. The history of such concealment has the character of a "mystery" (*das Geheimnis*).

Now, Heidegger makes a distinction between inauthentic metaphysics and the "essence of metaphysics": "*The essence of metaphysics consists in that it is the history of the secret of the promise (des Versprechens) of Being itself*" (227, Heidegger's Italics). So, there are two kinds of metaphysics: the "metaphysics of presence" tout court that Heidegger seems to reject, and "essential metaphysics," which has the veiled character of a "promise."[53] Since the character of the "promise" unfolds in the mode of a mystery, the essence of metaphysics cannot be assessed "positively or negatively." The promise has the character of a question.

But the question of Being in Heidegger's thinking is not coeval with perennial philosophy. Heidegger claims that the essence of metaphysics is attained by thinking in terms of the "history of Being" (227). This is the "essential provenance" of metaphysics. Every metaphysical "concept" bars access to the essence of metaphysics. Meanwhile, even the self-withdrawal of Being is part of the mode of the advent of Being: the thoughtful awareness of the self-veiling of Being admits its originary revealing unconcealment, "which is Being itself."

The inauthenticity of the history of metaphysics is not an isolated unfolding: "it takes place in an essential unity with the authenticity of nihilism" (228). The "metaphysics of presence" is not just a colossal mistake, but seems to be also a mode of *pathein mathein,* a learning through suffering that apparently goes from Plato to Nietzsche and that finds its fulfilment in the opening of the question of essential metaphysics. Hence, Heidegger claims that in the fulfilment of metaphysics "the essence of metaphysics reaches deeper than metaphysics itself."[54] At this stage in Heidegger's speculation, he asserts that "according to its essence nihilism is the history of the promise, in which Being itself saves itself in a mystery which is itself historical, and which preserves the unconcealment of Being from that history in the form of metaphysics" (228).[55] Heidegger calls the thought that engages in the "whole essence of nihilism" the "riddle" (*das Rätsel*).[56] As enigma or riddle Being gives "food for thought,"[57] "always" and from "every point of view." The question of Being is for Heidegger not perennial philosophy, because the origin of the question seems to lead beings to thoughtfully-singular ways in which they may find their substance. Heidegger, therefore, does not wish to imply that Being has an idiosyncratic character: in giving "food for thought," Being "gives what is to be thought."

Thought seems to be both wayfaring and "release." Heidegger's suggestion seems to be that a stark distinction between Being and nothingness *from a human perspective* loses its sharpness.[58] But Heidegger here takes a step back: doesn't this enthusiastic train of reasoning lead us to "romanticism" and hence to escape from "true reality"? (229).[59] Does not the fatefulness of this reasoning compromise our capacity for (political) "resistance"? Heidegger claims to be painfully aware of the "spreading violence of actual nihilism": a nihilism that Nietzsche himself foresaw and experienced spiritually. Again, the crisis of nihilism is not an abstract disembodied problem. It is an embodied problem that as such has a history. Ontologically speaking, the crisis is tied to the confusion as to whether the "'essence' of Being comes from beings," or "whether the effectuality that stems from Being itself calls forth everything actual" (230). From a human perspective, however, this appears to be an *either/or* between human "autonomy" and comprehensive "providence" that seems to do deep injustice to the complexity of history and human agency. Heidegger might be suggesting that at the core of nihilism there is a rift between our "autonomous" human experience, and an *either/or* mode of reason.

Heidegger takes us back to Nietzsche's account of nihilism in *The Will to Power* aphorism 2: "The upper values devalue themselves," which means that "the aim is lacking; the 'why' receives no answer." Heidegger puts emphasis on the "why" of the question. The why-question in Heidegger's reading is comprehensive and singular and pertains to the "vocation" of beings: it "interrogates beings as such and as a whole, *asking them why they are in being*" (230, emphasis mine). It asks about the ground or fundamental reason of "what is and the way it is." But Heidegger wonders: how does reasoning in terms of values provide a satisfactory answer to this question? To put the question in the language of values is to misplace the question: it takes the region of representational cogitation as the horizon for ultimate purposes—it is as such "bound to fall short" (230).

Nietzsche highlights that the answer to the question "why" is lacking. The lack of this question for Heidegger "governs all questioning": it is coeval with the "actual omission of the default of Being itself" (231). For Heidegger this omission is not an abstract point, but an occurrence in the "essential unfolding of the history of Being" of epic proportions. Nietzsche's "metaphysics" interprets Being in terms of value, that is, in terms of the metaphysics of will to power. Will to power seems to be the principle of the "new valuation"; a valuation that would presumably overcome nihilism. For Heidegger, however, this would be an inauthentic overcoming: an overcoming under the effectual guise of a "deracinated essence" (231).[60] The question for Heidegger at this stage of the meditation seems to be about the rootlessness of valuative thinking as being coeval with nihilism.

The "putative overcoming" of nihilism, the apparent "normative" triumph of valuative thinking, takes for granted the absolute absence of the question of Being, favoring the dominion of beings "in the form of valuative will to power." From this angle, being seems to "reign above and over all Being," leading to the most "extreme omission." This leads to the proud acquiescence to what is subject to measure as what is "most effectual," what is "palpable" and "makes an impression," what is "useful and its success" (232). Still, Heidegger wonders whether the unfolding of the will to power might be congruent with "essential nihilism," or whether it is only a mere "phantasy." Heidegger seems to draw from some kind of Hegelianism: in so far as nihilism is essential, it would thereby seem to be "real" in terms of unfolding in the history of Being.

But, naturally, questions arise about the approximation of the "real" and the "actual": how to envision the distinction between inauthentic and authentic nihilism? What is their degree of divergence? How, and to what "measure," is man to be affected by the withdrawal of Being? How to reconcile the evident cruelty of effective history with the concealed unconcealing of Being?

For Heidegger man is the "abode of the advent of Being" (233). Man here is a receptacle of such advent: the advent "grants itself the abode."[61] The advent of Being is a riddle, an "enigma for thinking." This thought in Heidegger not only is an admission but, as we have seen, also has the character of an unrelenting question. It insists on thinking the essence of the "self-veiled truth of Being." Heidegger contends, however, that this is a preparatory mode of thinking that is blocked by representational cogitation which takes "Being in the sense of the being as such," making it "lapse into beings," seizing thereby beings in a binary subject-object relation.

Representational thinking leads to the view of "truth" as "certainty for and against being" aiming at objectification and the "complete ordering of beings, in the sense of systematic securing of stockpiles, by means of which the establishment in the stability of certainty is to be completed" (234). Heidegger associates the primacy of will mediated by representational subjectivity with the "objectification of all being as such." This structure includes for Heidegger apparently "all transcendence, whether it be ontological or theological." Therefore, the metaphysics of subjectivity seems to rule "onto-theological" relations; the identification of "Being" with value leaves the "question of Being unthought, it is a product of the will to power." The modern "metaphysics of subjectivity" fore-closes the question of Being.

As a consequence, the "essence of man" understood as the "abode" of Being becomes more and more "uncertain," but the origin of this perplexity remains undefined. Man seeks the solution to this anxiety in the affirmation of the *ego cogitans*: doing one's "job" through the affirmation of human methodical will power. Despite the apparent success in the "ordering" and "securing" of beings, deep down the unspecified anxiety seems to increase. Heidegger takes the source of this anxiety to mean that "man, particularly in relation to his own essence, is at stake" (235). Heidegger's contention seems to be that the problem of "civilization and its discontents" has more relevant dimensions than those conceived by social scientific positivism.

Seven

Heidegger notes that Nietzsche tried to intimate his experience of metaphysical perplexity in a poem, under the theme of "Songs of Prince *Vogelfrei*," published as an appendix to the 1887 edition of *Die Fröhliche Wissenschaft*.[62]

Heidegger signals the expression "world-play" (Welt-Spiel)[63] as "the ruling" that gives manifestation to the will to power. Such will to power finds its basis in positing "Being" in "unity with 'semblance' (art) as the condition for its own enhancement" (236).[64] Yet, the blending of "Being" and will to power is referred to in the poem as "eternal fooling" (*das Ewig-Närrische*). "Being" as will to power is poetically expressed as "eternal fooling" and the "world-wheel, spinning by." Heidegger takes this to mean that in Nietzsche's poem man is a "configuration of will to power" that is mixed by "the blending power of the world-wheel 'into' the whole of becoming-being" (237). Heidegger thereby interprets the poem as depicting the human process of self-actualization or self-overcoming where becoming-and-being partake in a cyclical (but open) continuum. This is a "metaphysical domain of the thought of the will to power as the eternal recurrence of the same" which seems to lead to the final line: "eternally such fooling, mixes *us* in—the melee" (237).[65]

This perspective somehow seems to merge the cyclical eternal recurrence of the same and the linear will to power. But notice that it is not a vain glorious triumph, but rather an eternal fooling that affirms a melee, a skirmish, or scuffle that might be after all unnecessary. Heidegger claims that the language of traditional metaphysics—*essentia* and *existentia*—has defined this movement in the history of metaphysics. He also adds that the notion of "necessity" is not mentioned in the poem. Will to power as fundamental fact, would ultimately be a "will-to-will" based on the metaphysics of subjectivity, attaining its practical "peak" in its identification of the eternal recurrence of the same.[66]

In the transitional period of nihilism, Heidegger signals that "metaphysically" the being (*das Seiende*) "at times reveals itself as the will-to-will as such, and at times it conceals itself again" (238). This oscillation of bipolar voluntarism ("grit") and disenchanted self-oblivion seems to define large segments of modern subjectivity. This mode of cogitation is "structurally" oblivious of Being and seems therefore to be ruled by the liaison of the "I-and-we subject," an inner state of disoriented "vanity" and "averageness" Heidegger calls "the They" (*Das Man*).[67]

For Heidegger the centrality of the *ego cogito* means that the being operates in the mode of mere (inter)subjectivity: the subject under this mode grasps for means of certainty and security under the obliviousness of the default of Being. On the other hand, Heidegger claims that even in such circumstances *"Being itself occurs essentially as such keeping to itself"* (238, Heidegger's Italics). Being "manifests" itself not necessarily by means of "proofs" but, rather indirectly, by way of "hints." The affirmation of certainty is a mode of reasoning of the metaphysics of subjectivity. The question then becomes how to heed the hints, despite their evident lack of certainty (238).[68]

Eight

The omission of the default, the withdrawal that conceals itself, according to Heidegger, is in keeping with the "determination" (*Bestimmung*) of this epoch in the history of Being. This "temporizing" of Being in its default marks the epoch of the history of metaphysics of subjectivity. This epoch is coeval with the primacy of beings, which, as such, attempt to establish their exclusive "boundless" dominion through representational thinking. Beings appear as will to power ruled by valuative thinking: this seems to bring about the fulfillment of the epoch of subjective metaphysics. "Value thinking" is the mode of representation that epitomizes this epoch: the fixity on and progress toward security and permanence apparently closed off from the "truth of Being" (239). Yet this closing off offers a paradoxical condition: it appears as a "liberation [*die Befreiung*] from all metaphysics."[69] The closing off of the question under the mode of *Befreiung* marks according to Heidegger the predominance of nihilism and inauthenticity. Meanwhile, authenticity remains "submerged in the inaccessible and unthinkable" (239). Apparently, the nihilism of inauthenticity reveals "destructive features" in the realm of thinking. The "omission of the default of Being" leads to the confusion of seeking in metaphysics, antimetaphysics, and past metaphysics an anchor to overcome this confusion. Heidegger here associates non-essential metaphysics with what we would refer to as "ideology."

Ideological commitment, the fixing of valuative thought in terms of distinct willful "doctrines" made by representational subjectivity, believes it is overcoming nihilism by means of practice, but, since it starts from nihilistic premises—the metaphysics of subjectivity—it only furthers the oblivion of the question (240). It leads to the mistaken and naive self-complacency that it has overcome not only nihilism, but also metaphysics per se.

On the other hand, there seems to occur a "lapse" in the history of Being: "authentically existing history" does not find public space in inauthentic nihilism, and thus "lapses into the unhistorical." In the epoch of the default of the question there seem to be two venues for thinking: ideological "struggle" and a "retreat from historical consciousness" in the mode of "philosophies of consolation."[70] Heidegger, however, takes this "lapse" to lead to a third possibility: the emergence of the "scientific" study of history, that is, looking at history from the lens of "objectified" cause-and-effect: this mode of grasping history is tied to the goal of "mastery of beings" on the basis of willing a "comprehensible order" of "world-historical" proportions (240).[71] Despite these distinctions, Heidegger claims that "History as Being [*Geschichte als Sein*] . . . remains unthought" (241). The question for Heidegger seems to be how to remain attentive to the metaphysical character of history, while preventing "historiological thought" (i.e., "post-metaphysics") to claim that it can enlighten us when what it does is assert inauthentic nihilism.

What would Heidegger mean by "inauthentic nihilism"? In the withdrawal of the truth of Being, objectification of "human resources" transforms people into stockpiles, instrumentalizing man in the process of the "will-to-will." This process, depending on one's position in the chain, will seem, to some "free," to others "alienating" and merely mechanical. However, paradoxically because even the default of Being has been forgotten this process will even appear reasonably "spiritual": it will appear as if the process of enlightenment has reached some kind of apotheosis, and therefore the rational society, at least in principle, only needs to be implemented forward (241).[72]

The objectification of beings turns mankind into a "human resource," akin to "natural resources and raw materials" under the logic of safety and possession. What this means for Heidegger is that "the absolute objectification of the being as such results from the self-fulfilling dominion of subjectivity" (242). It is an increasing inner fragmentation of beings closed off from the default of Being "in the midst of the thoroughgoing securing of beings." This process finds "legitimacy" in the consensual public discourse of value thinking: mere "publicity" becomes a "necessary value for securing the permanence of the will to power." Such publicity takes Being to be a value, and as such turns being into non-being: "but the being (*das Seiende*), thus objectified, is nonetheless not what *is*." What "is" is what "is there" *in accordance with the essence of Being.* But for mere being there are no essential questions: "fortuna" does not control only about half of our circumstances[73] but is taken to encompass the whole human domain to be reasonably secured under valuative thinking.

Heidegger contends that "Being as the history of the default" occurs when man does not recognize that "his essence has been withheld from him" (243). But the process of seeking this awareness of the default does not seem to have the character of an overcoming. Rather, Heidegger tells us, "the historical relation of man to the essence of nihilism can only consist in his thoughtfully undertaking to think the encounter of the default of Being itself." This implies, somehow, coming "face to face" with nihilism in its essence. Nihilism cannot be overcome willfully: it cannot be "put behind" by mere volition because such overcoming would be an exercise in subjectivity, and it is precisely that mode of calculative "single-track" reasoning[74] that seems to have brought about non-essential nihilism in the first place.

Now, Heidegger claims that "thinking in terms of the history of Being lets Being arrive in the essential space of man" (243). Being cannot be willfully forced into appearance: it needs to be thoughtfully received in the human "abode." The unconcealment of Being finds "the same essential occurrence" in "lighting" (*lichten*), "arriving" (*ankommen*), "keeping to itself" (*ansichhalten*), "refusal" *(verweigern)*, "revealing" (*entbergen*), "concealing" (*verbergen*). But these are only allusions: upon examination, even the name

"Being" seems misleading, in so far as it suggests "presence and permanence (*Anwesenheit und Beständigkeit*).[75]

Perhaps another way to think the event would be that in *essential* "metaphysical thinking" man attempts to liberate his "essential space" (*Wesensraum*). This "essential space," Heidegger claims, is not a product of human subjectivity: it is "occasioned by Being in order that we think to encounter the advent of its default" (244). The aim of this presumably sacred or non-profane *being-there* would be to situate the meditative clearing facing "essential metaphysics," which would let-be the "open radius" for the experience of beings in dispositional as well as thoughtful attunement with the mystery of the *Seinsfrage*. But the "provenance" or "origin" (*die Herkunft*) of essential metaphysics still "remains to be thought." In our forgetfulness we seem to believe the sacred is either sentimental or irrational.

Heidegger reminds the reader that the withdrawal of the unconcealment of Being has the character of a "promise" (*Versprechen*). Again, Being finds relation to being in its concealed unconcealment: Being "compels" by laying claim to its abode in being. Such "compulsion" (*Nötigen*) of Being finds abode in man's essential calling. A calling where "Being itself is need." Man thereby experiences the "one thing needful"—his need for Being in Being's need. But this need manifests itself in the manner of an absence, which kindles a sense of longing: veiled "needful" Being remains away (245). But from another angle the "need for Being" does not seem particularly self-evident: being (*das Seiende*) thereby believes that it "is," and the illusion arises that "Being is without need."

For Heidegger the "compelling" need is not an unyielding necessity. It signals the abode of Being as the essence of man; it is such essence, the human abode, that is endangered by the oblivion of the default of Being. Heidegger claims that the "need of Being" ultimately comes to be the "need of needlessness." But the oblivion of the contemplative "need of needlessness" takes predominance in the non-essential, that is to say, inauthentic unfolding of nihilism. The oblivion "darkens beings" and seems to lead our age toward needless confusion, decay in human culture, fragmentation, and "impotence of willing" (245).

How can man regain the experience of essential need, especially if "in truth the need is a need of Being itself" (246)? Heidegger claims that the "need of Being" embodied in the essence of nihilism "perhaps" will bring "its authenticity to advent." But this is not a need that can be controlled or particularly forced by man. What man can do is experience as "needful" the needlessness as an essential occurrence of the quality of need; this seems to run parallel to the experience of the omission of the default of Being (246). The experience of the absence is the experience of the "essence of historical man." But this is a moment of danger: the absence of Being also threatens the historical essence of man. It is a dangerous mode of thinking that might be condemned as "irresponsible" and "groundless."

In other words, what did Nietzsche mean by his distinct exhortation to the free spirits to "live dangerously?"[76] Heidegger claims this expression of "active nihilism" belongs to the "metaphysics of the will to power." Heidegger, on the other hand, seems to evoke Kierkegaard at this point, but without mentioning him directly: the forceful "blindness" of the metaphysics of the will to power based on the omission of Being misses the thoughtful lament "in the face of the anxiety that experiences with trepidation the default of Being itself."[77]

The theoretically predictable clash of "wills" foreseen in the absence of the question finds itself resolving conflicts in terms of value-assessments: of optimistic "idealism" and of pessimistic "realism" *both* actualized through "merely brutal will." This seems to be a post-metaphysical but is in fact merely an ideological clash that ensues in terms of beings only. Both progressive and reactionary positions appear to miss thinking the "is" as determined by the truth of Being. Such "is" is taken for granted by beings: but the "is" becomes as questionable as the question of Being in the absence of the question (247). The return to the question is therefore a critique of political ideology.

More importantly, however, the absence of the question is also experienced as a closure of the divine: a process of disenchantment that consigns to homelessness the "essence of historical man." Man's homelessness, the lack of belonging to a "where," seems to signal the absence of a dwelling whereby "Being" itself could sensibly and thoughtfully find its abode (248).[78] Such homelessness, however, seems to drive man to attempt to overcome the oblivion in a future immanent conquest: this seems to be the origin of the hope that, once European nihilism be fully conquered, then the globe will become our "home."[79] In principle, for modern progressives this is their highest political goal, but for the classically oriented this is the source of the possibility of an unprecedented tyranny. It is in order to forestall this *either/or* that, in response to Heidegger and Marx, Hannah Arendt advocates an enlightened and classically aware *vita activa*.[80]

Increasingly, however, man seems to become fixated with the coordination and control of beings, becoming less inclined to "heed Being itself." The epoch of the "concealment of Being in the unconcealment of being," the apparent triumph of the consensually anthropocentric *ego cogito*, brings the "dominion of the nonessence of nihilism into its completeness" (248). This appears to be an epoch of unparalleled human empowerment: the fundamental questions appear to be practically solved, or at any rate practically solvable—all that is needed is to "proceed rightly to establish the dominion of justification as the supreme representative of the will-to-will" (248).

As man becomes unfamiliar with the destiny of Being, every time man thinks of Being he takes it to be an empty abstraction, mistaking is as "vacuous nothingness." Heidegger claims that the terms "Being" and "to be" are not recollected in their "essential historical fullness," and therefore sound only as "mere terms." The lack of "Being" is a lack of the "need of needlessness": a lack of meditative simplicity that, at times, might body-forth "in the stillness of Being's default" (249). But the man of the end of unessential metaphysics is drawn to "complexity" and ever-expanding "networks" that epitomize his "relational" control and power over beings. Such complexity is reinforced by the exertions of modern empirical science and increasingly global positive civil law.

Yet, for Heidegger the thinking of Being is neither a scientific nor an unscientific pursuit. It is a thinking that is not "for" or "against" but that would need to be attentive to the absence of the "is." The "need of needlessness" is coeval with the thinking of Being "according to its own essence in the history of Being" (249). The apparent triumph of 'metaphysics' has left our thinking of Being to occur in a tentative manner, at times borrowing the very tools that have been deployed in the history of metaphysics. Such *Seins-denken* at this point in time appears to be a reaching about uncertainly, staying in front of the question without sophistication, venturing a pathway toward the "open region" where the true mystery of Being is cleared essentially and freely (250).[81]

Heidegger finds in his reading of Nietzsche that the realm of man's essence is a "needlessness" of the most "extreme need."[82] A mode of freedom that evokes a destiny: a "call" that is a form of need, that nevertheless is not necessity.[83] Being reveals its worth in its "needful freedom," in the needlessness that nevertheless calls back to face the question. Man's thoughtful question—his need for truth—is Being's abode. This might well be "the very soul of hermeneutics."[84]

NOTES

1. Consider the following portrait of hermeneutics: "the experience of responding to and being captivated by a work of culture is not a solely an 'aesthetic' phenomenon, but rather, changes the very being who experiences it; [. . .] in confronting such a transformative object of understanding, one does not suspend who one is or where one comes from but attempts—in opening oneself to the truth of what is alien—to join what one already is with what addresses one; [. . .] the 'event' by which this truth discloses itself is not under the sovereign control of a 'subject,' but is rather the refutation of all subjectivism." Ronald Beiner *Philosophy in a Time of Lost Spirit: Essays on Contemporary Theory* (Toronto: University of Toronto Press, 1997), p. 102-103. Cf. Bernstein *Beyond Objectivism and Relativism*, p. 112-125.

2. Heidegger *Letter on Humanism*, p. 276. In the secondary literature *Besinnung* is also rendered in noun form as "mindfulness." The expression partakes in both verb and noun renditions, which seems consistent with Heidegger's intent. Cf. Martin Heidegger *Besinnung* (Klostermann: Frankfurt am Main, 1997).

3. In Gadamer's account of (Heideggerian) hermeneutics "the understanding of a text remains permanently determined by the anticipatory movement of the fore-understanding [. . .] not occasionally, but always, the meaning of a text goes beyond its author. That is why understanding is not merely reproductive, but always a productive attitude as well." *Truth and Method*, p. 261-62. There is, in the act of interpretation, a fidelity to the text that might expand toward the intelligibility of (creative) completion. We may wonder, however, whether Gadamer confuses "thinking" with "production" thereby assuming that knowing is a kind of making. Although some forms of knowing seem to be indistinguishable from "making" (poetry or architecture, for example), that does not mean that knowing in itself is a kind of *praxis*. At times, Gadamer misses that distinction.

4. Gadamer discusses the relation between movement, the forms of tradition, and the image of "horizon" in *Truth and Method*, p. 271-72. Intriguingly, Gadamer also references thinking as a "form of dancing" (102). This notion is explored in Nietzsche *Twilight of the Idols* "What the Germans Lack," sections 6-7; *Gay Science*, 366; see also Nietzsche's letter to Erwin Rohde (February 22nd, 1884). Hutter discusses the unification of Apollo and Dionysus in the figure of the "dancing Socrates" in *Shaping the Future*, p. 70-72; 179-199. The original reference of a "dancing Socrates" comes from Xenophon *Symposium* II, 1-24. The image of dance symbolizing harmonious movement as well as suppleness of mind might shed light on the apparent opposition between thinking and willing Arendt notices in Heidegger and in Nietzsche in *The Life of The Mind Vol. 2*, p. 179. Vallega-Neu *Contributions to Philosophy: An Introduction*, p. 5, depicts Heidegger's "tonalities" and the "movements of his thought" as a "dance lesson."On the other hand, the image of "meditation" conveys a sense of serene stillness and gathered repose that seems closer to classical *theoria*. "Dance" might be a released form of artful meditation. As a way to incorporate harmony and rhythm it is also of great political importance. Cf. Plato *Laws* 791a.

5. Heidegger *Being and Time*, Intro. I.4.B, p. 57; *What is Called Thinking?*, p. 207. Consider also W.W. Fortenbaugh *Aristotle on Emotion* (London: Duckworth, 2002), p. 67-69; Nietzsche *Dawn*, 306; 330. The qualified parallel between "*noeîn and aisthesis*" at some level might be analogous to Jane Austen's expression "sense and sensibility." Jesús Adrián Escudero discusses this theme along Aristotelian and Kantian lines in the thought of the young Heidegger in *Heidegger and the Emergence of the Question of Being* (London: Bloomsbury, 2015), p. 82-85.

6. Michel Haar *Nietzsche and Metaphysics*, p. 113, poses the following question: "Isn't Nietzsche a modern stoic?" But the eternal recurrence of the same, in Haar's reading, is a balancing act of Apollonian and Dionysian manifestations: "Dionysus regulated by the principle of reason, Apollo meets Dionysus. There is coincidence between the regulative principle of forms and the lucid dispensation of forces. Such paradoxical world, firm and lucid at the same time, both substantial and dreamlike excludes pure Apollonism and pure Dionysm" (p. 61). Contrast with Hegel *Phenomenology of Spirit*, Preface, Sections 10-11.

7. This seems consistent with Haar's Heideggerian reading of Nietzsche: "*Illusion* ('dream') recognized as such is illusion that has been [dispelled], not some illusion caught in the midst of its own confusion. The fact that the will to power can, and must, want illusion means that it is not mistaken itself, that it recognizes itself as the source of all perspectives, that it is 'in the true.'" Ibid. p. 61.

8. Heidegger *Basic Concepts*, p. 54-56; contrast with *Contributions to Philosophy*, Sections 33-34; 54-55.

9. Nietzsche *Thus Spoke Zarathustra*, III.15 "The Other Dance-Song." *Beyond Good and Evil*, 12; 19.

10. Heidegger *Letter on Humanism*, p. 275-76.

11. Otto Pöggeler *The Paths of Heidegger's Life and Thought*; Frederick Olafson "The Unity of Heidegger's Thought," in *The Cambridge Companion to Heidegger*, p. 97-121, make the case for the underlying unity of Heidegger's philosophical quest. I am not pursuing a study of Heidegger's entire *oeuvre* and exploring Heidegger's *Kehre* would be beyond the scope of this book. I can only flag the movement from Heidegger's early Husserlian focus on (Cartesian/Kantian) phenomenology, to a more classically attuned ontological receptivity that attempts to clear such dualism through the existential liaison of *aisthesis* and *noeîn*. Cf. *Being and Time*,

Intro. I.4.B, p. 57; Section 65, p. 370-380; Gadamer *Truth and Method*, 28; 111; 231; 258- 261; 325-33; 456-57; also, Heidegger's remarks on Plato's *Phaedrus* in *Nietzsche* Vol. I "The Will to Power as Art," Section 23. Raúl Echauri *Heidegger y la Metafisica Tomista*. Prefacio de Étienne Gilson. (Eudeba: Buenos Aires, 1970), links Heidegger's *Seinsfrage* with the Thomistic "historical discovery of being as *actus essendi*" (p. 14). Echauri coincides with Gilson that there seems to be a shared "trans-ontic" dimension in Heideggerian philosophy and Thomistic theology that would offer a speculative alternative to the clear-cut dualism, the subjective either/or of *noumena* and *phenomena* crystalized in Kantian philosophy (p. 8, 16). Heidegger, however, unlike Thomas Aquinas, does not seem to directly associate the question of Being with the creator God of the Abrahamic religions; rather, he seems to have in mind something like the *Nataraj*, the "dancing Shiva" of Hindu metaphysics, articulated in the language of Aristotelian philosophy. Consider Löwith *Nietzsche's Philosophy of the Eternal Return of the Same*, p. 113; Dallmayr *The Other Heidegger*, p. 112; J.L. Mehta "Heidegger and Vedanta: Reflections on a Questionable Theme," in Graham Parkes ed. *Heidegger and Asian Thought*, p. 15-45. Also, Nietzsche *Schopenhauer as Educator*, Section 3, p. 136-37; *Gay Science*, 335; *Dawn* 575. It might be worth noting that a large two-meter bronze statue of a "dancing Shiva," presented by the Department of Atomic Energy of India, stands on the grounds of the European Organization for Nuclear Research (CERN), in Geneva, near the Franco-Swiss border. CERN is known, among other things, for having been at the center of the invention of the internet, as well as for housing high-speed accelerators used for the study of sub-atomic particles. The image is meant to symbolize the "dance" of such particles.

12. Löwith *Nietzsche's Philosophy of the Eternal Recurrence of the Same*, p. 54-55.

13. In *Will to Power*, 749, Nietzsche brings up the notion of the "magic of the extreme," apparently in relation to the thought of utopia. Cf. Eric Voegelin "Wisdom and the Magic of the Extreme: A Meditation," in Ellis Sandoz ed. *Complete Works Vol. 12 Published Essays 1966-1985* (Baton Rouge: Louisiana State UP, 1990), Ch. 13. Löwith *Nietzsche's Philosophy of the Eternal Recurrence of the Same*, p. 176.

14. Heidegger here approximates the thought of Søren Kierkegaard. Cf. *Being and Time*, Section 40: "The Fundamental Mood of Anxiety as an Exceptional Disclosure of Dasein," and Sections 57-58: "Conscience as the Call of Care" and "Understanding the Call, and Guilt." In the second essay of the *Genealogy of Morals*, Nietzsche associates "guilt" with a sense of reciprocity, political promise-making, or the human awareness of having incurred "debt" ("the oldest and most primitive personal relationship," *GM* II, 8). Nietzsche, however, establishes a distinction between ontological "conscience" (*Gewissen*) and ontic "guilt" (*Schuld*) in *Gay Science*, 250 and 270-275. Nietzsche thinks highly of the former and seems to think that the latter, as a kind of fear, ought ultimately to be overcome. In other words, perhaps someone with Nietzsche's level of awareness (cf. *Dawn*, 233) would "promise" (that is to say, would overcome "forgetfulness" and gather trust) on the basis of conscience independent from guilt. This might shed light on the otherwise enigmatic aphorism 32 of *Beyond Good and Evil* where Nietzsche claims that the pre-historical "morality of consequences," and the succeeding "morality of intention" (which originated with the imperative "know thyself!") is, upon self-examination, undergoing in a certain sense a further self-overcoming in the most honest (*redlichsten*) "consciences of today" (*Gewissen von heute*). Such consciences in our *aussermoralische* period Nietzsche refers to as "living touchstones of the soul" (*lebendigen Probirsteinen der Seele*). Nietzsche is a conscientious thinker who learned to become guilt-free.

15. Cf. Heidegger *Being and Time*, Sections 55-57. Heidegger also names the call of conscience the "call of care." Care (*Sorge*) as the "Being of Dasein" is characterized by the unity of an existential constitution structured by finite projection, thrownness, and being with beings. Contrast with Nietzsche *Gay Science*, 270; *Dawn*, 53; 202.

16. Heidegger *Being and Time*, Section 55, p. 316: "We take the calling as a mode of discourse. Discourse articulates intelligibility. Characterizing conscience as a call is not just giving a 'picture,' like the Kantian representation of the conscience of a court of justice. Vocal utterance, however, is not essential for discourse, and therefore not for the call either; this must not be overlooked [. . .] the "voice" is taken rather as a giving-to-understand. In the tendency to disclosure which belongs to the call, lies the momentum of a push—of an abrupt arousal. The call is from afar unto afar. It reaches him who wants to be brought back." In my view,

Heidegger's thoughtful disclosure of conscience is not altogether incompatible with the Thomistic notion of "synderesis" or Platonic-Socratic "syn-eidesis." Cf. Etienne Gilson *The Philosophy of St. Thomas Aquinas*, Chs. XIII-XIV. Edward Andrew *Conscience and Its Critics: Protestant Conscience, Enlightenment Reason, and Modern Subjectivity* (Toronto: University of Toronto Press, 2001), p. 8-9; 21; 25, signals, in the context of British political history, features of the experience of conscience, particularly its antinomian character.

Consider also Joseph Ratzinger's interpretation of the Thomistic understanding of conscience as a mixture of *synderesis* and *anamnesis* (a balancing-act, it would seem, between the Platonic ideas and the myth of Er) in *El Elogio a la Conciencia: La Verdad Interroga al Corazón.* Spanish Trans. José Ramón Pérez Aranguena and L'Osservatore Romano. (Madrid: Ediciones Palabra, 2010), p. 26. In terms of Platonic psychology this might seem analogous to the attunement of heart and mind, *eros* and *thumos*, in the image of the chariot in Plato's *Phaedrus* 246a–254e.

17. Nietzsche *Will to Power, 2; Twilight of the Idols*, "The Four Great Errors," Sec. 7.

18. The difficulty seems to be that, for Heidegger, "freedom is the ground of the ground" *Pathmarks*, p. 134. How does Heidegger reconcile the ground of human freedom with the question of Being? This seems to be the "Grundfrage" of the *Letter on Humanism:* how, for what motive, and by whom the ontological and the ontic realms might be orchestrated together.

19. In Strauss' reading the key eidetic formulation for Plato's Socrates is the "what is" (*to ti esti*) question. Strauss remarks that: "the 'what is' questions point to 'essences,' to 'essential differences.'" Cf. *The City and Man*, p. 19; 119-121; Aristotle *Physics* 202 b35. From a more introspective level, Nietzsche also seems to share this "structural" focus; for instance, in the subtitle of *Ecce Homo* (his philosophical autobiography) he writes: "*Werde man wird, was man ist*" "How one becomes *what* one is." As Tracy Strong points out, the reference is to "what" and not "who." *The Cambridge Companion to Nietzsche* Bernd Mangus and Kathleen M. Higgins, eds. (Cambridge: Cambridge University Press, 1999), p. 147, footnote 68. Nietzsche, however, does offer a different rendition in *GS* 270: *Was sagt dein Gewissen?*—"Du sollst der werden, der du bist." *What does your conscience say?*—"You shall become the one you are." Here it is indeterminate whether Nietzsche is speaking of a "what" or a "who;" rather, he alludes to some kind of "unity." This exhortation seems to go back to the poet Pindar (*Second Pythian Ode*, 72). In Pindar it reads: "*genoi oios essi mathon*" "become or give origin (*genoi*) to what/who you know (*mathon*) you are." Nietzsche apparently turns it into an enthymeme, omitting, at least explicitly, the reference to "knowing" or "learning" (*mathein*). Babette Babich "Nietzsche's Imperative as a friend of Encomium: On Becoming the One You Are, Ethics, and Blessing," *Nietzsche-Studien*, 33 (2003), p. 29-58, references two possible translations of Pindar's line: *Archaic Greek Poetry: An Anthology.* Selected, and Trans. Barbara Fowler (Madison: U of Wisconsin P, 1992), p. 279: "be what you know you are." Alexander Nehamas *The Art of Living: Socratic Reflection from Plato to Foucault* (Berkeley: U of California P, 1998), p. 128: "having learned, become who you are." Although Heidegger would seem to favor Nehamas' translation, I think there is a fruitful indeterminateness between the epistemic "what" and the singular "who" that seems to shed light on the original Platonic intention. It might well be that the "why-question," the question about purpose, is what harmonizes the epistemic "what" with the personal "who."

20. Augustine *City of God* VIII; X.1; XII.10. Cf. also *Contra Academicos*, II.6.14. Contrast with Gilson *The Philosophy of St. Thomas Aquinas*, p. 354-55.

21. Heidegger misses completely the dialogical and "theatrical" structure of Plato's writings (Plato's dialogues being a kind of "essential theatre"). Thus, I agree with Rosen that Heidegger fails to unpack the Platonic intent to depict the universality of the ideas in light of the philosopher's way of life: the Socratic examined life in the Greek *polis*. Cf. Stanley Rosen "Heidegger's Interpretation of Plato," in *The Quarrel Between Philosophy and Poetry*, p. 139-40: Platonic "dialectic is for Heidegger exclusively the *techné* of division and collection in accordance with kinds [. . .] Heidegger ignores the playful or ironical dialectic of man [. . .] Heidegger [thus] 'epistemologizes' Plato."

22. Gadamer *Truth and Method*, p. 321-325, interprets this in the direct relation between "I" and "Thou": the "openness to one another [in] genuine human relationship[s]," expressed within the hermeneutic experience of language and tradition: "here the object of experience has

itself the character of a person, this kind of experience is a moral phenomenon, as is the knowledge acquired through experience, the understanding of the other person." Charles Taylor echoes this characterization: "the moment of vision" in authentic temporality, can also be an authentic relation of "I" and "Thou" understood as dialogical "significant others." *The Malaise of Modernity*, p. 34. Cf. Heidegger *Being and Time* Section 68a: "The Temporality of Understanding." Also, Martin Buber *I and Thou*. 2nd ed. Trans. Ronald Gregor Smith. (New York: Charles Scribner's Sons, 1958), p. 11, on the need for directedness in the I-Thou relationship.

23. Consider, for instance, the emphasis on concepts and types in *Ecce Homo* "Thus Spoke Zarathustra," Section 1: "Zarathustra himself as a type . . . overtook me"; Section 6: "my concept of the "Dionysian" here became supreme deed"; Zarathustra "experiences himself as the supreme type of all beings"; and, "into all abysses I still carry the blessings of my saying yes. But this is the concept of Dionysus once again." On the other hand, *Beyond Good and Evil* 295, highlights the humanity of Ariadne. The shameless philosophizing god Dionysus intimates that "under certain circumstances I love what is human – and with this he alluded to Ariadne, who was present."

24. For hermeneutic reasons Heidegger is criticizing Socrates' indictment of the poets in Book X of Plato's *Republic* (595a ff.). Hans-Georg Gadamer "Are the Poets Falling Silent?" in Dieter Misgeld and Graeme Nicholson eds. *Hans-Georg Gadamer on Education, Poetry, and History: Applied Hermeneutics* (New York: SUNY P, 1992), Ch. 7; "Plato and the Poets" in *Dialogue and Dialectic*, p. 39-72. On the need for the emergence of new poets consider Heidegger *Contributions to Philosophy*, Section 23.

25. Cf. Heidegger *Being and Time*, Section 25. While the "who" responds to a name the "what" is represented by number. The statistical modelling of modern social and political science is an instance of the metaphysics of "whatness."

26. Cf. Nietzsche *Gay Science*, 108; 124-125; 270; 280-281.

27. This theme is explored in Beiner *Civil Religion*, Chs. 30-31.

28. Cited in Dallmayr *The Other Heidegger*, p. 58. Dallmayr interprets this allusion in terms of *Gelassenheit* (Releasement), that is to say, a "willingness of *Dasein* to become engaged in a domain transgressing human will power."

29. Nietzsche *Birth of Tragedy*, Section 4.

30. In the language of Nietzsche, Heidegger seems to be saying that the Apollonian *principium individuationis* requires the "ground" of Dionysian "liberation" (*Birth of Tragedy*, 21). But the return of Dionysus also appears to take the form of some kind of "judgment." As Nietzsche puts it: "One only needs to pronounce the word 'Dionysus' in the presence of the best names and things, in the presence of Goethe perhaps, or Beethoven, or Shakespeare, or Raphael—at once we feel that our best things and moments have been judged. Dionysus is a judge! Have I been understood?" (*Will to Power*, 1051). It is the "lament of Ariadne" which softens the judgment of Dionysus. "Dionysus is a philosopher" and "therefore the gods also philosophize" (*Beyond Good and Evil*, 295). What this might mean is that the judgment of Dionysus in Nietzsche's view is attenuated by the love of Ariadne, and by the love of wisdom. Cf. *Thus Spoke Zarathustra*, III. 15 "The Other Dance-Song," section 2; also, Plato *Cratylus* 411d4-412-b3; *Timaeus* 40c4; 41b1-3. Contrast with *Truth and Method*, p. 442; 532, footnote 119, where Gadamer notes that the gods of Aristotle and of Hegel have "left 'philosophy' . . . behind." Pierre Hadot *Philosophy as a Way of Life*, p. 147-178, makes the case for bringing together Eros, Dionysus, and the "genius of the heart" in the "figure of Socrates."

31. Consider the opening line of Plato's *Phaedrus* 227a1. While Derrida is a critic of all "metaphysics of presence," Heidegger seems to tacitly grant that "presence," in the standing and simple saying of *Dasein*, gathers glimpses of the question. *Letter on Humanism*, p. 275-76.

32. In *Being and Time*, Section 65, p. 373, Heidegger speaks of "*Being* towards one's ownmost, distinctive potentiality for-Being." Cf. Michel Haar *Heidegger and the Essence of Man*, p. 139: "Does overcoming subjectivity inevitably mean renouncing individuation?" Attunement or affective disposition "is not a purely inner feeling, but a way in which all things 'stand out'; that is, take shape and offer themselves."

33. Politically speaking, one way to interpret this sense of particularity would be by means of "nationalism." I do not favor that interpretation: *citizenship*, in my view, is a better (ample but not massive) form to understand common ways of life. Here I am to a large extent sympa-

thetic to Habermas' conception of deliberative politics, though, I think Habermas' Kantian assertion of inter-subjectivity misses the essential question of trans-subjective "truth" that Heidegger is taking to heart. Habermas, it would seem, is both in history and *of history*: his mode of deliberation seems closed off from possibilities that could orient or thoughtfully question the willfulness of intersubjective human self-determination.

34. Heidegger has a romantic attachment to the "soil" that Nietzsche would have found questionable and probably not to his taste. Nietzsche, however, was also not a Kantian cosmopolitan: in *Beyond Good and Evil* 241, he speaks of "we 'good Europeans.'" Nietzsche particularly loved picturesque southern European cities like Nice, Genoa, and Venice. Cf. Safranski *Nietzsche*, p. 351-371.

35. Nietzsche *Uses and Disadvantages of History for Life*, Section 1, p. 63.

36. Aristotle *Nicomachean Ethics*, X.7.8. Cf. David Roochnik "What is theoria? *Nicomachean Ethics* 10. 7-8." *Classical Philology*, Vol. 1, 104, No. 1 (January 2009), p. 69-82. Roochnik highlights that, for Aristotle, the life of *theoria* is higher than practical wisdom (*phronesis*) mainly because "human beings are not the best of all things in the cosmos" (*N.E.* 1141 a21). There is in Aristotle an affirmation of man as political animal that is also aware that politics is important but essentially insufficient for human fulfilment.

37. Contrast with Heidegger *What is Called Thinking?*, p. 139; 244.

38. Contrast with Heidegger's remarks on silence and the "fittingness of the saying of Being," in *Being and Time*, Section 60; *Letter on Humanism*, p. 276. Cf. *Contributions to Philosophy*, Sections 30; 36-38.

39. Heidegger rejects the equation of Being and value in the *Letter on Humanism*, p. 265, because "by the assessment of something as a value what is valued is admitted only as an object of human estimation."

40. Cf. Nietzsche *Thus Spoke Zarathustra*, III.16.

41. Heidegger *Being and Time*, Section 42. Contrast with the intriguing mythical image in Plato's *Statesman* 269c7-d3, in which the cosmos itself experiences "reversals," or that there are cosmological "counter-normal epochs" in which the gods withdraw. There are two cycles of cosmic change in Plato's *Statesman*: the apparent "golden age" of Cronos, and the enlightened age of Zeus (cf. Plato *Laws* 713b ff.; *Republic* 376e-379b; *Gorgias* 523a-524b). Arendt discusses a variation of this theme drawing from the poetry of Virgil in *The Life of the Mind*, p. 212-215. Löwith also examines critically echoes of this topic in *Meaning in History*, p. 128-131. For interpretations of Plato's *Statesman* consider Cornelius Castoriadis *On Plato's Statesman*, p. 104-114; Stanley Rosen *Plato's Statesman: The Web of Politics* (South Bend, Indiana: St. Augustine Press, 2009), p. 40-66; "Plato's Myth of the Reversed Cosmos" in *The Quarrel between Philosophy and Poetry*, p. 56-77, with *The Mask of Enlightenment: Nietzsche's Zarathustra* (New Haven: Yale University Press, 2004), p. 10-11. Pierre Vidal-Naquet "Plato's Myth of the Statesman, the Ambiguities of the Golden Age and of History." *Journal of Hellenic Studies* 98 (1978), p. 132-41. Johannes M. Van Ophuijsen *Plato and Platonism* (Washington: Catholic University of America Press, 1999), Ch. 10. Marsilio Ficino *Platonic Theology*, Vol. 6. Bk. XVIII. Ch. VIII, p. 129-31; Ch. IX, p. 168-69; 176-77.

42. Heidegger *Being and Time,* Section 40. Dallmayr *The Other Heidegger*, p. 143; 209-210; Nishitani *The Self-Overcoming of Nihilism*, 154; 162.

43. See Nietzsche *Dawn*, 52-53

44. In other words, Freud's primary aim is to normalize the human subject to work and function with relative regularity in a civilized context. Nietzsche and Heidegger find this perspective insufficient. Their views go beyond the Freudian parameter toward spheres that, psychologically speaking, are difficult to fathom: consider, for instance, Nietzsche *Beyond Good and Evil* 150: "around the hero everything turns into tragedy; around the demi-god, into a satyr play; around a God—what? Perhaps into 'world'?—." Or Heidegger's claim in *Being and Time*, Section 45, p. 275, that in his analysis of "Dasein and temporality" he is pursuing an "ontological investigation." As far as I can tell, these passages signal that for both Heidegger and Nietzsche there is an oscillation between knowledge and belief that permeates human awareness and that cannot be overpowered by the Cartesian-Freudian ego (or "super ego"). That is to say, for Heidegger and Nietzsche there is a higher calling than what psychoanalytical normalization might conceive: in many ways they are much closer to Pascal than to Freud. Cf.

also Nietzsche *BGE* 45, with Heidegger *Zollikon Seminars.* Medard Boss ed. Trans. Franz Mayr and Richard Askay. (Evanston: Northwestern University Press, 2001), p. 224; *Poetry, Language, Thought*, p. 125. Fred Dallmayr "Heidegger and Freud" *Political Psychology* Vol. 14, No. 2 (June 1993), p. 235-53. There are indeed many shared themes in Nietzsche and Freudian depth psychology (e.g., *BGE* 3; 75, on the unconscious and *eros*), but Nietzsche's philosophy—read in conversation with Heidegger at any rate—encompasses a larger realm of questions than Freudian psychoanalysis would allow. See *BGE* 295 and the closing "Aftersong from High Mountains"; Heidegger *Nietzsche* Vol. II. Part 2: "Who is Nietzsche's Zarathustra?" p. 209-233. Haar *Heidegger and Metaphysics*, Ch. 3.

45. Nietzsche *Beyond Good and Evil*, 40.

46. Augustine *City of God*, XII.7. Jean Bethke Elshtain *Augustine and the Limits of Politics* (Notre Dame: University of Notre Dame Press, 1995), p. 76-77; 82-86.

47. Contrast with Augustine *City of God*, XII. 18-21.

48. Cf. Arendt *The Life of the Mind*, Part II. On the problem of "willing" consider Nietzsche *Genealogy of Morals*, III, 28; *Wagner in Bayreuth*, Section 5. *Gay Science*, 357: "We Germans are Hegelians even if there had never been any Hegel, in so far as we (unlike all Latins) instinctively attribute a deeper meaning and greater value to becoming and development than to what 'is.'"

49. Cf. Simone Weil *Gravity and Grace*, p. 26-31.

50. Heidegger, however, does not speak of the "saeculum" here. The critical emphasis in this statement is on the apparent "triumph" of voluntarism.

51. Here Heidegger also seems to have in mind the notion of *Gelassenheit*. Cf. Haar *Heidegger and Metaphysics*, p. 138; Dallmayr *The Other Heidegger*, p. 58.

52. Cf. Nietzsche *Dawn*, 350. Plato *Republic* 363 d6.

53. This is a central distinction between Heidegger and Nietzsche. While Heidegger envisions the "promise" ontologically, Nietzsche for the most part emphasizes promise-making in a genealogical manner. Cf. *Genealogy of Morals*, II.1. This section is analyzed drawing parallels between Homer and Nietzsche in Lawrence Hatab *On the Genealogy of Morality: An Introduction* (Cambridge: Cambridge University Press, 2008), p. 69-75. Keep in mind that Nietzsche's *Genealogy of Morality* is "a polemic" (that is the book's subtitle), and a "nay-saying" book. Keith Ansell-Pearson *How to Read Nietzsche* (London: Granta, 2005), p. 4, notes that *Beyond Good and Evil, Twilight of the Idols, The Anti-Christ*, and *Ecce Homo*, are also characterized by Nietzsche as "nay-saying" texts, "timely" negations, whose purpose is to prepare the reception of the "yes-saying" *Thus Spoke Zarathustra.*

54. Heidegger *Being and Time*, Section 48, p. 288.

55. At this juncture, Heidegger seems to evoke the Book of Job.

56. Nietzsche *Thus Spoke Zarathustra*, III. 46: "The Vision and the Riddle."

57. Heidegger *What is Called Thinking?*, p. 35.

58. Bull *Anti-Nietzsche*, Ch.6. Perhaps Heidegger's meditation here alludes to Taoist teachings: the harmonious interplay of action and inaction, depth and height, light and darkness. Cf. Graham Parkes ed. *Heidegger and Asian Thought* (Delhi: Motilal Banarsidass, 1992), p. 79-92. Otto Pöggeler *The Paths of Heidegger's Life and Thought*, p. 266-293. Peter Sloterdijk *Eurotaoismus.* (Frankfurt am Main: Suhrkamp, 1989).

59. Gadamer, on the other hand, speaks of "the romantic faith in the 'growth of tradition,'" as a kind of Burkean response to the Cartesian method underlying the European enlightenment. *Truth and Method*, p. 250.

60. There are echoes of this allusion in Simone Weil *The Need for Roots: Prelude and Declaration towards Mankind* (London: Routledge, 2002). See also Weil's distinction between will and the attention of non-attached desire in *Gravity and Grace*, p. 116-122.

61. Heidegger associates the resonances of "advent" (*die Ankunft*) and "abode" (*die Unterkunft*).

62. The Krell/Capuzzi version translates the "*Lieder des Prinzen Vogelfrei*" as "Songs of an outlaw Prince." Cf. Walter Kaufmann's explanatory footnote introducing the Appendix in his translation of Friedrich Nietzsche *The Gay Science: with Prelude in Rhymes and an Appendix of Songs* (New York: Vintage, 1974), p. 348-49. In *Ecce Homo* "La Gaya Scienza," Nietzsche depicts the *Prince Vogelfrei* as a Provençal poet—"that unity of singer, knight, and free spirit."

Nietzsche also tells the reader that the poem was written "for the most part in Sicily." The poem, addressed "to Goethe," goes as follows:

> The Ever-enduring
> Is but your conceit!
> And God, the alluring,
> A poet's retreat.
> World-wheel, spinning by,
> Skims goals on its way: Calamity! Is rancor's cry;
> The jester calls it Play!
> World-play, the ruling,
> Mixes "Seems" with "To Be":
> Eternally, such fooling Mixes *us* in—the melee!

63. Cf. Nietzsche *Beyond Good and Evil*, 94; *Thus Spoke Zarathustra*,. I.1 "The Three Metamorphoses." Gadamer discusses "play as the clue to the ontological explanation" in *Truth and Method*, p. 91-119. Strauss weaves together *paidia* (play) and classical *paideia* in *The Argument and the Action of Plato's Laws* (Chicago: University of Chicago Press, 1992), p. 17. See also Paul Friedländer *Plato: An Introduction* (Princeton: Princeton University Press, 1969), p. 32 ff.

64. Heidegger *Nietzsche* Vol. 1 "Will to Power as Art," Section 12.

65. Cf. Arendt *Lectures on Kant's Political Philosophy*, p. 42-55; *The Life of the Mind* Vol. I, p. 209-210.

66. Heidegger takes this signal to refer to a close proximity between Goethe's view of nature and the eternal cosmos of Heraclitus' Frag. 30: an eternal cosmos, "ever-living fire, kindling in measures, dwindling in measures" uncreated by the gods and man (p. 238). Krell notes that Heidegger does not refer to Heraclitus' Fragment 52 which deals explicitly with cosmic "eons": "ion is a child at play, playing at draughts; dominion is the child's." The implication seems to be that beyond the eons of cosmological cycles, beyond "gods and men," there would be a source of unfathomable "measure" that would, presumably, orient the question.

67. Heidegger *Being and Time*, Section 27.

68. Cf. Heidegger *Letter on Humanism*, p. 274-276. Nietzsche *Ecce Homo*, "Thus Spoke Zarathustra," 1.

69. Heidegger references Nietzsche's *Twilight of the Idols*, "How the 'True World' finally became a Fable." Cf. *Nietzsche* Vol. I "Will to Power as Art," Section 24.

70. Nietzsche *Beyond Good and Evil*, 212. Hadot *Philosophy as a Way of Life*, ch.1.

71. Eric Voegelin defines this development in terms of "gnostic" immanent politics in *New Science of Politics*, p. 109; 134.

72. See Nietzsche *Dawn*, 500.

73. Cf. Nietzsche *Gay Science*, 258; Machiavelli *Prince* Ch. XXV. For a discussion on *fortuna* that might suggest a link between Machiavelli and Heidegger, cf. Anthony Parel *The Machiavellian Cosmos*, Ch. 4.

74. Michel Haar *Heidegger and the Essence of Man*, p. 135.

75. Contrast with Simone Weil *Gravity and Grace*, p. 109-113.

76. Nietzsche *Gay Science*, 283.

77. Cf. Heidegger *Being and Time*, Section 40. Hubben *Dostoievsky, Kierkegaard, Nietzsche and Kafka*, p. 41; 100-101.

78. Cf. Nietzsche, *Wagner in Bayreuth*, Section 10, p. 322. Heidegger *Letter on Humanism*, p. 257; Liébert *Nietzsche and Music*, p. 34.

79. Cf. Heidegger *Letter on Humanism*, p. 247. Nietzsche *Gay Science*, 124.

80. Arendt *The Human Condition*, p. 322-325. In Arendt's Tocquevillian approach, there are quite positive aspects in the modern democratic conception of equality and freedom, but there are also totalitarian dangers in the potential "tyranny of the majority" and "soft despotism" of large centralized public administration beyond due proportion (cf. Tocqueville *Democracy in America*, II.4.6). In Arendt's view of public life, in the modern human condition it is decisive to

understand and face these questions—questions of political freedom that, as such, cannot be dictated upon free men. For Arendt, the truly unprecedented or unforeseen is always possible, and therefore we need to navigate our political dangers and prospects with active sense and practical understanding keeping in mind that political action takes place *inter pares*. Hence, for political reasons, Arendt does not provide a final answer to this vital question in contemporary political philosophy.

I think this Arendtian view, attractive as it is in many respects, is not fully persuasive in the face of the enormous challenges of the twentieth and twenty-first centuries. On the political plane at any rate, to respond to the problem of global politics in our technological era, it seems fitting to begin re-thinking in terms not only of utilitarian pragmatism, or Kantian practical reason, or even Aristotelian *phronesis* (each of which can have valuable and fine things to say), but more importantly in terms of Aristotelian "political science" (*episteme politiké*, cf. *N.E.* VI.7.7; VI.2.8). Aristotle demarcates clearly the distinction between theory and practice, and, generally speaking, puts forth key distinctions between regime-types and their predictable correlations in terms of character-formation. For the contemporary Platonic-Aristotelian political philosopher the challenge seems to be a double-edged one: his ultimate wish is not for political action, but for the overcoming of his inner "political" strife and fragmentation, so that he (or she, particularly for Plato) can attain further clarity on what it means to live the examined life. From my perspective, in our time this need not be incompatible with liberal politics in so far as liberal freedom allows the examined life to unfold in a plurality of ways. Freedom in the classical view is for the purpose of "the good life" rather than "mere life" (it is good that we respectfully disagree, sometimes strongly, on what the good life is: it makes us more thoughtful). But the inherent dynamism of liberal politics also requires a clear-eyed approach—an always difficult balance between epistemic distinctions and *l'esprit de la finesse*—to powerfully defend true liberal ways of life from both dogmatism and relativism. In practice, this would have to partake in and be sensible to distinct political cultures, where a sense of timing, relevant proportion, standing, face-to-face acquaintanceships and tactfulness, steadfast loyalties, resilience, uncompromising proven friendships, sensible judgment, as well as shared objects of longing and a spirit of deep historical awareness constitute some of the key aspects for any concerted inter-generational course of action. More generally, however, the question for the present generation would seem to be how to benefit from the humanistic opportunities of our vibrant global expansion without letting it dictate a kind of boundless or undifferentiated homogeneity that would no doubt be the very opposite to the classically-attuned spiritual development encouraged by Plato and Aristotle.

81. The section "Snow" in Thomas Mann's *The Magic Mountain*. Trans. John E. Woods. (New York: Vintage, 1996), p. 460-489, may be a way to depict, in narrative form, echoes of this allusion.

82. Cf. Heidegger *Nietzsche* Vol. I "The Will to Power as Art," Sections 14, 20, 25. *What is Called Thinking?*, p. 182. Also, Weil *Gravity and Grace*, p. 128-133.

83. Heidegger *Nietzsche* Vol. I "Will to Power as Art," Section 10, p. 64; also, "What are Poets For?" in *Poetry, Language, Thought*, p. 89-139 (especially his interpretation of the "figure of Nietzsche's Zarathustra," p. 131).

84. The expression comes from Gadamer *On Education, Poetry, and History*, p. 153.

Conclusions

Contrary to the many different appropriations of Nietzsche's writings in the twentieth and early twenty-first centuries, Heidegger finds in Nietzsche's philosophy an underlying metaphysical vision. Heidegger claims that Nietzsche's intellectual development moved in the direction of a major opus, which would have crystalized his thoughts on the overcoming of nihilism. Heidegger lectured extensively on Nietzsche at the level of ontology, for two related reasons: (1) to ensure that the cultural diagnosis that Nietzsche so compellingly offered would not be mistaken with "biologism,"[1] that is, the erroneous notion that there is no ontological justification for the humanities; and (2) to disentangle Nietzsche's thinking from mere "psychologism": the view that logic is a subset of idiosyncratic "psychology," or that autobiographical confession would be a necessary and sufficient condition for doing philosophy. Heidegger took up Nietzsche's philosophy to gather the momentous question "what does it mean to be?"

Heidegger traced Nietzsche's writings in a developmental or maturing manner. Quite often, however, the reader gets the impression that this is meant to suit Heidegger's mode of reasoning—pursuing a line of thinking not from first principles to its analytical implications, but in the opposite direction: from seemingly fragmented remarks towards the gathering of an ever more unitary question. Although the tone of the discussion is always exploratory, it is not uncommon to find a teleological and synoptic rhythm in Heidegger's mode of reading Nietzsche. Heidegger seems to have been persuaded that in order to explore Nietzsche's philosophy, or at any rate to lecture on him, it was advisable to focus not only on the published works of what Nietzsche scholars refer to as the "early and middle periods," but especially to dwell on Nietzsche's later works. Most of these writings were in the form of extensive notes taken from 1883 through 1888, and were initially edited by Peter Gast (virtually the only person who could decipher Nietzsche's handwriting at the time) and the infamous Elisabeth Förster-Nietzsche. The reader of Heidegger's *Nietzsche* therefore always has to keep in mind that Heidegger privileges the unpublished texts, and this brings about questions particularly at the level of authorial intent. The publication of *The Will to Power*, although planned by Nietzsche, was not carried out by him. But we should also keep in mind that Heidegger did not claim to take the book itself as his object of study: Heidegger's approach is to focus on a *selected set of aphorisms* from Nietzsche's *Nachlass*, offering his interpretation of distinct sections and passages all written by Nietzsche. Why did Heidegger find in the "late Nietzsche" the springboard for his interpretation? More importantly: what can we learn from this epic confrontation? In the introduction to "The Will to Power as Art," Heidegger makes the claim that:

> Nietzsche knew what philosophy is. Such a knowledge is rare. Only great thinkers possess it. The greatest possess it purely in the form of a persistent question. The genuinely grounding question, as the question of the essence of Being, does not unfold in the history of philosophy as such. Nietzsche too persists in the guiding question. [2]

Heidegger makes a key distinction between the "guiding question" (*Leitfrage*) and the "ground question" (*Grundfrage*) of philosophy.[3] Heidegger calls the *Leitfrage* the "penultimate question" of philosophy: it appears to be a subset, a preliminary stage prior to the question of "the ground." Heidegger does not quite put it this way, but perhaps we may venture to say that the *Leitfrage* pertains to the realm of "epistemology" (the question of beings or entities) and the *Grundfrage* points toward the realm of "ontology" (the question of Being). Heidegger claims that the history of western philosophy, beginning with the legacy of Plato and culminating in Nietzsche, gives an account of the "guiding question," but such "metaphysical" account seems to occlude the grounding question. In Heidegger's view, the brightness of the Platonic ideas, which unfolded as the history of "Platonism" and culminated in the apparent triumph of "valuative thought" and modern global technology, has prevented western philosophy from carefully attending (and tending) to a deeper experience of "truth" heeding the *Seinsfrage*. According to Heidegger, we have forgotten *the question*, and as a result assume that "Being" as well as the "is" in our use in normal discourse are given. We believe we know what Socrates apparently didn't: we believe we have self-knowledge.[4]

The structure of "Platonism"[5] crafts a dualistic cleft between Being and becoming. This dichotomy is subsequently interpreted "onto-theologically" in Augustine's Christianization of Plato. Augustine effects a key "transvaluation" in the history of Platonism because he introduces the notion of "will."[6] In the Augustinian view, the possibility of redemption requires man's alignment of his human will with the will of God, thereby participating, by his own *liberum arbitrium*, in the providential plan. Because of man's essential freedom, he can always miss the mark in this attunement, thereby declining to participate in this essential "pilgrimage"—"a road which is not a road from place to place but a road of the affections."[7] For Augustine it follows that the man who proudly chooses not to will the will of God errs by foolishly choosing to behave in vain. This is how Augustine explains the problem of evil within an overarching divine plan.[8] In the history of western culture the *either/or* of Being and becoming mediated by the Augustinian will transfigured "classical Platonism,"[9] and created the framework of western Christianity that shaped European culture at least until the Renaissance.

In Heidegger's account, however, the central protagonist in the "effective history" of Platonism is Rene Descartes. Apparently on the basis of the Augustinian pathway, Descartes offered a version of the body/soul distinction that articulated in methodical form the structure of modern subjectivity. Descartes shifts the emphasis from the epic history of salvation that Augustine portrayed in the *City of God,* and, instead, conceived that the primary task of a thinker was to cleanse the mind from historical presuppositions and the traditionalist spell of "old books": to "start anew," on the basis of the seemingly indubitable experience of thoughtful doubt. But the mind that doubts can doubt everything except that it is engaged in doubting. This process appeared to give Descartes a "clear and distinct"[10] beginning to methodically grasp and shape the world around him. In Heidegger's estimation it is the Cartesian turn to the primacy of the *ego cogitans*—the Cartesian subject as *hypokeimenon*—which twists the historical legacy of Plato in the direction of modern thought. Heidegger's argument is that within the history of Platonism the "representational thought" of Descartes finds its completion or "fulfillment" in Nietzsche's "will to power."[11]

On the basis of the Cartesian distinction between *res cogitans* and *res extensa,*[12] linked together by the fiat of the Augustinian will, Heidegger interprets the thought of the originator of the German idealist tradition: Immanuel Kant. The Kantian dichotomy of *noumena* and *phenomena*[13] mirrors for Heidegger Cartesian dualism. We seem to find in Kant that the *noumenal* world is beyond the limits of pure (mechanical) reason, it is a realm of "moral freedom" that can only be approached "practically" on the basis of conditional speculative intuitions. According to Kant, the realm of natural "phenomena" is ruled by Newtonian mechanics, inexorable cause-and-effect that nevertheless is only an "appearance" governed by the categories of the understanding. "Phenomena" therefore only appears to lack the freedom of our *noumenal* intuitions.[14] This is significant because the human being appears in the phenomenal realm, so, naturally, the question then becomes: how can man act freely and therefore morally? Man can act morally on the basis of "practical reason" guided by the *good rational will* that we apprehend noumenally. This is the speculative basis for the practice of Kantian autonomy.

Hegel inherits the Kantian dualistic construction and proposes to merge the division between the noumenal and phenomenal realms by means of a *phenomenology* of spirit. *Der Geist* or "spirit" or the "rational will" (*Vernunftswille*) from Hegel onwards becomes the realization of "immanent transcendence" (hence the joining of "phenomenon" or appearance and "spirit," in a single "logos") actualized through the phenomenon of world history: the history of the "rational will."[15] Hegel takes Cartesian/Kantian dualism and grasps it as an unfolding of "reason in history": a series of epochal teleological developments which for Hegel appear to be the world-historical actualization of "spirit." Hegel's philosophy of history takes the long process of the apparent legacy of Platonism—the historical shaping of Being over becoming—and encapsulates it, at long last, in the modern rational *Rechtsstaat.* The argument seems to end in that the Cartesian "subject" finds in the Hegelian state reconciliation with a sense of communal roots while partaking in a process of ethical acculturation and social recognition that Hegel calls *Sittlichkeit.*[16]

It is at this point of the story that Nietzsche, much like Søren Kierkegaard, finds that the Hegelian final synthesis tends to suffocate the life of the spirit. In *On the Uses and Disadvantages of History for Life,*[17] the young Nietzsche decries a series of consequences of this "oversaturation of an age with history":

1. The weakening of personality: "you are no longer capable of holding on to the sublime, your deeds are shortlived explosions, no rolling thunder."
2. The vain illusion that the problem of justice, "that rarest of virtues," has been finally and definitively grasped.
3. The critical skepticism toward our qualified "affective dispositions," which prevents the harmonious development of individual and cultural maturity: "thus the individual grows fainthearted and unsure and dares no longer believe in himself."
4. The belief that the old age of mankind has been reached, such that we become "latecomers and epigones": "for it almost seems that the task is to stand on guard over history to see that nothing comes out of it except more history, and certainly no real events!"
5. The slide into a "dangerous mood of irony . . . and cynicism," that saps man of his thoughtful authenticity: "anything that constrains a man to love less than unconditionally has severed the roots of his strength: he will wither away, that is to say, become dishonest."

Although these are sweeping propositions, the more general question still remains: what is Nietzsche's overarching concern with the modern condition? Nietzsche thought that the late-modern consensual belief in immanent historical progress closes us off from the dimension of *self-overcoming,* and left to its own devices, it would produce more and more (in the words of Max Weber) "specialists without spirit, sensualists without heart." The reason for this lies in the Hegelian belief that actual social structures have reached, at least in principle, the apotheosis of the human condition. We therefore seem to assume that fitting into socially given categories is what it means to be a good man. For Nietzsche, however, man as a manifestation of self-overcoming "incorporates" or "bodies-forth" (Heidegger's Shakespearian expression[18]) the "fundamental fact" of will to power. In the history of western culture, the Augustinian *voluntas* seems to find its final expression in Nietzsche's will to power in the apparent absence of the will of God: this is what Nietzsche *emotionally* understood as nihilism.

Heidegger, as we have seen, interprets this epochal process originating in the historical legacy of Plato and concluding in Nietzsche as a "fulfillment" (*Vollendung*). Nietzsche, however, would have probably been uneasy about this characterization. What Nietzsche seems to have had in mind was a combination of "ancient" and "modern" insights to "heal" the malaise of modernity: the educational return to Greek and Roman classics,[19] and an "enlightened" critique of the foundations of late-modern rationalism.[20] At the peak of modernity, Nietzsche urges a poetic-and-philosophical return to the sources of our tradition "for the benefit of a time to come."[21]

At this point, we seem to encounter a paradox in Nietzsche's "valuative thinking" or the view that knowing would be coeval to willing: his perhaps equally important attention to the Greek view of "nature."[22] Nietzsche was conflicted as to how to articulate the problem of self-knowledge in modernity: yes, his experience, and especially his bodily dispositions, seemed to be profoundly shaped by his historical acculturation,[23] but Nietzsche also seems to have understood that there is a "natural" permanent quality in man, "a granite of spiritual fatum" (*einen Granit von geistigem Fatum*) "of predetermined decision and answer to predetermined questions" that is *"unteachable* very deep down."[24] Nietzsche's mind "tensed the bow" of genuine thought and spirited historical unfolding to the limit. Nietzsche was torn by this dichotomy—the life of the mind and the spirit of history battling in his soul, as it were.

Nietzsche seems to have thought that there is not in the ultimate analysis a difference between "ideas" and "values." It is on the basis of this "categorical" plane, Nietzsche's polemical misreading of Plato, that Heidegger finds in Nietzsche an intricate link to the Platonism he so ardently seeks to overcome. Heidegger contends that Nietzsche's thinking is the culmination of the western tradition of "metaphysical thinking," beginning with "Plato"—extending itself by way of Augustine, Descartes, Kant and Hegel, and finding its last representative in the philosophy of the will to power.

Heidegger asserts that in his reading of Nietzsche he is only "preparing for a simple and inconspicuous step in thought. What matters to preparatory thinking is to light up that space within which Being itself might again be able to take man, with respect to his essence, into a primal relationship. To be preparatory is the essence of such thinking."[25] Heidegger also claims that he is not engaged in "onto-theology," but is rather pursuing a mode of philosophical thinking that is attentive to the rhythm and philosophical meaning of words, as they may convey deep "conditions of possibility" for being-in-the-world.[26] If we take seriously the perspective of epic theorizing that Nietzsche and Heidegger exemplify, as I do, it would seem that our contemporary confusion about whether we live in a secular or "post-secular" age[27] reflects to a significant extent Heidegger's thinking.[28] In Heidegger's reading of Nietzsche, the history of metaphysics appears to run its course and we seem to find ourselves in a "period of transition"[29] between "European nihilism" and the prelude to a "philosophy of the future."

Thus, we seem to have come to an impasse. As students of political philosophy, we can always choose to leave the old quarrel between ancients and moderns as a permanent *either/or*. At times, intellectual honesty seems to demand that position. However, the fact that we live in the modern world seems to require of us that we at least try to look at this question differently. As we saw throughout the book, Heidegger's reading of Nietzsche responds to the problem of "lost spirit" in modern culture: it has been our task to examine the distinction between classical and modern philosophy in order to explore how their non-identity might clear a pathway for returning to the examined life: to the question of "becoming who we are."[30]

Our reading of Heidegger's Nietzsche has been a contribution in the task of "enlightening the enlightenment":[31] to see whether the clearing (*die Lichtung*) of the question can shed some light on our deeper sources of thought and action. This might give us reasons to take classical thought and modern practice in their own terms—a measured sense of their distinction may well benefit us as we continue to navigate the history of political philosophy. This would involve gathering again, at the "peak of modernity," our need for truthfulness in a manner that is sensible to beauty and freedom.[32] Despite their profound differences, Heidegger and Nietzsche need not only be Plato's rivals in that epic recollection.

NOTES

1. In the context of the European *Kulturkampf* of the late 1930s and early 1940s over the cultural legacy of Nietzsche (which was already enormously influential and contested), one of Heidegger's purposes was to disassociate Nietzsche from "biologistic" renditions and misinter-

pretations by going directly to the primary sources, as well as by being an early advocate for what subsequently became the Colli-Montinari critical edition of Nietzsche's *Complete Works* (*Kritische Studiensausgabe* in 15 Vols.). In *Nietzsche* Vol. III. "The Will to Power as Knowledge," Section 6, p. 47, Heidegger notes: "One thinks that if one only pursues one's impressions one has understood Nietzsche. We must first unlearn this abuse that is supported by current catchwords like *biologism*. We must learn to read." In Heidegger's interpretation, appearances to the contrary, Nietzsche's philosophy is ontological and metaphysical, and closer than otherwise expected to Aristotle (cf. *De Anima* 414 b18-20; 427 b7-15; *Politics* 1253a10-18; contrast with Hobbes *Leviathan* XV, 21).

2. Heidegger *Nietzsche* "Will to Power as Art" Section 1, p. 4.

3. Heidegger *Nietzsche* "Will to Power as Art" Sections 11; 25.

4. Aristotle *N.E.* VI, 8. 1141 b3; 1142 a30. Nietzsche *Beyond Good and Evil*, 202.

5. Let me reiterate this point: Heidegger makes a distinction between Plato and "Platonism." This is a fundamental divide: it is not Heidegger's intent to pursue a close reading of Plato. Heidegger says explicitly that "we say 'Platonism' and not Plato, because here we are dealing with the conception of knowledge that corresponds to that term, not by way of an original and detailed examination of Plato's works." *Nietzsche* Vol. I. "Will to Power as Art," Section 20. From the perspective of the history of political philosophy, the implication seems to be that Heidegger, as heir of Machiavelli, is taking his bearings from the "effective history" of the legacy of Plato. Cf. Gadamer's *Truth and Method*, p. 267 ff. Dallmayr notes that Heidegger "rejects the definition of exegesis as a reconstruction of the *mens auctoris* (author's intention). . . . Rather, interpreting a text requires dynamic participation and involvement on the part of the reader—who, in turn, is not a sovereign master." *The Other Heidegger*, p. 138.

6. Augustine *City of God*, Bk. V. *De Doctrina Christiana* I. XVI–XXXI. Cf. *Confessions* VIII.9. Heidegger discusses at length the notion of "will" in *Nietzsche* Vol. 1 Sections 7-10. Cf. Hannah Arendt's discussion of "Augustine, the first philosopher of the Will" in *The Life of the Mind*, p. 84-110; see also Albrecht Dihle *The Theory of Will in Classical Antiquity* (Op cit.). Löwith traces back to the God of the Old Testament the linear notion of will as opposed to the cyclical motion of nature in *Meaning in History*, p. 221-22. Charles Taylor marks a distinction between the Augustinian will and Aristotelian deliberate choice (*prohairesis*) in *Sources of the Self*, p. 137-142. Cf. Nietzsche *Beyond Good and Evil*, 50; 200.

7. Augustine *De Doctrina Christiana* I. XXVII.

8. Augustine *City of God*, Bks. XI.9; 22. XII.7-9. Evil, according Augustine, lacks "ontological" reality: what we call "evil" is vain self-assertion that does not will the real "good" (*summum bonum*). Cf. Hannah Arendt *Love and Saint Augustine* (Chicago: U Chicago P, 1996), p. 23.

9. This interpretation seems consistent with Charles Taylor *Sources of the Self*, p. 177. Taylor notes that "Augustine's inward turn was tremendously influential in the West; at first in inaugurating a family of forms of Christian spirituality, which continued throughout the Middle Ages, and flourished again in the Renaissance. But then later this turn takes on secularized forms." Contrast with Gadamer *Truth and Method*, p. 440-41. Gadamer offers a qualified distinction between the Neo-platonic and Augustinian "metaphysics of light," and the "metaphysics of substance" of the Aristotelian-Thomistic tradition. See also Löwith *Meaning in History*, p. 247, footnote 6; Nietzsche *WP* 214.

10. In part II of the *Discourse on Method* Descartes points out that he will order his thoughts on the basis of four rules: (1) "Clarity," that is, avoiding *non-sequiturs* or "leaps," (2) analytical division into as many parts as possible, (3) simplicity and order; and (4) comprehensive enumeration.

11. Heidegger *Nietzsche* Vol. IV, Sections 19-20.

12. Descartes *Discourse on Method*, part IV.

13. Kant *Critique of Pure Reason* A 235ff. / B 294 ff.

14. Ibid. B 143. *Critique of Practical Reason*, p. 120. *Critique of Judgment* Intro. I.

15. In *Nietzsche* Vol. II. Part 2, "Who is Nietzsche's Zarathustra?", p. 222, Heidegger quotes Schelling's *Philosophical Investigations into the Essence of Human Freedom and the Objects Pertaining Thereto* (1809) on the attributes of Being as willing. Schelling claims that "in the final and highest instance there is no other Being than willing. Willing is primal Being,

and to it [willing] alone all the predicates of the same [primal Being] apply: absence of conditions; eternity; independence from time; self-affirmation. All philosophy strives solely in order to find this supreme expression." F.W.J. Schelling *Sämliche Werke* (1860), VII, 350. The identification of Being and willing is perhaps the definitive feature of German Idealism, and it originates in nominalist theology. Contrast with Michael Gillespie, *The Theological Origins of Modernity*, p. 75, for a comparison between Medieval nominalists and Renaissance humanists, and their shared emphasis on "names" and "rhetoric" over strict syllogistic logic (cf. Aristotle *Rhetoric* 1404a 1-16). Gillespie mentions, but does not seem to emphasize the Renaissance Platonic humanism of Marsilio Ficino. Ficino is the key link between Nietzsche and Plato in terms of Renaissance philosophy. I explore this theme in my essay "'Who Educates the Educators?' Nietzsche's Philosophical Therapy in the Age of Nihilism," in Hutter and Friedland eds. *Nietzsche's Therapeutic Teaching*, p. 54-56.

16. "Ethical life" as defined in Part III of the *Philosophy of Right*. Trans. with notes by T. M. Knox (London: Oxford University Press, 1967). In his notes to Hegel's text Knox defines *Sittlichkeit* as "the union of a subjective will with the objective order" (p. 346). Cf. Shlomo Avineri *Hegel's Theory of the Modern State* (Cambridge: Cambridge University Press, 1972, p. 32; 84-86; 132.

17. Nietzsche *Uses and Disadvantages of History for Life*, Sec 5. *Gay Science, 377.*

18. Heidegger *Nietzsche* Vol. III "The Will to Power as Knowledge," Section 12.

19. See Nietzsche *On the Future of Our Educational Institutions.* (South Bend: St. Augustine Press, 2004). Alexander Nehamas *Nietzsche: Life as Literature.* (Cambridge: Harvard University Press, 1985), p. 184. Robert Ackermann *Nietzsche* (Amherst: MIT Press, 1990), p. 25-26. Tom Darby, Bela Egyed, Ben Jones eds. *Nietzsche and the Rhetoric of Nihilism*, p. 55-69. In this context, consider also Heidegger's suggestion to his students at the University of Freiburg in 1951-1952 (the last lecture course he taught before his formal retirement from the university): "it is advisable, therefore, that you postpone reading Nietzsche for the time being, and first study Aristotle for ten to fifteen years." *What is Called Thinking?*, p. 73.

20. This is the origin of Jürgen Habermas' concern about the French deconstructive, post-Hegelian, appropriation of Nietzsche/Heidegger in *The Philosophical Discourse of Modernity*, p. 83 ff. For Habermas, the core of the enlightenment project is the dialectical overcoming of mythical power-relations, towards more transparent intersubjective "communicative action." The radical critique of reason that he associates with Nietzsche's philosophical heirs in the twentieth century, devolves, in Habermas' view, through non-ontological aesthetic judgment, toward unreflectively traditional forms of life with no categorical distinction between myth and *logos* (107). Although Habermas does not want to compromise the emancipatory integrity of the enlightenment, he ends his chapter on the "entwinement between myth and enlightenment" with a conciliatory note, in favor of a "discourse that . . . might break the spell of mythic thinking without incurring in a loss of the light radiating from the semantic potentials also preserved in myth" (103). The classic book on mythical motifs in Nietzsche is Ernst Bertram *Nietzsche: Attempt at a Mythology.* Trans. with and Intro. by Robert E. Norton. (Chicago: University of Illinois Press, 2009).

21. Nietzsche *Uses and Disadvantages of History for Life*, Foreword; *Dawn* 169. Cf. Aristotle *Poetics*, Ch. 9.

22. Paul van Tongeren "Nietzsche's Greek Measure" *The Journal of Nietzsche Studies*, Issue 24, Fall 2002, p. 5-24; Richard Capobianco discusses the Greek view of nature, grounded on Being, as "the temporal-spatial emerging and shining-forth of beings in their beingness" in *Heidegger's Way of Being*, p. 7.

23. Contrast with the image of the statue of the "god Glaucus" in Plato *Republic* 611d.

24. Nietzsche *Beyond Good and Evil, 231*; *Uses and Disadvantages of History for Life,* Section 4.

25. Heidegger "The Word of Nietzsche: God is Dead," in *The Question Concerning Technology*, p. 55.

26. Generally speaking, Heidegger's thinking seems to have moved from nominalist theology, to philosophy (of history), and eventually to some kind of meditative and poetic thought. See Heidegger's letter to Löwith (August 19th, 1921), in Karl Löwith *Martin Heidegger and European Nihilism*, p. 236. The overall theme of the letter involves (among other things)

Heidegger responding to certain concerns of the then doctoral candidate Löwith about Heidegger's teaching in relation to *Wissenschaft*, university life, and the deep influence he had on his students.

27. Cf. Nietzsche *Schopenhauer as Educator*, Section 4, p. 148-49. Charles Taylor *A Secular Age* (Cambridge: Harvard UP, 2007), p. 14; 548; 568; 630.

28. Beiner *Political Philosophy*, p. xxi, puts it well when he says that "epic theory does what Flaubert suggested all great art does: 'it pursue[s] an idea to its furthermost limits.'" In this light, consider also Robert Sparling's characterization of Socratic political philosophy in *Johann Georg Hamman and the Enlightenment Project* (University of Toronto Doctoral Dissertation, 2008). Sparling makes a persuasive case for the study of authors that challenge our fundamental presuppositions: "as a child of the Enlightenment, I fear that we post-theistic, post-metaphysical and now even post-secular (!) persons have all too much spiritual comfort and I consider the engagement with Enlightenment's opposite to be a central duty of political thought" (p. 10).

29. Gadamer dissents with the view that an epochal period of transition may indeed be unfolding: "I do not believe *at all* that we live between two worlds. I can follow neither Heidegger nor Buber on this [...] I *remember,* instead of this, the one world which I alone know." Gadamer to Strauss (April 5th 1961). Correspondence Concerning *Wahrheit und Methode. Independent Journal of Philosophy* (2), 1978, p. 10 (Gadamer's italics). Consider, on the other hand, a series of affirmations of an epochal crossing in Nietzsche *Gay Science*, 356; 377. *Dawn*, 164, 171, 453. Hegel *Phenomenology of Spirit*, Preface, Section 11; Michel Haar *Nietzsche and Metaphysics*, p. 131-149. Heidegger, *What is Called Thinking?*, p. 51; *Contributions to Philosophy*, Sections 5; 40. Arendt *Between Past and Future*, p. 3-16; Trías *La Edad del Espíritu*, p. 525 ff.

30. Contrast Nietzsche *Ecce Homo,* (subtitle) with *Gay Science,* 270. See also, Eugenio Trías *Meditación sobre el Poder* (Barcelona: Anagrama, 1993), p. 157-162.

31. Nietzsche *Dawn,* 197. Cf. Mazzimo Montinari "Enlightenment and Revolution: Nietzsche and the Later Goethe," in *Reading Nietzsche.* Trans. Greg Whitlock (Urbana: University of Illinois Press, 2003), p. 50-56.

32. Plato *Statesman* 309c. Heidegger *Pathmarks*, p. 166-67; Nietzsche *Gay Science, 281.*

Bibliography

Adrián Escudero, Jesús. *Heidegger and the Emergence of the Question of Being* Trans. Juan Pablo Hernández. London: Bloomsbury, 2015.

Aloni, Nomrod. *Beyond Nihilism: Nietzsche's Healing and Edifying Philosophy*. Lanham, MD: University Press of America, 1991.

Anderson Torsten. *Polis and Psyche: A Motif in Plato's Republic*. Göteborg: Studia Graeca et Latina Gothoburgensia, 1971.

Andrew, Edward. *Conscience and Its Critics: Protestant Conscience, Enlightenment Reason, and Modern Subjectivity*. Toronto: University of Toronto Press, 2001.

———. "Heidegger's Führerprinzip: Leadership out of and into Nihilism," in Joseph Masciulli, Mikhail Molchanov and W. Andy Knight eds. *The Ashgate Research Companion to Political Leadership*. Farnham: Ashgate, 2009.

———. "The Unworthiness of Nietzschean Values" *Animus* 14, 2010.

Ansell-Pearson, Keith. ed. *A Companion to Nietzsche*. Oxford: Blackwell, 2009.

Ansell-Pearson, Keith. *An Introduction to Nietzsche as Political Thinker*. Cambridge: Cambridge University Press, 1999.

———. *How to Read Nietzsche*. London: Granta, 2005.

Aquinas, Thomas. *On Being and Essence*. Trans. with and intro. by Armand Maurer. Toronto: PIMS, 1968

———. *Selected Writings*. Ed. and trans. with and intro. by Ralph Mcinerny. London: Penguin, 1998.

———. *Shorter Summa*. Manchester: Sophia Institute Press, 2002.

Arendt, Hannah. *Between Past and Future*. New York: Penguin, 1972.

———. *Essays in Understanding 1930-1954*. Jerome Kohn ed. New York: Harcourt, 1994.

———. *Lectures on Kant's Political Philosophy*. Edited with an Interpretative Essay by Ronald Beiner. Chicago: University of Chicago Press, 1989.

———. *Love and Saint Augustine*. Ed. With an Interpretative Essay by Joanna Vecchiarelli Scott and Judith Chelius Stark. Chicago: University of Chicago Press, 1996.

———. *The Human Condition*. Chicago: University of Chicago Press, 1974.

———. *The Life of the Mind, 2 Vols*. New York: Harcourt, 1978.

Aristotle. *De Anima*. Trans. J.A. Smith. In Richard Mckeon ed. *The Basic Works of Aristotle*. New York: Modern Library, 2001.

———. *Metaphysics*. 2 vols. Tredennick trans. Cambridge: Harvard University Press, 1977, 1980.

———. *Nicomachean Ethics* Trans. H. Rackham. London: Loeb Classical Library, 1934.

———. *Physics*. 2 vols. Wickstead trans. Cambridge: Harvard University Press, 1968, 1980.

————. *Poetics.* Trans. Ingram Bywater. In Richard Mckeon ed. *The Basic Works of Aristotle.* New York: Modern Library, 2001.

————. *Politics.* Trans. C.D.C. Reeve. Indianapolis: Hackett, 1998.

————. *Rhetoric.* Trans. Rhys Roberts. In Richard Mckeon ed. *The Basic Works of Aristotle.* New York: Modern Library, 2001.

Ascheim, Steven. *The Nietzsche Legacy in Germany 1880-1990.* Berkeley: University of California Press, 1994.

Assman, Jan. *The Price of Monotheism.* Stanford: Stanford University Press, 2010.

Augustine. *City of God against the Pagans.* London: Penguin, 2003.

————. *Confessions.* London: Penguin, 1961.

————. *On Christian Doctrine.* Trans. D.W. Robertsson Jr. New York: Library of Liberal Arts Press, 1997.

Babich, Babette. "Nietzsche's Imperative as a friend of Encomium: On Becoming the One You Are, Ethics, and Blessing." *Nietzsche-Studien,* 33 (2003), p. 29-58.

Bambach, Charles. *Heidegger's Roots: Nietzsche, National Socialism, and the Greeks.* Ithaca, NY: Cornell University Press, 2003.

Beck, Ulrich. *Risk Society: Towards a New Modernity.* London: Sage Publications, 1992.

Behnegar, Nasser. Leo *Strauss, Max Weber and the Scientific Study of Politics.* Chicago: University of Chicago Press, 2003.

Beiner, Ronald, ed. *Theorizing Nationalism.* New York: SUNY Press, 1999.

Beiner, Ronald. *Civil Religion : A Dialogue in the History of Political Philosophy.* Cambridge: Cambridge University Press, 2011.

————. *Philosophy in a Time of Lost Spirit: Essays on Contemporary Theory.* Toronto: University of Toronto Press, 1997.

————. *Political Philosophy: What it is and Why it Matters.* Cambridge: Cambridge University Press, 2014.

Benjamin, Walter. *Illuminations.* Trans. Harry Zohn. New York: Shocken, 1969.

Benson, Brice Ellis. *Pious Nietzsche: Decadence and Dionysian Faith.* Indianapolis: Indiana University Press, 2008.

Berlin, Isaiah. *Four Essays on Liberty.* Oxford: Oxford University Press, 1992.

Bernstein, Richard. *Beyond Objectivism and Relativism: Science, Hermeneutics, and Praxis.* Philadelphia: University of Pennsylvania, 1991.

Bertram, Ernst. *Nietzsche: Attempt at a Mythology.* Trans. with and Intro. by Robert E. Norton. Chicago: University of Illinois Press, 2009.

Blondel, Eric. *Nietzsche: The Body and Culture.* Trans. Sean Hand. Stanford: Stanford University Press, 1991.

Bortoft, Henri. *The Wholeness of Nature: Goethe's Way toward a Science of Conscious Participation in Nature.* New York: Lindisfarne Press, 1996.

Buber, Martin. *I and Thou.* 2nd ed. Trans. Ronald Gregor Smith. New York: Charles Scribner's Sons, 1958.

Bull, Malcolm. *Anti-Nietzsche.* London: Verso, 2014.

Burke, Edmund. *Reflections on the Revolution of France.* Oxford: Oxford University Press, 2009.

Capobianco, Richard. *Heidegger's Way of Being.* Toronto: University of Toronto Press, 2014.

Castoriadis, Cornelius. *On Plato's Statesman.* Trans. David Ames Curtis. Stanford, CA: Stanford University Press, 2002.

Cicero. *The Republic and The Laws.* Trans. Niall Rudd. Oxford: Oxford University Press, 2008.

Dallmayr, Fred. "Heidegger and Freud" *Political Psychology* Vol. 14, No. 2 (June 1993), p. 235-53.

————. "Heidegger on *Macht* and *Machenschaft*" *Continental Philosophy Review* 34 (3), September 2001, p. 261-263.

————. *The Other Heidegger.* Ithaca, NY: Cornell University Press, 1993.

Darby, Tom, et al. (eds.) *Nietzsche and the Rhetoric of Nihilism.* Ottawa: Carleton University Press, 1989.

Darby, Tom. (ed.) *Sojourns in the New World: Reflections on Technology.* Ottawa: Carleton University Press, 1986.

———. *The Feast: Meditations on Time.* Toronto: University of Toronto Press, 1990.

Deleuze, Giles. *Nietzsche and Philosophy.* London: Continuum, 1983.

Derrida, Jacques. *Dissemination.* Trans. Barbara Johnson. Chicago: University of Chicago Press, 1981.

———. *Of Grammatology.* Trans. Gayatri Chakravorty Spivak. Baltimore, MD: Johns Hopkins, 1974.

Descartes, Rene. *Discourse on Method.* Trans. Desmond M. Clark. London: Penguin, 2006.

———. *Meditations on First Philosophy.* Trans. Laurence Lafleur. London: Library of Liberal Arts, 1951.

Dihle, Albrecht. *The Theory of Will in Classical Antiquity.* Berkeley: University of California Press, 1982.

Dodds, E.R. *The Greeks and the Irrational.* Berkeley: University of California Press, 1951.

Duff, Alexander. *Heidegger and Politics: The Ontology of Radical Discontent.* Cambridge: Cambridge University Press, 2015.

Duns Scotus, John. *A Treatise on God as First Principle.* Chicago: Franciscan Herald Press, 1966.

Echauri, Raúl. *Heidegger y la Metafísica Tomista.* Prefacio de Étienne Gilson. Buenos Aires: Eudeba, 1970.

Elshtain, Jean Bethke. *Augustine and the Limits of Politics.* Notre Dame: University of Notre Dame Press, 1995.

Farías, Victor. *Heidegger and Nazism.* Trans by Paul Burrell. Ed, with a foreword by Joseph Margolis and Tom Rockmore. Philadelphia: Temple University Press, 1989.

Faye, Emmanuel. *Heidegger: L'Introduction du Nazisme dans la Philosophie.* Paris: Albin Michel, 2005.

Ficino, Marsilio. *Platonic Theology.* 6 Vols. Trans. Michael J.B. Allen with John Warden. Cambridge: Harvard University Press, 2001.

Fink, Eugen. *Nietzsche's Philosophy.* London: Continuum, 2003.

Finkielkraut, Alain. *Nous Autres, Modernes.* Paris: Gallimard, 2005.

Fortenbaugh, W.W. *Aristotle on Emotion.* London: Duckworth, 2002.

Foucault, Michel. *Madness and Civilization: A History of Insanity in the Age of Reason.* London: Routledge, 2005.

———. *Politics, Philosophy, Culture: Interviews and Other Writings, 1977-1984.* Ed. with Intro. by Laurence Kritzman. New York: Routledge, 1990.

———. *The Care of the Self: The History of Sexuality Vol. 3.* New York: Vintage, 1986.

———. *The Courage of Truth: The Government of Self and Others II.* Trans. Graham Burchell. New York: Picador, 2012.

———. *The Hermeneutics of the Subject* Ed. Frédéric Gross. Trans. Graham Burchel. Intro. By Arnold I Davidson. New York: Picador, 2004.

———. *The History of Sexuality* Vol. 3. New York: Vintage, 1988.

———. "Nietzsche, Genealogy, History" in *The Foucault Reader.* Paul Rabinow, ed. New York: Vintage, 2010.

Frazer, Michael. "The Compassion of Zarathustra: Nietzsche on Sympathy and Strength." *Review of Politics* 68 (2006), p. 49-78.

Friedländer, Paul. *Plato: An Introduction.* Princeton, NJ: Princeton University Press, 1969.

Gadamer, Hans-Georg. *Dialogue and Dialectic: Eight Hermeneutical Studies on Plato.* Trans. with and intro by P. Christopher Smith. New Haven, CT: Yale University Press, 1980.

———. *Heidegger's Ways.* Trans. John Stanley. New York: SUNY Press, 1994.

———. *Nietzsche L'Antipode: Le Drame de Zarathoustra.* Trad. Christophe David. Paris: Éditions Allia, 2000.

———. *Philosophical Apprenticeships.* Cambridge: MIT Press, 1985.

———. *Truth and Method.* Sheed and Ward Trans. New York: Continuum, 1975.

Gillespie, Michael Allen, and Tracey Strong eds. *Nietzsche's New Seas: Explorations in Philosophy, Aesthetics, and Politics.* Chicago: University of Chicago Press, 1991.

Gillespie, Michael. "Heidegger's Nietzsche." *Political Theory*, Vol. 15, No. 3 August 1987, p. 424-435.

———. *Nietzsche's Final Teaching*. Chicago: University of Chicago Press, 2017.

———. *Nihilism Before Nietzsche*. Chicago: University of Chicago Press, 1995.

———. *The Theological Origins of Modernity*. Chicago: University of Chicago Press, 2009.

Gilson, Etienne. *Philosophy of Thomas Aquinas*. Trans. Edward Bullough. New York: Barnes and Noble, 1993.

Goethe, Johann Wolfang von. *Conversations of Goethe with Johann Peter Eckermann*. Trans. John Oxenford. Ed. J.K. Moorhead. Intro. by Havelock Elis. Cambridge: Da Capo Press, 1998.

Grant, George. *English Speaking Justice*. Toronto: Anansi, 1974.

———. *Technology and Empire*. Toronto: Anansi, 1969.

———. *Technology and Justice*. Concord, Ontario: Anansi, 1986.

———. *Time as History*. Toronto: Hunter Rose Company, 1969.

Guignon, Charles B. ed. *The Cambridge Companion to Heidegger*. Cambridge: Cambridge University Press, 1993.

Guillemain, Bernard. *The Later Middle Ages*. London: Burns, 1960.

Gutting, Gary. *French Philosophy in the Twentieth Century*. Cambridge: Cambridge University Press, 2001.

Haar, Michel. *Heidegger and the Essence of Man*. Trans. William McNeill. New York: SUNY Press, 1993.

———. *Nietzsche and Metaphysics*. Trans and ed. Michael Gendre. Albany: State University of New York, 1996.

Habermas, Jürgen. *Knowledge and Human Interests* Trans. J. Shapiro. London: Heinemann, 1972.

———. *The Philosophical Discourse of Modernity*. Trans. Frederick Lawrence. Cambridge: MIT Press, 1990.

Hadot, Pierre. *Exercises Spirituels et Philosophie Antique*. Préface d'Arnold I. Davidson. Paris: Albin Michel, 2002.

———. *Plotin ou la Simplicité du Regard*. Paris: Folio-Essai, 1997.

———. *Philosophy as a Way of Life*. Ed. With and Intro. By Arnold I. Davidson. Oxford: Blackwell, 1995.

Han-Pile, Beatrice. "Nietzsche and the 'Masters of Truth': the Pre-Socratics and Christ" in Mark A. Wrathall and Jeff Malpas, eds. *Heidegger, Authenticity and Modernity: Essays in Honor of Hubert Dreyfus, Volume I*. Cambridge: MIT Press, 2000.

Hatab, Lawrence. *Ethics and Finitude: Heideggerian Contributions to Moral Philosophy*. Oxford: Rowman and Littlefield, 2000.

———. *On the Genealogy of Morality: An Introduction*. Cambridge: Cambridge University Press, 2008.

Hegel, G.W.F. *Phenomenology of Spirit*. A.V. Miller Trans. Oxford: Oxford University Press, 1977.

———. *Philosophy of Right*. Trans. T.M. Know. London: Oxford University Press, 1967.

Heidegger, Martin. *Basic Concepts*. Trans. Gary Aylesworth. Indianapolis: Indiana University Press, 1989.

———. *Basic Problems of Phenomenology*. Trans. Albert Hofstaedter. Bloomington: Indiana University Press, 1988.

———. *Being and Time*. Trans John Macquarrie and Edward Robinson. New York: Harper, 1962.

———. *Besinnung*. Frankfurt am Main: Vittorio Klostermann, 1997.

———. *Brief über den Humanismus*. Frankfurt am Main: Vittorio Klostermann, 1974.

———. "Comments on Karl Jasper's Psychology of Worldviews." William McNeill ed. *Pathmarks*. Cambridge: Cambridge University Press, 1999.

———. *Contributions to Philosophy (From Enowning)*. Trans. Parvis Emad and Kenneth Maly. Indianapolis: Indiana University Press, 1999.

———. *Introduction to Metaphysics*. Trans. Gregory Fried and Ricard Polt. New Haven: Yale University Press, 2000

———. "Letter on Humanism" Trans. Frank A. Capuzzi, in William McNeil ed. *Pathmarks*. Cambridge: Cambridge University Press, 1999.

———. *Nietzsche*. 2 Vols. Pfullingen: Verlag Günther Neske, 1961.

———. *Nietzsche*. Vols. 1-2. Trans. with Notes and Analysis by David Farrell Krell. New York: Harper 1979.

———. *Nietzsche*. Vols. 3-4. Trans. Frank Capuzzi. Edited with Notes and Analysis by David Farrell Krell. New York: Harper, 1991.

———. "On the Essence and Concept of *Phusis* in Aristotle's *Physics* B, I." Trans. Thomas Sheehan, in William McNeil ed. *Pathmarks*. Cambridge: Cambridge University Press, 1999.

———. "On the Essence of Truth" Trans. John Sallis, in William McNeil ed. *Pathmarks*. Cambridge: Cambridge University Press, 1999.

———. *Pathmarks*. William McNeil ed. Cambridge: Cambridge University Press, 1999.

———. "Plato's Doctrine of Truth" Trans. Thomas Sheehan, in William McNeil ed. *Pathmarks*. Cambridge: Cambridge University Press, 1999.

———. *Poetry, Language, Thought*. Trans. Albert Hofstadter. New York: Harper, 2001.

———. "The Anaximander Fragment" in Martin Heidegger *Early Greek Thinking*. Trans. David Farrel Krell and Frank Capuzzi. New York: Harper, 1975.

———. *The Event*. Trans. Richard Rojcewicz. Indianapolis: Indiana University Press, 2009.

———. *The Question Concerning Technology and Other Essays*. Trans. William Lowitt. New York: Harper, 1977.

———. *What is Called Thinking?* Trans. J. Glenn Gray. New York: Harper, 2004.

———. *Zollikon Seminars*. Medard Boss ed. Trans. Franz Mayr and Richard Askay. Evanston, IL: Northwestern University Press, 2001.

Heim, Karl. *Spirit and Truth: The Nature of Evangelical Christianity* Trans. Edgar P. Dickie. London: Lutterworth, 1929.

Henry, Desmond Paul. *The Logic of Saint Anselm*. Oxford: Oxford University Press, 1967.

Hesse, Herman. *Magister Ludi*. London: Penguin, 1975.

Hobbes, Thomas. *Leviathan*. Ed. Richard Tuck. Cambridge: Cambridge University Press, 2012.

Hollingdale, R.J. *Nietzsche*. London: Routledge, 1939.

Hubben, William. *Dostoievsky, Kierkegaard, Nietzsche and Kafka: Four Prophets of Our Destiny*. New York: Collier, 1972.

Husserl, Edmund. *Phenomenology and the Crisis of Philosophy*. Trans. Quentin Lauer. New York: Harper, 1965.

Hutter, Horst and Eli Friedland eds. *Nietzsche's Therapeutic Teaching: For Individuals and for Culture*. London: Bloomsbury, 2013.

Hutter, Horst. "Philosophie et religions comme gymnastiques de la volonté dans la pensée Nietzschéenne." *Conjonctures,* (2008), No.45/46, Été-Automne, 2008, p. 89-120.

———. *Shaping the Future: Nietzsche's New Regime of the Soul and Its Ascetic Practices*. New York: Lexington, 2006.

Jackson, Roy. *Nietzsche and Islam*. New York: Routledge, 2007.

Janssens, David. *Between Athens and Jerusalem: Philosophy, Prophecy, and Politics in Leo Strauss' Early Thought*. New York: SUNY Press, 2008.

Jonas, Hans. "Heidegger and Theology." *The Review of Metaphysics,* Vol. 18, No. 2 (Dec.,1964), pp. 207-233.

———. *The Imperative of Responsibility: In Search of an Ethics for the Technological Age*. Chicago: University of Chicago Press, 1985.

Jung, Carl. *Seminar On Nietzsche's Zarathustra* (abridged version). James Jarrett ed. Princeton: Princeton University Press, 1998.

Kant, Immanuel. "An Answer to the Question: What is Enlightenment?" in *Perpetual Peace and other Essays*. Trans. Ted Humphrey. Indianapolis: Hackett, 1983.

———. *Critique of Judgment*. Trans. Werner S. Pluhar. Indianapolis: Hackett, 1987.

———. *Critique of Practical Reason*. Trans. Werner Pluhar. Intro. Stephen Engstrom. Indianapolis: Hackett, 2002.

———. *Critique of Pure Reason*. Trans. Norman Kemp Smith. New York: St. Martin's, 1965.

———. "Idea for a Universal History with a Cosmological Intent" in *Perpetual Peace and Other Essays.* Trans. Ted Humphrey. Indianapolis: Hackett, 1983.

———. "Perpetual Peace: A Philosophical Sketch" in *Perpetual Peace and Other Essays.* Trans. Ted Humphrey. Indianapolis: Hackett, 1983.

Kemal et al. *Nietzsche, Philosophy and the Arts.* Cambridge: Cambridge University Press, 1998.

Kierkegaard, Søren. *Fear and Trembling.* Ed. and Trans. with and Intro. and notes by Howard Hong and Edna Hong. Princeton, NJ: Princeton University Press, 1983.

———. *The Concept of Irony with Continual Reference to Socrates* Trans. and ed. Howard Hong and Edna Hong. Princeton, NJ: Princeton University Press, 1992.

King, Magda. *A Guide to Heidegger's Being and Time.* Albany, NY: SUNY Press, 2001.

Klein, Jacob. *A Commentary on Plato's Meno.* Chicago: University of Chicago Press, 1989.

Klossowski, Pierre. *Nietzsche and the Vicious Circle.* Trans. Daniel Smith. Chicago: University of Chicago Press, 1997.

Kojève, Alexandre. *Introduction to the Reading of Hegel.* Assembled by Raymond Quenau. Allan Bloom ed. Trans. James H. Nichols, Jr. Ithaca, NY: Cornell University Press, 1980.

Kolakowski, Leszek. *God Owes Us Nothing: A Brief Remark in Pascal's Religion and on the Spirit of Salvation.* Chicago: University of Chicago Press, 1996.

———. *Modernity on Endless Trial.* Chicago: University of Chicago Press, 1990.

———. *The Alienation of Reason: A History of Positivist Thought.* New York: Double Day, 1968.

Konstan, David. *A Life Worthy of the Gods: The Materialist Psychology of Epicurus.* Athens: Parmenides, 2008.

Kuhn, Thomas S. *The Copernican Revolution: Planetary Astronomy in the Development of Western Thought.* Cambridge: Harvard University Press, 1985.

Lacoue-Labarthe, Philippe. *Heidegger, Art and Politics.* Oxford: Blackwell, 1990.

———. *La Fiction du Politique.* Paris: Bourgeois, 1987.

Lampert, Laurence. "Heidegger's Nietzsche Interpretation." *Man and World*, 11/1974, Volume 7, Issue 4, p. 353–378.

———. *Leo Strauss and Nietzsche.* Chicago: Chicago University Press, 1996.

———. *Nietzsche and Modern Times: A Study of Bacon, Descartes, and Nietzsche.* New Haven, CT: Yale University Press, 1993.

———. *Nietzsche's Task: An Interpretation of Beyond Good and Evil.* New Haven, CT: Yale University Press, 2001.

———. *Nietzsche's Teaching: An Interpretation of Thus Spoke Zarathustra.* New Haven, CT: Yale University Press, >1986.

Lerner, Ralph and Muhsin Mahdi eds. *Medieval Political Philosophy.* Ithaca, NY: Cornell University Press, 1963.

Liébert, Georges. *Nietzsche and Music.* Trans. David Pellauer and Graham Parkes. Chicago: University of Chicago Press, 1991.

Lilla, Mark. *G.B. Vico: The Making of an Anti-Modern.* Cambridge: Harvard University Press, 1993.

———. *The Reckless Mind: Intellectuals in Politics.* New York: New York Review of Books, 2006.

Lobkowicz, Nicolas. *Theory and Praxis.* South Bend, IN: Notre Dame University Press, 1968.

Locke, John. *Two Treatises of Government.* Peter Laslett ed. Cambridge: Cambridge University Press, 2003.

Löwith, Karl. *From Hegel to Nietzsche: The Revolution in 19th Century Thought.* Trans. David Green. New York: Holt, Rinehart and Winston, 1964.

———. *Martin Heidegger and European Nihilism.* Richard Wolin ed. Trans. Gary Steiner. New York: Columbia University Press, 1995.

———. *Meaning in History.* Chicago: University of Chicago Press, 1949 [Ninth impression 1967].

———. *Nietzsche's Philosophy of the Eternal Recurrence of the Same.* Trans. J. Harvey Lomax. Berkeley: University of California Press, 1997

Machiavelli, Niccolo. *Discourses on Livy* Trans. by Mansfield and Tarcov. Chicago: University of Chicago Press, 1996.

———. *The Prince.* Trans with Intro. and Notes by Leo Paul S. de Alvarez. Prospect Hills, IL: Waveland Press, 1989.

MacIntyre, Alasdair. *After Virtue.* South Bend, IN: University of Notre Dame Press, 1984.

Macquarrie, John. *Heidegger and Christianity.* New York: Continuum, 1994.

Magnus, Bernd. and Kathleen M. Higgins, eds *The Cambridge Companion to Nietzsche.* Cambridge: Cambridge UP, 1999.

Mann, Thomas. *The Magic Mountain.* Trans. John E. Woods. New York: Vintage, 1996.

Martin, Nicholas. Ed. *Nietzsche and the German Tradition.* Bern: Peter Lang, 2003.

Maurer Armand. *Medieval Philosophy: An Introduction.* With Preface by Etienne Gilson. Toronto: PIMS, 1982.

McIntyre, Alex. *The Sovereignty of Joy: Nietzsche's Vision of Grand Politics.* Toronto: University of Toronto Press, 1997.

Meier, Heinrich. *Leo Strauss and the Theologico-Political Problem.* Cambridge: Cambridge University Press, 2006.

Menn, Stephen. *Plato on God as Nous.* South Bend, IN: St. Augustine Press, 1995.

Milosz, Czeslaw. *Native Realm: A Search for Self-Definition.* New York: Farrar, 2002.

Misgeld, Dieter and Graeme Nicholson eds. *Hans-Georg Gadamer on Education, Poetry, and History: Applied Hermeneutics.* New York: SUNY Press, 1992.

Mitchel, Joshua. *Not By Reason Alone: Religion, History, and Identity in Early Modern Political Thought.* Chicago: University of Chicago Press, 1996.

Montiglio, Silvia. *Silence in the Land of Logos.* Princeton, NJ: Princeton University Press, 2000.

Montinari, Mazzimo. *Reading Nietzsche.* Trans. Greg Whitlock. Urbana: University of Illinois Press, 2003.

Morrison, Robert G. *Nietzsche and Buddhism: A Study in Nihilism and Ironic Affinities.* Oxford: Oxford University Press, 1997.

Musil, Robert. *The Man Without Qualities* 2 Vols. Trans. Sophie Wilkins. New York: Vintage, 1996.

Nehamas, Alexander. *Nietzsche: Life as Literature.* Cambridge: Harvard University Press, 1985.

Newell, Waller. *Tyranny: A New Interpretation.* Cambridge: Cambridge University Press, 2103.

Nietzsche, Friedrich. *Antichrist.* Trans. with an Introduction by H.L. Menken. New York: Knopf, 1920.

———. *Beyond Good and Evil* in *Basic Writings of Nietzsche.* Intro. by Peter Gay, Trans. Walter Kaufmann. New York: Modern Library, 2000.

———. *Birth of Tragedy* in *Basic Writings of Nietzsche.* Intro. by Peter Gay, Trans. Walter Kaufmann. New York: Modern Library, 2000.

———. *Ecce Homo* in *Basic Writings of Nietzsche.* Intro. by Peter Gay, Trans. Walter Kaufmann. New York: Modern Library, 2000.

———. *Genealogy of Morals* in *Basic Writings of Nietzsche.* Intro. by Peter Gay, Trans. Walter Kaufmann. New York: Modern Library, 2000.

———. *Dawn.* Trans. Brittain Smith. Intro. Afterword by Keith Ansell-Pearson. Stanford, CA: Stanford University Press, 2011.

———. *Human, All Too Human.* Trans. Marion Faber, with Stephen Lehman. Lincoln: University of Nebraska Press, 1986.

———. *Sämtliche Werke: Kritische Studienausgabe.* G. Colli and M. Montinary (eds.) Berlin: Walter de Gruyter, 1967.

———. *The Gay Science.* Trans. with Commentary by Walter Kaufmann. New York: Vintage, 1974.

———. *The Will to Power.* Trans. Walter Kaufmann and R.J. Hollingdale. New York: Vintage, 1967.

———. *Thus Spoke Zarathustra.* Trans. Graham Parkes. Oxford: Oxford University Press, 2008.

————. "Uses and Disadvantages of History for Life" in *Untimely Meditations*. Ed. Daniel Breazeale. Trans. R.J. Hollingdale. Cambridge: Cambridge University Press, 1997.

————. "Schopenhauer as Educator" in *Untimely Meditations*. Ed. Daniel Breazeale. Trans. R.J. Hollingdale. Cambridge: Cambridge University Press, 1997.

————. *Untimely Meditations*. Ed. Daniel Breazeale. Trans. R.J. Hollingdale. Cambridge: Cambridge University Press, 1997.

————. "Wagner in Bayreuth" in *Untimely Meditations*. Ed. Daniel Breazeale. Trans. R.J. Hollingdale. Cambridge: Cambridge University Press, 1997.

Nigiosian, S.A. *The Zoroastrian Faith: Tradition and Modern Research*. Montreal: McGill-Queen's University Press, 1993.

Nishitani, Keiji. *The Self-Overcoming of Nihilism*. Trans. Graham Parkes and Setsuko Aihara. New York: SUNY Press, 1990.

Oakeshott, Michael. *Rationalism in Politics and Other Essays*. Indianapolis: Liberty Press, 1991.

Pangle, Thomas. *Leo Strauss: An Introduction to his Thought and Intellectual Legacy*. Baltimore: Johns Hopkins University Press, 2006.

Parkes, Graham. ed. *Heidegger and Asian Thought*. Delhi: Motilal Banarsidass, 1992.

————. *Nietzsche and Asian Thought*. Chicago: University of Chicago Press, 1996.

Parel, Anthony. *The Machiavellian Cosmos*. New Haven: Yale University Press, 1992.

Parra, José Daniel. "The Rhetoric of Action: A Reflection on Plato's Gorgias" *Práxis Filosófica* 28, Enero-Junio, 2009, p. 55-75.

Pascal, Blaise. *Pensées and the Provincial Letters*. New York: Modern Library, 1941.

Peters, H.F. *Zarathustra's Sister: The Case of Elisabeth and Friedrich Nietzsche*. New York: Crown, 1977.

Pippin, Robert. *Interanimations: Receiving Modern German Philosophy*. Chicago: University of Chicago Press, 2015.

Plato. *Alcibiades I*. Trans. D. S. Hutchinson, in John M. Cooper ed. *Complete Works of Plato*. Indianapolis: Hackett, 1990.

————. *Cratylus*. Trans. C.D.C. Reeve, in John M. Cooper ed. *Complete Works of Plato*. Indianapolis: Hackett, 1990.

————. *Laws*. Trans. with Notes and Interpretive Essay by Thomas L. Pangle. Chicago: University of Chicago Press, 1980.

————. *Meno*. Trans. G.M.A. Grube, in John M. Cooper ed. *Complete Works of Plato*. Indianapolis: Hackett, 1990.

————. *Phaedo*. Trans. G.M.A. Grube, in John M. Cooper ed. *Complete Works of Plato*. Indianapolis: Hackett, 1990.

————. *Phaedrus*. Trans. Alexander Nehamas and Paul Woodruff, in John M. Cooper ed. *Complete Works of Plato*. Indianapolis: Hackett, 1990.

————. *Protagoras*. Trans. Stanley Lombardo and Karen Bell, in John M. Cooper ed. *Complete Works of Plato*. Indianapolis: Hackett, 1990.

————. *Republic*. Trans. with notes and Interpretative Essay by Allan Bloom. New York: Basic Books, 1991.

————. *Statesman*. Trans. C.J. Rove, in John M. Cooper ed. *Complete Works of Plato*. Indianapolis: Hackett, 1990.

————. *Symposium*. Alexander Nehamas and Paul Woodruff, in John M. Cooper ed. *Complete Works of Plato*. Indianapolis, Hackett, 1990.

————. *Timaeus*. Trans. Donald. J. Zeyl, in John M. Cooper ed. *Complete Works of Plato*. Indianapolis: Hackett, 1990.

————. *Theaetetus*. Trans. M.J. Levett, rev. Myles Burnyeat, in John M. Cooper ed. *Complete Works of Plato*. Indianapolis, Hackett, 1990.

Plutarch. "Alcibiades" in *Greek Lives*. Oxford: Oxford University Press, 2008.

Pöggeler, Otto. *The Paths of Heidegger's Life and Thought*. Trans. John Bailiff. London: Humanities Press, 1992.

Popper, Karl. *Open Society and its Enemies*. Princeton, NJ: Princeton University Press, 1971.

Possenti, Vittorio. *Nihilism and Metaphysics*. New York: SUNY Press, 2014.

Ratzinger, Joseph. *Einfürhrung in das Christentum*. Spanish Trans. José L. Domínguez Villar. München: Kösel-Verlag, 2000
————. *El Elogio a la Conciencia: La Verdad Interroga al Corazón*. Spanish Trans. José Ramón Pérez Aranguena and L'Osservatore Romano. Madrid: Ediciones Palabra, 2010.
————. *Jesus von Nazareth. Prolog. Die Kindheistgeschichten*. Spanish Trans. J. Fernando del Rio. Barcelona: Planeta, 2012.
Rawls, John. *A Theory of Justice*. Cambridge: Harvard University Press, 1971.
Richardson, John. *Nietzsche's System*. New York: Oxford University Press, 1996.
————. "Nietzsche's Problem of the Past" in M. Dries (ed.). *Nietzsche on Time and History*. New York: Walter de Gruyter, 2008.
Richardson, William, S.J. *Heidegger: Through Phenomenology to Thought*. With Preface by Martin Heidegger. New York: Fordham, 2003.
Romilly, Jacqueline. *The Great Sophists in Periclean Athens*. Trans. Janet Lloyd. Oxford: Clarendon Press, 1998.
Roochnik, David. "What is theoria? *Nicomachean Ethics* 10. 7-8." *Classical Philology*, Vol. 1, 104, No. 1 (January 2009), p. 69-82.
Rosen, Stanley. *Hermeneutics as Politics*. 2nd ed. New Haven, CT: Yale University Press, 2003.
————. *Nihilism: A Philosophical Essay*. New Haven, CT: Yale University Press, 1969.
————. *Plato's Statesman: The Web of Politics*. South Bend, IN: St. Augustine Press, 2009.
————. *The Quarrel Between Philosophy and Poetry*. New York: Routledge, 1993.
Rubenstein, Richard. *Aristotle's Children: How Christians, Muslims and Jews Rediscovered Ancient Wisdom and Illuminated the Middle Ages*. New York: Harcourt, 2003.
————. *When Jesus became God: The Struggle to Define Christianity During the Last Days of Rome*. New York: Harcourt, 1999.
Safranski, Rüdiger. *Martin Heidegger: Between Good and Evil*. Trans. Ewald Osers. Cambridge: Harvard University Press, 2002.
————. *Nietzsche: A Philosophical Biography*. Trans. Shelley Frisch. New York: Norton, 2003.
Schacht, Richard. *Nietzsche*. New York: Routledge, 1995.
Schmitt, Carl. *The Leviathan in the State Theory of Thomas Hobbes: Meaning and Failure of a Political Symbol*. Trans. George Schwab and Erna Hilfenstein. With Intro. By George Schwab and new foreword by Tracy Strong. Chicago: University of Chicago Press, 2008.
Schrift, Alan. *Nietzsche and the Question of Interpretation: Between Hermeneutics and Deconstruction*. New York: Routledge, 1990.
Schutte, Ofelia. *Beyond Nihilism: Nietzsche without Masks*. Chicago: University of Chicago Press, 1984.
Sheehan, Thomas. *Making Sense of Heidegger*. New York: Rowman and Littlefield, 2014.
Skinner, Quentin. "Meaning and Understanding in the History of Ideas." *Visions of Politics Vol. I*. Cambridge: Cambridge University Press, 2002.
Sloterdijk, Peter. *Eurotaoismus*. Frankfurt am Main: Suhrkamp, 1989.
Smith, Steven B. "An Exemplary Life: The Case of René Descartes." *Review of Metaphysics*, Vol. 57, No.3 (March 2004), p. 571-97.
Steiner, George. *Martin Heidegger*. Chicago: University of Chicago Press, 1989.
Strauss, Leo. *Natural Right and History*. Chicago: University of Chicago Press, 1965.
————. "Notes on the Concept of the Political." In Carl Schmitt *The Concept of the Political*. Trans. with an Introduction by George Schwab. With a foreword by Tracy Strong. Chicago: University of Chicago Press, 1996. [first published in 1932].
————. *On Tyranny: Including the Strauss-Kojève Debate*. Gourevich and Roth eds. Chicago: University of Chicago Press, 2000.
————. *Studies in Platonic Political Philosophy*. Chicago: University of Chicago Press, 1983.
————. *Spinoza's Critique of Religion*. Chicago: University of Chicago Press, 1997.
————. *The Argument and the Action of Plato's Laws*. Chicago: University of Chicago Press, 1992.
————. *The City and Man*. Chicago: University of Chicago Press, 1978.

————. *The Rebirth of Classical Political Rationalism*. Chicago: University of Chicago Press, 1989.

————. *Thoughts on Machiavelli*. Chicago: University of Chicago Press, 1978.

————. *What is Political Philosophy? And Other Studies*. Chicago: University of Chicago Press, 1988.

Strong, Tracy. *Friedrich Nietzsche and the Politics of Transfiguration* (Expanded Edition). Berkeley: University of California Press, 1988.

Tanguay, Daniel. *Leo Strauss: An Intellectual Biography*. New Haven, CT: Yale University Press, 2007.

Taylor, Charles. *A Secular Age*. Cambridge: Harvard University Press, 2007.

————. *Hegel*. Cambridge: Cambridge University Press, 2005.

————. *The Malaise of Modernity*. Toronto: Anansi, 1991.

————. *The Sources of the Self: The Making of Modern Identity*. Cambridge: Harvard University Press, 1989.

Thucydides. *The History of the Peloponnesian War*. Trans. Martin Hammond. Oxford: Oxford University Press, 2009.

Tocqueville, Alexis. *Democracy in America*. Trans. and ed. with an intro by Harvey Mansfield and Delba Winthorp. Chicago: University of Chicago Press, 2000.

Trías, Eugenio. *El Artista y la Ciudad*. Barcelona: Anagrama, 1997.

————. *Filosofía del Futuro*. Barcelona: Ariel, 1983.

————. *La Edad del Espíritu*. Barcelona: Penguin, 2014.

————. *Meditación sobre el Poder*. Barcelona: Anagrama, 1993.

Turgenev, Ivan. *Fathers and Sons*. Ed. and Trans M. Katz. New York: Norton 2009. [first published in 1862].

Valadier, Paul. *Nietzsche et la Critique du Christianisme*. Paris: Éditions du Cerf, 1974.

Vallega-Neu, Daniela. *Contributions to Philosophy: An Introduction*. Bloomington: Indiana University Press, 2003.

Vattimo, Gianni. *Dialogue with Nietzsche*. Trans. William McCuaig. New York: Columbia University Press, 2000.

————. *Introducción a Heidegger*. Barcelona: Gedisa, 2002.

————. *Nietzsche: An Introduction*. London: Continuum, 2002

————. *The End of Modernity: Nihilism and Hermeneutics in Postmodern Culture*. Trans. with Intro. by Jon R. Snyder. Baltimore: Johns Hopkins University Press, 1988.

Velkley, Richard. *Heidegger, Strauss, and the Premises of Philosophy: On Original Forgetting*. Chicago: University of Chicago Press, 2001.

Verdicchio, Massimo and Robert Burch eds. *Between Philosophy and Poetry: Writing, Rhythm, History*. New York: Continuum Press, 2002.

Verne, Donald Phillp. *Philosophy and the Return to Self-Knowledge*. New Haven, CT: Yale University Press, 1997.

Viroli, Maurizio. *Niccolo's Smile: A Biography of Machiavelli*. New York: Farrar, 2002.

————. *Redeeming the Prince: The Meaning of Machiavelli's Masterpiece*. Princeton, NJ: Princeton University Press, 2014.

Voegelin, Eric. *Complete Works Vol. 12 Published Essays 1966-1985*. Ellis Sandoz ed. Baton Rouge: Louisiana State University Press, 1990.

————. "Nietzsche, the Crisis and the War" *The Journal of Politics*. Volume 6. Issue 2, May 1944, p. 177-212.

————. *New Science of Politics: An Introduction*. With a foreword by Dante Germino. Chicago: University of Chicago Press, 1987.

Weber, Max. "Science as a Vocation" in *From Max Weber: Essays in Sociology*. Trans. and ed. H. Gerth and C. Wright Mills. New York: Oxford University Press, 1946.

Weil, Simone. *Gravity and Grace*. Trans. Emma Crawford and Mario von der Ruhr. London: Routledge, 1999.

————. *The Need for Roots: Prelude and Declaration towards Mankind*. Trans. Arthur Wills. London: Routledge, 2002.

White, Alan. *Within Nietzsche's Labyrinth*. New York: Routledge, 1990.

Wolin, Sheldon. "Political Theory as a Vocation" *American Political Science Review* 63, 1969.

Young, Julian. *Nietzsche's Philosophy of Religion.* Cambridge: Cambridge University Press, 2007.
Zeitlin, Irving. *Nietzsche: A Re-examination.* Cambridge: Polity Press, 1994.
Zweig, Stefan. *Nietzsche.* Trans. Will Stone. London: Hesperus Press, 2013.

Index

affect, 33, 54, 71, 84, 93, 96, 97, 98,
106n65, 113, 170, 187
Aristotle and, 107n80
as *Bestimmung*, 163, 165, 180n32, 188
aletheia, 23n58, 76, 128, 139n3, 142n24;
See *phusis*.
amor fati, 21n38, 149n102
anamnesis, 179n17
Andrew, Edward, 23n67, 147n79, 179n17
Apollo: and Dionysus, 2,
148n101–149n102, 161, 165, 177n4,
177n6; and *principium individuationis*,
180n30
Archimedean point, 34, 38, 46, 61n11,
101n24
Arendt, Hannah, 52, 61n9, 62n14, 63n36,
65n47, 69n76, 101n25, 105n59,
106n64, 119, 144n38, 146n71, 147n84,
148n101, 149n105, 175, 177n4,
181n41, 183n80–184n81, 191n6
Ariadne, 95, 97, 107n71, 158, 180n23,
180n30
Aristophanes, 65n53, 146n61
Aristotle, 5, 21n43, 33, 37, 40, 42, 55, 56,
62n15, 63n32, 64n40, 66n59, 72, 77,
85, 92, 100n12, 101n32, 107n80, 110,
119, 124, 128, 129, 132, 142n22,
143n35–144n36, 144n38, 145n52,
146n57, 147n72, 147n86, 155, 159,
163, 180n30, 181n36, 184n81, 191n2,
192n19; *Politics*, 3, 7, 24n68, 67n71,

148n101
Asclepius, 90
askesis: philosophical, 102n36
Athens, 21n38, 99n6
Augustine, 61n9, 63n32, 78, 101n25,
104n52, 106n70, 136, 149n107, 158,
186–187, 189, 191n6
Auseinandersetzung, 4, 5, 19n18
authenticity, 8, 63n35, 164–166, 167, 168,
172, 174, 188

Beiner, Ronald, 19n16, 24n69, 63n25,
99n5, 101n32, 141n11, 144n38, 176n1,
193n28
Benjamin, Walter, 148n101
Bestimmung, 2, 61n5, 151, 172; as
attunement, 139n1; as affective
disposition, 163
Bible, 68n75–69n76
biologism, 24n69, 185, 191n2
bodhisattva, 100n14–101n15

care, 9, 16, 116, 139n6, 142n23, 158, 186;
call of, 11, 64n39, 156, 178n15; of self,
107n71
compassion, 12, 34, 68n75,
107n80–108n81, 149n102
conscience, 11, 16, 60n3, 64n39, 99n5,
156, 161, 178n14–179n17, 179n19
contemplation, 23n58, 32, 49, 78, 97, 157;
as *vita contemplativa*, 69n76; and

About the Author

José Daniel Parra has a Ph.D. in political philosophy from the University of Toronto. From 2016 to 2018 he was a visiting postdoctoral scholar in the Humanities at Universität Pompeu Fabra, Barcelona, Spain. Currently, he is lecturer and research associate in government and international relations at Universidad Externado de Colombia. He has published articles and book chapters on Platonic political psychology, the history of political thought, and philosophical therapy.

www.ingramcontent.com/pod-product-compliance
Lightning Source LLC
Chambersburg PA
CBHW022312280326
41932CB00010B/1072